19077

# Evangelicals
# and
# Inerrancy

# Evangelicals and Inerrancy

edited by

# Ronald Youngblood

THOMAS NELSON PUBLISHERS
Nashville • Camden • New York

Published in the United States in Nashville, Tennessee, by Thomas Nelson, Inc., Publish-ers and distributed in Canada by Lawson Falle, Ltd., Cambridge, Ontario.

Permission was granted to reprint Roger Nicole, "The Old Testament Quotations in the New Testament With Reference to the Doctrine of Plenary Inspiration," from *Revelation and the Bible* (ed. C. F. H. Henry; Grand Rapids: Baker, 1958).

Library of Congress Cataloging in Publication Data
Main entry under title:

Evangelicals and inerrancy.

  Bibliography: pp. 253-265
  1. Bible—Evidences, authority, etc.—Addresses,
essays, lectures. 2. Bible—Inspiration—Addresses,
essays, lectures. 3. Evangelicalism—Addresses,
essays, lectures. I. Youngblood, Ronald F.
BS480.E82               1984            220.1'3            84-19050
ISBN 0-8407-5933-9

# Contents

## Essays published in the *Journal of the Evangelical Theological Society*, 1969-79

# List of Authors

Anderson, Stanley E. Late Director of Correspondence School, Northern Baptist Theological Seminary and Judson College.

Bahnsen, Greg L. Dean, Newport Graduate School.

Coleman, Richard J. Teaching Minister, Community Church of Durham.

Geisler, Norman L. Professor of Systematic Theology, Dallas Theological Seminary.

Gundry, Stanley N. Executive Editor, Academic Books, Zondervan Publishing House.

Harris, R. Laird. Emeritus Professor of Old Testament, Covenant Theological Seminary.

Holmes, Arthur F. Professor of Philosophy, Wheaton College.

Koivisto, Rex A. Associate Professor of Bible, Multnomah School of the Bible.

Lewis, Gordon R. Professor of Theology and Philosophy, Denver Conservative Baptist Seminary.

Lindsell, Harold. Editor Emeritus, *Christianity Today*.

Montgomery, John Warwick. President, Simon Greenleaf School of Law.

Nicole, Roger. Professor of Theology, Gordon-Conwell Theological Seminary.

Osborne, Grant R. Associate Professor of New Testament, Trinity Evangelical Divinity School.

Payne, J. Barton. Late Professor of Old Testament, Covenant Theological Seminary.

Pinnock, Clark H. Professor of Systematic Theology, McMaster Divinity College.

Poythress, Vern S. Associate Professor of New Testament, Westminster Theological Seminary.

Preus, Robert. President, Concordia Theological Seminary.

Saucy, Robert L. Professor of Systematic Theology, Talbot Theological Seminary.

Stonehouse, Ned B. Late Professor of New Testament, Westminster Theological Seminary.

Tenney, Merrill C. Emeritus Professor of Bible and Theology, Wheaton College.

The chapters that follow conform to the "Instructions for Contributors" section printed on pages 57-72 in the March 1977 issue of the *Journal of the Evangelical Theological Society*.

# Preface

"The Bible alone, and the Bible in its entirety, is the Word of God written and is therefore inerrant in the autographs." That single sentence has served—and served well—as the doctrinal basis of the Evangelical Theological Society since its organization thirty-five years ago.

We believe that only the Bible, the sixty-six books of the Old and New Testaments, is the inspired Word of God. No other book or group of books is "God-breathed" (2 Tim 3:16); No other book or group of books is authoritative for Christian faith and life.

All the books, all the paragraphs, all the words of the Bible, we believe, constitute the inscriptured messages given by God to the world. Nothing contained in the sixty-six books of the Old and New Testaments lies outside the pale of his intended revelation to humanity. "All Scripture...is useful" (2 Tim 3:16).

Because the Bible is God's Word, he originally gave it to us in a form that was without error and that spoke truthfully on whatever subject it treated. God is true, and therefore his Word sets forth the truth without any admixture of falsehood. It is profitable "for teaching, rebuking, correcting and training in righteousness," and its purpose is to enable and to empower us (2 Tim 3:16-17).

The above convictions (and others like them) have guided the work and interaction of the Society ever since its inception. The present volume is a modest attempt to provide some samples of how we have traditionally understood our doctrinal basis. All twenty-three chapters are reprinted from the Society's previously published papers and journals and are here gathered together conveniently in one place. We decided to begin with Roger Nicole's classic essay on how the authors of the New Testament quoted their Old Testament counterparts and to conclude with Stanley Gundry's programmatic presidential address that focused on what many of us consider the most important theological issue facing us today: Given an inerrant and inspired Scripture, how shall we most accurately and faithfully interpret it in all of its parts?

A quarter century of thoughtful and devout scholarship on Biblical inspiration and inerrancy is included in the following pages. We send them forth with the prayerful hope that they will stimulate us to further research and strengthen the faith of God's people everywhere.

Ronald Youngblood
Bethel Seminary West
San Diego, California

# The Old Testament Quotations In The New Testament With Reference To The Doctrine Of Plenary Inspiration

## ROGER NICOLE

The study of the OT quotations in the NT has led many authors to view them as an argument for plenary inspiration. The frequency of such quotations, the authority ascribed to them, the formulae of introduction used do indeed tend to indicate on the part of the NT authors a great confidence in the divine origin of OT Scripture. On the other hand, the freedom with which the quotations are adduced and the alleged forced interpretations have been considered by many authors as an invalidation of plenary inspiration. Two main lines of argumentation have been followed in this respect: (1) The authors of the NT, it is urged, not having taken care to quote in absolute agreement with the original texts of the OT, cannot have held the doctrine of plenary inspiration. Otherwise they would have had greater respect for the letter of Scripture.[1] (2) The authors of the NT, in quoting the OT inaccurately as to its letter or improperly as to its sense, or both, cannot have been directed to do so by the Spirit of God.[2]

The first argument attacks mainly the plenary inspiration of the OT; the second, mainly that of the NT. It is the aim of this paper to examine this line of difficulties and to suggest certain principles on the basis of which the facts of the matter can be harmonized with the doctrine of the plenary inspiration of the Scriptures. The paper does not aim to prove inspiration through the quotations, but rather its aim is to discover whether the facts of the quotations are such as to be an irrefutable invalidation of verbal inspiration. It must be recognized at the outset that each one of the following principles does not find application in each case, but it is the opinion of the present writer that, singly or in combination, as the case may be, they provide a very satisfactory explanation of apparent discrepancies in almost all cases and a possible explanation in all cases.

1. *The NT writers had to translate their quotations*. They wrote in Greek, and their source of quotations was either in Hebrew or in Aramaic. They had either to translate themselves or to use existing translations, and it is a well-recognized fact that no translation can give a completely adequate and coextensive rendering of the original. A very literal translation often does not at all convey in the new language what the text of the original suggested. An elaborate paraphrase may carry over the meaning with considerable accuracy, but the very length of it is a departure from the simplicity and directness of the original text. Therefore anyone who does have to quote in translation, even if he is under inspiration, will recognize that there is a certain measure of change that will occur.[3]

When the NT authors wrote, there existed one Greek version of the OT, the LXX. It was widespread, well known, and considered with great respect in spite of some defects obvious from the standpoint of modern scholarship. In most cases it was a fair translation of the Hebrew text and, furthermore, had distinctive literary qualities. Its position in the ancient world is comparable to that of the KJV before the RV was published. A conscientious scholar writing nowadays in a certain language will use for his quotations from foreign sources the translations that his readers generally use. He will not attempt to correct or change them unless there be a mistake bearing directly on his point. When slight errors or mistranslations occur, he generally will neither discuss them, because he would then direct the reader's attention away from his own point, nor correct them without notice, because he would risk arousing the reader's suspicion and thus again distract his attention from the main argument.

> To quote from a version unknown to his readers and not trusted by them,
> or to overload his pages with perpetual teasing emendations of the version
> which he employs, would be foolish, as it would debar him from the world
> and render his work futile.[4]

This is what many preachers and writers did who used the KJV or Luther's translation. They were often well aware that some verses render rather inadequately the Hebrew or the Greek, but no blame can be laid on them so long as they did not actually base an argument on what is mistaken in the translation. So the writers of the NT could use the LXX, the only Greek translation then existing, in spite of its occasional inaccuracy, and even quote passages that were somewhat inaccurately translated. They must never have profited by its errors, however, and we should not find any example of a deduction logically inferred from the LXX that cannot be maintained on the basis of the Hebrew text.[5]

Whenever they wanted to emphasize an idea that was insufficiently or inadequately rendered in the LXX, the NT writers may have retranslated wholly or in part the passage in question. In certain cases the reason why they introduced changes may remain unknown to us, but we are not on that account in a position to say either that a careful reproduction of the LXX is illegitimate or that a modification of that text is uncalled for. The whole case is well summarized by Gaussen:

> First, when the Alexandrine translators seem to them correct, they do not hesitate to conform to the recollections of their Hellenist auditors, and to quote the Septuagint version *literatim* and *verbatim*.
> Secondly, and this often occurs when dissatisfied with the work of the Seventy, they amend it, and make their quotations according to the original Hebrew, translating it more correctly.[6]

In their use of the LXX the NT writers have not attributed inspiration to this version. *A fortiori* they have not given inspiration to the translation of the passages they have used. They were inspired, however, to quote those texts as they did in the same way as they were inspired to record as they did the language of Herod, Pilate, the Pharisees, etc. Thus we should be careful not to derive any conclusion from those parts of the quotation that are somewhat mistranslated and not to the point of the sacred writers, as their presence in the Bible does not sanction the possible mistakes of the LXX. S. Davidson has a serious misconception on this point when he writes: "It will ever remain inexplicable by the supporters of verbal inspiration, that the words of the Septuagint became literally inspired as soon as they were taken from that version and transferred to the New Testament pages."[7] First, if it were inexplicable, it would not necessarily be false. Second, the supporters of verbal inspiration do not believe that and therefore cannot feel constrained to explain it.

Such a use of the LXX is not a case of objectionable accommodation. That the inspired Word is accommodated to humanity is an obvious fact—it is written in human language, uses human comparisons, its parts are determined by the circumstances of those to whom they were destined at first, etc. But we cannot admit of an accommodation in which the inspired writers would be giving their formal assent to what is considered to be an error of their time (for instance, Matt 12:40 concerning Jonah; Matt 22:43 concerning David's authorship of Psalm 110; etc.). In the use of the LXX, however, we are so far from actual agreement with error that the best scholars of all times have used similar methods.

2. *The NT writers did not have the same rules for quotations as are nowadays enforced in works of a scientific character.* In particular, they did not have any punctuation signs, which are so important in this respect.

a. They did not have any quotation marks, and thus it is not always possible to ascertain the exact beginning or the real extent of their quotations. They were not obliged by any means to start their actual citation immediately after the introductory formula, nor have we a right to affirm that the quotations end only when every resemblance with the source disappears. They may very well, in some cases, have had in mind shorter citations than is generally believed and have then added developments of their own, using still some words taken from the same source but not intended as part of the real quotation. Criticism of such passages as if they were intended as actual citations is evidently unfair.

b. They did not have any ellipsis marks. Thus the attention is not drawn to the numerous omissions they made. These ellipses, however, are not to be considered as illegitimate on that account.

c. They did not have any brackets to indicate editorial comments introduced in the quotation. Thus we should not be surprised to find intended additions, sometimes of one word, but possibly more important (cf. Eph 6:2).

d. They did not have any footnote references by which they could differentiate quotations from various sources. Thus we find sometimes a mixture of passages of analogous content or wording without being justified in charging the writers with having mishandled or misused the OT.

We readily recognize that the NT writers used the above methods, whose legitimacy is universally granted, much more than a present-day author would. The requirements of our punctuation rules make such practices tiresome and awkward, and one tries nowadays to omit, insert or modify as little as possible in quotations in order to avoid the complexity of repeated quotation marks, ellipsis marks, brackets, etc. But this common present usage is by no means a standard to judge the ancient writers. It would be interesting to apply to the NT quotations our rules of punctuation even far beyond what Nestle, Westcott and Hort, and others have done.

3. *The NT writers sometimes paraphrased their quotations.*

a. We might at first mention under this heading the use of expressions that are rather free translations of the Hebrew than real paraphrases. Such a procedure certainly needs no justification, since everybody knows that frequently a free translation renders better the sense and impression of the original than a literal one.

b. Slight modifications, such as a change of pronouns, a substitution of a noun for a pronoun or vice versa, transformations in the person, the tense, the mood or the voice of verbs, are sometimes introduced in order to suit better the connection in the NT. These are perhaps the most obviously legitimate of all paraphrases.

4

c. There are cases in which NT writers have obviously forsaken the actual tenor of the OT passage in order to manifest more clearly in what sense they were taking it. In this they are quite in agreement with the best modern usage, as represented by Campbell: "A careful paraphrase that does complete justice to the source is preferable to a long quotation."[8]

d. In certain cases the reference to the OT is not alluding to any single passage of the canonical books but rather summarizes their general teaching on certain subjects, and this in terms that are proper to the NT authors, although they want to express their indebtedness to, or their agreement with, the OT as to the thought.[9] This method of referring to the OT teachings is obviously legitimate.

e. Finally, we have to consider the possibility that the writers of the NT, writing or speaking for people well acquainted with the OT, may in certain cases have intended simply to refer their readers or hearers to a well-known passage of Scripture. Then, in order to suggest it to their memory, they may have cited accurately some expressions contained therein which they may have placed, however, in a general frame different from that of the original. This is today, as of old, the ordinary method of alluding to a well-known citation.[10]

4. *The NT writers often simply alluded to OT passages without intending to quote them.*

a. This distinction is of considerable importance and has been recognized by many authors—for example, Patrick Fairbairn, who says:

> It is proper, however, to state at the outset, that a very considerable number of the passages, which may, in a sense, be reckoned quotations from OT Scripture, are better omitted in investigations like the present. They consist of silent, unacknowledged appropriations of OT words or sentences, quite natural for those who from their childhood had been instructed in the oracles of God, but so employed as to involve no question of propriety, or difficulty of interpretation. The speakers or writers, in such cases, do not profess to give forth the precise words and meaning of former revelations; their thoughts and language merely derived from these the form and direction, which by a kind of sacred instinct they took, and it does not matter...whether the portions thus appropriated might or might not be very closely followed, and used in connections quite different from those in which they originally stood.[11]

Only in cases where NT authors have definitely manifested the purpose of citing by the use of a formula of introduction can we expect of them any strong measure of conformity.

b. Only that quotation that follows immediately such a formula is to be certainly considered as a formal citation. In such instances of successive quotations, *kai palin* always introduces an actual citation (Rom

15:11; 1 Cor 3:20; Heb 1:5; 2:13; 10:30). But with *kai* and *de*, or in the case of successive quotations without any intervening link, criticisms are quite precarious, since it is always possible to answer that no formal quotation is intended.[12]

c. Even when a definite formula points directly to an OT passage, we will not expect strict adherence to the letter of the source when this quotation is recorded not in the direct discourse but in the indirect discourse, whether it be with *hoti*, with *hina*, or with the objective construction in the accusative. In cases like that we often meet with remarkable verbal accuracy, but we cannot criticize departure from the original when the very form of the sentence so naturally allows for it.

d. We must also consider as in a special category the quotations that report not the word of Scripture itself but the sayings of individuals recorded in Scripture. In cases like that, the forms of *legō*, *eipon*, etc., that generally introduce a citation may very well be part of the narrative, and the saying itself an informal reference not subjected to the same requirements of exactness as an actual quotation. One clear instance of such legitimate freedom is found in Acts 7:26, where a declaration of Moses is recorded that is not found at all in the OT and is certainly not intended as a quotation. The following passages may belong to this category: Matt 2:23; 15:4; 22:32; 24:15; Mark 12:26; Acts 3:25; 7:3, 5-7, 26-28, 32-35, 40; 13:22; Rom 9:15; 11:4; 2 Cor 4:6; Gal 3:8; Heb 1:5, 13; 6:14; 8:5; 10:30; 12:21, 26; 13:5; Jas 2:11; 1 Pet 3:6; Jude 14.

5. *The NT authors sometimes recorded quotations made by others.* All quotations found in the NT are not introduced by the writers themselves for the purpose of illustrating their narrative or bolstering their argument, but they sometimes recorded quotations made by some of the characters who appear in the history they relate: Jesus, Paul, Peter, James, Stephen, the Jews, Satan. In two cases we have a record of a reading: Luke 4:18-19 and Acts 8:32-33. The NT writers had at their disposal at least three legitimate methods of recording such quotations:

a. They could translate them directly from the original text.

b. They could use the existing LXX and quote according to this version (as suggested under 1. above).

c. They could translate directly from the form used by the person quoting, often presumably an Aramaic translation of the Hebrew text. A few words are needed here only with reference to the last possibility. Of course we expect the persons quoting, at least those who were inspired (Jesus, Paul, Peter, James and possibly Stephen), to quote accurately, so that in these cases no divergence from the original can be explained by the mere fact that somebody else's quotation is recorded. Since, however, probably most of these quotations were originally made in Aramaic according to a current oral or written Aramaic translation, certain discrepancies between the OT and NT, which cannot be accounted for on the basis of the LXX, may have their true explanation in the use of this probable Aramaic version.[13]

6. *Other principles whose application must be limited.* Under this heading we need to consider briefly three additional principles of explanation of apparent discrepancies between the text of the OT and that of the NT. These principles, in the writer's opinion, may well be the ground of a legitimate explanation, but they ought to be handled with the utmost care and one should have recourse to them only as a last resort, because indiscriminate use of them may tend to overthrow the very thing for which the conservative scholar contends in the doctrine of plenary inspiration—to wit, the assured present authority of the Bible.

a. The texts are uncertain. Everybody knows that the ancient texts now in our hands are not altogether exact reproductions of the original mss. In the study of the quotations we have to deal almost exclusively with the Greek text of the NT, the Hebrew text of the OT, and the LXX translation. The NT possesses a degree of certainty unequaled by any other ancient text transmitted to us by manuscript. There are, however, numerous variants and instances in which the best authorities are divided in a puzzling way. Thus, while arguments based on the general scope of a passage or on several different passages have a probability practically equal to certainty, arguments based on single details—and many criticisms of the quotations are of this kind—must always be handled with utmost care. We cannot always preclude completely the possibility that our text of the Greek NT may be corrupt at a given point.

The text of the OT has received the most painstaking attention from the Jews, who exercised the utmost care in its preservation. The recently discovered mss of the Cave have tended to underscore the reliability of the MT. Nevertheless we cannot glibly equate the latter with the original autographs, and "it is conceivable that a New Testament writer has preserved a true reading of the Hebrew, current in his time, which the Masoretic text exhibits in corrupt form."[14]

The text of the LXX is quite corrupted. There were three classes of mss widely divergent in places already at the time of Jerome. Thus the present readings that we have may often fail to represent this translation in the form available to the NT authors.

In the case of the quotations all these different textual uncertainties must be considered, and sometimes the principle of compound probability must be applied. Nevertheless the present writer views it as dangerous to indulge in a boundless correction of the text on the grounds of the quotations, and he has not found any instance in the NT where such a correction might appear as the only possible legitimate explanation of the difficulty. If one begins arbitrarily—that is, without the support of actual manuscript evidence—to introduce corrections in the text of the OT or of the NT, there appears to be hardly any limit to the length to which one might go along this line and no logical stopping place on that road.

b. In the quotations, as well as in other inspired texts, the personality of the writers has been respected. It is an unsearchable mystery that the Holy Spirit could inspire the sacred writings so as to communicate his inerrancy to their very words and, at the same time, respect freedom and the personalities of the writers so that we might easily recognize their style and their characteristics. The same thing is true of the quotations, for there also we may recognize the individuality of the writers in their use of them, in the sources employed and in the method of quoting. Perhaps some slight modifications of the original text may be explained on the ground of this principle in a way that is not inconsistent with the highest view of inspiration. Elsewhere in Scripture we do find round numbers, slight differences in parallel passages, etc.—all things that are perfectly legitimate adaptations of the Holy Spirit to human habits and conventions. Although this remark may have its application in reference to quotations, it must be urged that it should be handled with utmost care. There is a dangerous distortion of this principle in the numerous appeals made by some to slips of memory in order to explain certain difficulties. If the NT authors might have slips of memory when quoting the OT, they could also have them when recording the life of Jesus or of the early Church, and the whole principle of inerrancy would be seriously undermined. Therefore the above principle should be used with such discrimination that a basic surrender will not be made of the very point at issue. In fact, as Toy himself recognized—and he cannot easily be charged with being biased in favor of inspiration—so many quotations show verbal agreement with the LXX "that we must suppose either that they were made from a written text, or, if not, that the memory of the writers was very accurate."[15]

c. The Spirit of God was free to modify the expressions that he inspired in the OT. This again is a principle that must be handled with great care lest its application lead to a destruction of the idea of verbal inspiration. In the present writer's opinion, conservative people have been too quickly ready to advocate this approach when other less precarious solutions might be proposed. Nevertheless in this connection one may well give assent to the judgment of Patrick Fairbairn:

> Even in those cases in which, for anything we can see, a closer translation would have served equally well the purpose of the writer, it may have been worthy of the inspiring Spirit, and perfectly consistent with the fullest in-

spiration of the original Scripture, that the sense should have been given in a free current translation; for the principle was thereby sanctioned of a rational freedom in handling of the Scripture, as opposed to the rigid formalism and superstitious regard to the letter, which prevailed among the Rabbinical Jews. . . . The stress occasionally laid in the New Testament upon particular words in passages of the Old . . . sufficiently proves what a value attaches to the very form of the Divine communications and how it is necessary to connect the element of inspiration with the written record as it stands. It shows that God's words are pure words, and that, if fairly interpreted, they cannot be too closely pressed. But in other cases, when nothing depended upon a rigid adherence to the letter, the practice of the sacred writers, not scrupulously to stickle about this, but to give prominence simply to the substance of the revelation, is fraught also with an important lesson; since it teaches us that the letter is valuable only for the truth couched in it, and that the one is no further to be prized and contended for, than may be required for the exhibition of the other. [16]

## Conclusion

1. In the above remarks we have addressed ourselves only to the problem of verbal differences between the OT texts and the NT quotations. The question of the alleged difference of the meaning between the original Hebrew in its context and the sense that is given to the quotation by the NT authors should also be the object of a careful investigation. Yet the problems raised in this area are probably less embarrassing to the advocate of plenary inspiration, since few people will have the presumption of setting forth their own interpretation as normative when it runs directly counter to that of the Lord Jesus and of the apostles, while verbal differences are simply matters of fact. This whole subject is closely related to the great topic of messianic prophecy, and even a summary discussion of the principles involved would take us too far afield.

2. It may not be out of order to quote here a remark of Warfield with which the writer is in hearty agreement:

We are not bound to harmonize the alleged phenomena with the Bible doctrine; and if we cannot harmonize them save by strained or artificial exegesis they would be better left unharmonized. We are not bound, however, on the other hand, to believe that they are unharmonizable, because we cannot harmonize them save by strained exegesis. Our individual fertility in exegetical expedients, our individual insight into exegetical truth, our individual capacity of understanding are not the measure of truth. If we cannot harmonize without straining, let us leave unharmonized. It is not necessary for us to see the harmony that it should exist or even be recognized by us as existing. But it is necessary for us to believe the harmony to be possi-

ble and real, provided that we are not prepared to say that we clearly see
that on any conceivable hypothesis...the harmony is impossible—if the
trustworthiness of the Biblical writers who teach us the doctrine of plenary
inspiration is really safeguarded to us on evidence which we cannot disbelieve. In that case every unharmonized passage remains a case of difficult
harmony and does not pass into the category of objections to plenary inspiration.[17]

3. It has been the writer's privilege to devote substantial time to the
consideration of all quotations of the OT in the NT. This study has led
him to the conclusion that the principles mentioned above can provide in
every case a possible explanation of the difficulties at hand in perfect harmony with the doctrine of the inerrancy of Scripture. There is no claim
here that all of the difficulties are readily dispelled or that we are in possession of the final solution of every problem. Nevertheless, possible if not
plausible explanations are at hand in every case known to us. It is thus
with some confidence that this presentation is made, and it gives joy to
state that the quotations, which at the start of the work were viewed as
one of the major difficulties to be raised against the doctrine of plenary
inspiration, have turned out to be upon examination a confirmation for
this doctrine rather than an invalidation of it. To this concur the judgments of men who can certainly be advanced as impartial witnesses in
statements such as the following, made precisely with reference to OT
quotations in the NT:

> For our evangelist [Matthew], the Scripture is literally inspired. Every-
> thing it says is true; and not with a relative truth subordinated to the general
> sense of the context, but with an absolute truth, each word having its pecu-
> liar value. Every word of Scripture is the manifestation of a special will of
> God.[18]

> We know, from the general tone of the New Testament, that it regards the
> Old Testament, as all Jews then did, as the revealed and inspired Word of
> God, and clothed with His authority.[19]

> Our authors look upon the words of the Old Testament as immediate
> words of God, and adduce them expressly as such, even those of them which
> are not at all related as direct sayings of God. They see nothing at all in the
> sacred volume which is simply the word of its human author and not at the
> same time the very Word of God Himself. In all that stands "written" God
> Himself speaks to them.[20]

In quoting the Old Testament, the New Testament writers proceed consistently from the presupposition that they have Holy Scripture in hand. The actual author is God or the Holy Spirit, and both, as also frequently the *graphē*, are represented as speaking either directly or through the Old Testament writers.[21]

Such statements from such authors mean more than anything a conservative scholar could say. They may be allowed to stand at the end of this study as expressing in a striking way the writer's own conclusions on the subject.

[1]Cf., among others, S. Davidson, *Sacred Hermeneutics* (Edinburgh: T. & T. Clark, 1843) 513.

[2]Cf., among others, M. Dods, *The Bible—Its Origin and Nature* (New York: Scribner, 1905) 113-114.

[3]This line of consideration was strengthened by comments made at the ETS meeting by [Faith Theological Seminary] President [Allan] MacRae.

[4]F. Johnson, *The Quotations of the New Testament from the Old Considered in the Light of General Literature* (London: Baptist Tract and Book Society, 1896) 20.

[5]Heb 10:5-7 is not, in the writer's opinion, an exception to this principle. Although the word *sōma* is found in the context (v 10), this does not appear to be derived from the form in which Psalm 40 has been quoted, and the reverse substitution of *ōtia* to *sōma* in v 5 would not impair the validity of the argument nor the appropriateness of the use of *sōma* in v 10.

[6]L. Gaussen, *Theopneustia* (Chicago: Bible Institute Colportage Assn., n.d.) 163.

[7]S. Davidson, *Hermeneutics* 575.

[8]W. G. Campbell, *A Form Book for Thesis Writing* (New York: Houghton Mifflin, 1939) 15.

[9]The following might be viewed as examples of such "quotations of substance," as Johnson calls them: Matt (2:23); 5:31, 33; 12:3, 5; 19:7; 22:24; 24:15; 26:24, 54, 56; Mark 2:25; 9:12, 13; 10:4; 12:19; 14:21, 49; Luke 2:22; 6:3; (11:49); 18:31; 20:28; 21:22; 24:27, 32, 44-46; John 1:45; 5:39, 46; 7:38, 42; 8:17; 17:12; 19:7, 28; 20:9; Acts (1:16); 3:18; 7:51; 13:22, 29; 17:2-3; Rom 3:10; 1 Cor 2:9; 14:34; 15:3-4, (25-27); 2 Cor 4:6; Gal 3:22; 4:22; Eph 5:14; Jas 4:5; 2 Pet 3:12-13.

[10]This particular principle, as suggested by MacRae, may sometimes account for the fact that the truths derived from the quotation cannot be logically deduced from the very words quoted, although it is contained in the general context from which the quotation is taken and of which the words quoted will be simply a reminder. Such a form of quotation would be almost necessary when there was no division of chapter and verses to make reference easy. Cf. for further elaboration and examples from general literature Johnson, *Quotations* 62-73.

[11]P. Fairbairn, *Heremeneutical Manual* (2d ed.; Philadelphia: Smith, English, 1889) 390-391.

[12]Matt 5:43; Luke 22:37; 1 Pet 1:17; 2 Pet 2:22; and Matt 5:21; 21:13; Mark 11:17; Luke 19:46 are examples of cases in which *kai* or *de* following the quotation introduces some additional material that itself can hardly be viewed as a quotation.

[13]It would appear that in those cases alone where others' quotations are adduced can this hypothesis be rightfully used to explain difficulties, for one would hardly claim that the NT authors writing in Greek could legitimately introduce on their own account mistranslations drawn from an Aramaic version. This remark limits sharply the validity of Eduard Boehl's explanations based frequently, and indiscriminately for the whole NT, on the hypothesis of what he calls the "Volksbibel" (*Die Alttestamentlichen Citate im Neuen Testament* [Vienna: W. Braumueller, 1878]).

[14]C. H. Toy, *Quotations in the New Testament* (New York: Scribner, 1884) xix.

[15]Ibid., p. xx.

[16]Fairbairn, *Manual* 453-454.

[17]B. B. Warfield, "The Real Problem of Inspiration," *Presbyterian and Reformed Review* (1893) 215-216 (reprinted in *Revelation and Inspiration* 219 and *The Inspiration and Authority of the Bible* 219-220).

[18]Massébieau, *Examen des Citations de l'Ancien Testament dans l'Evangile de Matthieu* (Paris: Fischbacher, 1885) 74.

[19]Toy, *Quotations* xxx.

[20]R. Rothe, *Zur Dogmatik* (2d ed.; Gotha: Perthes, 1869) 177-178.

[21]E. Huehn, *Die Alt-testamentlichen Citate und Reminiscenzen im Neuen Testament* (Tübingen: Mohr, 1900) 272.

# Verbal Inspiration Inductively Considered

## STANLEY E. ANDERSON

Verbal inspiration is that extraordinary and supernatural influence exerted by the Holy Spirit upon the writers of the sixty-six books of the Bible by which their words were rendered also the words of God and were preserved from all error and omission, thus producing an infallible original record. Each writer was guided so that his choice of words was also the choice of the Holy Spirit, thus making the product the Word of God as well as the work of man. This definition disavows mechanical dictation, although some parts of revelation were given by direct dictation.

Revelation is that direct divine influence that imparts truth to the human mind. Inspiration is that divine influence that secures the accurate transference of this truth into language by the writers of Scripture. Revelation is what God gives; inspiration is his method of insuring the precise record of what he gives.

The inductive method of studying inspiration may be defined in the words of Webster's dictionary as "the act or process of reasoning from a part to a whole, from particulars to generals, or from the individual to the universal." Let us then consider the inspiration of the Bible from ten different particulars, or viewpoints, and see if they lead us to a general conclusion.

1. Let us turn to history and archaeology to see what they say in support of an infallible record and hence in support of verbal inspiration. Many excellent volumes on the archaeology of the Bible have appeared in recent years. They all support the accuracy of the Bible, even though some were written by liberals. Current newspaper and magazine articles give us fresh news of recent discoveries, all corroborating the validity of the sacred records. Ezekiel 26:4-5 prophesied of Tyre, "I will also scrape her dust from her, and make her like the top of a rock. It shall be a place

13

for the spreading of nets in the midst of the sea: for I have spoken it, saith the Lord God." Compare this with Myers' *Ancient History* (p. 88): "The larger part of the once great city [Tyre] is now bare as the top of a rock—a place where the fishermen that still frequent the spot spread their nets to dry." Many other examples of the verbal accuracy of the sacred text may be cited.

2. Prophecy confirms the exact inspiration of the Bible. The many predictions in Deuteronomy 28, for instance, have been fulfilled literally in Jewish history. The dozen or more prophecies concerning Christ in Psalm 22 were fulfilled literally. The many unlikely prophecies concerning such ancient nations as Babylon, Medo-Persia, Greece, Egypt, Sidon and Nineveh have been fulfilled. When Jeremiah was commissioned to prophesy the future of nations he was given assurance of verbal inspiration for that superhuman task. The Lord said to him, "Behold, I have put my words in your mouth. See, I have set you this day over nations and over kingdoms, to pluck up and to break down, to destroy and to overthrow, to build and to plant" (Jer 1:9-10 RSV).

3. Science supports an accurate record and hence accurate inspiration. The first chapter of Genesis records the creation and formation of fifteen different things. No scientist has yet shown them to be in wrong order. According to the mathematical law of permutation, Moses had only one chance in 1,307,674,368,000 to record these fifteen items in their correct order, but he got them all right. How could he have done that apart from verbal inspiration? The law of genetics, "after its kind," is still binding upon all nature, in spite of the many frantic efforts to prove a theory of evolution. Moses wrote in Lev 17:11 that "the life of the flesh is in the blood," and it took medical scientists many centuries to discover the same truth. Isaiah 40:22 speaks of the "circle" of the earth, meaning a sphere, and Job 26:7 says that the Lord "hangs the earth upon nothing." These examples of scientific accuracy, among many others, indicate precise inspiration, especially in view of the fantastic cosmology current among nations in Bible times. We should be reminded here that these evidences of divine revelation and exact inspiration are not like links in a chain whose strength depends on its weakest part. Instead, each proof is like a strand in a cable whose strength is increased by a proper combination of all strands.

4. Logic argues for a unique Bible and thus for unique inspiration. Every effect must have an adequate cause. When we consider the vastness of Christendom with its many buildings, publications, missions, and worldwide beneficences of Bible-believers, we must postulate an ade-

quate cause. To base the immensity of all Christian philanthropies upon a book of man's own phrasing is like placing the pyramid of Cheops upon its apex or the Empire State building upon its slender television mast.

The objection that we do not now have the original autographs of Scripture is met by this observation: We who hold to verbal inspiration begin with an infallible Bible, whereas others must begin with faulty Scriptures. We have an excellent analogy in the history of the British yardstick. Their official standard yardstick was destroyed by fire in 1834, and not until 1855 was a new one prepared and legalized. During those twenty-one years many yardsticks were in use and served satisfactorily for all practical purposes, for they were reasonably accurate copies of the original. Then by studying many yardsticks inductively, a new one was arrived at and declared to be official. So now our Biblical scholars are meticulously studying a great many old mss in order to arrive at the original wording of the autographs. Incidentally, their diligent study of words indicates that they themselves hold to the importance of word-inspiration. While many scholars deny verbal inspiration in theory they seem to accept it in practice.

If we hold to inspiration at all, we should not be afraid of verbal inspiration. In syllogistic form we may put it this way: All Scripture is inspired of God; each word is a part of Scripture; therefore each word is inspired of God. Surely God could inspire the words for the Bible as well as the thoughts. And since words are necessary to convey thoughts, the words of the Bible must all be inspired in order to guarantee an accurate transcript of God's will.

5. The facts of psychology seem to imply verbal inspiration. The conversion of an individual involves a radical change in his thinking and emotions. Conversion is both a regeneration of a person's *psychē* or soul and a reformation of his mental habits. And since this regeneration is a supernatural event, it must have a supernatural cause. We know that the words of Scripture as applied by the Holy Spirit have converted millions of hard hearts, and that no other literature has ever done so. Once again we are driven to the conclusion that the words of Scripture have unique power.

The deep insight into human nature as revealed in the psalms, gospels and epistles show a knowledge of psychology far beyond the human ability of Scripture writers. Only God knows the heart of man, and only he could enable chosen men to write the Word of God, which is "living and active, sharper than any two-edged sword, piercing to the division of soul and spirit, of joints and marrow, and discerning the thoughts and intentions of the heart" (Heb 4:12).

The world's greatest scholars have not yet plumbed the depths of the writings of Peter and John, who were called uneducated and common men (Acts 4:13). These two ex-fishermen were utterly incapable of phrasing divine revelation in their own words apart from inerrant verbal inspiration.

6. The philosophy of the Bible is superior to all other systems. The book of Proverbs is still unsurpassed for practical wisdom. The book of Psalms outshines pagan philosophies as the sun outshines the moon. The sermon on the mount exceeds all the wisdom of ancient and contemporary philosophers, from Plato to John Dewey. Moreover, the ethics of the Bible are vastly superior to those of all other books combined. Divine inspiration is the only reason. And in the realm of metaphysics the Bible is suggestive if not exhaustive, and yet it is a corrective of many false philosophies.

7. The universality of the Bible's appeal argues for its divine origin, for it meets the needs of all nations. In every land those who accept the Bible are transformed by it. No nation can say that the Bible is provincial. But it would be a provincial book if those who wrote it had been left free to choose their own words for it. Jonah is one example. The Hebrews, in some senses the most proud and provincial of all races, would surely have needed divine inspiration to make the Bible appeal to all men. Apart from such inspiration, the Jewish writers would have produced merely another Jewish book of little interest or value to the world of Gentiles. But God, who loves all men without respect of persons, caused the Jewish writers to produce a book with universal appeal.

8. The moral influence of the Bible implies a divine author. No other book in the world even approaches the Bible in the extent and purity of its wholesome effects. The Bible is the fountainhead of Christian missions, driving out superstition, ignorance, idolatry, animism and self-immolation. The Bible wrought the miracle in *The Mutiny of the Bounty*. The Bible and its Christ are the mainspring in rescue missions, saving alcoholics and dope fiends where no other force in the world can save. This unique power of the Bible is not due to the superiority of the Jews over other people. David, Solomon and Peter had plenty of faults, yet their writings are faultless. "The law of the Lord is perfect" only because it is wholly of the Lord.

Charles G. Finney was a young pagan lawyer until he read the Bible, and then he became a miracle-working preacher with the Bible as his only visible instrument. Billy Graham has shaken the world with his one phrase, "The Bible says." Even illiterate preachers can win converts by using Bible texts. All this leads us to recognize the dominance of the divine factor in the inspiration of our Bibles.

9. The Christology of the Bible demands a high view of its inspiration.

The prophecies and types of Christ in the OT are beyond the ingenuity of man. The NT records of Christ's birth, life, death, resurrection and promised return are likewise beyond man's inventive ability. Who could describe a character like his or compose such sentences of authority as those spoken by him? The French infidel Rousseau wrote, "It is more inconceivable that a number of persons should agree to write such a history, than that one should be the subject of it; for the inventor would be a more remarkable character than the hero."

Those who say they hold to Christ but not to the Bible are utterly without foundation, for we know almost nothing of our Savior apart from the Bible. Further, how did the gospel writers record Christ's matchless words? They did not take shorthand, we may be sure, and they likely wrote many years after they had heard their Master speak. With the human memory as uncertain and faulty as it is, we simply must assume divine inspiration in recording the words of our Lord. This amounts to verbal inspiration, for no other explanation is adequate. Jesus emphasized the importance of words in John 17:8: "I have given them the words which thou gavest me."

The evidences so far given are incomplete without the testimony of Scripture to its own inspiration. Since we believe that God inspired his Word, we may logically assume that he revealed the manner of its inspiration.

10. Scripture itself is its own best testimony to the kind of inspiration that produced it. The mineralogist assays ore to determine its nature; the chemist tests all sorts of materials to discover their composition; and so the Christian searches the Scriptures to learn if they describe its manner of transmission from heaven to earth. We have reason to expect such information, and our search has been abundantly satisfying.

We believe that the Bible gives a clear explanation of its inspiration in 1 Cor 2:10-13: "God has revealed to us through the Spirit. For the Spirit searches everything, even the depths of God. For what person knows a man's thoughts except the spirit of man which is in him? So also no one comprehends the thoughts of God except the Spirit of God. Now we have received not the spirit of the world, but the Spirit which is from God, that we might understand the gifts bestowed on us by God. And we impart this in words not taught by human wisdom but taught by the Spirit, interpreting spiritual truths to those who possess the Spirit." Notice that this passage declares that no one can comprehend the thoughts of God, thus disposing of the dynamic or thought-inspiration theory of inspiration. And the truths of God are imparted not in words of human wisdom, but in words taught by the Holy Spirit. How could verbal inspiration be stated more precisely?

1 Thess 2:13: "And we also thank God constantly for this, that when

you received the word of God which you heard from us, you accepted it not as the word of men but as what it really is, the word of God, which is at work in you believers."

2 Tim 3:16: "All Scripture is inspired by God and profitable for teaching, for reproof, for correction, and for training in righteousness."

2 Pet 1:21: "Because no prophecy ever came by the impulse of man, but men moved by the Holy Spirit spoke from God."

The OT alone has over 2600 references to the fact that its writers were aware of the divine origin of their messages. The phrase "The Word of the Lord" is found about five hundred times in the Bible; "The Word of the Lord came" twenty-three times; "God spoke" or "The Lord spoke" over one hundred fifty times; "Thus saith the Lord," "The Lord saith," and "saith the Lord of hosts," 816 times.

Exod 20:1: "And God spoke all these words, saying." Exod 24:4: "And Moses wrote all the words of the Lord." Exod 34:27: "And the Lord said to Moses, 'Write these words; in accordance with these words I have made a covenant with you and with Israel.'" Lev 4:1: "And the Lord said unto Moses." Num 11:24: So Moses went out and told the people the words of the Lord." Num 22:38: "Balaam said to Balak, 'Lo, I have come to you! Have I now any power at all to speak anything? The word that God puts in my mouth, that must I speak.'" Num 23:13: "And he answered, 'Must I not take heed to speak what the Lord puts in my mouth?'" (These latter two verses are all the more remarkable proof of verbal inspiration since Balaam was a "hireling prophet.")

Deut 4:2: "You shall not add to the word which I command you, nor take from it." Deut 18:18: "I will raise up for them a prophet like you from among their brethren; and I will put my words in his mouth, and he shall speak to them all that I command him."

Josh 24:26: "And Joshua wrote these words in the book of the law of God." 1 Sam 8:10: "So Samuel told all the words of the Lord to the people." 2 Sam 23:2: "The Spirit of the Lord speaks by me, his word is upon my tongue."

1 Kgs 17:24: "And the woman said to Elijah, 'Now I know that you are a man of God, and that the word of the Lord in your mouth is truth.' " 1 Kgs 22:14: "But Micaiah said, 'As the Lord lives, what the Lord says to me, that I will speak.' "

1 Chr 17:15: "In accordance with all these words, and in accordance with all this vision, Nathan spoke to David."

Ezra 1:1: "In the first year of Cyrus king of Persia, that the word of the Lord by the mouth of Jeremiah might be accomplished, the Lord stirred up the spirit of Cyrus king of Persia so that he made a proclamation throughout all his kingdom and also put it in writing."

Ps 19:7: "The law of the Lord is perfect, reviving the soul; the testimony of the Lord is sure, making wise the simple." (Consider the high degree of inspiration necessary for these words of Scripture, which are said to be perfect, sure, right, pure, clean, eternal, true and altogether righteous.) Ps 138:2: "Thou hast exalted above everything thy name and thy word." (The RSV marginal reading agrees with the KJV: "Thou hast exalted thy word above all thy name.")

Prov 30:5: "Every word of God proves true; he is a shield to those who take refuge in him."

Isa 59:21: "My words which I have put in your mouth." (Four times in Isaiah this expression is found: "The mouth of the Lord hath spoken it.")

Jer 1:9: "The Lord said to me, 'Behold, I have put my words in your mouth.'" Jer 30:2: "Thus says the Lord, the God of Israel: Write in a book all the words that I have spoken to you." Jer 36:1 ff.: "This word came to Jeremiah from the Lord, 'Take a scroll and write on it all the words that I have spoken to you.'... Then Jeremiah called Baruch the son of Neriah, and Baruch wrote upon a scroll at the dictation of Jeremiah all the words of the Lord which he had spoken to him.... 'You shall read the words of the Lord from the scroll which you have written at my dictation.' " (Also indicative of verbal inspiration in chap. 36 are vv 8, 10, 11, 13, 16-20, 27, 28, 32. The RSV has the word "dictation" six times and "words" eighteen times in this one chapter.) Jer 45:1: "The word that Jeremiah the prophet spoke to Baruch the son of Neriah, when he wrote these words in a book at the dictation of Jeremiah."

Ezek 3:10: "Moreover he [God] said to me, 'Son of man, all my words that I shall speak to you receive in your heart, and hear with your ears.' "

Dan 12:8-9: "I heard, but I did not understand. Then I said, 'O my Lord, what shall be the issue of these things?' He said, 'Go your way, Daniel, for the words are shut up and sealed until the time of the end.' "

Hos 1:1: "The word of the Lord came to Hosea." Amos 1:1: "The words of Amos, who was among the shepherds of Tekoa, which he saw concerning Israel." Hab 2:2: "And the Lord answered me: 'Write the vision; make it plain upon tablets, so he may run who reads it.' " (See also Joel 1:1; Zeph 1:1; Hag 1:1; Mal 1:1.)

The NT seems to be quite explicit as to the manner of its inspiration. Matthew 5:18 reads, "For truly, I say to you, till heaven and earth pass away, not an iota, not a dot, will pass from the law till all be fulfilled." (Here inspiration is more than verbal; it extends to you the smallest parts of the words.) Matt 10:20: "It is not who speak, but the Spirit of your Father speaking through you." Mark 12:36: "David himself, inspired by the Holy Spirit, declared, 'The Lord said to my Lord.' " Luke 16:17: "But it is easier for heaven and earth to pass away, then for one dot of the law to become void."

John 3:34: "For he whom God has sent utters the words of God, for it is

19

not by measure that he gives the Spirit." John 6:63: "The words that I have spoken to you are spirit and life." John 8:47: "He who is of God hears the words of God; the reason why you do not hear them is that you are not of God." John 10:35: "Scripture cannot be broken." John 11:51: "He [Caiaphas, Christ's lethal enemy] did not say this of his own accord, but being high priest that year he prophesied that Jesus should die for the nation." John 14:10: "The words that I say to you I do not speak on my own authority."

Acts 1:16: "Brethren, the scripture had to be fulfilled, which the Holy Spirit spoke beforehand by the mouth of David." Acts 28:25: "The Holy Spirit was right in saying to your fathers through Isaiah the prophet."

1 Cor 14:37: "If anyone thinks that he is a prophet, or spiritual, he should acknowledge that what I am writing to you is a command of the Lord."

2 Pet 3:16: "There are some things in them [Paul's letters] hard to understand, which the ignorant and unstable twist to their own destruction, as they do the other scriptures."

Rev 1:10-11: "I was in the Spirit on the Lord's day, and I heard behind me a loud voice like a trumpet saying, 'Write what you see in a book and send it to the seven churches.' " Rev 2:1: "To the angel of the church in Ephesus write: 'The words of him who holds the seven stars in his right hand.' " Rev 2:8: "The words of the first and the last." Rev 2:12: "The words of him who has the sharp two-edged sword." Rev 2:18: "The words of the Son of God." Rev 3:1: "The words of him who has the seven spirits of God and the seven stars." Rev 3:7: "The words of the holy one, the true one." Rev 3:14: "The words of the Amen, the faithful and true witness, the beginning of God's creation."

Rev 14:13: "And I heard a voice from heaven saying, 'Write this: Blessed are the dear who die in the Lord henceforth.' " Rev 19:9: "And the angel said to me, 'Write this: Blessed are those who are invited to the marriage supper of the Lamb.' And he said to me, 'These are the true words of God.' " Rev 21:5: "And he who sat on the throne said, 'Behold, I make all things new.' Also he said, 'Write this, for these words are trustworthy and true.' "

Rev 22:18-19: "I warn everyone of you who hears the words of the prophecy of this book: If any one adds to them, God will add to him the plagues described in this book, and if any one takes away from the words of the book of this prophecy, God will take away his share in the tree of life and in the holy city, which are described in this book."

Since the Bible itself gives repeated witness to its own verbal inspiration, then every Christian ought to accept it and hold to it loyally. We believe that objections to verbal inspiration can be answered quite as readily as objections to any other. And we have yet to find an adequate text for any other kind of inspiration. Why, then, should any Christian hesitate to accept the Bible's own doctrine of its inspiration? The evidences of history, prophecy, science, logic, psychology, philosophy, universality, moral influence and Christology all corroborate the scriptural doctrine of verbal inspiration.

# THE INFALLIBILITY OF SCRIPTURE AND EVANGELICAL PROGRESS

## NED B. STONEHOUSE

On the occasion of this fellowship banquet, which is appropriately more informal than our regular sessions, I have in view a rather broad and general treatment of the topic that has been announced. If my recollections are correct I have good precedents for following this course rather than endeavoring to make a scholarly contribution to the understanding of some carefully circumscribed topic.

The joining of these two phrases—"the infallibility of Scripture" and "evangelical progress"—indicates that in my judgment there is a very intimate connection between the maintenance of the infallibility of Scripture and the attainment of any significant progress so far as the evangelical cause is concerned. The burden of what I have to say is indeed that the former is indispensable to the latter, that in fact the more clearly and consistently we take our stand upon the position to which this Society is committed the more assuredly and rapidly we shall make some genuine advance in the field of Biblical and theological studies.

We are painfully aware indeed that this estimate is not shared by many of our contemporaries. We know that the doctrine of the infallibility of Scripture is widely regarded as an egregious error, reflecting obscurantism and inevitably leading to further obscurantism. Rather than being a liberating force it is regarded as an intolerable burden. It is sometimes said that it must result in religious and ecclesiastical paralysis. Our view of the Bible is thought to place us in bondage to a paper pope.

It will be recognized that this point of view, while hardly a novelty in our day, has been given considerable impetus and has found increasing acceptance because of the colossal impact of the teaching of Karl Barth. In view of the fact that his volume on *The Doctrine of the Word of God* has now become available in English and his theological position is becoming better and better known in our day, we may anticipate an increasing impact in the years ahead. Barth's clear-cut position that the Bible is itself fallible and that it may not be regarded even as containing infallible elements is presented in an attractive light because it is insisted that precisely on his view of the relationship between God and Scripture there is a recognition of "the free grace in which the Spirit of God is present and active before and above and in the Bible."

The Barthian point of view is reflected in scores of volumes that are coming from the press in these days, one of the most recent of these being the book of J. K. S. Reid of Glasgow on *The Authority of Scripture* (New York: Harper, 1957). Reid maintains, for example, that "the movement towards literal inerrancy can repeatedly be diagnosed as the sickness or torpor that succeeds a 'first fine careless rapture.' It is the mark of the ebb tide setting in, when the flood having reached its peak subsides" (p. 25). In another connection Reid maintains that according to the position of Biblical infallibility "God's Word is petrified in a dead record" (p. 279).

In the face of the modern evaluations of Scripture, shall we still maintain our historic position? And in particular may we insist that it is precisely as we lay hold with energy upon Scripture, acknowledged as coming to us with plenary and verbal inspiration and as possessing divine authority, that we are given the indispensable basis for genuine progress?

Certainly the issue raised by these questions is not of a peripheral or isolated character. We are confronted here with the profoundest questions as to the very nature of God and his relationships with man. The modern view maintains that the doctrine of the infallibility of Scripture is derogatory to God and involves an abridgement of man's essential liberty. If on the other hand we are to maintain this doctrine it can only be because we recognize that our doctrine of Scripture is an aspect of our doctrine of God. To acknowledge Scripture as infallible is to acknowledge the absolute supremacy of the God of the covenant in the sphere of truth. Accordingly submission to that truth is a profoundly religious act.

In seeking now to come to grips more particularly with the specific theme of my address, I wish first of all to make the point that our position concerning Scripture, and it alone, involved the recognition of a qualitative distinction between Scripture and tradition, and that precisely as we recognize this distinction in all our labors and carry out its implications we may be assured of a measure of progress.

In insisting upon the distinction between Scripture and tradition and in pleading for greater consistency in working out the implications of this Protestant principle, I would not indeed suggest that we should despise tradition or in general minimize its historical significance. Tradition, in truth, is a factor of great significance within the history of special revelation itself. This is bound up especially with the fact that the special revelation of the Bible is a revelation in history. As such the truth of revelation is often presented as that which on the one hand is received and on the other hand is delivered over. To make this point more specifically it may now suffice to recall the words of Paul in 1 Cor 15:3: "For I delivered unto you first of all that which I also received."

In addition to the tradition within Scripture there is the tradition beyond Scripture, the tradition of the Church. And though this tradition is on a different level from that of which Paul has spoken, it remains true that for one who recognizes the providence of God, the kingship of Jesus Christ and the presence and power of the Holy Spirit in the life of the Church, historical tradition may oftentimes be of very great significance. To put the matter in a somewhat different way, it must be recognized that Scripture itself has made a profound impact upon the life and thinking of the Church, and this is of course especially true as it has been accompanied by the operations of the Spirit in the hearts of men.

Nevertheless the distinction between Scripture and tradition must prevent us from absolutizing tradition. No matter how high our estimate of the scriptural significance of any phase of history, including for example the Reformation, we may not make the judgments and practices of any such phase our starting point for our evaluations of truth or our standard concerning it.

In emphasizing this point as I do I am deeply concerned with a tendency that seems to me to be widely prevalent among evangelicals to obliterate or obscure this basic distinction.

This tendency is found, for example, in dealing with questions concerning the origin of the NT. My impression is that it is reflected even in the terminology that is in common use in dealing with problems of NT introduction. Although I cannot speak confidently with regard to present practices in the classroom and elsewhere, I may illustrate what I have in mind when I observe that in treating questions of special introduction it seems to me to be rather common to deal first with "external evidence" and then with "internal evidence" as if these two types of evidence were simply coordinate. As a consequence the conclusions drawn seem to be based upon a kind of synthesis of these two types of evidence. We would, however, reflect our basic principle more fully if, even in this matter of terminology, we distinguished carefully between the testimony of historical tradition and the infallible testimony of Holy Scripture by which the voice of tradition is to be tested and judged. We need, I believe, a far more thoroughgoing way to observe to what extent it must be rejected and to what extent it is to be maintained.

May I illustrate what I have in view by referring more particularly to the subject of gospel origins? We are confronted today with two extremes in dealing with the synoptic problem. On the one hand there is present an uncritical acceptance of the two-document theory even on the part of some conservatives. This is in spite of the fact that this theory commonly conceives of the evangelists as mere editors, and indeed often as editors who more or less consciously distort or manipulate the contents of the gospel. On the other hand, there appears to be a tendency, because of these fundamental objections to the two-document theory, to reject it as simply the product of unbelief. This would preclude in advance the possibility of recognizing that there may be component features of the theory that are of a different character from the estimate of the editors to which I have just referred, features that may be quite acceptable and indeed preferable to certain traditional views. In particular, as one is concerned with such questions as the authorship and the order of the gospels it is vital that one should draw a line between conclusions that flow from the testimony of Scripture itself and those that enjoy only the support of tradition.

In particular, with regard to the order in which the gospels were written, one may not rest heavily upon tradition. This is true, in the first place, because that testimony is not unitary. The Anti-Marcionite Prologue of Luke places Matthew and Mark before Luke, whereas Clement of Alexandria says that the gospels with genealogies were written before Mark. Moreover, in the nature of the case such testimony would not rest upon as secure a foundation as, for example, the tradition concerning the authorship of a gospel. Whereas the latter would have been associated with the individual gospels from the time of their original publication, the former would have arisen presumably only as the gospels were brought together, and especially as there developed the necessity of assigning them a particular order in the ms transmission. In any case, one must apparently allow for the lapse of a period of time following the publication of individual gospels before such judgments could have been formed. It is not possible at the present time to give further consideration to this question of the order of the gospels and in particular to the question of whether Matthew is earlier than Mark or Mark earlier than Matthew. What I "am concerned to stress, however, is that such decisions should not be largely influenced by tradition, and that the testimony of the gospels themselves, as that is disclosed by an intensive study of their individual characteristics, must be given the decisive weight.

The question may now be appropriately raised concerning whether the discounting of the authority of tradition in such a matter as the order of the gospels applies in similar fashion to the traditions concerning their authorship. In my opinion this does not necessarily follow. If one reflects, for example, upon the tradition relating to the authorship of Matthew it will appear that the tradition of apostolic authorship is early and consistent in all the witnesses. And in view of the significance of the attestation of the gospel there is a strong presumption that such testimony goes back to the very beginning of its circulation. It is remarkable, moreover, that the Church's interest in attestation, and its understandable concern with the witness of the apostles, did not result in a development in which, without regard to the actual facts, apostolic names were assigned to all four gospels. The consideration that as many as two of the four gospels have been handed down as the writings of Mark and Luke, who were not numbered among the apostles, constitutes weighty evidence that the association of the apostle Matthew's name with a particular gospel must be due to the Church's belief that he was responsible for it.

Regardless of our judgment as to the reliability of this tradition, however, we remain under the necessity of giving priority to internal evidence. Pursuant to this approach one must examine with the greatest possible care such objections to the testimony of tradition as have been or may be offered. My own opinion is that the objections to the apostolic authorship of Matthew advanced in modern times are not impressive unless one shares to a considerable degree the modern skepticism with regard to the trustworthiness of the gospel tradition as a whole. I personally am strongly persuaded of the apostolic authorship of Matthew. Nevertheless, in keeping with the main point that I have been making, it appears to me to be essential to distinguish qualitatively in this matter also between the testimony of tradition and that of Scripture itself. Matthew is an anonymous work in that it does not make any claim to Matthean authorship. One may therefore be influenced by the strength of the tradition and by the complete congruity of the contents of Matthew therewith firmly to maintain the traditional position concerning its authorship. Nevertheless we should not elevate such a conclusion to the status of an article of the Christian faith. Such articles of faith should be based securely upon the teaching of Scripture.

First of all, therefore, I have argued that as a matter of principle we must take great care not to ascribe more authority to tradition than properly belongs to it. A qualitative distinction between Scripture and tradition must be observed all along the line, and this I am convinced is the only way in which we may anticipate genuine evangelical progress in dealing with many basic questions.

It is necessary now, however, to indicate a second implication of our basic position that is even more fundamental. This is that in every area of life and thought we should more fully and constantly recognize and take into account the final authority that rightly belongs to Holy Scripture.

The fact of our common commitment in the Society to the infallibility of Scripture possesses indeed far-reaching significance for fellowship and cooperation. Yet we may not rest content with this common affirmation with regard to the Bible. This affirmation itself challenges us to reflection upon its implications. As a matter of fact there might be relatively little significance in such a commitment if it should turn out to be agreement with regard only to our doctrine of Scripture and if in our total understanding of Scripture we should be basically at odds with one another. It is well that we remind ourselves from time to time that heretical and sectarian groups commonly also appeal to the infallibility of Scripture and insist that their peculiar views flow from this starting point.

If the word "evangelical" in the name of our Society and in its broader applications in our day is to possess genuine meaning, we may not be satisfied with a lowest common denominator of Christian belief. Rather, taking with full earnestness our avowed commitment to the divine inspiration and authority of Scripture and putting more fully into practice our theoretical acknowledgment of the primacy of exegesis, we must search out diligently what the Scriptures teach concerning basic questions on which evangelicals are seriously divided. There can be no hope of evangelical progress apart from energetic labors in this direction.

Let me mention a few areas in which it seems to me it is especially urgent that we give fresh attention to the testimony of Scripture.

In the first place, our commitment to the infallibility of Scripture imposes upon us the obligation of reflecting constantly upon the testimony of the whole of Scripture to its own character. Unless we are alert and conscientious in this matter there is considerable danger that we shall conceive of infallibility or inerrancy in an *a priori* or abstract manner. In dealing with such matters as the harmony of the gospels and quotations of the OT in the NT, for example, there is danger that we shall draw inferences from the affirmation of infallibility, or apply this doctrine in such a way, as actually to do violence to the total witness of Scripture. A satisfactory evaluation of the testimony of Scripture will include indeed a responsible dealing with the most specific reflections upon the character of Scripture, which are found, for example, in 2 Tim 3:15-16. In order to insure, however, that our evaluation of Scripture corresponds with the nature of Scripture as that is disclosed by its entire self-testimony, it is necessary to expound and thus constantly keep before us the comprehensive character of this task.

My impression is indeed that we are largely aware of our responsibility in this matter. The publication of our own volume on *Inspiration and Interpretation* and of other recent volumes by members of our Society, the "Wheaton Report on Inspiration," and a "Report on Inspiration" to be presented to the 1958 Assembly of the Reformed Ecumenical Synod are heartening evidences of this fact. It will be necessary to continue to insist, however, that it is precisely we evangelicals, committed as we are to the infallibility of Scripture, who are under the most solemn responsibilities to search the Scriptures without ceasing in order to assure ourselves that we have come to the fullest possible understanding of what Scripture really is.

In the second place, our particular evaluation of Scripture constrains us, as no other view can, to interpret correctly the message of Scripture. An affirmation of inspiration without regard to sound hermeneutics is of little or no significance. As John Murray has expressed it:

> In all questions pertinent to the doctrine of Scripture we must remember that the intent of Scripture is Scripture; it is what Scripture means to say that is Scripture. We cannot deal, therefore, with the inerrancy of Scripture apart from hermeneutics. In dealing with the bearing of a particular passage on the inerrancy of Scripture we must, first of all, bring the science of hermeneutics to bear upon that particular passage and insure that it is the intended import of the text that is brought into consideration and not some other import which it may, on *prima facie* reading, appear to convey.

The problem of hermeneutics is acutely before us at the present time as we are under the compulsion to distinguish between literal historical affirmation and symbol or allegory as well as that which is alleged to be mythical or mythopoeic. The task of distinguishing between the literal and the figurative is clearly not an easy one, especially because figurative features are commonly present in every form of writing. It should become increasingly obvious that the suggested rule, "as literal as possible," is not particularly helpful. Although one may sympathize with the apprehension lest the affirmations of history should dissolve into myths, sober reflection upon the character of language will compel the abandonment of any such simple approach to the problems of interpretation. In general it is safe to say only that a particular passage must be evaluated in the light of all the evidence that is pertinent to its elucidation. But in the mind of the evangelical there will be in the foreground the recognition that his view of Scripture carries with it the implication that "the infallible rule of interpretation of Scripture is Scripture itself." It appears again therefore that the evangelical will be a sound interpreter only as he consistently acknowledges the authority of Scripture.

In the third place, as we take account of the Biblical message of the redemption accomplished by God in Christ it is incumbent upon us that we set forth this doctrine in the perspective of the whole of Scripture. Only as it is understood in connection with the revelation of the whole counsel of God will we begin to understand it not only in terms of its breadth and height and depth but even in its essential character. It is in Christ that God was reconciling the world unto himself and it was in a *Son* that he spoke at the end of these days. But if we are not to impoverish or distort the gospel it is imperative that we recognize that it is God who was reconciling the world unto himself and it is God who has spoken unto us. There is an important sense indeed in which the message of the Bible is centered in Christ, but modern viewpoints that define their position in Christocentric or Christological terms only too often fall far short of measuring up to the God-centered character of the redemption and revelation presented in the Bible. A person who does not hold to the authority of Scripture may not be under compulsion to take account of the whole counsel of God and may seek to justify a more selective approach, but we evangelicals cannot escape the responsibility bound up with our view of Scripture that we shall seek to lay hold upon its testimony in its entirety.

Finally, there is the matter of eschatology. If we are fully agreed on our doctrine of Scripture but remain as divided as we apparently are on the subject of eschatology, one may gravely question whether our unity is as substantial and basic as we may have supposed. One influential factor that accounts for the present diversity is the lack of progress in the development of sound hermeneutics to which reference has previously been made. Another factor, in my judgment, has been the tendency to assign central significance to peripheral matters and to fail to recognize that which is truly central. To be more specific on this point, I believe, for example, that the interpretation of Revelation 20 has been accorded a place far beyond its relative significance both for the understanding of the book of Revelation as a whole and of the general questions of eschatology. On the other hand, the elemental aspects of eschatology, concerned as they are with the ultimate consummation of the plan of God and the coming of his kingdom in all its perfection, are often lost sight of or obscured. The result has been tragic impoverishment both theologically and religiously. Thus the cosmic scope and sweep of the divine salvation have been neglected. And the perspective that is gained for the understanding of every aspect of our present life by a proper estimate of the world to come is also blurred. Has not eschatology generally been considered in a fragmentary way with the result that it is isolated from our theology as a whole and is viewed largely in terms of the interpretation of a few passages of Scripture?

At this point also accordingly our belief in the divine authority of Scripture must constrain us to renewed efforts to enter into a larger and more adequate understanding of eschatology. If we are successful in this endeavor we may anticipate not only a far greater meeting of minds than has heretofore been manifest but also a deepening of religious commitment and life as with greater penetration of meaning and intensification of our spirit of worship we exclaim: "The kingdom of the world is become the kingdom of our Lord and of his Christ, and he shall reign forever and ever."

From our commitment to the inspiration of Scripture there issues a liberating and energizing force that frees us from bondage to the doctrines and commandments of men. It should also spur us on to lay hold with all our powers upon the Word of God in order that all our thoughts and ways may come under his control.

# THE LEGITIMATE LIMITS OF
# BIBLICAL CRITICISM

## MERRILL C. TENNEY

Biblical criticism is a comparatively recent development in the history of
the Christian Church. Except for the sporadic attacks of its enemies, like
that of Celsus in the second century, the authenticity and integrity of the
Biblical books were largely taken for granted. Occasional observations
like Martin Luther's on James, that it was "a right strawy epistle," represented casual opinion rather than studied research. From the Council of
Nicea (325) to the end of the Reformation movements (1775) the Church
as a whole was more interested in discussing theology than it was in the
historical and textual background of the Scriptures.

Beginning with the rise of rationalism in the seventeenth century under
Spinoza and later with the encyclopedists of the French Revolution,
Christian scholars were confronted with the problems of the historical origins and validity of the Biblical records. If, as their opponents contended, much of its content was a mass of legend, written at a time later
than the traditional dates demanded and composed by men who possessed no first-hand knowledge of the facts, the genuineness and authority of the Bible would be seriously impaired. How could a jumbled
miscellany of legends, shaped by the limited knowledge and concepts of
an unenlightened or bigoted era, convey any imperative message that
modern scientific thinkers would accept?

In attempting to meet this attack the present science of Biblical criticism was developed. The connotation of the term "criticism" is unfortunate, for it implies a negative attitude. Biblical criticism is not necessarily
an attack on the Scriptures but is an examination of their historical and
literary relation to the times and events concerning which they were written. This study is not in itself destructive. It can confirm and illumine the
Biblical text just as well as it can cast doubt upon it or devaluate it. Insofar as historical and literary evidence can be used to find out exactly what

the Bible means and to remove difficulties in understanding it, the study is beneficial.

In understanding the procedure of Biblical criticism, however, what limits should be set for it? Is not any questioning of the Bible a piece of impertinence? If the Scriptures are the Word of God, as most evangelicals believe, are they not above criticism? Would not any challenge to their truthfulness or integrity be blasphemous impudence?

Since the Bible was written by human beings who lived at definite times in definite places, it must be related to the circumstances and places in which it was produced. The historical events of which it speaks or from which it springs, the personalities who wrote it or whose deeds it chronicles, and the ideas that it contains are all a part of a setting to which other records and literature belong. A comparison between the facts and concepts in the Bible and those in contemporary literature may be a valuable means of interpreting its meaning for modern readers.

If the Bible is the revelation of God to men it must be superior to any ordinary book. Not only must its teachings be reliable, but the historical framework in which they are contained must also be accurately formulated. It is true that psychological truth can be conveyed by historical fiction, as many novels demonstrate, but the Bible does not purport to be fiction. The events it narrates are recounted as actual happenings, its characters are treated as actual men and women, and its ideas are set forth as the Word of God to men. If we take the Bible at face value it demands not only attention but also obedience.

Where, then, shall Biblical criticism begin, and where shall it stop? Can we commence the process of historical and literary evaluation, only to halt at a fixed point because to go beyond it would be sacrilege? Can we curtail our investigations without placing an unwarranted curb on honest scholarship?

In order to determine the proper sphere of Biblical criticism, the following limitations are suggested:

1. *The limitation of inspired character.* One should begin by recognizing the unique character of the Bible. Its dynamic is different from that of any other piece of writing that has survived from antiquity. The reality of this dynamic is amply attested by its effect on history. Throughout the period in which the Scriptures have been known and circulated, they have produced a moral impact upon men that cannot be duplicated by any other literature. The reading of the Law by Josiah moved the king to repentance and reform (2 Kgs 22:10-13; 23:1-25). The public translation by Ezra stimulated a sweeping change in the conduct of the people (Neh 8:1-6; 9:1-3). And in more recent times the Bible, wherever it has gone, has proved to be a potent force in producing righteousness. Not all of its

characters were moral and not all of its history can serve as a model for present behavior, but the standards by which it measures both those characters and that history are far above those of contemporaneous religious belief. Neither Homer not Plato nor any other writer or philosopher has had the influence for moral change or given such a lofty concept of God as has the Bible.

Any criticism that seeks to explain the Bible must take this fact into account. To treat the Bible simply as the Hebrew-Christian contribution to the literary achievements of the race, neither better nor worse than the other surviving documents of antiquity, is to undervalue it and to ignore the most striking characteristic of the book. A criticism that does not allow for this dynamic and that does not recognize its existence will draw partial if not faulty conclusions. Such criticism will tell as much about the Bible as dissection of a corpse will tell about the living man. It fails to recognize its living quality.

2. *The limitation of evidence.* To conclude that the Bible is incorrect in its statements because it does not accord with the information that we possess overlooks the fact that not all the necessary evidence may be available. The narratives of the Bible do not pretend to give a complete account of all the events that take place, nor even to deal exhaustively with the phenomena that concern them most. Historical records of past ages have largely perished because of the wars, vandalism and neglect that they have suffered. Many statements of the Scriptures cannot be corroborated because they have hitherto remained the sole witness to the facts of which they speak, but they must not consequently be regarded with suspicion. As new discoveries enlarge the knowledge of the ancient world they tend to confirm rather than to contradict the Bible. All interpretative hypotheses that are formed from known facts should be regarded as tentative until sufficient evidence is available to afford concrete confirmation.

3. *The limitation of personal understanding.* Sometimes the critic rather than the evidence may be at fault. He may not have seen the evidence in its proper light, and so have drawn hasty or false conclusions. Biblical language can be misunderstood because it is not in the idiom of our own times. Numerous small misinterpretations of the NT have been cleared up by the discovery of papyri that have not changed the readings of the mss but have shown that a well-known word had been wrongly translated. Any previous critical judgment on the text, however learned, would have been erroneous because of imperfect understanding on the part of the critic.

The critical student of the Scriptures should learn to discount his own prejudices when dealing with evidence. Complete objectivity is probably impossible, for—even unconsciously—human beings think in molds. But if the theologians of the past have failed to interpret the Scriptures correctly because of an "unscientific" bias, it is equally true that many critics of the present fail even more lamentably because of an antisupernaturalistic bias. In cases where positive evidence is lacking, suspended judgment is imperative. The benefit of the doubt should be given to the Bible's claims for itself.

4. *The limitation of purpose.* In forming any conclusion concerning the historicity and truthfulness of the Scriptures, we should always keep in mind the purpose for which they were written. The writers of the Bible did not include more than their purpose of writing demanded, nor did they explain contemporary phenomena for the benefit of scholars in the twentieth century. To charge them with omission or obscurity is to presuppose an obligation that they would not have recognized. Their readers or hearers would have easily understood allusions that are obscure to us and would have been able to fill in gaps by commonplace knowledge that is not now available.

Furthermore, one should assume that these writers were normally truthful. Apart from any question of inspiration, the authors of the OT and NT were not impelled by a perverted ambition to victimize a gullible public. They were not making a point of producing religious fiction. Most of them were prophets and preachers who jeopardized their lives to proclaim what these mss contain. They would not have wasted their efforts in trivia, nor would they have propagated untruth. Falsehood is not unknown in religious literature, but there is no reason for beginning Biblical research with the assumption that the subject of study is untrustworthy.

5. *The limitation of positive contribution.* The unfortunate connotation of Biblical criticism that has brought it into disrepute is that it is characterized by destructive denial. Generally it has been accused of constantly attempting to find discrepancies in the Bible and to discredit its truth. To enumerate apparent inconsistencies or disagreements in its text may be a part of the total procedure of investigation, but to conclude on the basis of insufficient evidence evidence that these indicate unreliability is quite another thing. The aim of a healthy criticism should be to seek a fuller understanding and confirmation of the purpose of sincere writers and to clarify their obscurities rather than to make these obscurities a reason for rejecting their testimony.

These limitations do not circumscribe the scholar in his investigative work. He has the utmost liberty to search for evidence, to classify and to interpret it, to view the Bible in its light, and to formulate hypotheses of interpretation that may prove helpful. They do mean that he cannot honestly entertain a hostile bias to the Scriptures and at the same time do them justice, nor should he treat an hypothesis as fact when it has not sufficient material evidence to support it. He should be sure of his premises before he asserts emphatically the finality of his conclusion.

As an illustration of the application of these limitations one may cite the work of E. R. Thiele, *The Mysterious Numbers of the Hebrew Kings.* For years the chronologies of the kings of Israel and Judah had defied reconciliation, and many scholars had concluded either that the Biblical text was corrupt or that it was historically untrustworthy. Thiele, operating on the principle that the record was truthful though obscure, showed quite satisfactorily that it involved two methods of reckoning that changed without notice in the text. While he did not solve all the problems of chronology immediately, his simple explanation reconciled the conflicting figures and confirmed the existing account. Accepting the presupposition of essential truthfulness led to fuller investigation and to sounder conclusions.

The recognition of these limitations is not a plea for obscurantism but for more persistent research. Where the Bible seemingly disagrees with history, we need to probe deeper into the available evidence and to be ready to rearrange our thinking if necessary. Hypotheses may come and go; understanding may be imperfect; but truth is eternal and is available to those who will pay the price for it.

# WHAT DOES BIBLICAL INFALLIBILITY MEAN?

## GORDON R. LEWIS

The purpose of this study is to investigate the meaning of infallibility, not to establish the grounds on which infallibility rests. The writer, however, questions the view that inerrancy is not "required" by the Biblical teaching of its own inspiration.[1] Rather, he here assumes with Frederick C. Grant that in the NT "it is everywhere taken for granted that Scripture is trustworthy, infallible and inerrant. . . . No New Testament writer would ever dream of questioning a statement contained in the Old Testament."[2]

Neither does the paper intend to lay a foundation for the doctrine of propositional revelation. We assume a position similar to that of Bernard Ramm.[3] Nor is it the purpose of this paper to discuss the implications of textual criticism for the nature of inspiration. It is assumed that textual criticism has generally confirmed the trustworthiness of by far the greatest part of the Greek and Hebrew texts. References to the Bible may be regarded as being to those passages on which there is not such variation in the mss as to affect in any material way the meaning conveyed.

An important distinction between the Bible as given and the Bible as interpreted should also be noted. The doctrine of infallibility applies to the Bible as given, not to the interpretation of any individual. Therefore is not the province of this paper to deal with the complex issues of hermeneutics, although they cannot be avoided entirely. It is assumed, however, that an objectively infallible standard is not in vain. Although no interpreter can claim inerrancy for himsef, interpreters are not equally in a morass of subjectivity since there is an objective standard of comparison in Scripture. The Bible's meaning can be approximated by the use of sound principles of hermeneutics, the witness of the Holy Spirit, and the help of previously Spirit-illumined interpreters in the history of the Church.

Positively this paper explores a means of understanding and communicating the significance of Biblical infallibility to our generation. One of the most influential schools of thought is called philosophical analysis, a recent development from earlier logical positivism. In order to help young people familiar with philosophical analysis to understand the import of Biblical infallibility we may employ its terms as far as possible for meaningful communication. In so doing our own concept of the applicability of the doctrine of Biblical infallibility to our times may be enriched and expressed with increased precision.

## I. Meaning and Language

Contemporary philosophical analysis and semantics vigorously stress the difference between logical meanings and the verbal sentences conveying them. Long ago Augustine had classically expressed the distinction in his dialogue "On the Teacher" (*De Magistro*). The words uttered by a teacher are not identical with the thought he hopes to teach or the realities to which they refer. As a result of this analysis Augustine cautioned against confusion of linguistic signs with their meanings or with the things they signify. The NT itself distinguishes to some extent *logos* (emphasizing the meaning of words) from *rhēma* (underlining the uttered or written terms).

Although this distinction has a long and noble ancestry it has frequently been ignored in discussions of Biblical inerrancy. Logically, errorlessness or truth is a quality not of words but of meanings. Ben F. Kimpel explains, "Language...is only a means for articulating a proposition. Hence the truth-character of an affirmed proposition is not a feature of its language-form....Language is not essential for having true beliefs. It is essential only for *affirming* them."[4] How can this important distinction be related to the doctrine of inspiration? May we not preserve it by employing "inerrancy," which explicitly claims truth, only for the propositional content of Scripture, and by using "infallibility," which may mean "not liable to fail," only for the verbal expressions of Scripture?

Acknowledging that the Bible is both inerrant in content and infallible in expressing it, we do not maintain mere conceptual inspiration or mere "record" inspiration[5] but both. That seems to have been the point of verbal inspiration. Furthermore we shall seek to determine how verbal inspiration may be understood plenarily in these terms. It will be helpful to note not only the distinction between content and wording but also a number of subdivisions within each of these categories. To facilitate reference to these classifications in the remainder of the paper, the following chart lists rather widely-accepted kinds of meaning in the left-hand column and parallel uses of language in the right-hand column.

# AN ANALYSIS OF MEANING AND LANGUAGE[6]

## KINDS OF MEANING

### A. *Cognitive Meanings*
Assertions that are either true or false.

1. Formally
The truth or falsity is determined by the definitions of the terms, the principles of logic, or principles of mathematics.

2. Empirically
The truth or falsity is determined by observable, sensory, scientific evidence. Any proposition that is cognitively meaningful must be verifiable. Some empirical evidence must be relevant to the confirmation or disconfirmation of it. Such meaning may also be designated as literal.

### B. *Noncognitive Meanings*
1. Emotive
Vent the speaker's emotions or evoke similar emotions in others.

2. Motivational
Stimulate volitional action.

3. Interrogative

4. Exclamatory

5. Pictorial, imaginative

### C. *Meaningless Nonsense*
Alleged assertions about unverifiable existences or realities.

## USES OF LANGUAGE

### A. *Informative Sentences*
Usually declarative

1. Formally informative
Convey nothing about matters of fact but only about definitions of words and logical or mathematical relations.

2. Empirically informative
Convey propositions regarding matters of fact, states of affairs, existence, or reality.

### B. *Noninformative Sentences*
1. Expressive
Convey emotive meaning (e.g., poetry).

2. Directive
Convey exhortations, commands.

3. Questions

4. Exclamations

5. Figures of speech

### C. *Pseudo-Sentences*
Declarative sentences conveying nonsense.

## II. Inerrancy and Kinds of Meaning

The term inerrancy here specifically designates meaning that is not false but true. By definition cognitive meanings alone can be true or false of objective reality—that is, reality independent of the speaker. Noncognitive meanings on the other hand express something only of the speaker. We shall consider the relation of inerrancy first to those Biblical meanings that are related to the objective world. Cognitive meanings themselves have a twofold classification, as the chart reveals. There are those assertions that may be regarded as true or false formally—that is, by reason of their definition or by reason of the principles of mathematics or logic. In the second place, there those cognitive propositions which are true or false empirically—that is, by reason of some observable scientific evidence which tends either to confirm or disconfirm them. Are there such cognitive propositions in the Bible? And if so, what does it mean to say to our contemporaries that they are inerrant?

1. *Formally cognitive meanings.* In order to keep the discussion within reasonable limits, we shall consider of the formal types of cognitive assertions only the logical. Formal logical principles seem to be implied in Rom 11:6. The content of the verse is clearly dependent upon such basic laws of logic as the principle of identity, the principle of excluded middle, and the principle of noncontradiction. Israel's election, Paul argues, is by grace, not works. "And if by grace, then is it no more of works: otherwise grace is no more grace. But if it be of works, then is it no more grace: otherwise work is no more work." No experimental inquiry need be instituted here. The argument is settled by application of these logical principles. Assuming the principle of identity, grace is grace and works are works; assuming the validity of the principle of excluded middle, Israel's election must be either by grace or works; and assuming the validity of the principle of noncontradiction, it cannot be by grace and not by grace. What, then, does inerrancy mean in a passage like this? If the Scriptures teach inerrancy concerning their own content, then are not their assertions in didactic passages formally true and not false?

Syllogistic reasoning appears in the argument of Gal 3:15-17. Paul argues: No confirmed covenant is one that is disannulled or altered. The covenant with Abraham is a confirmed covenant. Therefore the covenant with Abraham is not one that is disannulled or altered (by the law 430 years later). Again Paul's case depends upon formal principles; it does not require any experiential confirmation. The truth of his conclusion rests squarely on the validity of the principles of syllogistic reasoning. The rules of a valid syllogism are followed. In a passage like this, what does inerrancy mean? Would not the doctrine of inerrancy mean that assertions dependent on formal logical principles in didactic passages are cognitively true and not false? Can the reasoned case of an inspired author be based on fallacious logic?

Although this is not the place to examine the status of formal logical principles, a few words are necessary. According to the analysts, propositions true on formal logical grounds are true because (1) we have arbitrarily ruled that the game be played that way, or (2) we have surreptitiously hidden the conclusion in the premises so that our argument is tautologous. However, Paul in the two Biblical passages mentioned hardly seeks to spell out the implications of arbitrarily conceived rules of thought or first premises. Rather, he employs formal logic to support what is in fact the case concerning God's gracious election and the Abrahamic covenant. How can these passages be made to fit the analyst's shibboleths of "merely formal," "arbitrary" and "tautologous"? Indeed they are formally valid, but the contexts imply more than that. These propositions are both formally and actually true. And how can these passages be made to fit the neo-orthodox shibboleth of "mere witness" to the mighty covenant acts of God? They are that, but they are more than that. They spell out the propositional implications of these divine acts. If these passages are inerrant, the truth of their propositional content is certified both formally and actually.

2. *Empirically cognitive meanings.* Some cognitive assertions are true or false not in virtue of formal logical principle but in virtue of empirically observable evidence. The Bible contains many assertions whose truth is not formally validated but could be tested through human experience. Under the continuing influence of logical positivism, many contemporary analysts still limit human experience that attests cognitively true propositions to the witness of the five senses. And the Bible includes many such propositions. The descriptive statement of Acts 1:12 is a verifiable one. The disciples, after the ascension, "returned to Jerusalem from the Mount called Olivet which is from Jerusalem a Sabbath day's journey." That event was testable by the senses on the day it occurred. And by means of sensory observation, the disciples had confirmed the bodily resurrection of Christ from the dead. They heard him speak; they saw him eat before them; and they were invited to touch him (Luke 24:36-43; John 20:25-28). What then can it mean to say that such passages are inerrant? It cannot mean merely an accurate record of what may not have happened. Rather, if inerrant the assertions are true and therefore the facts specified real. The disciples did take the trip from Olivet to Jerusalem; Christ in his scarred body did talk, walk and eat with the disciples after his death.

Now to account for Scripture data it is necessary to broaden the criterion of verifiability as held by positivistically inclined contemporaries.

The positivists themselves have been forced to adopt a weakened form of the verification principle, such as that of A. J. Ayer in his *Language, Truth and Logic*. Nonpositivists consider it arbitrary to limit the meaningful experience to that of our bodily senses. Because of the complexity of human experience, the verification principle as applied to the five senses may be only one clue to meaning; there may be many others. Empirical philosophies of religion like that of the late Edgar S. Brightman have stressed the richness of all human experience, including experience of values and of God. We may well expand the verification principle after the pattern suggested by F. W. Copleston to the effect that there must be some difference between that situation in which an empirically meaningful proposition would be true and those in which it would be false. "We can conceive or imagine facts that would render it true or false," or "some experiential data are relevant to the formation of the idea."[7] It cannot dogmatically be asserted that no prehistorical and no metaphysical proposition satisfies this general requirement. Nor does this criterion open the door to snarks and boojums that make no conceivable difference in any situation whether alleged to exist or not.

On such a broadened criterion, the following Biblical statements must be considered as empirically cognitive. "They were all filled with the Holy Spirit" (Acts 2:4). The disciples' reception of the invisible Spirit on the Day of Pentecost made an experiential difference in their lives. The assertion to that effect is either true or false, and if inerrant it is true. In such a passage as Gen 2:10-14 describing four rivers flowing out from Eden the content is not verifiable on a strict positivistic view of history. The alleged state of affairs antedates extant writing from the time, and there is no known way now of confirming or disconfirming such propositions. However, if the Scriptures in fact intend to assert the actual existence of the four rivers, then what does inerrancy of such statements imply? Must we not conclude that there were such rivers? There is conceivable empirical difference between the ancient world that had these four rivers and an ancient world that did not have them.

The Scriptures also make assertions concerning the being of God as in Exod 3:14, "I AM THAT I AM," or Heb 11:6, "He that cometh to God must believe that he is, and that he is the rewarder of them that diligently seek him." What does inerrancy mean in relation to these passages? Does it not imply the truth of the propositions even though they are not verifiable in the strict positivistic sense? Is it not the case that, although no man has seen him at any time, an eternally active God exists? Admitting frequent metaphor, parable, and other figures of speech, must we not acknowledge that if a concept of inerrancy applies at all, every literal assertion made by didactic passages of Scripture is true? If so, the state of affairs or the reality designated actually existed, exists, or will exist as the Scriptures specify.

Again it is impossible here to attempt anything like a full justification of this position or its enormous implications. However, a brief consideration may indicate the writer's position on some of the problems involved. To assert inerrancy is not to assert full comprehension of any of the events or things designated. Granting propositional revelation and a high view of inspiration, we still know only in part. But we *know* in part! Following the Biblical writers, can we not call knowledge of God truth?

Someone may object that the limited character of the concepts God had available as he began to reveal himself rule out cognitive truth ontologically. A father puts things in a very circumscribed way to "get through" to his child—even to the point of distortion. How much more then does God have to abandon infinite truth to get through to finite man! Such an argument fails to take into account several important factors. God did not decide to communicate with man after all possible temporal conditions contributed to make this impossible. Communication with man was among his eternal purposes, was it not? Providence from the moment of the first creative act worked toward the realization of that purpose in the cultures, the moral ideas, the thought patterns and the languages. Revelation was not frustrated by unforeseen limitations of earlier creative activity! On a Biblical view, provision for communication was planned and equipment for it was included in the mind of man from the beginning.

Overlooking these points, Eugene Heideman argues that verbal inspiration necessarily implies fallibility. In choosing to use Hebrew, God was limited to its available erroneous concepts. The belief that the sun went around the earth and low moral concepts exemplify his point.[8] May we ask Heideman if he has considered sufficiently the fact that truth-claims must always be evaluated in terms of the writer's purpose? It could be no part of the Biblical writer's intention to scoop Copernicus' view of the solar system. The language of phenomenal appearance (the sun going around the earth) is true within its intended realm of discourse. But what about the concept of Hebrew justice? Did not God have to make use of a crude, vengeful idea in revealing his justice? No, the principle of an eye for an eye also must be judged in its historical setting and purpose. The law did not provide freedom for all to take personal vengeance on wrongdoers. Whereas people had taken justice into their own hands, the national judges were now provided with an objective law of retribution. Its point was that in Israel's courts the punishment should fit the crime, a principle not foreign to our allegedly high views of justice nor to that of the divine judgment seat. Admittedly in the progress of revelation God took the Israelites where they were and accomplished amazing things with them for his redemptive purposes. But where they were at the beginning was no accident. God in his providence had long before intended the use of the Hebrew language and its concepts for a medium of his revelation to mankind.

No attempt is made here to deny that the divine revelation does, like the divine incarnation, stoop to man and make use of anthropic and cosmic modes of revelation. It is claimed, however, that these forms of revelation are true as far as they go and not distortive. They are true, however, not as the very archetypal ideas in the mind of God himself, but as a copy of them expressed to man, his image. The knowledge of propositional revelation then is true as a copy or ectype of the original, because revealed truth is the object of worship. However, it is no service to worship to deny the accuracy of Biblical propositions concerning God. Neither is it the part of piety to allege that the Bible is full of nonsense.

3. *Noncognitive meanings.* Noncognitive propositions, according to the analysts, are those that do not assert any matter of fact in the objective world but simply express something about the speaker. While the earliest positivists may have denied the meaningfulness of emotive, motivational, interrogative, exclamatory and pictorial types of meaning, recent analysts have extended their concept of meaning to include at least these. On this theory, when a football fan screams "Hurrah!" he is not asserting a verifiable state of affairs but simply venting his emotions and possibly seeking to evoke a similar reaction in others. Are there statements in the Bible that do not intend to assert states of affairs in publicly observable reality but rather to express the writer's emotions? Such a meaning may be in view when a prophet like Isaiah cries, "Woe is me!" We shall not expect archaeology to confirm or disconfirm the truth of that proposition. What then does inerrancy mean for content like this? If these Biblical expressions are inerrant, is not their point about the speaker or writer in fact true concerning him? Emotive meanings may be said to be inerrant in that they adequately convey what the writer felt or sought to evoke in others.

There are also in the Bible other noncognitive materials, such as motivational statements, exhortations and commands, expressing the speaker's will and stimulating others to action. Is it not beside the point to look for confirmation or disproof of these meanings on the part of any objective science? If so, then it is irrelevant to assert their cognitive inerrancy in the sense analysts commonly understand. However, such a phrase as "Love one another" (John 15:17) may meaningfully be considered inerrant in truly stating the speaker's will and desire. Interrogative meanings also tell us something true of the questioner. A question from Satan, for example, inerrantly expresses his challenge of God's word: "Yea, hath God said ye shall not eat of every tree of the garden?" (Gen 3:1). Exclamations also adequately state the speaker's feeling: "Woe unto you, scribes and Pharisees...!" (Matt 23:14). If such noncognitive thoughts are inerrant, do they not truly assert what was the desire, the question and the emphatic feeling of the one who said them at the time they were spoken? Pictorial language inerrantly portrays the author's view of a given thing. The metaphor, "The tongue is a fire" (Jas 3:6), does not teach a literal matter of fact but vividly illustrates James' concept of the potential dangers of speech.

What then does inerrancy mean in such noncognitive passages of the Bible? In these cases the point of infallibility is simply that we have a true assertion of what the writer felt, commanded, asked, exclaimed or pictured. The question of whether those feelings and exclamations are exemplary must be determined by the context. If there is no explicit indication of approval or disapproval in the immediate context, then we must resort to the broader context of the thought of the Bible in its entirety. The applicability of commands must be similarly judged.

These noncognitive categories of the analysts may seem arbitrarily to exclude implicit cognitive elements in them. Men like E. L. Mascall, university lecturer in philosophy of religion at Oxford, argue that there are no completely noncognitive forms of language. Mascall goes so far as to say that art is essentially a cognitive activity revealing truth.[9] If the noncognitive types of meanings here listed do carry some implicit objective implications that may be regarded true or false in an external state of affairs, as the points of figures of speech clearly do, then all that we have said concerning cognitive inerrancy applies to those implications. However, what has been said concerning the inerrancy of the emotive, motivational, interrogative, exclamatory and pictorial types of subjective meaning also holds. In other words, to the extent that the Biblical materials are noncognitive they are here regarded as inerrant in reference to the speaker, and to the extent that they teach cognitive assertions they are also regarded as inerrant objectively. The knotty problem of determining what is cognitively taught and what is not can only be resolved in individual passages by devout scholars employing sound principles of hermeneutics and respecting the judgment of other Spirit-led exegetes throughout the Church's history.

Some may fear possible consequences of leaving to interpreters the distinguishing of objectively inerrant propositions from the subjectively inerrant ones. Admitting the dangers of misinterpretation in determining the objective or subjective reference of Biblical statements, we cannot escape the responsibility. Such decisions are as unavoidable as those between what is literal and figurative, or between narratives that are exemplary and those that are not. There is no virtue in denying the necessity of facing these issues of interpretation with louder affirmations of belief in inspiration. Evan a stalwart like A. T. Pierson frankly acknowledged, "Every student must observe what in Holy Scripture carries authority and what only accuracy." After citing Satan's words to Eve and the questionable counsel given Job by his friends, Pierson adds, "Even prophets and apostles apart from their character and capacity as such, being only fallible men, were liable to mistakes (I Kings 19:4; Gal. 2:11-14)." What is Pierson's conclusion? "Any theory would be absurd that clothes all words found in Scripture with equal authority or importance. But whatever is meant to convey God's thought is used with a purpose and adapted to its end, so that, as the angel said to John on Patmos: 'These are the true sayings of God' (Rev. 19:9)."[10]

We might well ask what criteria Pierson used to determine which narrative passages carried authority and which only accuracy of recording. In some cases, he suggests, God's disapproval is evident in the context, whereas in other cases the sentiments and acts are obviously controlled by the Holy Spirit and represent the mind and will of God. Where no such contextual indications are available the judgment must be made in accord with general scriptural teaching on the subject. May we not suggest similar standards for judging passages cognitive or noncognitive? If contextual evidence indicates that a proposition has no cognitive import, we abide by that. If an assertion that displays the characteristics of cognitive propositions is taught by Christ himself, or prophets and apostles, the content inerrantly conveys truth concerning reality. If the context fails to clarify the cognitive intent of a proposition, its intention can only be determined in accord with the general tenor of Scripture on the subject or related subjects. The interpreter who faces these issues will work with sound principles of hermeneutics and avail himself of the judgment of Spirit-led exegetes from the past as safeguards against dangerous misinterpretation.

4. *Inerrancy and meaninglessness or nonsense.* If inerrancy applies to the Bible in any respect, does it not mean that in any didactic passage there can be no nonsense? Although there may be serious assertions incapable of verification on a strict positivistic principle, if the Holy Spirit kept the thought of Scripture free from error he preserved the writers from including any assertions that were not true to the facts. Employing a broadened sense of verification, we may say that inerrancy means that there is no intended assertion of Scripture that does not make some difference in the total complex of reality.

Let us sum up the discussion of inerrancy and the content of Scripture. As inspiration is applied to Scripture content it guarantees the objective inerrancy not of every thought conveyed in the Bible but of everything cognitively taught in it.[11] Insofar as the Bible chooses to assert the existence of scientifically verifiable or unverifiable realities, the Bible is true; the events or realities specified are actual. Furthermore there is no nonsense in Scripture. This is not to say, however, that the Bible's propositional truth is presented with twentieth century technical precision. Its accuracy must be judged in terms of the writer's own purpose. Needless to say, the Bible writers' purpose was not to address specialists in an honorary scientific society. In accord with the popular purpose, if the Scriptures are inerrant at all we must conclude that their didactic assertions are true. Furthermore noncognitive assertions about the speaker or writer are held to be inerrant for their particular purposes. From the consideration of the content of Scripture, we turn to a discussion of the verbal expressions through which the meanings are conveyed.

## III. INFALLIBILITY AND USES OF LANGUAGE

Infallibility is here used to emphasize the nonfailing character of God's written Word as a vehicle for its meanings. This concept applies fruitfully to Biblical sentences. The Word of God through the prophets and apostles will not return void; it will accomplish the purpose for which he sent it (Isa 55:11). Not one jot or tittle will fail until all God purposed through it is fulfilled (Matt 5:17-18; Luke 16:17; John 10:35).

How then does infallibility apply to informative sentences that convey formal or empirical truth? B. B. Warfield has well stated the point: "Inspiration is a means to an end and not an end in itself; if the truth is conveyed accurately to the ear that listens to it, its end is obtained."[12] In other words, to assert the infalliblity of Scripture is to assert that it is grammatically adequate in conveying the divinely-intended meanings. "A sentence is grammatically adequate when it clearly articulates meaning, and it is grammatically inadequate when it does not do so."[13]

Viewed in this light, the writers' sentences are infallible even though their purpose may be not to present cognitive propositions but to convey noncognitive meanings. Thus noninformative sentences are clear and adequate to their respective tasks. Emotive expressions in the poetical books are as infallible as empirically informative statements in Acts. The directive sentences of the ten commandments are as infallible as the informative statement that God cannot deny himself. The meaning of questions is conveyed as accurately as the content of John 3:16. Exclamations clearly portray the intended spirit, and figures of speech adequately present their point. All of the Bible, whatever its kinds of sentences, is equally infallible and equally effective in conveying the various meanings intended by the Holy Spirit through the inspired writers. From the fact that the Bible contains no nonsense it follows that the writers were preserved from penning any pseudo-sentences.

As a result of this understanding of infallibility we may appreciate the Reformers' doctrine of the Scriptures' perspicacity. In terms common to our generation, would not the Reformers assert that the Bible is capable of adequately accomplishing its goal of communication apart from any external interpretive authority?

In view of contemporary understanding of the limitations of culturally conditioned languages, is such a concept of infallibility tenable? Are the grammatical structures of Hebrew and Greek so readily adaptable for mediating the divine meanings? Many contemporary theories of the origin of language assume that meaningful sounds evolved from earlier grunts and that all terms were devised with physical or phenomenal referents. If that be assumed, it is indeed difficult to transmit infinite meanings through finite vocables. But must a Bible believer accept the naturalistic theories of the origin of language? Eugene Nida assumes that we must.[14] He claims that language was first used for the naming of animals. And language originated not by God's naming of them but Adam's. This, he argues, means that language is primarily a human convention participating in the finiteness of all that is human. We would not deny that the naming of the animals may be the origin of certain human words, but what of the communication between God and Adam? Dialogue between God and man presupposes that two-way conversation is possible. May not the Bible-believer also hold that God created man's capacity for linguistic communication? Of course this is impossible on a positivistic world view! But on a theistic world view, Gordon Clark argues, God created man and revealed himself to him in words. Language is adequate for theology.[15]

It may be well then to observe some of the advantages of the view proposed in this paper for the use and understanding of the terms "infallibility" and "inerrancy." One benefit of regarding truth a quality of propositions rather than sentences is a diminishing of the problem of some of the variations in the gospel accounts, in other historical passages relating to the same event (Kings and Chronicles) and in the NT wordings of OT references. One and the same logical content can be expressed by different wordings—that is, active or passive, direct or indirect discourse, etc. The major point of inerrancy is to assert the truth of the meaning rather than the wording. Verbal inspiration in this context stresses the functional value of whatever sentences are used to convey accurately the intended meaning. Verbal inspiration would not imply that alternative expressions are necessarily falsifying.

A second value of this analysis may be a clarification of the role of the witness of the Holy Spirit. A factual or cognitive proposition has both an intension and an extension. "Its intension is its meaning. Its extension is the reality to which its meaning refers."[16] Independently of the gracious witness of the Holy Spirit a grammarian can examine Biblical sentences and a logician analyze their precise intension. But only via the witness of the Holy Spirit can any man come into personal communion with God himself, the reality to whom the sentences refer. This at any rate was Augustine's view of illumination, which stimulated Calvin's thought on the testimony of the Spirit.

What then are the conclusions of this paper?

1. Although there is a clear distinction today between meaning and sentences, inspiration may be viewed as implying neither merely conceptual nor merely verbal supervision on the part of the Holy Spirit. Inspiration in this realm of discourse applies to both content and wording, meanings and sentences.

2. "Inerrancy" may be used most clearly for meanings that are cognitively taught by those with delegated authority as spokesmen for God, and for noncognitive meanings relating to the speakers themselves.

3. "Infallibility" most helpfully designates the verbal media of the Scriptures as effective communicators of the Spirit-intended meaning through the Biblical writings.

4. All that is written in Scripture is infallible. All that Scripture teaches cognitively is objectively true. All that Scripture teaches noncognitively is subjectively true—that is, true of the one whose idea is expressed. This then is a plenary view of verbal inspiration. All sentences are infallible, and all meanings are inerrant for their respective purposes.

[1]E. F. Harrison, "The Phenomena of Scripture," in *Revelation and the Bible* (ed. C. F. H. Henry; Grand Rapids: Baker, 1958) 238, 250.

[2]F. C. Grant, *Introduction to New Testament Thought* (New York: Abingdon-Cokesbury, 1950) 75.

[3]B. Ramm, *Special Revelation and the Word of God* (Grand Rapids: Eerdmans, 1961).

[4]B. F. Kimpel, *Language and Religion* (New York: Philosophical Library, 1957) 93.

[5]E. J. Carnell, *The Case for Orthodox Theology* (Philadelphia: Westminster, 1959) 92-112.

[6]These classifications are not presented as final or absolute but suggestive. Additional categories may well be required by the scriptural materials. See H. Feigl, "Logical Empiricism," *Twentieth Century Philosophy* (ed. D. D. Runes; New York: Philosophical Library, 1943) 379.

[7]F. W. Copleston, *Contemporary Philosophy* (London: Burns and Oates, 1956) 46, 48.

[8]E. W. Heideman, "The Inspiration of Scripture," *RefR* 15 (September 1961) 29.

[9]E. L. Mascall, *Words and Images* (London: Longmans Green, 1957) 93.

[10]A. T. Pierson, *Knowing the Scriptures* (Los Angeles: Biola Book Room, 1910) 16-17.

[11] Cf. J. I. Packer, *"Fundamentalism" and the Word of God* (Grand Rapids: Eerdmans, 1958) 169, and Smedes' comment.

[12]B. B. Warfield, *The Inspiration and Authority of Scripture* (Philadelphia: Presbyterian and Reformed, 1948) 438.

[13]Kimpel, *Language* 138.

[14]E. Nida, *Message and Mission* (New York: Harper, 1960) 224-225, as summarized by E. Heideman, "Inspiration."

[15]G. H. Clark, *Religion, Reason and Revelation* (Philadelphia: Presbyterian and Reformed, 1961) 146.

[16] Kimpel, *Language* 134.

# An Historian Looks At Inerrancy

## HAROLD LINDSELL

During the summer of 1964, *Christianity Today* polled the membership of the Evangelical Theological Society. Its members were asked to designate the major areas of conflict in the theological arena. Two-thirds of the 112 responders to the poll said that Biblical authority is the main theological theme now under review in conservative circles in America. The replies left this writer with the definite impression that the overall theological viewpoint of any man will ultimately be a reflection of his answer to the question, "What is the nature of inspiration and authority?"

Now I am not a theologian in the formal sense of that term. However, this does not disqualify me from speaking on the subject of Biblical authority, for I shall deal with it in a perspective consonant with my formal training. Just as a judge must be familiar with the law and make decisions about matters outside the realm of his intimate knowledge, so the historian can come to conclusions about men and movements that operate within complex disciplines outside his own competence but that can be subjected to historical scrutiny competently. I speak therefore as an historian, and as a member of that craft I wish to take a hard look at the inerracy of the Bible, a subject that is intrinsic to the question of Biblical authority.

One of the historian's first conclusions is that in every period in the history of man some central issue has dominated that age. This is true both for profane and sacred history. We are concerned here with sacred history, and to that area I will limit myself.

Any serious study of the OT and NT will show that the writers devoted little space to the careful formulation of a doctrine of revelation, inspiration and inerrancy. Nowhere in Scripture is there any reasoned argument along this line such as will be found for justification by faith alone in Romans and for the resurrection of Jesus Christ from the dead in 1 Corinthians. This may appear strange at first until we recognize that this is true for many of the key doctrines of the Christian faith. There is no great apologetic for the existence of God or for the trinity. Everywhere these truths are enunciated and taken for granted, however. Yet they are not the subject of formal treatment in the same sense that justification by faith and the resurrection from the dead are dealt with.

Search the gospels and you will find little that deals directly with this question of the Scriptures. Jesus Christ constantly refers to the OT Scriptures, but nowhere does he speak with the view to defend them. Rather he takes it for granted that the Scriptures are inspired, authoritative and inerrant, and on the basis of this assumption he interprets the Scriptures and instructs friend and foe alike. He assumes that they, like himself, are controlled by a view similar to his own. Thus when Jesus addresses himself to the Jews concerning his relationship to God, he defends himself and his claim to deity by using the expression, "Scripture cannot be broken." It was this claim that the Jews would not and could not deny. They believed it. What they did not believe was the claim of Jesus to be God. This they held to be blasphemy.

Read the Acts of the Apostles. What do you find there? Surely there is nothing that deals decisively with the phenomena of Scripture. Central to the Acts of the Apostles is their witness to the resurrection of Jesus Christ from the dead, not to that of an inerrant record. Later when Paul deals with the truth or the falsity of the gospel in 1 Corinthians 15, he never makes reference to the authority, inspiration or inerrancy of Scripture. But he does state that the faith rises or falls on the resurrection of Jesus Christ from the dead.

One can read the balance of the NT, and search in vain he must, for anything that suggests that the writers sought to formulate a carefully defined doctrine of an inspired, authoritative and inerrant revelation. There is adequate material dealing with this subject, but not in the context of a disputed issue and not with the intention of forging an apologetic to answer the opponents of such a viewpoint. Indeed there was no need for the writers of the NT to spend much time dealing with this subject. They embraced the common view of the OT held by the Jews of every age. There is a sense in which it may be said that the NT deals with the inerrancy of the Scriptures much the same way that it deals with the virgin birth. Both are stated and affirmed. But neither one is the object of real definitive treatment. Both are taken for granted.

In the early centuries of the Church, the theologians and church councils faced grave problems. But none of them devoted much time to the question of an inspired and inerrant Bible. The question of Christology agitated every fishmonger in the Eastern Church. The philosophically-minded Greek world wrestled with the question of the preincarnate

Christ. The Arian controversy symbolized this struggle, and from it came decisions that firmly imbedded into the theology of Christendom the teaching that Jesus Christ is coeternal with the Father, of one substance in essence and yet distinct in person.

The Christological controversy did not stop with the preincarnate Christ. It continued as the Church sought answers to the questions raised by the incarnation. If Christ is God, is he also true man? Or is his appearance as man simply an appearance and nothing more? Under the guise of docetism, the humanity of Christ was obscured and the Church had to fight its way through that miasma of speculation until the formula was devised of one person in two natures, with a human nature and a divine nature, separate and distinct without fusion or confusion. And then it was declared that Christ had both a human and a divine will as over against the teaching of the monothelites.

Still later the Church was gripped by the anthropological controversy, better known under the label of Pelagianism and semi-Pelagianism. There, as in the other controversies, the problem was not one that involved the inspiration and inerrancy of the Bible. It was a matter of interpretation. Augustine of course was part and parcel of this period of strife, and lines he laid down influenced John Calvin, as any reading of *The Institutes of the Christian Religion* will demonstrate.

The Reformation period did nothing to change the picture materially relative to inspiration and inerrancy. It is true that the Reformation involved the Scriptures, but never was it a question of either the authority or the inspiration of the Scriptures. Both Romanists and Reformers alike held firmly to an inerrant Word of God. The problem did center in the addition of tradition as a source of belief and authority, which addition the Reformers repudiated vehemently. *Sola Scriptura* was the key phrase in the mouths of the Reformers. But it is also true that the question of *interpreting* Scripture was central in the Reformation. Thus Luther's formula *sola fide*, or justification by faith alone, involved the problem of Biblical interpretation, not Biblical inspiration and inerrancy, which both Romanists and Reformers accepted cordially. The authority of the Bible alone and without anything else was the formal principle of the Reformers. Justification by faith alone, which repudiated the view that the Church's interpretation of Scripture must prevail, was the material principle of the Reformation.

It may be said without fear of contradiction that the Roman Catholic Church in its official position has always clung to an inerrant Scripture. And this Church has constantly defended itself against any other teaching. Thus *The Catholic Encyclopedia* of 1910 (p. 48) says:

For the last three centuries there have been authors—theologians, exegetes, and especially apologists such as Holden, Rohling, Lenormant, di Bartolo, and others—who maintained, with more or less confidence, that inspiration was limited to moral and dogmatic teaching, excluding everything in the Bible relating to history and the natural sciences. They think that in this way a whole mass of difficulties against the inerrancy of the Bible would be removed. But the Church has never ceased to protest against this attempt to restrict the inspiration of the sacred books. This is what took place when Mgr. d'Hulst, Rector of the Institut Catholique of Paris, gave a sympathetic account of this opinion in "Le Correspondant" of 25 Jan. 1893. The reply was quickly forthcoming in the Encyclical "Providentissimus Deus" of the same year. In that Encyclical Leo XIII said: "It will never be lawful to restrict inspiration to certain parts of the Holy Scriptures, or to grant that the sacred writer could have made a mistake. Nor may the opinion of those be tolerated, who, in order to get out of these difficulties, do not hesitate to suppose that Divine inspiration extends only to what touches faith and morals, on the false plea that the true meaning is sought for less in what God has said than in the motive for which He has said it." In fact, a limited inspiration contradicts Christian tradition and theological teaching.

As for the inerrancy of the inspired text it is to the Inspirer that it must finally be attributed, and it matters little if God has insured the truth of His scripture by the grace of inspiration itself, as the adherents of verbal inspiration teach, rather than by a providential assistance![1]

Luther and Calvin both accepted and taught the doctrine of an inerrant Scripture. This has been documented and is beyond denial.[2] Curiously enough, some of the followers of Luther went beyond anything taught by him and formulated a view that few if any conservative theologians would accept today. I quote: "The Lutherans who devoted themselves to composing the Protestant theory of inspiration were Melanchthon, Chemnitz, Quenstadt, Calov. Soon, to the inspiration of the words was added that of the vowel points of the present Hebrew text. This was not a mere opinion held by the two Buxtorfs, but a doctrine defined, and imposed under pain of fine, imprisonment and exile, by the Confession of the Swiss Churches, promulgated in 1675. These dispositions were abrogated in 1724" (*The Catholic Encyclopedia*, p. 48).

The eighteenth century witnessed no radical departure from the view of Scripture that had been normative through the centuries. Indeed in 1729 the Westminster Confession of Faith was adopted. When propounding a doctrine of Scripture, the Confession spoke of "the consent of all the parts...and the entire perfection thereof" (chap. 1, sec. 5). The Westminster Confession was used as the basis for the Savoy Declaration of 1658, which became normative for the Congregational Churches. And the Baptists in the United States in 1742 adopted what is generally known as the Philadelphia Confession of Faith based upon the Westminster Confession for the most part and retaining its statement on the Scriptures. A century later in 1833 the New Hampshire Confession of Faith was adopted by Baptists in America and included a statement that the Word of God is "without any mixture of error" (Declaration 1).

Of course there always were dissenting voices that did not believe the Word of God to be infallible and inerrant. But these voices were neither normative nor dominant. They did not exercise a determinative voice in the historic churches at this moment in history. Following the Reformation there was a mighty struggle waged between the Arminians and the Calvinists that extended from the sixteenth well into the nineteenth century. The battle was not waged, however, over the nature of inspiration but over questions relating to a proper understanding and interpretation of the Scriptures.

The eighteenth century marked a definite point of departure on the subject of inspiration. Sparked by the writing of John Locke in the seventeenth century, the next two centuries were characterized by the rise of rationalism, romanticism, evolution and higher criticism. Many great names are connected with this period of change: Hume, Paley, Paine, Hegel, Kant, Darwin, Nietzsche, Schopenhauer, Spencer, Comte, Marx, and the like. Included in this list should be scores of Germans popularly associated with higher criticism in the nineteenth and twentieth centuries, not to mention the various schools of thought represented by university centers such as Berlin, Tübingen and Heidelberg. Whereas earlier ages argued whether ultimate religious authority was to be found in the Bible alone, or the Bible through the teaching of the Church, or the Bible through the Pope, or by the addition of tradition, now there was a direct frontal assault on the Bible itself. Just about everything was questioned and discarded. The Bible under this attack ceased to be a book with the stamp of the divine upon it. It became to the critics a human document composed by men who were no more inspired than other literary figures and certainly not to be fully trusted for ultimate truth in theological or other areas of witness. The storm generated by the higher critics gathered in intensity and seemed to sweep everything before it. Citadels crumbled rapidly; seminaries capitulated; liberalism or modernism with all of its trappings became the order of the day in the twentieth century. In the battle, the fundamentals of the Christian faith that had stood for almost two millennia were discarded. Clifton Olmstead, in his *History of Religion in the United States*, speaks of the resistance forged against this attack on the Bible:

> In the Protestant world the theses of liberal theologians went not unchallenged. Many a theological school, especially those in the Calvinist tradition, produced scholars who were sharply critical of the new currents in

religion and clung rigidly to the doctrine of the plenary inspiration of the Bible. Among the leaders in this camp were the Presbyterians A. A. Hodge, Francis L. Patton, and Benjamin B. Warfield, and the Baptists John A. Broadus and Asahel Kendrick. At the Niagara Bible Conference, which opened in 1876 and continued to meet annually until the end of the century, conservatives regrouped their forces for a frontal attack on the new theology. Their leaders were A. J. Gordon, Arthur Pierson, C. I. Scofield, and James Gray. At the meeting in 1895 the conference formulated its famous "five points of fundamentalism" or necessary standards of belief. They were the inerrancy of Scripture, the Virgin Birth of Jesus Christ, the substitutionary theory of the atonement, the physical resurrection of Christ, and his imminent bodily return to earth. These doctrines were taught as essential at such conservative centers as Moody Bible Institute in Chicago and Los Angeles Bible Institute. In 1909 two wealthy Californians, Lyman and Milton Stewart, financed the publication of twelve small volumes entitled *The Fundamentals: A Testimony of the Truth*, nearly three million copies of which were circulated among ministers and laymen in the United States and abroad. The effect was to stir up a militant antagonism toward liberalism which would reach its height in the decade which followed the First World War. By that time the new theology would have grown old and about to be replaced by theologies which dealt more positively with contemporary issues.

It hardly seems necessary to detail the contributions rendered in the defense of orthodoxy by the Princetonians Hodge, Warfield and Green. They and others with them constructed an apologetic that has been neither equaled nor surpassed in the last generation. They worked out conservative Christianity's finest defense. Their writings are still the chief source of fact and fuel for contemporary conservative Christianity. The debt that is owed them is almost beyond estimation. It was their work that preserved the Presbyterian Church from rapid and complete surrender to the claims of higher criticism. Other denominations were infiltrated and their walls breached, but the onslaughts were thrown back by the Presbyterians. Again Olmstead speaks a word from history about this:

In several of the major denominations the fundamentalist-modernist controversy grew to gigantic proportions. None was more shaken by the conflict than the Presbyterian, U.S.A. During the painful theological controversies of the late nineteenth century, the church had held to its official position of Biblical inerrancy. In 1910 when a complaint was made to the General Assembly that the New York Presbytery had licensed three ministerial candidates whose theological views were somewhat suspect, the Assembly ruled the following articles of faith were necessary for ordination: the inerrancy of Scripture, the Virgin Birth of Christ, the miracles of Christ, the substitutionary atonement, the Resurrection of Christ. No mention was made of premillennialism, a necessary article for fundamentalists. Though the Assembly of 1910 and the Assemblies of 1916 and 1923, which reiterated the five-point requirement, had no intention of reducing the church's theology to these five articles, the conservative element in the church tended to treat the articles in precisely that manner. The general effect was to increase tension and encourage heresy-hunting.

At last the Presbyterian Church was breached. J. Gresham Machen and others continued their apologetic for a trustworthy Scripture from without the Church. At no time during this struggle within the Presbyterian Church could the defenders of an inerrant Scripture be called fundamentalists, nor would they themselves have desired the appellation. It was reserved for another group of theologically conservative people more largely connected with the Bible institute movement and with independent Bible churches throughout the land. It was the accretions to fundamentalism that gave it a bad name among so many people in America. And here one must make a distinction between theological fundamentalism and sociological fundamentalism. At no time could the Machen movement be called sociologically fundamentalist, but it certainly could be called theologically fundamentalist in the best sense of that term.

The Second World War saw the rise might be called the new evangelicalism that was keenly aware of the plight of a fundamentalism that majored on codes of conduct and defected to liberalism in the area of Christian social ethics. Earlier Carl F. H. Henry's contribution, *The Uneasy Conscience of Modern Fundamentalism*, brought some of this into sharp focus. The new evangelicals started with certain presuppositions in mind: (1) a desire to create a new and vigorous apologetic for the conservative position by raising a new generation of well-trained scholars with all of the badges of academic respectability who could speak to the current issues of the day, talk the language of the opposition, and present cogently and compellingly the viewpoint of historic Christianity in the present milieu; (2) a desire to move more vigorously into the area of social ethics and do something about the renovation of society from the vantage point of conservative theology; (3) a desire to meet and overcome the rise of neo-orthodoxy, which had replaced the decadent liberalism of the 1920s; (4) a desire to engage in dialogue with those with whom it was in disagreement, based upon the suppositions that the best defense is a good offense and that to man the walls behind barricades had led to nothing constructive in former years; and (5) a desire to move away from the negativism in personal conduct of the older fundamentalism.

This effort began to bear fruit. New and able exponents of the orthodox faith came on the scene. Their names are as familiar to you as they are to me. Books, monographs and articles were written. Even a magazine like *Time* could conclude, as did its religion editor, that conservative

Christianity had depth, strength, scholarship, and something to offer. The evangelistic ministry of Billy Graham, the establishment of *Christianity Today*, the opening of Fuller Theological Seminary, and other events evidenced the new trend. Moreover, the voices of evangelical spokesman were listened to and heard in places where they long had been silent. And all of this was accomplished within the context of a conservative theology that included a belief in an inerrant Scripture.

But now the scene is changing. In getting to the opponents of orthodox Christianity the opponents, in turn, have gotten to some of the new evangelicals. And this is no isolated phenomenon. With the new learning there had come new leaven. And the leaven is to be found in Christian colleges and theological seminaries, in books and articles, in Bible institutes and in conservative churches. The new leaven, as yet, has nothing to do with such vital questions as the virgin birth, the deity of Christ, the vicarious atonement, the physical resurrection from the dead or the second advent. It involves what it has always involved in the first stages of its development—the nature of inspiration and authority. It could not be otherwise, for one's view of the Bible ultimately determines his theology in all of its ramifications. It is like the Continental Divide in the United States, which marks off the flow of waters either to the Atlantic or the Pacific Oceans depending on which side of the Divide the waters fall. Inexorably and inevitably the waters find their way to their ultimate destiny, just as one's view of the Bible determines ultimately what his theology will be. No man in good conscience or in sanity could hold to an inerrant Scripture after forsaking the deity of Christ, the virgin birth, the vicarious atonement, the physical resurrection from the dead and the second advent.

Today there are those who have been numbered among the new evangelicals, some of whom possess the keenest minds and have acquired the apparati of scholarship, who have broken, or are in the process of breaking, with the doctrine of an inerrant Scripture. They have done so or are doing so because they think this view to be indefensible and because they do not regard it as a great divide. In order for them to be intellectually honest with themselves they must do it. Logically, however, the same attitude, orientation, bent of mind and approach to scholarship that makes the retention of an inerrant Scripture impossible also ultimately makes impossible the retention of the vicarious atonement, imputed guilt, the virgin birth, the physical resurrection and miraculous supernaturalism.[3] The mediating voices among the new evangelicals who have begun by forsaking inerrancy while retaining inspiration, revelation, authority, and the like still have this hard lesson to learn.

The new-school adherents often feel that those evangelicals who hold to an inerrant Scripture do so because they have "closed minds," or are not truly "scholarly," or are psychologically maladjusted with a defensive mechanism that precludes "openness." What they fail to realize is that the very opinions they hold in regard to those who cling to inerrancy are applied to themselves by those who have not only scrapped inerrancy but also the basic doctrines to which these same people are still committed. Thus they cannot avoid wearing the same labels they apply to the people who adhere to inerrancy, and if they think that by their concession they have really advanced the cause of dialogue with those outside the conservative tradition they are grossly mistaken.

Moreover the possession of the "closed mind," and the failure to enjoy "openness," and the problem of being truly "scholarly" does not haunt the conservative alone. Liberals are among those who have most thoroughly enjoyed and displayed the very traits they militate against in others. And the mind that is closed because it believes it possesses the truth cannot truly be unscholarly, since the pursuit of truth is the goal of scholarship; and "openness" is not a virtue when it allows for dilution and diminution of the truth one feels he possesses. Of course men may mistakenly but honestly hold to what is false, but unless there is something that is commonly held by all men, neither those who believe nor those who disbelieve can be sure of the rightness or wrongness of their positions unless they have some outside validating authority to which final reference can be made. And this the Word of God is.

One can predict with almost fatalistic certainty that in due course of time the moderating evangelicals who deny inerrancy will adopt new positions such as belief in the multiple authorship of Isaiah, the late date of Daniel, the idea that the first eleven chapters of Genesis are myth and saga. And then these critical conclusions will spill over into the NT, and when the same principles of higher criticism are applied this can only lead to a scrapping of the facticity of the resurrection, etc. This has ever been the historical movement, and there is nothing to suppose that such a repetitive process will not follow.

Rarely does one hear of a journey from liberalism to orthodoxy, from an errant Scripture to an inerrant Scripture. For the most part it is a one-way street in the wrong direction. It is the opinion of this writer that the moderating proponents among the new evangelicals stand in mortal danger of defecting from the foundation on which the new evangelicalism was built, of evacuating that which it came into being to defend, of surrendering to an inclusive theology that it opposed, and of hiding its deception in a plethora of words semantically disguised so as to curry favor with those who deny inerrancy and at the same time to retain the allegiance of those who cling to the old doctrine.

This is no obscurantist pose. Nor does it in any sense threaten or underestimate the good in the new evangelicalism. Nor is it intended to downgrade Christian scholarship of the highest order. Rather it is intended to make plain the fact that just as Christology, anthropology and justification by faith were key issues in the theological struggle of bygone ages, so today the key theological issue is that of a wholly trustworthy or inerrant Scripture. Moreover it is designed to impress upon all that the most significant conservative movement of the twentieth century, labeled by many the new evangelicalism, has already been breached by some and is in the process of being breached by others. And the Evangelical Theological Society that has been such a vital part of the new evangelicalism had better be aware of the turn of events. It has been infected itself, and its own foundations need to be reexamined. For what this Society does and how it reacts to this challenge may well determine the direction that churches, denominations and institutions take in the years immediately before us.

¹It should be noted here that the question of the means by which an inerrant Scripture came into being is not the subject of discussion. One can honestly disagree with the person who believes in the mechanical dictation theory as over against the view that God by his Spirit allowed the writers to speak consonant with their linguistic talents and peculiarities. Yet whatever the means were, the end product is the same: an inerrant Scripture.

² In *Scripture Cannot Be Broken*, Theodore Engelder adduces overwhelming evidence to support this assertion about Luther. Luther endorsed Augustine by saying: "The Scriptures have never erred"; "the Scriptures cannot err"; "it is certain that Scripture cannot disagree with itself." Augustine's famous statement is: "To those books which are already styled canonical, I have learned to pay such reverence and honour as most firmly to believe that none of their authors has committed any error in writing. If in that literature I meet with anything which seems contrary to truth, I will have no doubt that it is only the maunscript which is faulty, or the translator who has not hit the sense, or my own failure to understand" (*A Catholic Dictionary* [New York: Addis and Arnold, 1884] 450). In the case of Calvin there are those who have argued on both sides of the issue. In favor of inerrancy are H. Banke, *Das Problem der Theologie Calvins*; R. E. Davies, *The Problem of Authority in the Continental Reformers*; E. A. Dowey, *The Knowledge of God in Calvin's Theology*; A. M. Hunter, *The Teaching of Calvin*; J. Mackinnon, *Calvin and the Reformation*. Mackinnon senses as everyone must that Calvin the scholar over against Calvin the theologian had problems: "When he (the scholar) sees an obvious error in text before him, there is no indication that it makes any *theologial* impression on him at all....Again, why, if not because the error is a trivial copyist's blunder, not a misunderstanding of divine 'dictation' by an apostle or prophet?" In other words, Calvin would have been in agreement with Augustine. In both cases it means that they were looking to the autographs, not to copies that were in some measure defective due to copyists' mistakes. Ernest R. Sandeen, of North College, in his paper "The Princeton Theology," *CH* (September 1962), says that Hodge and Warfield "retreated" to "lost and completely useless original autographs" as though this was an innovation. He labels it "the Princeton argument." He failed to see that Hodge and Warfield followed both Augustine and Calvin. Thus the problem was not a new one, but it was "new" in the sense that for the first time in the history of the Church it was *the* central issue being discussed and fought.

³It is true that men do not always press their views to their logical conclusions. Thus one can hold to an errant Scripture while not forsaking other cardinal doctrines. It is for this reason that those who accept Biblical inerrancy should not break with those who disagree with them unless the divergence includes a further departure from other major doctrines of orthodoxy. Perchance the continuance of closest contacts will convince those who reject inerrancy what the logical consequences of such rejection involve.

# INSPIRATION AND INERRANCY: A NEW DEPARTURE

## JOHN WARWICK MONTGOMERY

If I have told you earthly things, and ye believe not, how shall ye believe, if I tell you of heavenly things? (John 3:12)

In his classic work, *The Progress of Dogma*, James Orr contended that the Christian Church, in each great epoch of its history, has been forced to come to grips with one particular doctrine of crucial significance both for that day and for the subsequent history of the Church.[1] In the patristic era the issue was the relation of the persons of the Godhead, and particularly the Christological problem of Jesus' character. The ecumenical creeds represent the success of orthodox trinitarian theology over against numerous Christological heresies, any one of which could have permanently destroyed the Christian faith. Medieval Christianity faced the issue of the meaning of Christ's atonement, and Anselm's "Latin doctrine," in spite of its scholastic inadequacies, gave solid expression to Biblical salvation-history as represented by the epistle to the Hebrews. In the Reformation era the overarching doctrinal problem facing the Church was the appication of redemption in justification. Luther's stand for *sola gratia, sola fide* arrested an anthropocentric trend that could have turned the Christian faith into little more than pagan religiosity.

And contemporary Christianity? What great doctrinal issue does the modern Church face? Writing just before the turn of the present century, Orr thought that he could see in eschatology the unique doctrinal challenge for modern Christianity. Subsequent events, however, have proven this judgment wrong: The doctrinal problem that above all others demands resolution in the modern Church is that of the authority of Holy Scripture. All other issues of belief today pale before this issue, and indeed root in it. For example, ecumenical discussions, if they are doctrinal in nature, eventually and inevitably reach the question of religious

59

authority: What is the final determinant of doctrinal truth, and how fully can the Bible be relied upon to establish truth in theological dialog? As the patristic age faced a Christological watershed, as the medieval and Reformation Churches confronted soteriological crises, so the contemporary Church finds itself grappling with the great epistemological question in Christian dogmatics.[2] And let it be noted with care: Just as the Church in former times could have permanently crippled its posterity through superficial or misleading answers to the root questions then at issue, so we today have an equal obligation to deal responsibly with the Scripture issue. If we do not, future generations of theologians may find that no criterion remains by which to solve any subsequent doctrinal problems, and the theologians of the twentieth century will have gained the dubious distinction of having made their discipline (and the Church that looks to it for its doctrinal guidance) totally irrelevant.

## I. THE OSTENSIBLE NATURE OF THE ISSUE

To the unsophisticated observer of the twentieth-century theological scene it might seem that the present epistemological issue in theology is simply whether the Bible is inspired or not. (Later we shall be reminded that the unsophisticated, like children, often have disarming insight.) However, those who are dissatisfied with the traditional formulations of the Scripture doctrine argue in the strongest terms that the real issue is not whether the Bible is inspired or not, but the *character* and *extent* of inspiration. The claim is made that a nontraditional approach to Biblical authority in no way denies the existence of inspiration. It merely defines more closely what is meant by inspiration and how far such inspiration extends in Holy Writ.

Thus it is held that Scripture is inspired as a theological norm—as God's authoritative message in matters spiritual—but that in matters historical and scientific we must recognize the human, fallible element in the Biblical witness. "So," writes Roy A. Harrisville of Luther Seminary, "we admit to the discrepancies and the broken connections in Scripture, we let them stand just as they are—this is part of what it means that faith has its sphere in this world and not in some cloud cuckoo-land."[3] And the editors of *Dialog*, in a recent issue devoted to "Scripture and Tradition," are willing (albeit grudgingly) to continue the use of the expression "Scripture is inspired" if by it is meant that "Scripture is God's absolutely authoritative and authorized fundamental witness to revelation"—as long as no attempt is made to apply such inspiration to "an inerrancy of the 'parts,' of the historical and scientific opinions of the biblical authors."[4] In a subsequent issue of *Dialog* the Lutheran Church-Missouri

Synod's *Report of the Commission on Theology and Church Relations* ("A Study Document on Revelation, Inspiration, Inerrancy," 1964) is criticized for not labeling as erroneous the *Brief Statement's* inclusion of the historical and scientific data of the Bible in its definition of inspiration.[5] A more esoteric expression of the same general view is that the Bible is totally inspired—indeed, infallibly inspired—but that such inspiration does not necessarily produce inerrant results in matters historical or scientific, since God's word infallibly accomplishes only what he *intends* it to accomplish (that is, the revelation of theological truths, not the imparting of historical or scientific absolutes).

In sum, then, the present controversy over Biblical authority ostensibly centers on a split between inspiration and inerrancy. It is claimed that the former can and should be held without the latter. Not only will the Christian no longer have to defend the Bible against scientific and historical criticism, but he will be freed to enter more fully into a purely faith-relationship with Jesus Christ.

> In the last analysis, a rejection of the doctrine of inerrancy involves primarily a mental readjustment. Nothing basic is lost. In fact, when all the evidence is examined, those essential elements which the advocates of the doctrine of inerrancy have cherished and sought to protect are more firmly supported than ever before. Scripture is the product of inspiration and it is the indispensable source for coming to know God's claim upon us and his will for us.[6]

The contention of the present writer, over against these views expressed above, is that inspiration and inerrancy cannot be separated—that like "love" and "marriage" in *Annie, Get Your Gun*, "you can't have one without the other." This traditional position may seem on the surface to necessitate a traditional defense of it, along the lines of the vast number of admittedly drab works on the subject produced by "fundamentalists" since the days of the Scopes evolution trial. However, nothing could be farther from the truth. Note carefully that I have not said merely (as others have said) that inspiration and inerrancy *should* not be separated (that is, that they *can* be separated but for various Biblical and theological reasons *ought* not to be), but rather than scriptural inspiration and inerrancy *cannot* exist apart from each other (that is, that to separate them results not just in error but in plain and simple *meaninglessness*). I am convinced that the dullness and the sameness in standard orthodox defenses of Biblical inerrancy point to an impasse in previous thinking on the subject and constitute a demand for ground-breaking along different lines. By way of certain new techniques derived from the realm of analytical philosophy I believe that one can see exactly where the central difficulty lies in the present-day attempt to dichotomize inspiration and inerrancy. The result of this investigation will, it is believed, leave the reader with but two meaningful alternatives: a Bible that is both inspired and inerrant (or, better, inerrant because it is inspired), or a Bible that is not different qualitatively from other books.[7] The superficially attractive halfway-house of an inspired, noninerrant Bible will be seen to evaporate in the mist as a concept having neither philosophical nor theological but only emotive significance.

## II. THE PECULIARITY OF THE ISSUE

The contemporary advocates of an inspired but noninerrant view of the Bible appeal constantly to the pressure of recent scholarship as justifying and indeed demanding their viewpoint. A recent letter from a well-known professor of NT interpretation took me to task for my Biblical position on the ground that "a new era of biblical theology began to dawn some twenty-five years ago; and, I believe, any biblical matters cannot ignore what has happened in this field." Warren A. Quanbeck of Luther Seminary has recently argued in more explicit terms that inerrancy was unable to survive the onslaughts of modern historical and scientific scholarship:

> Theologians read the Bible as a collection of revealed propositions unfolding the truth about God, the world, and man. Because the Holy Spirit was the real author of Scripture, every proposition in it was guaranteed infallible and inerrant, not only in spiritual, but in secular matters.
>
> Because of this insistence on the Bible's inerrancy in historical and scientific matters, the blows struck by studies in historical and natural science were crushing in their force. When men approached the Bible as a collection of historical books they saw plainly the human character of its writers and their obvious dependence upon the sources of information available in their day. They recognized also that the scientific outlook of the writers was that of their time, and could not be a substitute for present-day scientific investigation and experiment. When theologians insisted that the religious message of the Bible stood or fell with its scientific and historical information they assumed an impossible apologetic task.[8]

The strangeness in this line of argumentation lies in two principal considerations: (1) The alleged factual errors and internal contradictions in Scripture that are currently cited to demonstrate the impossibly archaic nature of the inerrancy view are themselves impossibly archaic in a high proportion of instances; and (2) the most recent scholarly investigations and intellectual trends bearing on the validity of Biblical data have never been more hospitable to inerrancy claims. Let us consider in this connection the recent series of anti-inerrancy arguments adduced by Robert Scharlemann:

Unless one makes all sorts of special qualifications for the term "error," this statement [that "the scientist can accept the entire Bible and God's inspired Word for it is inerrant"] can simply not be supported by an examination of the Bible itself. Let me cite two examples which, since they are not from the area of "science," are likely to be less provocative.

A reporter could ask the question, "Was the Greek word *houtos* the first or last word in the superscription on the cross at Jesus' crucifixion?" From Luke (23:38) he would receive the reply, "It was the last." From Matthew (27:37) he would receive the reply, "It was the first." By any normal definition of error, either Matthew or Luke is in error concerning this reportorial matter; perhaps both of them are.

As second example is the classical one. Matthew 27:9 ascribes to Jeremiah a quotation which is actually found in Zechariah.

These are not isolated cases. Numerous examples can be found if one is interested in hunting for them. When was Jesus crucified? According to Matthew, Mark, and Luke it was on the 15th of Nisan; according to John it was on the 14th of Nisan. At least one of them must be in error. Unless one so defines "error" that it does not really mean an error in the normal sense; or unless one holds to the word "inerrancy" with a sort of blind dogmatism, the assertion that the Bible is inerrant, "that is, contains no error," simply cannot be supported by the Biblical evidence itself.[9]

This account of representative "contradictions" derives in no sense from modern scholarship. The alleged discrepancies have been recognized for centuries and have been dealt with in a variety of effective ways. Haley, in his great work on supposed Biblical contradictions, stated in 1874 what had been obvious to readers of the superscriptions since the accounts were originally set down: "It is altogether improbable that three inscriptions, in three different languages, should correspond word for word."[10] And in reference to the Zechariah quotation in Matthew he presents two perfectly reasonable ways of dealing with the problem, both of which are derived from earlier scholarship:

> According to the Jewish writers, Jeremiah was reckoned the first of the prophets, and was placed first in the book of the prophets; thus, Jeremiah, Ezekiel, Isaiah, etc. Matthew, in quoting this book, may have quoted it under the name which stood *first* in it; that is, instead of saying, "by the Prophets," he may have said, "by Jeremy the prophet," since *he* headed the list.
>
> Or, the difficulty may have arisen from abridgment of the names. In the Greek, Jeremiah, instead of being written in full, might stand thus, "Iriou"; Zechariah thus, "Zriou." By the mere change of Z into I [i.e., by later scribal copyists], the mistake would be made. The Syriac Peshitto and several MSS. have simply, "by the prophet."[11]

Alleged contradictions of this kind were, in fact, more than adequately handled by such orthodox fathers of the Reformation era as Andreas Althamer.[12] As for the 14th/15th-Nisan crucifixion difficulty, which has also had much attention through Christian history, the most recent Biblical scholarship has provided what may well be the final answer to the problem: A. Jaubert, a French specialist on the Dead Sea scrolls, has shown that two calendars were employed in first-century Palestine (the official lunar calendar and a Jubilees-Qumran calendar) and that there is every reason to believe that the double dating in the gospel accounts of the crucifixion, far from being a contradiction, simply reflects these two calendar systems.[13]

In point of fact, as Jaubert's investigations illustrate, the present climate of research is more hospitable to an inerrancy approach than was the nineteenth century or the early decades of the twentieth. Archaeological work daily confirms Biblical history in ways that liberal criticism would have regarded as patently impossible a few decades ago.[14] The Einsteinian-relativistic reinterpretation of "natural law" has dealt a death-blow to Hume's arguments against the miraculous and has removed the rational possibility of using antimiraculous presuppositions for dehistoricizing such Biblical accounts as Jonah-and-the-Leviathan.[15] The collapse of form-critical techniques in Homeric and other classical literary criticism, and the presently recognized debility of that approach even in the literary study of English ballads, has raised overwhelming doubts as to the whole presuppositional substructure of the Dibelius-Bultmann approach to the NT documents.[16] All in all, the traditional position on inspiration is able to command more respect today than it has during any generation since the advent of rationalistic higher criticism.

However, there is obviously something to the claim that "a new era of biblical theology began to dawn some twenty-five years ago"—an era that, in spite of developments such as those just described, could not tolerate plenary inspirationism. What has constituted the enormous pressure against the inerrancy view? Why have contemporary theologians found it necessary to ridicule the position and to treat it as a hopelessly outmoded one, in spite of such formidable proponents of it as the philosopher Gordon Clark, the theologian Edward John Carnell, and the NT lexicographer W. F. Arndt? Why have such considerations as archaeological findings and classical scholarship not moved the mainstream theologians in the direction of plenary inspiration? The answer is most definitely not (in spite of loud protests continually voiced) the weight of new factual evidence against an inerrant Bible. Such "evidence" simply does not exist. As we have noted and illustrated, the contemporary critic of an inerrant Scripture is still citing alleged discrepancies and supposed scientific objections that have been adequately dealt with over and over again.[17] *The issue is not empirical; it is philosophical.* That is to say, there has been an alteration in the philosophical *Zeitgeist* that, apart from the question of particular factual evidence, makes scriptural inerrancy offensive to much of contemporary theological thought. What precisely is this new element in the current climate of theological opinion?

A hint of an answer is provided by Rupert E. Davies in his attempt to refute John Wenham's inerrancy position. Writes Davies:

> I cannot believe that truths which go away into mystery can be expressed once for all in propositional form; and the Bible never claims that they can. Its purpose is to draw attention in many different ways to the saving Acts of God.[18]

Here a suggestion is made that the Bible deals with a different kind of subject matter than is capable of being expressed propositionally. Biblical truth is not propositional and static but dynamic and active; its focus is on acts, not assertions.

For the late A.G. Hebert, one of the prime modern opponents of plenary inspiration, the "propositional" view of Biblical truth is a relatively recent and unfortunate result of applying scientific categories in the religious sphere.

> The doctrine of Inerrancy was not very harmful in an age which thought of "truth" primarily as belonging to the revelation of God and of the eternal meaning of man's life. The Bible was regarded as teaching chiefly spiritual truths about God and man. It was otherwise when the "scientific age" had begun; truth was now commonly understood as the matter-of-fact truth of observable phenomena, and so great a man as Locke could make the outrageous statement that the existence of God was as certain as the propositions of geometry. The Inerrancy of the Bible was understood as guaranteeing the literal exactness of its every statement. This is the Fundamentalism which has been a potent cause of modern unbelief. This materialistic Inerrancy needs to be carefully distinguished from the theological and religious Inerrancy in which earlier ages believed.[19]

Even if one leaves aside the minor fallacies in this statement (for example, the confusion of geometry with observable phenomena),[20] one cannot accept the historical explanation of the inerrancy position here presented. Throughout the history of the Church there has been continual concern to maintain and defend the total factual reliability of the Bible. To take only one prominent example, St. Augustine, by all odds the most important theologian of the patristic age, argued with vehemence for an inerrant Bible. As the definitive study of his Biblical position asserts:

> There is no point of doctrine more plainly asserted or more vigorously defended by St. Augustine, than the absence of falsehood and error from the divine Scriptures....Indeed inerrancy is so intimately bound up with inspiration that an inspired book cannot assert what is not true....It is impos-

sible for Scripture to contain contradictory statements. One book of Scripture cannot contradict another, nor can the same author contradict himself.[21]

From earliest times the Church was concerned with the propositional accuracy of the Biblical text, for such a concern followed directly from the Church's commitment to the inspiration of Scripture. Actually the so-called "dynamic," nonpropositional view of truth has its origin not in pre-scientific times but in very recent thinking.

The source of this essentially new approach to the nature of Biblical truth over against traditional plenary inspiration will become more evident if we look closely at a typical recent expression of it. Let us hear Warren Quanbeck's "re-examination of theological presuppositions":

> Since human language is always relative, being conditioned by its historical development and usage, there can be no absolute expression of the truth even in the language of theology. Truth is made known in Jesus Christ, who is God's Word, his address to mankind. Christ is the only absolute. Theological statements, which have an instrumental function, find their meaning in relation to him; they do not contain the truth nor give adequate expression to it. At best they point to Jesus Christ as the one in whom one may know the truth. Truth is not a matter of intellection only, but of obedient discipleship. Only by "abiding in Christ" can one know the truth.[22]

To any historian of philosophy the antecedents of this view are patently obvious, and they lie not in the realm of Biblical/theological presuppositions, as Quanbeck and other adherents of this position believe, but in the realm of philosophical a priori. The idea that "there can be no absolute expression of the truth" in propositional form has clear alignment with the venerable philosophical position known as metaphysical dualism, which in one form or other has always claimed that the Absolute cannot be fully manifested in the phenomenal world. From Plato's separation of the world of ideas from the world of things and the soul from the body, to the medieval "realists" with their split between universals and particulars, through the Reformation Calvinists' conviction that *finitum non est capax infiniti*, to the modern idealism of Kant and Hegel, we see this same conviction in various semantic garbs. It is this absolute separation of eternity and time that lies at the basis of the contemporary theological split between *Geschichte* and *Historie*, as I have indicated elsewhere.[23] And it is most definitely the same aprioristic dualism that motivates much of contemporary theology in its refusal to allow the Eternal to express himself in absolutely veracious Biblical propositions.

But metaphysical dualism is only the minor element in the anti-inerrancy position taken by Quanbeck and others. "Truth," he writes, "is not a matter of intellection only, but of obedient discipleship," and "Christ is the only absolute." Here we see the redefinition of truth in personal, as opposed to propositional, terms. Truth is arrived at not through words or through investigation but "only by 'abiding in Christ.' " Martin Scharlemann, in an unpublished paper presenting this same general approach to Biblical inspiration, concludes: "In a very real sense, therefore, it is impossible to speak of revelation as an objective reality, independent of personal reaction on the part of him to whom a disclosure is made. ...Knowledge is not a matter of acquiring information but of being confronted with God Himself as He is revealed as His Son."[24] Such terminology and conceptual content point unmistakably to the existentialist movement in modern philosophy, which, stemming from Kierkegaard, has affirmed that "truth is subjectivity" and that "existence," as manifested in personal relationships, precedes and surpasses in quality "essence"—that is, formal, propositional assertions or descriptions concerning reality.[25] In the hands of its most influential contemporary Protestant advocate, Rudolf Bultmann, existentialist theology claims to "cut under the subject-object distinction"[26] so as to arrive at a "dynamic" view of Biblical truth untrammeled by questions of propositional facticity or objective validity.

No philosophy has so captured the minds and hearts of the contemporary world as existentialism, for how can one listen to "propositional" assertions of "objective" ideals when the West has barely survived two terrible self-created holocausts and seems bent on nuclear self-destruction? Only in personal existential relationships does any hope seem to lie. So speaks the average member of the Western intelligentsia. And, as has happened not a few times in the history of theology, the professional theologian does him one better: In religious life as well, truth can only be found in personality (Christ), and one should discard as irrelevant and harmful excess baggage the traditional view that Scripture offers propositionally objective truth to man. Thus the cultural pressure to existentialism, combined with a powerful tradition of metaphysical dualism,[27] impels much of modern theology to reject inerrancy. Modernity is indeed the source of the new approach to Scripture, but it is not a modernity characterized by new discoveries of empirical fact that have forced modifications of traditional thinking. Rather, it is a modernity of philosophical *Zeitgeist*.

Bultmann has argued, in defense of his use of existentialistic categories in interpreting Biblical data, that existentialism is really not an alien philosophy but a heuristic methodology that does not commit one to extra-Biblical positions. It is almost universally agreed, however, both by professional philosophers and by lay interpreters of existentialism, that this viewpoint does indeed constitute a philosophy and that its presuppositions (that is, "existence precedes essence," "the objective-subjective distinction must be transcended," "truth is found only in personal encounter," etc.) can and must be subjected to philosophical analysis and criticism. Such a process of critical anaylsis has been going on now for some years, and the results have been devastatingly negative for the existentialist position. Indeed, faced with the blistering criticism directed against existentialism by analytical philosophy in particular, contemporary thought is now beginning to move away from Albert Camus's dread city of Oran into more congenial philosophical habitats.

It is now our task to apply the techniques of analytic philosophy to the anti-inerrancy position on Scripture that derives from an existentialistic-dualistic *Weltanschauung*. In doing so we shall discover, possibly to our amazement, that contemporary theological denials of inerrancy necessarily tie themselves to philosophical stars that are rapidly burning out.

## III. The Meaninglessness of Existentialistic and Dualistic Affirmations

We shall commence our critical task with an examination of analytical technique in general and its application to existentialism and dualism in particular. The relevance of the following discussion to the inerrancy issue will become evident in the subsequent sections of the paper.

While theologians of the last two decades have been especially concerned with the epistemological problem of Biblical authority, contemporary philosophy (particularly in England) has likewise focused attention on central epistemological issues. Faced with the welter of conflicting philosophical and theological world views propounded through the centuries, twentieth-century analytical philosophers have attempted to cut back to the basic question: How can truth-claims be verified? In a brief paper such as this it would be impossible to discuss the history of this analytical movement, arising from the pioneering *Principia Mathematica* of Russell and Whitehead, extending through the "logical atomism" of Wittgenstein's amazing *Tractatus Logico-Philosophicus*, and culminating in the (misnamed) "logical positivism" of Von Mises and the "linguistic analysis" or "ordinary language philosophy" of the later Wittgenstein and Ryle.[28] But in very general terms the conclusions of these analytical thinkers can be summarized in regard to the problem of verifiability.

> The criterion which we use to test the genuineness of apparent statements of fact is the criterion of verifiability. We say that a sentence is factually significant to any given person, if, and only if, he knows how to verify the proposition which it purports to express—that is, if he knows what observations

would lead him, under certain conditions, to accept the proposition as being true, or reject it as being false.[29]

This "verifiability criterion of meaning" arose from the discovery (set forth by Whitehead and Russell in the *Principia*) that assertions in mathematics and deductive logic are tautologous—that is, they state nothing factual about the world but follow from the a priori assumptions of the deductive system. Such "analytic" sentences can be verified without recourse to the world of fact, since they say nothing about the world. But other assertions (nontautological or "synthetic" affirmations) must be tested by the data of the real world if we are to discover their truth or falsity.

Thus any proposition, upon inspection, will fall into one of the following categories: (1) Analytic sentences, which are true or false solely by virtue of their logical form, *ex hypothesi*. Such assertions, though essential to thought and potentially meaningful, are often termed "trivial" since they never provide information about the world of experience. Example: "All husbands are married," whose truth follows entirely from the definition of the word "husband." (2) Synthetic sentences, which are true or false according to the application of the verifiability criterion set forth above. Such sentences are sometimes termed "informative" because they do potentially give information about the world. Example: "Jesus died at Jerusalem," which can be tested through an examination of historical evidence. (3) Meaningless sentences, embracing all affirmations that are neither analytic nor synthetic. Such sentences are incapable of testing, for they neither express tautological judgments (they are not statements whose truth depends on their logical form) nor do they affirm anything about the real world which is testable by investigating the world. Example: the philosopher F. H. Bradley's claim that "the Absolute enters into, but is itself incapable of, evolution and progress." Such a statement is clearly not tautologous, for it is not deduced from the a prioris of logic nor is it capable of any test that could conceivably determine its truth or falsity. Thus it is meaningless or nonsensical (in the technical meaning of "nonsense"—that is, without verifiable sense).

The importance of the analytic approach to questions of truth and falsity cannot be overestimated. As a result of its application, vast areas of philosophical speculation and argument have been shown to lie in a never-never land of meaninglessness, a land where discussion could continue forever without any possibility of arriving at truth or falsity. The analysts have successfully cleared the philosophical air of numerous positions about which discussion of truth-value is a waste of time because their verifiability is impossible in any case.[30].

It should be emphasized, however, that "category three" statements are meaningless only in the special sense of nonverifiability. When Ayer speaks of the analytical "elimination of metaphysics," one should not conclude that nontestable philosophical or religions assertions do not deserve study. They do, but only from an historical or psychological viewpoint. Such statements as "The Absolute enters into evolution and progress," while not telling us anything about logic or about the constitution of the world, do tell us something (a great deal, in fact) about its formulator, Bradley, and about the history of philosophical ideology. Wittgenstein illustrates the matter well by one of his typically striking parables:

> Imagine that there is a town in which the policemen are required to obtain information from each inhabitant, e.g. his age, where he came from, and what work he does. A record is kept of this information and some use is made of it. Occasionally when a policeman questions an inhabitant he discovers that the latter does not do *any* work. The policeman enters this fact on the record, because *this too* is a useful piece of information about the man![31]

Malcolm, who relates the parable, comments: "The application of the parable is, I think, that if you do not understand a statement, then to discover that it has no verification is an important piece of information about it and makes you understand it better. That is to say, you understand it *better*; you do not find out that there is nothing to understand." Thus analytical philosophy does not, *pace* its detractors, attempt to silence all discussion of nonverifiable matters. Rather, it attempts to limit discussions only to the "understandable" aspects of these matters— namely, to the emotive considerations represented by metaphysical assertions. It is in light of this qualification that we must interpret Wittgenstein's two great assertions, which have so powerfully influenced all subsequent analytical work:

> Alles was überhaupt gedacht werden kann, kann klar gedacht werden. Alles was sich aussprechen lässt, lässt sich klar aussprechen.

> Wovon man nicht sprechen kann, darüber muss man schweigen.[32]

Now in practice how does the verifiability principle achieve this desirable limitation of speech to what can be said meaningfully and clearly? Let us consider several examples, which will progressively move us into the philosophical-theological application of analytical technique.

1. *"There are angels living on the planet Uranus."*[33] This might seem on the surface to be a meaningless proposition, for no present test of verifiability exists by which the truth or falsity of the claim can be determined. However (on the assumption that angels are visible creatures), a test can

be conceived: It would involve the use of spacecraft to make the journey to Uranus, whereby through direct observation the proposition could be tested as to its truth-value. Thus the proposition, being hypothetically testable, is meaningful. However, let it be noted well that if "angels" are defined in such a way that there is no conceivable way of determining their presence even if one succeeds in arriving at their habitat, then proposition 1 would indeed be meaningless (except as an emotive assertion, such as "I like angels"). Consider Antony Flew's parable, developed from a tale told by John Wisdom:

> Once upon a time two explorers came upon a clearing in the jungle. In the clearing were growing many flowers and many weeds. One explorer says, "Some gardener must tend this plot." The other disagrees, "There is no gardener." So they pitch their tents and set a watch. No gardener is ever seen. "But perhaps he is an invisible gardener." So they set up a barbed-wire fence. They electrify it. They patrol with bloodhounds. (For they remember how H.G. Wells' *The Invisible Man* could be both smelt and touched though he could not be seen.) But no shrieks ever suggest that some intruder has received a shock. No movements of the wire ever betray an invisible climber. The bloodhounds never give cry. Yet still the Believer is not convinced. "But there is a gardener, invisible, intangible, insensible to electric shocks, a gardener who has no scent and makes no sound, a gardener who comes secretly to look after the garden which he loves." At last the Sceptic despairs, "But what remains of your original assertion? Just how does what you call an invisible, intangible, eternally elusive gardener differ from an imaginary gardener or even from no gardener at all?"[34]

This parable shows with utmost clarity how meaningless are religious assertions that are removed entirely from the realm of testability. Is not one of the most fundamental reasons for the strength of the Christian proclamation that "God was *in Christ*"—since apart from God's revelation of himself in our midst, we could never know with certainty whether the garden of this world had a loving Gardener at all? But more of this later.

2. "*The world was created in 4004 B.C., but with built-in evidence of radiocarbon dating, fossil evidence, etc., indicating millions of years of prior developmental growth*." This assertion, given current popularity by Whitcomb and Morris in their controversial, anti-evolutionary book, *The Genesis Flood*, is a nonsensical proposition.[35] Why? Because it excludes all possible testability. *Any* alleged scientific fact marshaled against 4004 B.C. creation is, by the nature of the original proposition, discounted as having been built into the universe at its creation. Moreover, the statement is reconcilable with an infinite number of parallel assertions, such as "The world was created ten years ago (or ten minutes ago) with a built-in history." Such assertions as proposition 2 are really no different from mean-

ingless cosmological affirmations of the type "The universe is continually increasing in size at a uniform rate" (obviously, in such a case, our instruments of measurement would *also* be increasing in size uniformly, and would not therefore be capable of yielding any evidence of the increase!). The Christian can take comfort that his God is not like Descartes's "Evil Genius"—that he does not introduce deceptive elements into his universe, thereby driving his creatures to meaningless affirmations about the world.

3. *"The resurrection of Christ, though an historical event in the full sense of the term (Geschichte and Historie), nonetheless cannot be verified by the methods of objective historical scholarship; it is evident only to the eyes of faith."* This position, developed by Karl Barth and emphasized in his 1952 debate with Bultmann, is revealed as meaningless when placed under the searchlight of the verifiability principle. For how could one possibly know if Christ's resurrection (or any other event) was in fact historical if it could not be tested by the ordinary methods of historical investigation? As a parallel, consider the following argument: "In my backyard is an orange hippopotamus. He is really there, but his presence cannot be tested by any techniques employed to show the existence of the other things in my backyard." Such a claim is nonsense. Either the hippopotamus is there or he is not there; and if no empirical test will show that he is, then one must conclude that assertions concerning his existence are meaningless. Likewise, if Christ's resurrection really occurred in history (*Historie*), then historical investigation will indicate it; if not, then one must give up any meaningful claim to the resurrection as a *historisch* event. Either the orthodox theologians are right, or Bultmann is right: No meaningful middle ground exists.

But, it is argued, can we not speak of Christ's resurrection, virgin birth, and other such religious events on the level of *Geschichte*, "metahistory" or "suprahistory"? It is exactly here that we encounter the dualistic tradition, which as already noted constitutes one of the two essential elements in the contemporary anti-inerrancy view of the Bible. What about this eminent tradition of metaphysical dualism that serves as the most extensive "footnote to Plato" in Western thought? Should we not think of the Absolute apart from the earthly flux—God as Otto's "Wholly Other" or as Tillich's "Ultimate Concern," never fully identified with institutions, persons, books or events in this world? Is it not of tremendous value to hold, with Plato and the medieval realists, that the phenomenal world can never dim the beauties of the eternal world of Ideas, and to affirm with Tillich that the "truth of faith" cannot be "judged by any other kind of truth, whether scientific, historical or philosophical"?[36] The answer is simply that, whatever the supposed advantages of metaphysical or theological dualism, and however praiseworthy the motives leading to such dualisms, their result is analytical meaninglessness. Why? Because by definition, insofar as any statement about the "Absolute" or "God" does not touch the world of human experience, to that extent it cannot be verified in any sensible way. Thus have the analytical philosophers devastatingly criticized the metaphysical affirmations of the modern philosophical tradition represented by Hegel and Kant, and thus do the theological dualists on the contemporary scene fall under the critical axe of the same verifiability test. If for example claim is made that Christ rose from the dead, but in the suprahistorical realm of *Geschichte*, not in the empirical realm of *Historie*, one has every right to ask, "What precisely do you *mean* by the realm of *Geschichte*, and how do you know anything—much less a resurrection—goes on there?" A supra-experiential realm is *ex hypothesi* untestable and therefore, like my orange hippopotamus mentioned earlier, irrelevant as a theological concept. It may (and does) tell us much about the theologians who rely upon it (particularly, that they fervently wish to avoid criticism from secular historians!), but it tells us nothing whatever about the truth-value of alleged events of a *geschichtlich* character. We know (or can know) whether a resurrection occurred in this world, and we know (or can know) whether God was incarnated in this world, but about a realm beyond all human testability we can know nothing. To theological dualisms, Wittgenstein's final proposition has precise applicability: "Whereof one cannot speak, thereof one must be silent."

Existential affirmations, however, would seem to fall within the sphere of verifiable meaning, since they (unlike dualistic assertions) treat of "existence" rather than of "essence." What of this area of modern philosophy, which forms an even more important element than dualism in the makeup of anti-inerrancy views of Scripture?

One must understand, first of all, that the assertions of existentialism are not simply statements about verifiable, existent things or events. Rather, they are specialized philosophical claims about the nature of man's existence in the universe—that is, they are genuinely metaphysical affirmations. Consider such basic tenets of the existentialist world-view as the following: "Truth cannot be found in abstract propositions." "Truth is discovered in responsible decision." "Personal encounter is the only sure avenue to truth." "The subject-object distinction must be transcended."[37] Such beliefs as these are very definitely claims as to the nature of the world and of man's relationship to it, and as such they deserve analytical inspection in the same way as other truth-claims.

And what is the result when existentialist affirmations are subjected to verifiability tests? An excellent illustration has been provided in Rudolf Carnap's examination of the following typical argument in *Was Ist Metaphysik Heideggers?*:

What is to be investigated is being only and—*nothing* else; being alone and further—*nothing*; solely being, and beyond being—*nothing. What about this Nothing?...Does the Nothing exist only because the Not, i.e., the Negation, exists?* Or is it the other way around? *Does Negation and the Not exist only because the Nothing exists?...*We assert: *the Nothing is prior to the Not and the Negation....*Where do we seek the Nothing? How do we find the Nothing?...We know the Nothing....*Anxiety reveals the Nothing* ....That for which and because of which we were anxious, was "really"— nothing. Indeed: the Nothing itself—as such—was present....*What about this Nothing?—The Nothing itself nothings.*

This argument, asserting the primacy of existence ("the Nothing") over essence ("the Negation and the Not") and the necessity of embracing it through personal recognition of estrangement ("anxiety"), is shown by Carnap to consist of analytically meaningless "pseudo-statements," whose "non-sensicality is not obvious at first glance, because one is easily deceived by the analogy with...meaningful sentences." To assert that "the rain rains" is meaningful, but to argue that "the Nothing nothings" is something else again! "Even if it were admissible to introduce 'nothing' as a name or description of an entity, still the existence of this entity would be denied in its very definition, whereas [Heidegger] goes on to affirm its existence."[38] In point of fact all the basic metaphysical affirmations of existentialism, in purporting to unfold the very heart of existent reality, overreach themselves and arrive not at reality but at nonsense.

The fundamental cause of meaninglessness in existentialism lies in its convictions that the subject-object distinction must be overcome and that "I-thou" personal encounter must be substituted for propositional truth. One can certainly appreciate the historical factors that gave rise to these affirmations: the breakdown of idealistic philosophy, the coldness of "dead-orthodox" theology (cf. Kierkegaard's *Attack upon "Christendom"*), the depersonalization of Western man in modern technological, scientific society, and the anxieties produced by decades of hot and cold wars. But appreciation of existentialist motives must not obscure the fundamental facts that meaningful thought absolutely requires the subject-object distinction and that questions of truth cannot even be formulated apart from propositions. "Bohr has emphasized the fact that the observer and his instruments must be presupposed in any investigation, so that the instruments are not part of the phenomenon described but are used."[39] The absolute necessity of the subject-object distinction is the source of the riotous humor in Robert Benchley's story of his experience in a college biology course: He spent the term carefully drawing the image of his own eyelash as it fell across the microscopic field! If in any investigation— whether in science or in theology—the observer loses the distinction between himself and his subject matter, the result is complete chaos: not a "transcending of the subject-object barrier," but a necessary fall into pure subjectivity. The more perceptive existentialists have indeed seen this. Sartre for example asserts that what all existentialists, atheistic and Christian, "have in common is that they think existence precedes essence, or, if you prefer, that subjectivity must be the starting point."[40] Such subjectivity, however, is utterly nontestable, and utterances concerning "estrangement," "existential anxiety" and "nothingness" stand outside of meaningful discourse.[41]

Like logic itself, both the subject-object ditsinction and propositional thinking must be presupposed in all sensible investigations. Why? Because to argue against their necessity is to employ them already! When one asserts: "Personal encounters, not propositions, yield truth," one is in fact stating a proposition (though a meaningless one) and is implying that there is sufficient distinction between "truth" and those who claim to possess it to warrant a clarifying statement on the subject! Existentialism's passionate attempt to dissolve subject-object boundaries and to escape from propositions about reality to reality itself is thus bound to fail and necessarily to arrive at nonsense. Of objective propositional truth, as of logic itself, one must say what Emerson said of Brahma: "When me they fly, I am the wings."[42]

## IV. THE ANALYTICAL MEANINGLESSNESS OF A "NONINERRANT INSPIRED SCRIPTURE"

Our study to this point has yielded the following conclusions: (1) Biblical inerrancy is under severe attack in our time not because of the discovery of empirical data militating against the view, but because of the climate of philosophical opinion presently conditioning Protestant theology. (2) The current theological *Zeitgeist*, as pertains to the issue of Biblical authority, is governed by existentialistic and dualistic a prioris. (3) The fundamental axioms of both dualism and existentialism are analytically meaningless. From these conclusions it is but a short step to the central claim of this paper: that the current attempt to maintain a divinely-inspired but noninerrant Bible is as analytically nonsensical as are the dualistic and existential assumptions upon which the attempt rests. We shall proceed to make this point through an examination of four major anti-inerrancy inspiration-claims. These four positions, it is believed, cover the gamut of non-verbal-inspiration views in contemporary Protestantism.

1. *"Holy Scripture is inspired, not in conveying inerrant propositions about God and the world but in acting as a vehicle for true Christian exis-*

*tential experience.*" This is, in substance, the position taken by Bultmann and by those who follow in his train. For Bultmann, "self-understanding of one's existence" arises from the kerygma of the primitive Church; for the "post-Bultmannians," who, like Günther Bornkamm, Käsemann, Fuchs and Ebeling, are engaged in a "new quest of the historical Jesus," this "self-understanding" arises from a correlation between our personal existential situation and Jesus' own self-understanding of his existence.[43] But both Bultmann and his former disciples accept in general the same critical presuppositions and existential a prioris. For both, inerrancy is a hopeless, pre-existential identification of truth with propositions instead of with vital existential experience.

This approach to Biblical inspiration is seen, on analysis, to be completely unverifiable and therefore nonsensical. For what is meant by "Christian existential experience"? And what gives one any reason to suppose that the Bible will serve instrumentally in promoting it? To determine what "Christian existential experience" is, one would have to define it in propositional terms (but "propositions" are ruled out in the original statement of the view!), and one would have to set up criteria for distinguishing truly salvatory experience from nonsalvatory experience, and the Bible from other, nonexistentially pregnant religious works (but all objective tests are ruled out by the existential refusal to employ the objective-subjective distinction!). Thus one is left in a morass of untestable subjectivity.

C. B. Martin, in discussing this problem of "a religious way of knowing," asks how one can know whether someone has a direct experience of God—or how the believer himself can know if he has this direct experience. Martin correctly points out that the claim to immediate existential experience on a believer's part is not analogous to experience claims in general and is *per se* analytically meaningless.

> In the case of knowing a blue sky in Naples, one can look at street signs and maps in order to be sure that this is the really blue sky in question. It is only when one comes to such a case as knowing God that the society of tests and check-up procedures that surround other instances of knowing, completely vanishes. What is put in the place of these tests and checking procedures is an immediacy of knowledge that is supposed to carry its own guarantee.[44]

In actuality, however, "tests and checking procedures" for truly Christian existential experience have not "vanished"; they have been obliterated by those who refuse to take the objective fact of an inerrant Bible seriously. It is only a Bible capable of standing the acid test of objective verifiability that will provide the "map" of God's blue sky of religious truth. And apart from such a map, the domain of immediate religious experience will forever remain a *terra incognita* of confusion and meaninglessness.

2. *"Holy Scripture is inspired, not in its scientific or historical statements, but in the theological truths it conveys."* Relatively few Lutherans on the American scene are prepared to move fully into the Bultmannian position on Scripture represented by anti-inerrancy argument 1. The more usual approach among American Lutheran theologians who would bring the Church out of "captivity" to verbal inspirationism is to argue for a distinction between the religious and the nonreligious content of the Bible: The former is indeed inspired and fully reliable, while the latter is subject to the human fallibility that besets all of man's undertakings.[45]

The problem here is twofold: First, how do we distinguish the religious from the historical-scientific (including the sociological and the moral!) element in the Scriptures? Second, how do we show that the "theological" affirmations of the Bible are indeed inspired of God? The first of these questions we postpone temporarily (for consideration in the next section of this paper, where it will be shown that a dichotomy between "sacred" and "secular" is antithetical to the very heart of the Biblical faith). The second question alone, however, sufficiently reveals the meaninglessness of anti-inerrancy argument 2. For here, obviously, one again encounters dualism: a split between eternity (the theological element in the Bible: *Heilsgeschichte*) and time (the scientific-historical content of Scripture: *Historie*).

An effort is being made to free the Bible from secular criticism. In effect, the proponents of this view argue, "It doesn't matter what historical and scientific errors or what internal contradictions are discovered in the Bible; its theological truth stands firm!" But note well: Every theological "truth," to the extent of its isolation from empirical reality, becomes unverifiable and therefore meaningless. As one approaches the realm of idealistic "Absolutes," refutability does indeed become less and less possible, but this chimerical advantage is achieved by the corresponding loss of meaningless relevance. The (theoretical) possibility of proving a claim wrong is the *sine qua non* for the claim's meaningfulness, since those assertions, which are so separated from the world that they are devoid of testability, are a waste of time to discuss, except in psychological or sociological terms. The theologian who pleads for a "theologically inspired," historically errant Bible pleads a meaningless case, for insofar as theological truths are removed from the world of testable experience, nothing at all can be said of their truth-value. Like the "eternal truths" of Tantrism, such "theological truths" of Christianity might as well remain unexpressed. In avoiding the necessary offense of defending the Bible's histori-cal and scientific content, the dualistic theologians have succeeded in ren-dering the Bible utterly irrelevant.

It should, moreover, be a sobering thought to those who have accepted the above-described dualistic approach in principle to be reminded that, carried to its logical conclusion, such dualism will eventually necessitate the denial of infallibility *even to the "theological" content of Scripture.* Why? Because the "theological," just like the "historical-scientific," ele-ment of the Bible was conveyed to human agents (the Biblical writers) and therefore (on the dualistic a priori) must also have been touched by human fallibility. Martin Scharlemann overlooks this point completely when he argues:

> The very limitations of the individual authors in terms of language, geo-graphical, historical, and literary knowledge testify to the specifics of divine revelation. This is part of the "scandal" of the Bible. An insistence on its "in-errancy" is often an attempt to remove this obstacle. The use of the term al-most invariably results in a docetic view of the Bible and so tends to overlook the fact that our Sacred Scriptures are both divine and human documents.[46]

Actually, if one is to avoid all "docetism," the inevitable conclusion is that even in its theological affirmations the Bible is touched by the falli-bility of its human writers (or perhaps *especially* in its theological affir-mations, since these evidently constitute the major part of the Bible?).

Paul Tillich does not blink at the consequences of such a consistent (though, as we have seen, meaningless!) dualism. For him *everything* in the Bible must in theory at least stand under judgment. Nothing on earth can be identified fully with Being Itself, which constitutes the only true "ultimate concern." This is Tillich's "Protestant principle": "The only in-fallible truth of faith, the one in which the ultimate itself is uncondition-ally manifest, is that any truth of faith stands under a yes-or-no judgment."[47] Thus the Bible loses even theologically normative force; and what then constitutes the basis of "yes-or-no judgment" in religion? Clearly, as Gordon Clark has argued in reference to Barth's theology, one must then accept as a norm or canon "something or other external to the Bible," and "since this external norm or canon "something or other exter-nal to the Bible," and "since this external norm cannot be a wordless reve-lation, for a wordless revelation cannot give us the necessary information, it must be secular science, history, or anthropology."[48] The result is a re-duction of special revelation to a vague and secularistic "natural revela-tion," which lands us again in the hopeless maze of unreconstructed modernism. From the heights of the Unconditioned we are plummeted to the depths of a world lacking any inspired word from God. Such is the in-evitable effect of analytically nonsensical revelational dualisms.

3. *"Holy Scripture is inspired, not as a conveyer of infallible informa-tion, but insofar as it testifies to the person of our Lord and Savior Jesus Christ."* Tillich himself employs this approach when he identifies (but symbolically only, to be sure) the "yes-or-no judgment" on all things hu-man with "the cross of the Christ." But it is especially the contemporary Lutheran anti-inerrantists who present argument 3, since they—in spite of Reu's impeccable historical case[49]—hold that Luther himself took this position. Writes M. Scharlemann: Biblical "knowledge is not a matter of acquiring information but of being confronted with God Himself as He is revealed in His Son."[50] Robert Schultz expresses his "hope that Lutheran theologians generally will move back through the accumulated traditions of verbal inspiration and reappropriate Luther's dynamic insight that the Scripture is that which teaches Christ."[51]

Argument 3 incorporates the existential element from argument 1 and the dualistic element from argument 2, thus acquiring a double dose of analytical meaninglessness. The argument must be regarded as dualistic if it is not to avoid condemnation for simple circularity: The "Jesus Christ" spoken of must be a *geschichtlich* "Christ of faith," not a *his-torisch* "Jesus of history," for the latter would be describable proposition-ally and subject to inerrancy tests—which obviously would defeat the whole point of the argument. The idea here, as in argument 2, is to raise Biblical inspiration beyond the level of historical, scientific judgment by focusing it upon a Christ-figure who stands above the realm of verifiabil-ity. But, as emphasized in analyzing argument 2, such supra-empirical claims by definition pass into irrelevant nonsense. And, as we shall see in the next section of this paper, a "Christ" of this kind is theologically non-sensical as well, for the Biblical Christ entered fully into the empirical sphere, subjecting himself to the full "offense" of verifiability.

The existential side of argument 3 is pointed up in its anti-"informa-tional" character. Scriptural inspiration allegedly leads to confrontation with Christ, not to theological data. But, as we saw in our discussion of argument 1, meaningful "confrontation" is possible only on the basis of verifiable data, for otherwise there is no way of knowing whether one has engaged in a real confrontation at all! Particularly in the realm of religion it is desperately important to know the difference (to speak irreverently but precisely) between Christ-in-the-heart and heartburn. Apart from an objectively reliable, inerrant Biblical description of Christ the result is al-ways, on the part of sinful man, the creation of subjective Christs to fit one's needs. This has, in fact, been the tragic history of twentieth-century theology: the creation of God in our philosophical or cultural image in-stead of the straightforward acceptance of his portrait of us and of his sal-vation for us as presented in Holy Writ.[52]

Schultz is, we fear, unaware of the ghastly implication of his position when he expresses the hope "that Lutherans will once again find themselves bound to all in Scripture and tradition that teaches Christ, compelled to change all that is contrary to Christ, free to use creatively everything that does not matter, as well as to create new tradition."[53] What, we ask, will serve as the criterion for determining what in Scripture is "contrary to Christ" and "does not matter"? For setting the pattern of scriptural "change"? For the "creative use" of the "unimportant" in the Bible? Obviously not the Biblical Christ himself, who was concerned about the inerrancy even of scriptural jots and tittles! The theological criterion has clearly become an existential Christ-in-the-heart, who, because of his nonpropositional, analytically indefinable character, can take on, chameleon-like, the qualities of his spokesman. Perhaps we are not as far away as we think from the *Deutsche Christen* of the Third Reich, whose "Christ" conveniently supported all aspects of their demonic ideology. It is well not to forget that from analytical meaninglessness, as from logical contradiction, *anything* can be "deduced," depending on the predilections, conscious or unconscious, of the deducer.

4. *"Holy Scripture is inerrant, but in its intent—in its dynamic ability to fulfil God's purposes—not in its static accord with objective scientific or historical fact."* Here we consider an argument that would not deserve attention were it not for its deceptive quality. Argument 4 in reality says nothing that has not already been expressed more directly in the preceding three arguments. However, it conceals its analytic meaninglessness under the guise of the word "intent."

The question, of course, is not whether the Bible infallibly or inerrantly achieves the purposes for which God intended it. The orthodox Christian would be the last to deny this. The question is simply: How does one determine God's intent? Only two answers are possible: from an inerrant revelation, or from a source or sources external to special revelation. The former answer is hardly what the proponent of argument 4 wants. His purpose in stating the argument is to move away from propositional inerrancy to an "inerrancy" that will focus on "theological" considerations, or on "existential experience," or on "personal encounter with Christ"—that is, on the existential-dualistic affirmations of arguments 1, 2 and 3. Scripture is "inerrant" only when it achieves the purpose that *he* (the nonplenary inspirationist) accepts as appropriate to it.

Thus again we encounter the analytical nonsense of dualism and existentialism, and the subtle importation of nonrevelational considerations by which revelation is judged. In point of fact only God's Word is capable of indicating God's intent. And if this Word is not propositionally inerrant and perspicuous, man will never know the divine intent in general—to say nothing of his intent as regards Holy Writ itself! But a study of the totality of Scripture confirms the historic claim of the Church that God intended by his special revelation to convey the truth of Christ within the solid framework of, and confirmed by, the entire truth of an infallibly inspired Bible.[54]

In our discussion of arguments 3 and 4 we have referred in passing to Christ's view of the Bible and the Bible's own attitude toward itself. These references lead us quite naturally to the theological evaluation of noninerrancy views of scriptural inspiration. We have found that analytically such views are nonsensical. It now remains for us to see that from the standpoint of Biblical theology also they are without any genuine meaning.

## V. The Theological Meaninglessness of a "Noninerrant Inspired Scripture"

Advocates of the anti-inerrancy positions discussed in the preceding sections of this paper are united in their contention that the Bible itself, and Christ its Lord, present a "dynamic," "personalized" view of truth that is irreconcilable with the propositional, objectively historical approach to truth characteristic of plenary inspirationists. Emil Brunner, for example, asserts: "In the time of the apostles as in that of the Old Testament prophets, divine revelation always meant the whole of the divine activity for the salvation of the world. Divine revelation is not a book or a doctrine."[55] Frequently appealed to in support of this contention is Albrecht Oepke's article in Kittel's *Wörterbuch*, where one is told that in the Bible "revelation is not the communication of rational knowledge" but rather "Yahweh's offering of Himself in mutual fellowship."[56] Though James Barr's revolutionary book, *The Semantics of Biblical Language*, has decisively shown that neo-orthodox, "Biblical-theology-movement" a priori, rather than linguistic objectivity, lies at the basis of such articles as Oepke's,[57] the general question remains as to whether the Biblical view of revelation is anti-objective, anti-propositional. It is worthwhile noting that if the latter is the case then the Bible, like many of its modern interpreters, will pass into the never-never land of analytical meaninglessness, for its content will be devoid of testability. Like the Scriptures of the Eastern religions its "truth" will be "known" only to those who read it through the glass of prior belief, and it will say nothing to all those who, not having had an (indefinable, unverifiable) experience in relation to it, are understandably wary of such "experiences"!

But in fact the Bible does not operate within an existential-dualistic frame of reference. Fundamental to the entire Biblical revelation are the twin convictions that subjective truth is grounded in and verifiable through objective truth and that the eternal has been made manifest in the temporal.

Consider such prominent OT events as Gideon and the fleece (Judges 6) and Elijah on Mount Carmel (1 Kings 18). Gideon, realizing how easy it is to deceive oneself in matters of subjective religious assurance, asks an objective sign from God by which he can know that the Lord will deliver Israel from her enemies. God willingly complies, not once but twice: First, dew falls on Gideon's fleece but not on the surrounding ground; second, dew falls on the ground but not on the fleece. The point? Gideon, like any spatio-temporally-bound member of the human race, was incapable of knowing by subjective, existential immediacy that the voice within him was God's voice. Yet he had to know, for the lives of others as well as his own safety depended upon his ability to make a true religious judgment. In this quandary God provided Gideon with external evidence—in concrete, empirical terms—showing that it was indeed he who spoke within Gideon's heart.

Elijah was faced with a common religious problem, one that existential immediacy is totally unable to solve. This is the problem of conflicting religious claims. The "false prophets" said one thing to the people, Elijah said another. How were the people to know who was proclaiming God aright and who was the idolater? An objective test was the only way of ridding the situation of endless confusion and meaningless claims. So Elijah gave the false prophets the opportunity to demonstrate the "reality" of their God through his ability to perform an act of divine power on earth. The inability of the false prophets' truth-claim to hold up under such a test, when coupled with Yahweh's positive response to the identical test, provided the needed ground for belief in the true God.

Such examples could be multiplied in the OT, but let us now turn to our Lord's own attitude toward religious verifiability. A close look at a frequently misunderstood event in his public ministry will be especially revealing. In all three synoptic gospels (Matthew 9; Mark 2; Luke 5) Jesus' healing of the palsied man is recorded in similar detail. Here is the Marcan account:

> And again he entered into Capernaum after some days; and it was noised that he was in the house. And straightway many were gathered together, insomuch that there was no room to receive them, no, not so much as about the door; and he preached the word unto them. And they come unto him, bringing one sick of the palsy, which was borne of four. And when they could not come nigh unto him for the press, they uncovered the roof where he was; and when they had broken it up, they let down the bed wherein the sick of the palsy lay. When Jesus saw their faith, he said unto the sick of the palsy, Son, thy sins be forgiven thee. But there were certain of the scribes sitting there, and reasoning in their hearts, Why doth this man thus speak blas-

phemies? Who can forgive sins but God only? And immediately when Jesus perceived in his spirit that they so reasoned within themselves, he said unto them, Why reason ye these things in your hearts? Whether is it easier to say to the sick of the palsy, Thy sins be forgiven thee; or to say, Arise, and take up thy bed, and walk? But that ye may know that the Son of man hath power on earth to forgive sins, (he saith to the sick of the palsy,) I say unto thee, Arise, and take up thy bed, and go thy way into thine house. And immediately he arose, took up the bed, and went forth before them all; insomuch that they were all amazed, and glorified God, saying, We never saw it on this fashion.

It is generally assumed that the answer to Jesus' question, "Is it easier to say, Thy sins be forgiven, or Take up thy bed and walk?" is "Take up thy bed and walk." Quite the opposite is the case. Perhaps it is easier to restore a sick man to health than to forgive sin, but Jesus' question has to do not with acts but with claims. Jesus asks not "Which is easier?" but "Which is easier to say?" Clearly it is easier to *claim* to be able to forgive sin than to be able to restore a palsied man to health miraculously, for the former is a theological affirmation that cannot *per se* be subjected to verification.

So what does our Lord do? Does he leave his forgiveness claim in the realm of the unverifiable, as have numerous religious leaders through the ages? By no means. He connects the theological claim with an empirical claim whose verifiability is not only possible but inevitable. The argument thus runs: "You do not believe that I can forgive sins. Very well; I cannot show you that directly. But if I show you that I can, by my divine power, remedy the empirical sickness that connects with the sin problem, will you have any reason left for denying my power to work in the theological sphere?" The empirical, objective healing of the palsied man was performed that men might "know that the Son of man hath power on earth to forgive sins"—a fact that, had our Lord not coupled it with an objective test, could have been dismissed as meaningless and irrelevant by those who had doubtless heard such claims many times before. In precisely the same way does the NT present Christ's resurrection as the objective ground for belief in the theological significance of his death on the cross.[58]

The picture of the Biblical conception of truth drawn from the foregoing passages is in no way altered by Jesus' affirmations, "I am the truth" (John 14:6) and "Everyone who is of the truth hears my voice" (18:37), or by any other "personalized" references to truth in the Bible. Of course such statements are part of the scriptural revelation. Plenary inspirationists have never denied their existence or importance. The question is not whether truth is ever conceived of personally in the Bible, but whether it is *only* conceived of personally there. We contend that the Biblical view of truth requires subjective (existential, if you will) truth to be grounded in objective, empirical facticity, for only then can existential truth be distinguished from existential error. Jesus' claim to be the truth hardly warrants the conclusion that the facticity of his earthly acts, or the precise veracity of his words, is unimportant. Quite the contrary: It is the truth of his acts and words that drives us to commit our lives to him as the only final answer to man's quest for truth.

The Biblical conception of truth not only stands over against analytically nonsensical existentialisms. It categorically opposes the equally meaningless notion of a dualistic split between the "theological" and the "historical/empirical" or between "personal encounter" and "objective facticity." Here, indeed, we find ourselves at the very heart and center of the Christian faith: the doctrine of incarnation. According to Biblical teaching, the OT revelation typologically introduces, and the NT writings express the fulfilment of, the genuine incarnation of God in human history. The prologue of John's gospel summarizes this superlative teaching in the simple words *ho logos sarx egeneto*. As the ecumenical creeds of the Church consistently testify, this incarnation was in every sense a real entrance of God into the human scene. The gap between eternity and time was fully bridged in Christ.

The soteriological necessity of this act has often been stressed through Christian history,[59] but at the same time the epistemological need for the incarnation ought never to be forgotten. Apart from empirical confrontation with God in Christ, man's religious aspirations and conceptions would have forever remained in the realm of unverifiable meaninglessness. This is why throughout the NT the apostles place such powerful stress on having "seen with their eyes" and "touched with their hands" the incarnate Word.[60] The Biblical message recognizes finite man's need to "try the spirits" representing diverse religious claims and ideologies, and the only meaningful test is objective verifiability: "Every spirit that confesseth that Jesus Christ is come in the flesh is of God" (1 John 4:1-3).

In Biblical religion it is impossible to conceive of theological truth divorced from historical, empirical truth. This divorce would destroy the whole meaning of incarnation. The theological truths of Scripture are thus inextricably united with earthly matters, and the truth of the one demands the truth of the other. The Bible recognizes as fully as does analytical philosophy that to speak of "theological truth" or of "existential encounter with God" apart from empirical veracity is to speak nonsense. When Bishop Wand asserts that "there is no external guarantee of inspiration"[61] he is asserting just such nonsense, for without the "external guarantee" of empirical facticity "inspiration" becomes no more than an emotive plea—on the same level with the innumerable and conflicting immediacy claims to inspiration by religious fanatics.

Even Beegle, in his recent attempt to demolish Biblical inerrancy, admits that "subjective truth cannot occur without some minimal amount of objective truth."[62] But here he gives his whole case away. For what amount of objective truth is "minimal"? The Bible declares, as does analytic philosophy, that only where objective truth is unqualifiedly present can one avoid meaninglessness on the subjective side. Thus the "minimum" is unrestricted objective truth, which in the case of the Christian revelation means nothing less than an inerrant Bible. For wherever the Scriptures were to err objectively, there doubt would be warranted subjectively; and wherever the words of Scripture were to carry historically or scientifically erroneous ideas, there the reader would have every right to reject the theological affirmations, which in the very nature of God's revelation are inextricably entwined with empirical facts.[63]

And here, like it or not, we arrive at verbal inspiration, for, as contemporary linguistic analysis has so fully demonstrated, every genuine word carries genuine meaning and influences the context in which it is used. Therefore each "jot and tittle" of Scripture has an impact, however slight, on the totality of the Bible, and this impact must be either for good or for ill. On the basis of the throughgoing incarnational theology of the Bible we can affirm that the verbal impact is always veracious, not only theologically but also in all other aspects touched. For in the final analysis the Biblical theology that centers on Christ the incarnate Word knows no distinction between "other aspects of life" and the religious: Biblical truth is holistic, and its claim to theological validity is preserved from meaninglessness by its verifiability in the empirical domains that it touches.[64]

## VI. A FINAL CLARIFICATION AND CAVEAT

It has been not infrequently argued by those who would move Lutheranism away from the inerrancy view of Biblical inspiration that the Lutheran Church is fortunate in lacking explicit statements on verbal inspiration in its historic creeds. We are informed that it is to our advantage that, unlike the Calvinists, our creeds contain no assertions concerning "the entire perfection" and "infallible truth" of Scripture.[65] Therefore, the argument continues, we are free to embrace fully, without loss of intellectual integrity, the nonpropositional, nonverbal view of inspiration that has become so popular in recent years.

The analytical discussions comprising the bulk of this paper should have prepared us to see the fallacy in this superficially attractive line of reasoning. Let us see what the last of the Reformation Lutheran Confessions, the *Formula of Concord*, does say on the subject of Biblical inspiration. The *Formula's* position in this matter is drawn from Luther:

[Luther] diesen Unterscheid ausdrücklich gesetzt hat, dass alleine Gottes Wort die einige Richtschnur und Regel aller Lehre sein und bleiben solle, welchem keines Menschen Schriften gleich geachtet, sondern demselben alles unterworfen werden soll.

Hoc discrimen (inter divina et humana scripta) perspicue posuit, solas videlicet sacras litteras pro unica regula et norma omnium dogmatum agnoscendas, iisque nullius omnino hominis scripta adaequanda, sed potius omnia subiicienda esse.[66]

Here, it is true, there is no reference to infallibility or inerrancy. Yet the Scriptures are declared to be the "only standard and rule," to which all other writings must be "subordinated." Clearly the Bible is held to stand in judgment over all other books—in all fields—and no man is permitted to judge the Scriptures in any particular. Such a view of Biblical authority differs in no way from the verbal inspiration position set out in this paper.

And indeed how could it, if Luther and the theologians of the Confessions understood the implications of scriptural inspiration? We have seen that the incarnational theology of the Bible demands the plenary truth of Scripture—that the "historical-empirical" elements in the Bible must be regarded as no less veracious than the "theological" truths intimately bound up with them and epistemologically dependent upon them. Though the Lutheran fathers were not acquainted with the technical concept of analytic meaninglessness, they understood the Bible too well to believe that it would retain its theological value if its truthfulness in other particulars were impugned. The writers of the Lutheran Confessions did not face the epistemological issue of Biblical reliability that we face today, but they knew full well that to allow the Scriptures to fall under *any* kind of negative criticism would tear the foundation out of all meaningful theology. That "the Word was made flesh" gripped them too powerfully to permit their losing the objective veracity of God's revelation.

Today the winds of philosophical change are veering away from existentialistic and dualistic world-views. The analytical tradition has delivered mortal body-blows to these metaphysical *Weltanschauungen*. And within the realm of analytical philosophy itself, every year that goes by sees greater stress placed upon "words," "language" and "propositions."[67] How unfortunate it would be if now, when the presuppositions of the anti-verbal inspirationists have been thoroughly undermined along with the a prioris of existentialism and dualism, and a new era of appreciation for the verbal proposition is on the horizon, Christians in the Reformation tradition should sell their Biblical heritage for a mess of outdated philosophical pottage! In the Bible and in the Christ to whom it testifies

God has given a *plērōma* of meaningfulness. May we not lose it in chasing the phantoms of analytical nonsensicality.

[1]J. Orr, *The Progress of Dogma* (4th ed.; London: Hodder & Stoughton, 1901) *passim*. The lectures comprising this book were originally delivered in 1897. Orr was professor of apologetics and systematic theology in the United Free Church College, Glasgow.

[2]In this connection it is instructive to note that a recurring theme in present-day "broad-church" Lutheran theological writing is that Bultmann should be regarded as a twentieth-century Luther. As Luther directed men from ethical works-righteousness to the saving Christ, so it is argued, Bultmann points men from intellectualistic works-righteousness (i.e., relying on an inerrant Bible) to Christ. (See for a typical statement of this view R. Scharlemann, "Shadow on the Tomb," *Dialog* 1 [Spring 1962] 22-29; cf. T. C. Oden, "Bultmann As Lutheran Existentialist," *Dialog* 3 [Summer 1964] 207-214.) This comparison has the single merit of emphasizing that, as justification was the key theological issue Luther faced, the Scripture problem is the theological watershed of our time. Otherwise the Luther-Bultmann parallel is completely wide of the mark. As I have written elsewhere: "Whereas Luther turned from moral guilt to confidence in the *objective* facts of Christ's death for his sin and resurrection for his justification, Bultmann turns from his intellectual doubts to *subjective* anthropological salvation—a direct about-face from the objective Gospel Luther proclaimed" (*The Shape of the Past* ["History in Christian Perspective," Vol. 1; Ann Arbor: Edwards, 1963] 160).

[3]R. A. Harrisville, "A Theology of Rediscovery," *Dialog* 2 (Summer 1963) 190.

[4]"Controversy on Inspiration," *Dialog* 2 (Autumn 1963) 273. The same editorial asserts that the inspiration controversy "is surely one of the emptiest." If so, why devote a journal issue to an attempt to demolish the traditional position on inspiration?

[5]Of the Commission's Report the *Dialog* editor writes: "The statement on biblical 'iner-rancy' does not come off very well. Admittedly this is a sensitive question and an emotionally laden word in the Missouri Synod; and if public opinion is a determinant, one can under-stand why the only point raised against *A Brief Statement*—the official document of the Synod which describes the Scriptures as the infallible truth even in 'historical, geographical, and other secular matters'—is the question whether it 'does justice to the rich variety present in the content and mode of the utterances of the Scriptures.' But, synodical public opinion aside, the objection to that sentence in *A Brief Statement* surely is not that it is insufficient but that it is wrong; and the Report ought to say so" ("Right Key—Wrong Melody," *Dialog* 3 [Summer 1964] 165).

[6]D. M. Beegle, *The Inspiration of Scripture* (Philadelphia: Westminster, 1963) 187.

[7]Such a Bible could of course have a higher (quantatitive) degree of *literary* inspiration than the average book (cf. Shakespeare as compared with Mickey Spillane), but this is clearly not the type of "inspiration" with which any theologian (except the unreconstructed, pre-World-War-I liberal) is concerned.

[8]W. A. Quanbeck, "The Bible," in *Theology in the Life of the Church* (ed. R. W. Bertram; Philadelphia: Fortress, 1963) 23. This book is an outgrowth of the Conference of Lutheran Professors of Theology and thus well reflects the general trends of Lutheran theo-logical thought in America today.

[9]R. Scharlemann, "Letter to the Editor," *The Lutheran Scholar*, April 1963.

[10]J. W. Haley, *An Examination of the Alleged Discrepancies of the Bible* (reprint ed.; Grand Rapids: Baker, 1958) 154.

[11]Ibid., p. 153. Cf. also W. F. Arndt, *Does the Bible Contradict Itself?* (5th ed.; St. Louis: Concordia, 1955) 51-53, 73-74; E. J. Young, *Thy Word Is Truth* (Grand Rapids: Eerdmans, 1957) 172-175.

[12]A. Althamer, *Conciliationes Locorum Scripturae, qui specie tenus inter se pugnare vi-dentur, centuriae duae* (Vitebergae: Zacharias Lehman, 1582). This excellent work, of which I possess a personal copy, treats 160 "discrepancies" and went through at least sixteen editions (1st ed., 1527).

[13]A. Jaubert, *La Date de la Cene. Calendrier biblique et liturgie chretienne* (Paris: Gabalda, 1957). I have treated this matter in some detail in my article, "The Fourth Gospel Yesterday and Today," *CTM* 34 (April 1963) 206, 213.

[14]For a semi-popular overview of this trend see W. Keller, *The Bible As History* (New York: William Morrow, 1956).

[15]On the invalidity of Hume's argument in light of the replacement of Newtonian by Einsteinian conceptions of scientific law see Montgomery, *Shape* 288-293; C.S. Lewis, *Miracles* (New York: Macmillan, 1947), esp. chap. 13.

[16]I have discussed this matter in considerable detail in my lecture series, "Jesus Christ and History," delivered on January 29 and 30, 1963, at the University of British Columbia. These lectures are currently being serialized in *HIS Magazine*, the first article having appeared in the December 1964 issue. See also in this connection H. J. Rose, *Handbook of Greek Literature from Homer to the Age of Lucian* (London: Methuen, 1934) 42-43; A. H. McNeile and C. S. C. Williams, *Introduction to the Study of the New Testament* (2d ed.; Oxford: Clarendon, 1955) 52-58.

[17]If the Genesis 1-3 problem here comes to mind, the reader should consult such classic refutations of suppposed "scientific error" in the Biblical account as are found in two monographs of the American Scientific Affiliation: *Modern Science and Christian Faith* (2d ed., 1950) and *Evolution and Christian Thought Today* (2d ed., 1960).

[18]*Is the Bible Infallible? A Debate between John Wenham, Vice-Principal of Tyndale Hall, Bristol, and Rupert E. Davies, Tutor at Didsbury College, Bristol* (London: Epworth, 1959) 27.

[19]A. G. Hebert, *The Authority of the Old Testament* (London: Faber & Faber, 1947) 306-307. Hebert's misrepresentations of Biblical orthodoxy as "fundamentalism" have been decisively answered in J. I. Packer's *"Fundamentalism" and the Word of God* (Grand Rapids: Eerdmans, 1958).

[20]Locke's statement is grounded in rationalism, not in empiricism, and as such offers no proper analogy to the Biblical inerrancy position. Russell and Whitehead in the *Principia Mathematica* and Wittgentstein in the *Tractatus Logico-Philosophicus* have shown that geometrical propositions are tautologous—i.e., they have no necessary connection with "observable phenomena." Neither the Biblical writers nor the plenary inspirationists have argued that Biblical truth is mathematical/tautologous. Rather, they have asserted that it is observationally reliable (as in the case of the historic revelation of Christ himself).

[21]C. J. Costello, *St. Augustine's Doctrine on the Inspiration and Canonicity of Scripture* (Washington: Catholic University of America, 1930) 30-31. Costello's work constituted his thesis for the doctorate in theology and is fully grounded in the primary works of Augustine. It is noteworthy that Augustine, in the fifth century, effectively treated the Zechariah-Jeremiah "contradiction" that R. Scharlemann presented in 1963 as a decisive counter to Biblical inerrancy (see Costello, *Augustine* 34-37, and cf. our text above at nn. 9-11).

[22]Quanbeck, "Bible" 25.

[23]J. W. Montgomery, "Karl Barth and Contemporary Theology of History," published both in *The Cresset* (November 1963) 8-14 and in the *BETS* 6 (May 1963) 39-49. In this article I deal primarily with the baleful implications of the *Geschichte-Historie* dualism in Christology and in theology of history.

[24]M. H. Scharlemann, "The Bible As Record, Witness and Medium" (mimeographed essay) 11. The same approach is found in W. Hordern, *Case for a New Reformation Theology* (Philadelphia: Westminster, 1959), where the amazingly circular statement appears: "Objectivity is possible only when there is a faith-commitment made to objectivity" (p. 44; cf. pp. 62-69).

[25]Cf. J. Wahl, *A Short History of Existentialism* (New York: Philosophical Library, 1949).

[26]P. Tillich, "Existential Philosophy: Its Historical Meaning," in his *Theology of Culture* (ed. R. C. Kimball; New York: Oxford University, 1959) 92.

[27]Ironically, to be sure, existentialism has sought to destroy all metaphysical speculation, including dualism. But since existentialism itself has a metaphysic it cannot successfully destroy metaphysics. And it often (as here) finds itself a strange bedfellow to other (uncongenial) metaphysical tendencies.

[28]For a short introduction to these movements see V. Kraft, *The Vienna Circle* (New York: Philosophical Library, 1953).

²⁹A. J. Ayer, *Language, Truth and Logic* (New York: Dover, 1946) 35. Since the publication of the first edition of his work (1936) Ayer has somewhat refined his statement of the "verifiability principle" (see his introduction to the new edition, pp. 5-16). However, in substance his original statement remains unaltered, and its classic simplicity warrants its continued use.

³⁰Attempts have been made, of course, to destroy the verifiability criterion. Few traditional, speculative philosophers have been happy with Feigl's remark that "Philosophy is the disease of which analysis should be the cure!" But the verifiability principle still stands as the best available road-map through the forest of truth-claims. One of the most persistent attempts to refute the criterion has been the effort to show that it is itself a meaningless assertion, being evidently neither an analytic nor a synthetic statement. However, this objection has been effeectively met both by Ayer, who argues that the criterion is actually a definition (*Language* 15-16) and by Hempel, who shows that it, "like the result of any other explication, represents a linguistic proposal which itself is neither true nor false" ("The Empiricist Criterion of Meaning," published originally in the *Revenue Internationale de Philosophie* 4 [1950] and reprinted with newly appended remarks by the author in *Logical Positivism* [ed. A. J. Ayer; Glencoe: Free Press, 1959] 108-129).

³¹The parable was told by Wittgenstein to Stout and is related by N. Malcolm in his *Ludwig Wittgenstein: A Memoir* (London: Oxford University, 1962) 66.

³²*Tractatus Logico-Philosophicus*, propositions 4.116 and 7.0 (cf. Wittgenstein's "Vorwort"). For a discussion of these propositions in light of the *Tractatus* as a whole see M. Black's long-awaited and just-published commentary, *A Companion to Wittgenstein's "Tractatus"* (Ithaca: Cornell University, 1964) *passim*.

³³This is a variation on M. Schlick's (now outdated!) propositional example: "There are mountains on the other side of the moon."

³⁴A. Flew, "Theology and Falsification," in *New Essays in Philosophical Theology* (ed. Flew and Macintyre; London:, SCM, 1955) 96.

³⁵This was shown in detail by T. H. Leith of York University, Toronto, Canada, in a paper titled "Logical Problems with Discussion of the Age and Origin of the Universe," delivered at the nineteenth Annual Convention of the American Scientific Affiliation, August 27, 1964.

³⁶P. Tillich, *Dynamics of Faith* (New York: Harper, 1958) 95.

³⁷Cf. J. Sartre, *Existentialism and Human Emotions* (New York: Philosophical Library, 1957).

³⁸R. Carnap, "The Elimination of Metaphysics through Logical Analysis of Language," in *Logical Positivism* (ed. Ayer) 69-73. Carnap's paper originally appeared in German in Vol. 2 of *Erkenntnis* (1932).

³⁹V. F. Lenzen, *Procedures of Empirical Science* ("International Encyclopedia of Unified Science" 1/5; Chicago: University Press, 1938) 28. That the Heisenberg indeterminacy principle does not in any sense break the subject-object distinction has been shown by Lenzen and by many others.

⁴⁰J. Sartre, *Existentialism* 13.

⁴¹To avoid misunderstanding, I must anticipate myself by pointing out here that my argument does *not* negate a "Christian existentialism" (Christian subjectivity) *founded upon testable, objective considerations* (specifically, upon an inerrant Scripture). Indeed, I myself have made much use of genuine Christian-existential categories (e.g., in my Strasbourg thesis for the degree of Docteur de l'Universite, mention Theologie Protestants, 1964). But it is this very idea of an objective basis for existential subjectivity that the contemporary philosophical and theological existentialists decry, and this is the reason for my above-stated counter to subjectivistic existentialism. Apart from an objective foundation, all existentialism is analytically meaningless.

⁴²Cf. my *Chytraeus on Sacrifice* (St. Louis: Concordia, 1962) 27.

⁴³Cf. the essays in H. Ristow and K. Matthiae, eds., *Der Historische Jesus und der kerygmatische Christus* (Berlin: Evangelische Verlagsanstalt, 1961).

⁴⁴C. B. Martin, "A Religious Way of Knowing," in *New Essays* (ed. Flew and Macintyre) 83. See also Montgomery, *Shape* 257-311.

⁴⁵This is the general position espoused in *Dialog* (see above our text at nn. 4 and 5).

⁴⁶M. Scharlemann, "Bible" 14.

⁴⁷Tillich, *Dynamics* 98.

[48]G. H. Clark, *Karl Barth's Theological Method* (Philadelphia: Presbyterian and Reformed, 1963) 224.

[49]M. Reu, *Luther and the Scriptures* (Columbus, Ohio: Wartburg, 1944), reprinted in The Springfielder 24 (August 1960). Cf. my review of W. J. Kooiman, *Luther and the Bible*, in *Christianity Today* 6 (February 16, 1962) 498.

[50]M. Scharlemann, "Bible" 11.

[51]R. C. Schultz, "Scripture, Tradition and the Traditions: A Lutheran Perspective," *Dialog* 2 (Autumn 1963) 281.

[52]When we do subject ourselves fully to the Biblical testimony concerning Christ, we find—note well—that we must simultaneously accept the plenary inspiration and inerrancy of *all* of Scripture, for this was the belief of the Biblical Christ himself. This fact has been emphasized by numerous writers across the centuries; for a succinct marshaling of the evidence for it see P. Marcel. "Our Lord's Use of Scripture," in *Revelation and the Bible* (ed. C. F. H. Henry; Grand Rapids: Baker, 1958) 119-134. Moreover, to employ kenotic arguments in an effort to lessen the binding force of Jesus' attitude toward Scripture is to board a vehicle whose logically inevitable destination is theological solipsism, since a Jesus who accomodates to the first century thought world in one respect cannot be assumed to have stated any absolutes in other respects. Thus all of Jesus' words lose binding force if his view of Scripture is not held to be normative.

[53]Schultz, "Scripture."

[54]On the Bible's view of itself see B. B. Warfield's classic essays published under the title *The Inspiration and Authority of the Bible* (Philadelphia: Presbyterian and Reformed, 1948). This volume is a new edition of Warfield's Revelation and Inspiration, published by Oxford University Press and now out of print.

[55]E. Brunner, *Revelation and Reason* (Philadelphia: Westminster, 1946) 8.

[56]A. Oepke, "*Kalyptō*," *TWNT*, 3.575.

[57]Barr takes Oepke as "a very bad example" of the absorption of philology by theological a priori in the *TWNT*. He shows that Oepke's *Apokalyptō article "is assimilated to modern theological usage to a degree that the actual linguistic material will not bear"* (*The Semantics of Biblical Language* [London: Oxford University, 1961] 230).

[58]See 1 Corinthians 15, and cf. my University of British Columbia lectures (see n. 16).

[59]One thinks immediately of Anselm's *Cur Deus Homo?* and Aulen's *Christus Victor*. Cf. my *Chytraeus on Sacrifice.*

[60]See e.g. 1 John 1:1-4, where existential "joy" (v 4) is grounded in objective empirical contact with the incarnate Christ (vv 1-3); cf. also John 20:24 ff.

[61]J. W. C. Wand, *The Authority of the Scriptures* (London: Mowbray, 1949) 61.

[62]Beegle, *Inspiration* 191.

[63]The fallacy of "minimum" objective facticity has been implicitly recognized in Käsemann's damning criticism of Bultmann's claim that Christian existential experience requires only the "thatness" of Jesus as an historical person—the mere fact that he existed. Says Käsemann (representing the "post-Bultmannian" reaction in contemporary European theology): Such minimal "thatness" will reduce the Christian gospel to a gnostic redeemer myth and docetism.

[64]I am not arguing (note well) that empirical verifiability of the historical and scientific content of Scripture automatically produces subjective *commitment* to the truth of its religious claims. The Pharisees could (and doubtless many of them did) refuse to believe that Jesus was able to forgive sin even after he had healed the palsied man. However, only where objective verifiability is present can genuine faith be distinguished from blind faith. To engage in existentialists' "leap of faith" is to topple headlong into the domain of analytic meaninglessness, where one man believes in "Christ" and another in a pantheon of six-headed monsters! Only Biblical inerrancy preserves Biblical faith from condemnation as nonsensically irrelevant.

[65]These phrases appear in the *Westminster Confession of Faith*, chap. 1, sec. 5.

[66]F. C. (Sol. Dec.), Preface, para6.

[67]The analytical stage is now being occupied particularly by the "linguistic analysts," such as the "ordinary language philosophers" Ryle and Toulmin. Here also is to be classed the work of the later Wittgenstein (the posthumous *Philosophical Investigations*).

# Notes On The Inerrancy Of Scripture

## ROBERT PREUS

This study is offered as an approach to the problem of the inerrancy of Scripture as it concerns evangelical Protestantism today. The attempt is to present a position that agrees with Scripture's testimony concerning itself and with the historic position of the Christian church. At the same time the attempt is made to be timely and to take into account contemporary issues raised by modern Biblical theology.

Here we shall try to delineate and clarify what is meant by the inerrancy of Scripture, what is the basis of this dogma, and what are its implications. It is not our purpose to become involved in the technicalities that have often obscured the doctrine or to traverse the labyrinth of intricate discussion that has not infrequently belabored studies of this basic theological truth.

Indeed, a brief treatment such as we are about to give cannot possibly solve the many hermeneutical and isagogical problems that touch upon the inerrancy of Scripture. Yet hermeneutical and isagogical concerns cannot be avoided in a study of this nature. Therefore we have endeavored to lay down general principles concerning these matters that will comport with the inerrancy and sole authority of Scripture.

## I. Thesis

In calling the Sacred Scriptures inerrant we recognize in them (A), as words taught by the Holy Spirit (B), that quality that makes them overwhelmingly (C) reliable witnesses (D-E) to the words and deeds of the God who has in his inspired spokesmen and in his incarnate Son disclosed himself to men for their salvation (F).[1]

Note: This definition is very general, seeking as it does to fit all the

Biblical data (for example, the bold language of prophecy and of adoration, the promises concerning the world to come for which human experience offers only imperfect and insufficient analogies, the expressive and indispensable anthropomorphisms and anthropopathisms used of God, the symbolic use of numbers and other referents in books like Daniel and Revelation, etc.). The definition also agrees, however, with what the Church catholic has believed and confessed through her entire history. We offer a few typical examples to bring out this fact.

Augustine, *Epist.* 82 *to Jerome*: "Only to those books which are called canonical have I learned to give honor so that I believe most firmly that no author in these books made any error in writing. I read other authors not with the thought that what they have thought and written is true just because they have manifested holiness and learning!"

Thomas Aquinas, *In Ioh.* 13, *lect.* 1: "It is heretical to say that any falsehood whatsoever is contained either in the gospels or in any canonical Scripture."

Luther (W² 15. 1481): "The Scriptures have never erred." W² 9. 356: "It is impossible that Scripture should contradict itself; it only appears so to senseless and obstinate hypocrites."

*Preface to the Book of Concord* (Tappert, p. 8): "We have in what follows purposed to commit ourselves exclusively and only, in accordance with the pure, infallible and unalterable Word of God, to that Augsburg Confession which was submitted to Emperor Charles V at the great imperial assembly in Augsburg in the year 1530." *Large Catechism* (Baptism 57. Tappert, p. 444): "My neighbor and I—in short, all men—may err and deceive, but God's Word cannot err." *Formula of Concord* (Epitome, 7. 13. Tappert, p. 483): "God's Word is not false nor does it lie."

Calov, *Systema locorum theologicorum* (Wittenberg, 1655-1677), 1. 462: "Because Scripture is God's Word which is absolutely true, Scripture is itself truth (Ps. 119:43.86.142.160; Jn. 17:17.19; 2 Sam. 7:28; Ps. 33:4; Gal. 3:1; Col. 1:5; 2 Tim. 2:18; 3:8; Tit. 1:1 and Jas. 1:8). Thus, whatever the sacred Scriptures contain is fully true and to be accepted with utmost certainty. Not only must we hold that to be true which is presented in Scripture relative to faith and morals, but we must hold to everything that happens to be included therein. Inasmuch as Scripture has been written by an immediate and divine impulse and all the Scriptures recognize Him as their author who cannot err or be mistaken in any way (Heb. 6:18), no untruth or error or lapse can be ascribed to the God-breathed Scriptures, lest God Himself be accused."

Turrettin, *Institutio Theologiae Elencticae* (Genevae, 1688), 1. 79: "We deny that there are any true and real contradictions in Scripture. Our reasons are as follows: namely, that Scripture is God breathed (2 Tim. 3:16), that the Word of God cannot lie or be ignorant of what has happened (Ps.

19:8.9; Heb. 6:18) and cannot be set aside (Matt. 5:18), that it shall remain forever (1 Pet. 1:25), and that it is the Word of truth (John 17:17). Now how could such things be predicated of Scripture if it were not free of contradictions, or if God were to allow the holy writers to err and lose their memory or were to allow hopeless blunders to enter into the Scriptures?"

Tromp, *De Sacrae Scripturae Inspiratione* (Romae, 1953) 121: "Everything which is contained in sacred Scripture, as attested by the author and in the sense intended by him, is infallibly true."

J. I. Packer, *"Fundamentalism" and the Word of God* (Grand Rapids: Eerdmans, 1958) 95: "Scripture is termed infallible and inerrant to express the conviction that all its teaching is the utterance of God 'who cannot lie,' whose word, once spoken, abides for ever, and that therefore it may be trusted implicitly."

Such statements written under different circumstances and at different times evince the remarkable unanimity on this matter that obtained in the Church throughout her history. The statements also indicate or infer the following six ektheses, which will serve to delineate and further explain our definition.

## EKTHESIS A

This "recognition" of the truthfulness of the written Word of God is not primarily intellectual. It takes place in the obedience of faith. The truthfulness and reliability of the Scriptures is an article of faith.

## EKTHESIS B

The basis of inerrancy rests on the nature of Scripture as God's Word. Inerrancy is an inextricable concomitant of inspiration. Our conviction is that since Scripture is truly and properly speaking God's Word, it will not deceive nor err.[2] Admittedly this is an inference (as in the case of the doctrine of the trinity or the two natures of Christ), but it is a necessary inference, because God is faithful and his Word (Scripture) is truth, and no Christian theologian until the period of rationalism ever shrank from this inference. It is to be noted that both Christ and the apostles drew the same inference (cf. not only John 10:34; Mark 12:24; Matt 5:18-19, but also Christ's and the apostles' use of the OT: They simply cite it as unconditionally true and unassailable).

## EKTHESIS C

Our recognition of the reliability of the witness of Scripture is graciously imposed upon us by the Spirit of God, and this through the power of Scripture itself.

## EKTHESIS D

The nature of inerrancy is essentially twofold: Scripture does not lie or deceive, and Scripture does not err or make mistakes in any affirmation it makes (*falsum formale* and *falsum materiale*). In other words the holy writers, moved by the Spirit of God, infallibly achieve the intent of their writing (cf. the statement of Tromp above). This is what is meant when we say that Scripture is a *reliable witness* to the words and deeds of God. Of his people God demands in the second and eighth commandments that they tell the truth, of his prophets and apostles that they do not lie: God will not countenance lying and prevarication (Prov 14:5; 19:22; Ps 63:11; Jer 23:25 ff.; Zeph 3:13; Acts 5:3; 1 John 2:21, 27). And God himself will not lie nor deceive (Prov 30:6-7; Num 23:19; Ps 89:35; Heb 6:18). In his written Word he will not break or suspend that standard of truth that he demands of his children. Thus we hear frequently from God's inspired witnesses the claim that they do not deceive, that they are not mistaken, that they tell the truth (Rom 9:1; 2 Cor 11:31; Gal 1:20; 1 Tim 2:7). The whole impact of entire books of the Bible depends upon the authoritative and truthful witness of the writer (John 21:24; 1 John 1:1-5a; 2 Pet 1:15-18). Pertinent to what was just said we must add the following: The truth of the sacred Scriptures must be determined from the sense that is intended (in verse, pericope, book) by the author. This sense in turn must be determined according to sound hermeneutical rules.

It is obvious that such a position on the nature of Biblical inerrancy is predicated on a correspondence idea of truth, which in part means this: Declarative statements (at least in those Biblical genres, or literary forms, that purport to be dealing with fact or history) of Scripture are, according to their intention, true in that they correspond to what has taken place (for example, historical statements), to what obtains (for example, theological affirmations and other affirmations concerning fact), or to what will take place (for example, prophecy). It really ought to go without saying that Scripture, like all cognitive discourse, operates under the rubrics of a correspondence idea of truth (see John 8:46; Eph 4:25; 1 Kgs 8:26; 22:16, 22 ff.; Gen 42:16, 20; Deut 18:22; Ps 119:163; Dan 2:9; Prov 14:25; Zech 8:16; John 5:31 ff.; Acts 24:8, 11; 1 Tim 1:15; cf. also the forensic picture that haunts all of Scripture—for example, such concepts as witness, testimony, judge, the eighth commandment, etc., John 21:24).

To speak of inerrancy of purpose (that God achieves his purpose in Scripture) or of Christological inerrancy of Scripture is indeed relevant to the general question of inerrancy but may at the same time be misleading if such a construct is understood as constituting the nature of inerrancy— for then we might speak of the inerrancy of Luther's Little Catechism or of a hymn by Paul Gerhardt, since they successfully achieve their purpose.

The first purpose of Scripture is to bring us to faith in Christ (John 20:31; 2 Tim 3:15). Involved with this prime purpose of Scripture is Luther's doctrine of the Christocentricity of Scripture (OT as well as NT). Such Christocentricity has a soteriological purpose. Only when I understand that Scripture and Christ are *pro me* will I understand the Scriptures (or the inerrancy thereof). But to say that Scripture is inerrant only to the extent that it achieves its soteriological purpose is a misleading position if it is made to be identical with inerrancy or confused with it. How does Scripture achieve this soteriological purpose? By cognitive language. By presenting facts, by telling a history (OT as well as NT). To say that there is a purpose in Scripture but no intentionality (for example, intent to give meaning) in the individual books or sections or verses, or to maintain that Scripture is inerrant in its eschatological purpose but not in the intentionality of its individual parts and pericopes, would not only be nonsense (mysticism), reducing all Scripture to the level of some sort of mystical utterances, but would be quite unscriptural (Luke 1:1-4, etc.). The eschatological purpose of Scripture does not cancel or vitiate or render trivial and unimportant the cognitive and factual content of assertions (and the truth of assertions) throughout Scripture but requires all this (Rom 15:4). And, on the other hand, formal and material inerrancy does not threaten or eclipse the Christological purpose of Scripture but supports it. Nor does such a position (formal and material inerrancy) become tantamount to reading Scripture atomistically. Language is a primary structure of lived experience and cannot be studied in isolation from it. Because the language of imagery in Scripture may not always be adequately analyzed or ever completely exhausted implies neither that it is meaningless (positivism) nor that it is errant ("Christian" positivism). Not orthodoxy but neo-orthodoxy has a positivistic, wooden theory of language.[3]

## EKTHESIS E

Inerrancy is plenary or absolute. (1) It not only pertains to the substance of the doctrines and narratives in Scripture but pertains also to those things that are nonessential, adjunct or *obiter dicta* (Quenstedt, *Systema*, 1. 77: "doctrine, ethics, history, chronology, topography or onamastics." (2) It covers not only the primary intent of the various pericopes and verses but also the secondary intent (for example, a passing historical reference within the framework of narrative—that is, that Christ was crucified between two thieves, that wise men visited him at his birth, that Joshua led the children of Israel into Canaan, that Ruth was a Moabitess, Nimrod a hunter, etc., etc.), not only soteriological, eschatological and religious intent and content of Scripture but also all declarative statements touching history and the realm of nature.

There are various reasons for this strict position. (1) The NT cites what might often be considered to be passing statements or negligible items from the OT, accepting them as true and authoritative (Matt 6:29; 12:42; John 10:35). Jesus accepts the basic framework of the OT history, even those aspects of that history that seem unimportant to many today—for example, Sodom and Gomorrah (Luke 17:27), Lot's wife turning to salt, the murder of Abel (11:51), Naaman (4:27). The NT does not recognize levicula in the OT (Rom 15:4; 2 Tim 3:16). (2) The primary intent of a passage or pericope is often dependent upon the secondary intent(s). This is so in the nature of the case. For instance, the exodus as a deliverance of God depends on the miraculous events connected with it. (3) The most common argument for the full inerrancy of Scripture as advanced by the older theologians was as follows: If errors are admitted in minor matters recorded in Scripture (matters that do not matter [?]), by what right may one then assume that there is no error in important or doctrinal concerns? How does one determine what matters are important? And does not, after all, everything pertain at least indirectly to doctrine (2 Tim 3:16)? In other words, to maintain that "things that matter" in Scripture (doctrinal matters) are inerrant and "things that do not matter" (nondoctrinal matters) are errant is both arbitrary and impossible to apply (cf. Calov, *Systema*, 1. 606 ff.).

## EKTHESIS F

The practical importance of the doctrine must always be recognized. It consists in this: that, as God is true and faithful, the reader of Scripture can have the assurance that he will not be deceived or led astray by anything he reads in God's Word, Holy Scripture. In no discussion of inerrancy do we find merely an academic interest in maintaining purely a traditional position or in hewing to a party line. Such a practical concern must also be emphasized in our day. Any approach to Scripture or method of interpretation that would make of Scripture something less than trustworthy is sub-Christian and does not take Scripture at its own terms. It must also be borne in mind that the truthfulness of Scripture is never an end in itself but serves the soteriological purpose of Scripture.

## II. Adjuncts to the Doctrine of Biblical Inerrancy

1. *Inerrancy does not imply verbal exactness of quotations* (for example, the words of institution, the words on Jesus' cross). The NT ordinarily quotes the OT according to its sense only, sometimes it only alludes to a pericope or verse in the OT, sometimes there are conflations, etc. In the case of extra-Biblical citations we ought to assume that the holy writer stands behind and accepts the truth of his quotation unless the context would indicate otherwise (cf. 2 Chr 5:9; 8:8, where there are citations from documents that say that a situation obtains "to this day"—that is, when the original document was written). It is helpful to distinguish between the *veritas citationis* (lies, statements of evil men, or, for example, the statements of Job's friends, etc.) and the *veritas rei citatae* (Acts 17:28; Num 21:14 and possibly 2 Kgs 1:18).

2. *Inerrancy does not imply verbal or intentional agreement in parallel accounts of the same event.* For instance, the portrayal of creation in Genesis 1 and in Job 38 are radically different because of a radical difference in the aim of the author. Again, the different evangelists write about our Lord from different vantage points and out of different concerns. Therefore their accounts will differ not only in details (as in the case of any two or three witnesses of the same event) but in aim. We must exercise caution here lest we impose a point of view upon an author which cannot be drawn inductively from Scripture itself. For instance, there is no certain evidence that Matthew is writing for Jews, tying up Christ's life with OT prophecy (John also cites the OT often: 22 times). This is merely a rather safe conjecture. The same may be said concerning John writing on Christ's divinity against Cerinthus. We have no right or good reason to assume that the holy writer tampers with or distorts facts to maintain a point of view. The evangelists claim to be faithful and careful witnesses (John 21:24; Luke 1:1 ff.). However, it must be clearly recognized that incomplete history or an incomplete presentation of doctrine in a given pericope is not false history or a false presentation.

3. *Scripture is replete with figures of speech*—for example, metonymy (Luke 16:29), metaphor (Ps 18:20), personification (Matt 6:4), synecdoche (Luke 2:1), apostrophe, hyperbole (Matt 2:3), etc. It should go without saying that figurative language is not errant language. To assert

that Scripture, by rounding numbers and employing hyperbole, meta-phors, etc., is not concerned about precision of fact (and therefore subject to error) is to misunderstand the intention of Biblical language. Figura-tive language (and not modern scientifically *"precise"* language) is *precisely* the mode of expression that the sacred writers' purposes demand. To imply that figurative language is *ex hypothesi* meaningless *or* that it cannot convey information—truthful and, from its own point of view, *precise* information—is the position of positivism, not the result of sensi-tive exegesis (for example, "Yanks slaughter Indians" is a meaningful and precise statement). How else does one speak of a transcendent God, of his epiphanies and revelations, than in metaphors and figures of speech? De-metaphorize, deanthropomorphize, and you are not getting closer to the meaning of such expressions but losing their meaning. Figurative lan-guage, then, meets all the canons necessary: (1) that statements perfectly represent the author's meaning, (2) that statements do not mislead the reader or lead him into error of any kind, and (3) that statements corre-spond to fact when they purport to deal with fact—and this in the case of poetry as well as in the case of straight narrative.

Note: When we interpret or read Scripture we identify ourselves with the writers, not only with their *Sitz im Leben* and their use of language but with their entire spirit and their faith (which is more important, 1 Cor 2:14-16). We not only understand them but feel and live and experi-ence with them. We become totally involved. To stand back dispassion-ately and assess and criticize as a modern man would Shelley or Shakespeare or Homer is to fail to interpret Scripture.

4. *Scripture uses popular phrases and expressions of its day—* for exam-ple, bowels of mercy, four corners of the earth. Joseph is called the father of Christ, etc. No error is involved in the use of such popular expressions. Cf. Ps 7:9; 22:10.

5. *In describing the things of nature Scripture does not employ scientif-ically precise language but describes and alludes to things phenomenally as they appear to our senses*—for example, the fixity of stellar constella-tions and the magnitude of the stars (Isa 13:10; Judg 5:20; Job 38:31; Amos 5:8; Job 9:9); the sun and moon called lights and the implication that the moon is larger than the stars (Gen 1:16) [it *is* larger from our van-tage point]; the earth as motionless in a fixed position (Eccl 1:4; Ps 93:1); the sun goes around the fixed earth (Eccl 1:5; Matt 13:6; Eph 4:26; note that in Hebrew there is even a phrase for the rising of the sun: *mizraḥ šemeš*, which means "east," Num 34:15). Phenomenal language also ex-plains why the bat is classified with birds (Lev 19:11; cf. Lev 11:6; Ps 135:6). Such a classification offers no attempt to be scientific. Many

things in the realm of nature are spoken of in poetic language: the spreading out of the heavens (Isaiah 40; Job 9:8), the foundations of the earth (Job 38:6), the pillars of the earth (9:6) and of heaven (26:11), the ends of the earth (Ps 67:7; 72:8). Note that there is much apostrophe and hyperbole (Mark 4:31) when Scripture speaks of the things of nature. In none of the above instances is inerrancy threatened or vitiated. The intention of the passages cited above is not to establish or vouch for a particular world view or scientific explanation of things. Because the language is not scientific does not imply that it is not true descriptively.

### 6. The various literary forms used by Scripture.

(1) Certain alleged forms are not compatible either with the purpose of Scripture or with its inerrancy. Specifically, any literary genre that would in itself be immoral or involve deceit or error is not compatible with Biblical inerrancy and is not to be found in Scripture—for example, myth, etiological tale, midrash, legend or saga according to the usual designation of these forms. None of these genres fits the serious theological purpose of Scripture. Thus we do not find Scripture presenting material as factual or historical when in truth it is only mythical (2 Pet 1:16 ff.; 1 Tim 1:4; 4:7; 2 Tim 4:4).[4]

(2) Apart from the above strictures any form of ancient literature is hypothetically compatible with Biblical inerrancy—for example, allegory (Galatians 4), fable (Judg 9:8-15), etc.—provided the genre is indicated directly or indirectly. At the same time it does no violence to inerrancy if the language of folklore or mythical elements serve as a means to clothe a Biblical author's presentation of doctrine (for example, "helpers of Rahab" in Job 9:13; "Leviathan" in Job 3:8 and in Ps 74:12-15; Idumea as inhabited by centaurs, satyrs, etc. [Is 34:14], meaning that Idumea will be devastated so that only such animals can live there). We do the same today if in a sermon a pastor refers to a "dog in the manger." As for the midrash, there is no reason to maintain that Scripture cannot employ midrashim any more than other literary forms. In many cases midrash approaches parable in form and purpose. However, the fanciful examples of midrash with the indiscriminate admixture of truth and error and the production of pure fiction to stress a certain lesson is not compatible with the historical character and the inerrancy of Scripture; cf. J. M. Lehrmann, The World of the Midrash (London, 1961).[5]

### 7. Biblical historiography.

(1) Some Biblical writers use and cite sources for their history. We must assume that the Biblical author by the way in which he cites sources believes that these sources speak the truth, that they are reliable sources. Therefore he follows them. The contrary contention is certainly possible,

but it must be proved in individual cases (implicit citations, cf. 2 Samuel). In the case of explicit citations (the words of a character in a history) we assume the truth of the matter cited, but this again depends upon the intention of the hagiographer. We can assume the truth of the matter cited only if the holy writer formally or implicitly asserts that he approved it and judges to be true what he asserts in the citation (cf. Acts 17:29).

(2) Historical events are not described phenomenally as are the data of nature.[6]

(3) The historical genre employed by Scripture is apparently a unique form. As it cannot be judged according to the canons of modern scientific historiography, it cannot be judged by the mythological and legendary or even historical forms of ancient contemporary civilizations—for example, we take the ancient Babylonian and Ugaritic accounts of creation as pure myth, but quite clearly the Biblical cannot be taken as such.[7]

(4) Chronology and genealogies are not presented in Scripture in the full and orderly manner in which we might present a chronicle or family tree today. Scripture often spreads out time for the sake of symmetry or harmony, hysteron proteron is often employed, and also prolepsis (John 17:4; 13:31). Again, genealogies often omit many generations (cf. 1 Chr 26:24, where Moses, Gershom, Shubael are given, covering a period of perhaps more than four hundred years; or cf. Heb 7:9-10, where Levi is said to be in the loins of Abraham, his father, when Melchizedek met him. Thus any ancestor is the father of all his descendants).

8. *We must grant that there is often a sensus plenior in Scripture pericopae in the sense of 1 Pet 1:10-12.* That is to say, the writer of Scripture is not in every respect a child of his time, conditioned by his own cultural milieu, but he often writes for a later age. However, we cannot countenance a *sensus diversus et disperatus relate ad sensus litteralem obvium hagiographi*, which would conflict with Biblical inerrancy and turn Scripture into a waxen nose. We hold only to a profounder and sometimes more distinct sense than the writer may have perceived as he expressed himself. This has serious implications relative to the NT use and interpretation of the OT. The NT does not misinterpret or do violence to the OT when it interprets. *Sensus litteralis Scripturae unicus est* does not imply that the sacred writer understands the full divine implication of all his words.

9. *Pseudepigrapha.* Pseudonymity in the sense of one writer pretending to be another in order to secure acceptance of his own work is illicit and not compatible with inerrancy. That the motives for such action may be

construed as good does not alter the fact that fraud or forgery has been perpetrated. The fact that such a practice was carried on in ancient times does not justify it nor indicate that the practice was considered moral. When in ancient times a pious fraud was found out and the authenticity of a work disproved, the work itself was suspect (cf. *Fragmentum Muratorianum* 5, where the *finctae* letters of Paul to the Laodiceans and the Alexandrians were not accepted by the Church for that very reason).

Pseudonymity must be carefully delimited. Pseudonymity is deliberate fraud (for any reason whatsoever). It has nothing to do with anonymity. Nor would it be pseudonymity if a later writer culled under inspiration all the wisdom sayings of Solomon, gathering them into a volume and presenting them for what they are—Solomon's wisdom. His contemporaries know that Solomon has not written the book but understand the sayings and the wisdom to be Solomon's (similar to this: that we have the words of Christ in the gospels). In such a case no deception is involved. In the case of the pastoral epistles this could not be assumed by any stretch of the imagination. The letters are written to give the impression that they come directly from Paul, claiming his authority. If they were not in fact Pauline a deception has taken place, a successful deception until lately.[8]

10. *Etymologies in Scripture are often according to sound and not (obviously) according to modern linguistic analysis.* This fact does not affect inerrancy. The ancients are not thinking of etymologies in the modern sense.[9]

11. *The inerrancy and the authority of Scripture are inseparably related.* This fact has been consistently recognized by Reformation theologians who have often included inerrancy and authority under the rubric of infallibility. What is meant is that without inerrancy the *sola scriptura* principle cannot be maintained or practiced. An erring authority for all Christian doctrine (like an erring Word of God) is an impossible and impracticable *contradictio in adjecto*.

12. *In approaching the Scriptures as children of God who are under the Scriptures it is well to recall and observe two basic principles of our Reformation fathers*:

(1) Scripture is *autopistos*—that is to say, we are to believe its utterances simply because Scripture, the Word of God, makes these utterances (inerrancy is always to be accepted on faith!), and we are to believe without the need of any corroborating evidence. This would apply to statements about God, but also to statements about events in history.

(2) Scripture is *anapodeiktos*—that is, self-authenticating. It brings its own demonstration, the demonstration of the Spirit and of power.

Again no corroborating evidence is necessary or sought for. Now *sola scriptura* means all this, and it means as well that there are no outside criteria for judging the truthfulness or factual content of scriptural assertions (for example, neither a modern scientific world view nor modern "scientific historiography"). We accept the assertions of Scripture on faith. For instance, the fact that the creation story or the flood or the story of Babel has some parallels in other Semitic and ancient lore gives no right to conclude that these accounts in Scripture are mythical (any more than we have the right to conclude that Christ's resurrection is not historical because there are mythical resurrections recorded in history). Such an interpretation would involve a violation of the *sola scriptura* principle. At the same time it is possible that a changed world view (for example, our modern view as opposed to the Newtonian view of absolute space and time) will open for consideration a new interpretation of a Biblical pericope, although it can never determine our interpretation of Scripture.

It is particularly important to maintain the above principles in our day in view of the tendency to allow extra-Biblical data (particularly historical and archaeological data) to encroach on the absolute authority of Scripture.

[1]Majuscule letters A-F refer to the six ektheses that will shortly be given in support and clarification of the major thesis.

[2]Cf. M. Nicolau and I. Salaverri, S. J., *Sacrae Theologiae Summa* (Madrid, 1958), 1. 1095: "Inerrantiam Scripturae non derivari praecise ex fine scriptoris, ad illa tantum quae ipse docere intendit, sed derivari ex natura inspirationis, ad illa omnis quae vi huius influxus asseruntur." The alluding to many contemporary Roman Catholic sources in notes does not necessarily imply full agreement with these statements or that we should use these statements in any final study on inerrancy. The statements are for the most part quite sound and useful. The fact is that Roman Catholics are the majority of those who write on inerrancy today from a point of view similar to ours.

[3]Hoepfl insists that inerrancy is made irrelevant when it is said that historical errors do not affect the intent of Scripture. Cf. *Introductio Generalis in Sacram Scripturam* (Romae, 1958) 123: "Pro ipsis Protestantibus liberalibus magis 'conservatoribus,' qui inspirationis notionem saltem valde deprimunt, quaestio inerrantiae omnino non exsistit, cum errores historici fini S. Scripturae non noceant."

[4]Cf. A. Bea, *De Inspiratione et Inerrantia Sacrae Scripturae* (Rome, 1954) 44: "Myth is the expression of some religious or cultic idea through personifications which are regarded as divine entities (e.g., the fertility of the earth and of animals—Astarte). Such myths must be distinguished from mythic literary elements (metaphors, personifications) employed from selected mythology for illustrative purposes. Cf. Is. 27:1 ( = Ugarit A + I, 1-2?); Ps. 74:12-17; 89:10-14; 48:3; Job 26:7; Ez. 32:20. Myth, properly so-called, cannot be found in the sacred Scriptures (cf. *EB* n. 60.333); however, that literary elements could be used to adorn or illustrate was already granted by the holy Fathers; cf. S. Greg. Nyss. *PG* 44, 973. On individual passages, see *Biblica* 19 (1938), 444-448; F. Porporato, *Miti e inspirazione biblica*, 1944; id. in *Civ. Catt.* 94 (1943/I), 329-340.

"*Midrashim* technically speaking are rabbinic literary efforts—writings from that era— which are not strictly exegetical but composed for establishing rules for living (*halachah*). 2 Chron. 13:22 and 24:27 do not use the term in this technical sense, but signify merely 'study' or 'work' (cf. Eissfeldt, *Einl.*, p. 605). Since it arbitrarily confuses true and false things, midrash *per se* is excluded by the holy Scriptures (cf. *EB* n. 474). It can be admitted only if the holy writer clearly indicated that he is writing only for the sake of edification and not for setting forth properly history (cf. *EB* n. 154)."

[5] Cf. *Sacrae Theologiae Summa*, 1. 1097: "All literary genres are quite compatible with inspiration, if they are not by their very nature immoral (as in the case of certain classical poetry) or if they do not tend to lead into error. Thus myths considered as false religious fables (e. g., the personification of natural things such as the fertility of the earth as divine beings is a literary form not consonant with inspiration). But a myth merely cited in Scripture or used as a mere literary adornment may be admitted, but as something merely cited, or as something purely metaphorical.... We can even allow that fictitious narratives (are present) in the Scriptures, provided that they are recognized as such and that of necessity the truth related by the words of the story is in the proper sense not historical. Thus, there is the allegorical mode of speaking in Scripture, such as we find in the Song of Songs which is an allegorical song describing the love and mystical union between Jahveh and His people. And it is true that in the different literary forms of Scripture, whether poetical or doctrinal or narrative, (fables) are interspersed."

[6] Cf. Bea, *De Inspiratione* 45: " 'History according to appearance' is based upon a false foundation, namely this, that principles which obtain relative to matters of nature can be transferred to historical concerns. Historical sources or general opinion are not 'appearances of happenings'; the telling of a certain happening *per se* does not amount to announcing that something appeared to the senses, as in the realm of nature, nor is it tantamount to say what the common people think about a happening; rather it is the announcing of the happening itself." Cf. also *Sacrae Theologiae Summa*, 1. 1097: "On the other hand, history is not concerned with phenomena which are continuously apparent and with things which men describe according to appearance, but history concerns itself with *things that have happened, just as they have happened*" (italics theirs).

[7] Cf. Bea, *De Inspiratione* 46-48: "In its own characteristics Israelite writing of history far surpasses all other Semitic historiography.... Albright, *The Archaeology of Pal.* (1932), 128.... In a certain sense Hebrew historiography can be compared with the Hittite (cf. *Annales Mursilis* II, ca. 1353-1325; *Apologia Hattusil.*, ca. 1295-1260), but the Israelitish writing of history surpasses this in liveliness, in its simple manner, and sincere way of narrating, in psychological depth and breadth; in particular it is not a 'courtly' or 'official' manner of narrating...."

"The manner of writing among the ancients definitely differs from the modern. Firstly, the ancients considered the writing of history to be an art (cf. Cicero). Thus it was adorned greatly, for instance, with fictitious speeches to express certain ideas. Such historiography pays more attention to giving the sense of a speech than to bringing out the exact words; it employs numerical schemata (30, 40, 70); it uses mnemonic techniques (such as etymologies); it is careless concerning exact chronology; it uses genealogies as shortcuts to history; it narrates in 'concentric circles' rather than in straight continuous exposition, etc. Now all of these devices, provided that they are properly considered, in no way conflict with the integrity of the narratives....

"Ancient history is not a genre of its own peculiar type which is less interested in telling the truth than modern history. Rather it has different aims, different ways of exposition from modern history. Therefore it is necessary in the case of all the individual authors to investigate accurately what sources they use, how they make judgments from these sources, what style they employ, what purpose they intend. Only then are we able to assess rightly and judiciously concerning their historical merit....

"The intention of the inspired historiographers is to write *true* history. When they made use of the narrative genre, this presupposes per se that they desire to tell of things that *have happened*....

"That these stories have a religious aim does not imply that the *facts* which they refer to are any less true. 'Religious history' is not necessarily fictional narrative. Thus, for instance, the evangelists, although they write with a religious aim in mind, are very careful about the truth of the facts (cf. Lk. 1:1; Jn. 19:35; 1 Jn. 1:1)....

"That the facts connected with revelation are sometimes (for example, in the first eleven chapters of Genesis) presented in a simple manner, a manner accommodated to the comprehension of less cultured men, that they are presented figuratively and anthropomorphically, does not imply that we can call these narratives any less truly historical although they are not history in our modern technical meaning of the term; cf. *EB* 581, and *Verb. Dom.* 25 (1946), 354-56.

"The Judaic as well as the Christian tradition understood the Biblical narratives in the strictly historical sense; cf. the sayings of Christ (Lk. 4:25; 6:3ff.; 17:32; Matt. 12:40) and the sayings of the apostles (Heb. 11:17-40; 2 Pet. 2:5-8), in which facts of minor or secondary importance are set forth as history....That Christ and the apostles simply 'accommodated' themselves to their own contemporaries cannot be asserted a priori, but must be proved in each individual case where there might seem to be some special reason for granting this."

[8]Cf. J. I. Packer, *"Fundamentalism" and the Word of God* (Grand Rapids: Eerdmans, 1958) 182 ff.

[9]Cf. J. Levie, *The Bible, Word of God in Words of Men* (New York, 1962) 220-221: "We know that in all countries the common people very often invent as an afterthought etymological explanations for the name of a given place or given tribe on the basis of quite arbitrary associations of ideas or words. Is it legitimate to admit that here too the sacred writer is content to hand down to us the popular derivations customary in his environment or should we be obliged to believe that, by virtue of inspiration, these derivations are the true linguistic explanations of the words in question, and should therefore be accepted by present-day scholars?

"It is now generally recognized that the inspired writer is only reporting these attempted etymologies as he found them in the folklore of his country. The literary form he adopts, which is that of popular history, clearly shows that he has no intention of offering us scientific derivations of the modern kind, but popular derivations in the style of his own times.

"Here are a few examples taken from ten chapters of Genesis, 16 to 26:—16.13 (Atta el Roi); 16.14 (Lachai Roi); 17.17; 18.12-15; 21.6 which give three derivations of the name Isaac (these clearly show by their differences that the writer intended to give a simple report and to make no attempt at criticism); 19.22 (Segor); 21.31 (Bersabee); 22.14 (Yahweh Yireh); 25.25 (Jacob); 25.30-1 (Edom); 26.20 (Eseq); 26.21 (Sitna); 26.22 (Rechoboth); 26.33 (Schibea)."

# The Basis For Our Belief In Inerrancy

## R. LAIRD HARRIS

Our subject is, simply, "Why I believe the Bible." And of course there are many reasons. We use the word "believe," however, not in a general sense. Generally speaking we may believe the reports of the war in Vietnam without believing them in detail. When we say we believe it we mean we believe it to be true, and true throughout. In short, we believe it to be without error.

It is obvious that this has been the historic Protestant position. The Reformation creeds do not use the terminology of today, yet candid examination has convinced most people that they express what we call Biblical inerrancy. The Roman Council of Trent is as explicit on this subject as any Protestant could wish. And the Nicene fathers who speak on the subject make express statements to the effect that the Scriptures show no real contradiction but are to be believed whole and entire. Earlier writings are scanty, but Irenaeus can be quoted as saying that "the Scriptures are indeed perfect since they were spoken by the Word of God and his Spirit" (*Against Heresies*, 2.28.2). And Justin Martyr near the middle of the second century says, "I am entirely convinced that no Scripture contradicts another" (*Dialogue with Trypho*, chap. 65). Such statements are found also in those scanty writings that remain of Polycarp, Ignatius and Clement, men who actually were contemporaneous with the apostles.

This doctrine of the inerrancy of Scripture is pervasive, ancient and basic. Why has it been held so universally in all ages? Whatever may be the bases for this belief, they must be strong and powerfully persuasive to Christian hearts and minds.

It is not of small moment that the Bible has also often been disbelieved. Indeed it has almost always been disbelieved by those outside of orthodox Christian faith. The early days had a Cerinthus. The Reformers were troubled by the Socinians. The age of rationalism produced a welter of skeptics. Our own days are more than usually afflicted in that the seats of unbelief are firmly emplaced within the visible Church and in particular in the halls of theological learning. None today are so skeptical as theologians. It is left to them to proclaim not only the mythology of the Bible but the very death of God.

We may learn, however, from Church history that those who are earnest believers in Jesus Christ as Lord are by and large believers also in the Bible. There have been and are exceptions. Some have tried to hold on to the teachings of Jesus while discounting the inerrancy of the Bible. But in general it does not work. The students of such men either go on to denial of Christ as he is revealed in the Scriptures, or they draw back to a more complete and consistent faith. There would seem to be a reason for this situation. It appears that belief in inerrancy is closely associated with a full-orbed Christian faith. And the converse seems also to be one of the lessons of history. Although belief in the Bible is not necessary to salvation, yet Christian faith has great difficulty in maintaining itself without this doctrine. I believe there are reasons for this, and we shall look at them. They concern the bases for our belief in inerrancy.

Calvin, in his *Institutes of the Christian Religion*, long ago set a pattern for our inquiry. At the beginning of his system of theology Calvin states the necessity of a written revelation for men to know God. He declares that there are proofs aplenty to convince any reasonable person of the truth and divine authority of the Scriptures. But he concludes that these are all the arguments of men and will not convince a single skeptic except when the certainty of it shall be founded on the "internal persuasion of the Holy Spirit." For, he says, the conviction that Scripture is the word of God "cannot be known without faith" (*Institutes*, 1.8.13).

Calvin's rational arguments in favor of Scripture are summed up in the Westminster Confession as "The testimony of the church...the heavenliness of the matter, the efficacy of the doctrine, the majesty of the style, the consent of all the parts, the scope of the whole (which is to give all glory to God), the full discovery it makes of the only way of man's salvation, the many other incomparable excellencies and the entire perfection thereof." I suppose that today we should add the argument from archeology! But the Confession goes on: "Our full persuasion and assurance of the infallible truth, and divine authority thereof, is from the inward work of the Holy Spirit bearing witness by and with the Word in our hearts" (chap. 1, sec. 5).

Here both Calvin, the Westminster Confession and others, too, leave the subject. This is thought to be the ultimate answer. Scripture is self-authenticating. This principle is sometimes extended also to the question of canon as in the French Confession of 1559 and in the *Systematic Theology* of my friend and colleague, J. Oliver Buswell, Jr.

Hodge on the other hand refers the question of canon to the authority of Christ and not at all to the inner testimony of the Holy Spirit. And he bases the proof of inspiration likewise on the authority of Christ and on the phenomena of Scripture, almost to the exclusion of the inner testimony.

In my own work on *Inspiration and Canonicity* I follow Warfield, Hodge, Alexander and others in giving the greatest weight to the authority of Jesus Christ as the basis of inerrancy. However, I do say that this position does not exclude the idea of the testimony of the Holy Spirit when rightly considered as is done, I believe, both correctly and extensively by A. Kuyper in his *Principles of Sacred Theology*.

It is a remarkable fact that the doctrine of the testimony of the Holy Spirit is not alluded to at all by the writers of the first two centuries. I am not a sufficient student of the Middle Ages to state a flat negative: that the doctrine was not held before the Reformation. But it appears not to have been widely held at least. Augustine was widely quoted as resting the authority of the gospels on the witness of the Church. Calvin takes up this quotation and declares that he only meant that the witness—not the authority—of the Church was vital. But it seems likely that the great name of Augustine plus the pretensions of the hierarchy made the Church the standard basis of Biblical inerrancy through the Middle Ages. Curiously this view was not openly espoused by the Council of Trent, which contented itself with ascribing inerrancy to the Scriptures because God was their author and because they derived from Christ.

The prominence of the teaching of the testimony of the Holy Spirit in Reformation times is probably due to the fact that questions of authority were under discussion. The Catholics alleged an ecclesiastical authority. The self-authentication of Scripture was a good rebuttal. It should be complemented, however, with that which the early Church constantly alleged: the historical evidence of the teaching of Christ.

Papias, for instance, in the fragments remaining of his works, tells how he minutely inquired after the sayings of the Lord from the followers of his disciples. Ignatius too rests all upon the authority of Christ: "When I heard some saying, 'If I do not find it in the ancient Scriptures I will not believe the Gospel,' on my saying to them, it is written, they answered me, 'That remains to be proved.' But to me Jesus is in the place of all that is ancient" (*Phld.*, chap. 8). Other such statements could be multiplied. The early believers were not called Christians for nothing. They based all their authority, their hope, their salvation, their duty on Christ. Indeed one problem in the study of the fathers on gospel origins is to determine whether their quotations of the words of Christ are authoritative because they come from him or because they are found in the gospels. Likely we should say both, because no words of Christ of any consequence are quoted outside of our canonical gospels. But in any event the appeal before the public was to well-authenticated words of the divinely-attested Christ.

It is an interesting experience to read through these early fathers from this angle. What is their source of authority? The answer shines on every page. It is Christ. As Ignatius said in the quotation given above, "His cross, and death, and resurrection and the faith which is by him are undefiled monuments of antiquity." The apostles are also highly elevated as a complete and closed circle.

But the apostles possess their high authority only in virtue of their relation to the divine Christ. The OT writings are of course also fully authoritative. But no conflict was felt here because they are the Word of God spoken by God's Spirit, and Christ also is God. In short, the OT Scriptures are authoritative because they are from God, and the NT writings are equally acceptable and found remarkably easy acceptance because in them the incarnate God speaks.

I remind ourselves that this is still a good basis for inerrancy. I do not need to belabor this point, for I have done it in print and so have others. One book I have found quite helpful is by Hugh McIntosh, *Is Christ Infallible and the Bible True?* Warfield has also developed this thought in his *Revelation and Inspiration*, as has Abraham Kuyper in his *Principles of Sacred Theology* (Grand Rapids: Eerdmans, 1954 reprint) 428-473. I must point out that this is a basis, a solid basis, and one that even a nonbeliever can appreciate—though he will naturally not be convinced.

The witness of Christ is plain. Standard verses are John 10:35; Luke 16:17, 29, 31; 24:25, 44; Matt 5:17; etc. Luke 24 gives Christ's resurrection testimony. Luke 16:29, 31 speak of the Bible as a more effective witness than a resurrection of the dead would be. Luke 16:17 declares that the Bible is true to the smallest letter. Matthew 5:17 is probably a parallel passage and declares that the book—the Law and the Prophets, which is a standard NT designation of the Jewish canon—is perfect to the jot and tittle. Clearly verbal inspiration was taught by Christ. Furthermore, Jesus' whole attitude to the OT is one of complete acceptance. He believed its prophecies and cited its miracles. He accepted the Mosaic authorship of the Pentateuch and the reality of Adam and Eve, of Jonah, of Noah. Happily it is admitted today that Jesus was no higher critic. The orthodox exegesis of these passages is at least admitted. The question now lies where it ought to lie. Shall we accept the teaching of Jesus or not? A. Kuyper in a masterful section shows that to speak of Jesus accommodating himself to the ideas of the day is now out of the question for a Christian who accepts the moral integrity of Christ. For the modern theologians themselves scorn to accommodate themselves to a Christian public holding older conservative ideas. He concludes, "Either Jesus' view of the Scripture is the true one, and then we should kneel in His presence; or Jesus' view of the Scripture is an enormous mistake, in which case the Rabbi of Nazareth can no longer be the absolute guide along the way of faith" (*Principles* 459). Of course modern skepticism has dissolved Jesus still more. If all we know of Jesus is his "thatness," it is of no value to discuss his teaching. But then nothing is of any value anyhow, and unbelief wallows deeper in its quicksands. What the answer of the early Church fathers to such ideas would have been is easy to suppose. They would have gone on declaring the facts and giving the evidence, not worrying too much about some seed falling on stony ground. For us the basis of inerrancy is clear enough, and if some will not see it we must conclude that the God of this world is still active.

For, as Kuyper declares, there is no middle ground. You cannot accept Jesus as Lord and be saved while holding that all we know of him is his "thatness." And if we know more, at once we see that what we know of him is that he believed in the inerrancy of Scripture. Thus if we have a regard to consistency we believe in Christ and Biblical inerrancy—both or neither. For the Christian the choice is plain. And Jesus himself laid this choice before us: "If ye believe not his writings, how shall ye believe my words?" (John 5:47).

I could add greatly to the details of this argument, but there is neither time nor need. The authority of Christ is an adequate basis for belief in Biblical inerrancy. I might say also, by the side, that the statements of Christ are a sufficient definition of the type of inerrancy to be held. This is one explanation of the curious fact mentioned at the start why the historic Christian faith has always included inerrancy but non-Christians just do not really believe the Bible except perhaps in a theoretical impersonal way—a grudging admission without intelligent investigation of the corollaries.

But as mentioned previously, this teaching is not antithetic to the doctrine of the witness of the Holy Spirit. However, this witness must be carefully defined. The Westminster Confession calls it a witness by and with the Word in our hearts. Calvin speaks of it as an opening of the eyes to behold inherent excellencies of Scripture. Buswell speaks similarly. John Murray well says, "The internal testimony does not convey to us new truth content" ("The Attestation of Scripture," in *The Infallible Word* [Philadelphia: Presbyterian Guardian, 1946] 50). There are no new revelations of the Spirit. And neither is this testimony a new work of God making the Bible the Word of God for us à la Barth. The Spirit testifies by and with the Bible that it is the Word of God and authoritative because it is from him.

Can such a testimony witness to inerrancy? If so, would it witness to an inerrant KJV? Not if the doctrine is appropriately defined as is done best, I

109

believe, by Kuyper (*Principles* 557 ff.). Briefly, his view is that the Spirit works "gradually and unobserved." First comes the *palingenesis*. But this involves both an acceptance of the greatest of miracles—Christ's resurrection—and a new way of looking at Biblical supernaturalism. At once the offense of the cross is gone. And this miracle of salvation is of a piece with Bible doctrine and specifically with the gospel records of Christ. Our hearts are strangely warmed by *these* doctrines and no others. "Thus the veil is gradually being pushed aside, the eye turns toward the Divine light that radiates from the Scripture, and now our inner *ego* sees its imposing superiority" (p. 558). Kuyper mentions the work of brother Christians and even of nonbelieving antagonists in sharpening the process. Finally of great significance is what we have just said. This Christ who thus brings peace and pardon also recommends to us the Scriptures in their minutest detail. Problems with such a view are solved first by a new look from the spiritual angle, then by a greater faith to lay some problems as it were on ice for later light. The help of brother Christian students accounts for more assistance. At last, as Kuyper says, "the assurance of his faith on this point is immovably established" (p. 562).

This formulation, I believe, agrees with the fact that a non-Christian who has not seen the light of the Spirit working on the evangelical history cannot appreciate or understand or accept the Bible as true because he does not accept the Christ of the Bible as his own. It also agrees with the fact that this testimony was not referred to in early times. They had it too but did not analyze it. They simply included this teaching in their understanding of what it meant to believe on Christ, as the Westminster Confession puts it in chap. 14 on saving faith: "A Christian believes to be true whatsoever is revealed in the Word, for the authority of God Himself speaketh therein."

# DIFFICULTIES WITH INERRANCY

## ROBERT L. SAUCY

It is not our present purpose to attempt to discuss in detail the whole gamut of problems connected with the inspiration of Scripture but rather to examine briefly some of the major objections, methods and thoughts behind these.

The charges against the inerrancy of the Scriptures can be broadly categorized under two heads: historical-critical and theological. Which of these is prior and which dependent on the other is perhaps open to question, but both have an affinity in their esteem of human opinion.

Difficulties arise from the area of the historical-critical, not because these areas have uncovered any new demonstrable facts contradictory to the words of Scripture but because they come from what has been termed a revolutionary historical approach to the Bible.[1] The essence of this new approach is the application of a naturalistic historical development methodology to the contents of the Word of God. The Bible is approached as any other book and scrutinized with the tools of modern and often spiritually uncommitted scholarship. The Biblical writers are historically enmeshed into their fallible human environment in varying degrees both as to form and content of their message. Thus a supernatural inspiration is denied and the doctrine destroyed with charges of error.

The radical conclusions of this method are not accepted by all advocates of an errant Bible today, but much of the erroneous methodology is. We refer to the plea for an inductive examination of the phenomena of Scripture.[2] Most certainly, inductive methodology must not be discarded in ascertaining the doctrine of inspiration, but it must include a thorough induction of the Bible's own relevant data on the subject. The modern advocates of errancy claim adherence to this principle. As Beegle affirms: "A truly Biblical formulation of inspiration must give equal weight to the teaching and to the facts of Scripture."[3] But one looks in vain through his recent study of the subject for a thorough inductive study of the Scriptural doctrine or of a reckoning with the exegetical studies of those who have made such studies. The problem with the modern inductive approach is just this: It imposes the contemporary scientific method of natural man upon the Word of God and makes it the standard of truth and error. The Bible is approached from outside of the faith as any human book, and the critical methods of humanistic unbelief are made the judge of all Biblical data. Whatever does not square with contemporary knowledge is wrong.[4]

It is not only the acceptance of the a prioris of unbelief that leads to difficulties with inerrancy but also the imposition of modern technical thought patterns upon the general nontechnical statements of Scripture. As genuine critical scholarship reveals the ancient methodologies of Biblical times, many of these difficulties disappear.[5] The data of the Bible must be judged by its own standards.

Unless one is willing to accept the radical naturalistic historical development a priori, modern scholarship on a factual basis has revealed few if any difficulties that have not been known for centuries and answered effectively in various ways. On the contrary, new research is gradually decreasing Biblical difficulties and giving stronger support to the belief that the difficulties yet remaining are due not to error but to lack of knowledge.

It appears then that the empirical problems raised today are done so only to buttress other deeper objections of theology and philosophy. This is quite evident when, for example, Thielicke answers the question of Biblical inerrancy negatively without mention of any historical data and makes a point of doing so.[6] From theology it is charged that an inerrant inspiration denies the humanity of the Word of God and is in fact guilty of docetism.[7] It denies the "gracious condescension of God into our history."[8]

In order to more fully justify this charge, the doctrine of verbal inspiration is often grotesquely caricatured into some theory of mechanical dictation. "Because he [God] thus enters into a history with us," Thielicke says, "he moves the hearts of his servants and is not content merely to guide their pen or goose quill for them."[9] Such a statement by itself might be ignored as jesting hyperbole, but he goes on to dogmatize:

> This is actually the way in which the advocates of the doctrine of verbal inspiration conceived it to have happened. What this was, expressed in modern terms, was a fantastic idea of heavenly cybernetics in which God was the guide of a process of automatic writing.[10]

Thielicke is not alone in the charge of dictation. Beegle states unequivocally that "the doctrine of inerrancy leads eventually into the mechanical or dictation theory of inspiration."[11] In the light of clear statements on inspiration to the contrary,[12] it is difficult to dissuade oneself of the opinion that these are exaggerated attempts to discredit an inerrant inspiration in favor of a lower view.

The demand that genuine humanity involves fallibility not only is based on an un-Biblical dualism that denies the sovereign control of God over the free actions of his creatures but also has serious ramifications concerning the person of the God-man. Admitting the mystery of both the incarnation and the process of inspiration it is difficult to see how, if humanity necessitates fallibility, the Lord himself could be free from such fallibility. Humanity and error do coincide in daily experience, but inspiration sees humanity not by itself but under the operation of the Spirit (2 Pet 1:21).

One of the most effective means of jarring the average believer from dogmatizing on inerrancy is the false comparison of the written Word with the living Word. Brunner says, "The vessel 'speech' could no longer contain the content of this new form of divine revelation." "When we say that Jesus is the real Word of God we alter the simple meaning of the notion 'word', since a person is different from a spoken word."[13] There is a vast qualitative difference made between subjective, personal I-Thou revelation from an encounter with the living Word and the impersonal, rational it-truth of a doctrinaire revelation.[14] Such a view has for its basis again the false metaphysical dualism that denies God entry into history, for such an entry into objective historical revelation is said to imprison God and deny his sovereign freedom.[15] Actually the opposite is true. His sovereignty is denied when he cannot enter history and still be Lord of it.

No advocate of an inerrant inspiration seeks to minimize the living Word in favor of a written word. However, the exaltation of a personal encounter with Christ at the expense of the derogation of the written Word to "sterile intellectualism" is neither logical nor Biblical.[16] A person may make himself known in ways other than speech. However, the usual and most fruitful method of making personal acquaintance is through rational conceptual speech. And when one comes to know a person, his speech does not then have less importance but more. The words of Jesus, far from barring the way, led to his person. "Lord, to whom shall we go?" Peter said. "Thou hast the words of eternal life" (John 6:68). The disciples encountered the person of Christ through infallible historical words. There is no reason to deny the same process today.

Coupled with the exaltation of Christ and a personal relationship to him is the subtle suggestion that inerrancy is after all a minor issue and actually dangerous to personal faith. Christianity is Christ, and he will take care of his Word. Thielicke states this forcefully in parable form. The disciples are out with Christ on the Sea of Galilee. While Christ sleeps the disciples are "prowling about the ship, listening to the creaking in the ship's sides and peering from the railings into the water to see whether they can discover some Bult- or frogman down there boring a hole in the ship's side." The fundamentalist, he concludes, is worrying about the ship even though the Lord is in it. He has reversed the true order of interest.[17] With the same reasoning, Barth makes verbal inspiration simply a product of rationalism as opposed to faith.[18]

Finally the doctrine of inerrancy is charged with hindering the work of the Church, a charge that no Christian relishes. After reminding us that we need to be about the affairs of God's kingdom proclaiming the gospel, Beegle pictures the doctrine of inerrancy as a " 'sound barrier' as it were," which "if we can get through... we will be ready to challenge the tremendous moral and spiritual problems that confront us on every side."[19] Unfortunately this nearsighted concern has a certain neutralizing effect on the maintenance of the doctrine of inerrancy among those oriented toward involvement on a minimal doctrinal basis.

The present controversy over inerrancy, as far as we can see, has revealed no new factual basis for departing from the orthodox stand. The issue today is much the same as that expressed by Warfield in his day and in fact extends back to the Garden of Eden—the Word of God versus the word of man. The scholarly and the scientific have saturated our time in all areas, including the Bible. In this milieu it behooves every believer to make certain to whom he is listening.

---

[1]A. Richardson, "The Rise of Modern Biblical Scholarship," in *The Cambridge History of the Bible* (ed. S.L. Greenslade; Cambridge: University Press, 1963) 294-298.

[2]W. Sanday, *Inspiration* (London: Longmans, Green, 1911) 391; D. Beegle, *The Inspiration of Scripture* (Philadelphia: Westminster, 1963) 11-14.

[3]Beegle, *Inspiration* 14.

[4]For full discussion see B.B. Warfield, "The Real Problem of Inspiration," in *The Inspiration and Authority of the Bible* (Philadelphia: Presbyterian and Reformed, 1948); T. Engelder, *Scripture Cannot Be Broken* (St. Louis: Concordia, 1944) 30-78.

[5]Cf. E. Thiele, *The Mysterious Numbers of the Hebrew Kings* (Chicago: University Press, 1951).

[6]H. Thielicke, *Between Heaven and Earth* (New York: Harper, 1965) 1-13.

[7]Ibid., p. 9; K. Barth, *Church Dogmatics*, 1. 2. 509-510.

[8]Thielicke, *Between* 13.

[9]Ibid., p.6.

[10]Ibid.

[11]Beegle, *Inspiration* 84.

[12]Cf. E. J. Young, *Thy Word is Truth* (Grand Rapids: Eerdmans, 1957) 65-109; B. B. Warfield, "Inspiration" 131-166.

[13]E. Brunner, *The Christian Doctrine of God* (London: Lutterworth, 1955) 27.

[14]Beegle, *Inspiration* 144-146.

[15]See K. Runia, *Karl Barth's Doctrine of Holy Scripture* (Grand Rapids: Eerdmans, 1962).

[16]Brunner, *Christian* 28.

[17]Thielicke, *Between* 33-34.

[18]Barth, *Dogmatics*, 4. 1. 368.

[19]Beegle, *Inspiration* 188.

# Apeitheō: Current Resistance To Biblical Inerrancy

## J. Barton Payne

"The whole Bible?" If such an inquiry into their beliefs were to be directed to today's theologians, the response of the large majority would be, "*Apeithō*: I am not persuaded, I disbelieve." Doubts about Scripture's veracity, moreover, are no longer limited to convinced doctrinal skeptics, whether of an unreconstructed sort of liberalism or of a more repentant kind of neo-orthodoxy. They are being currently voiced among theologians generally classified as evangelical, among men who would look to Jesus Christ as Lord and Savior. Furthermore their resistance to the authority of the entire written Word, which the ETS designates as Biblical inerrancy, is producing an effect in conservative institutions, conferences and denominations, especially among our more advanced students and younger scholars. But why should those who have been reared in Bible-believing environments now experience attraction to the posture of *apeitheō*? It is not too much to conclude that the very future of the ETS and of the Biblical position that it represents lies at stake as we ask how, and why, some of our former colleagues have turned against us and what the Christian's approach to Scripture really ought to be.

## I. The Nature of the Present Declension

Most modern skeptics prefer to cloak their opposition to the Bible beneath words of recognition, or even praise, for its authority. Except for communists and a few atheistic cranks, it is no longer the thing to ridicule scriptural inspiration. Among the more liberal this may be traced to a war-induced disenchantment with man's native capabilities and to an existentialistic yearning for a transcendent point of reference. Among the more conservative, whether they be Roman Catholic or ex-fundamental

Protestant, vested interests seem to require their continued use of the term "inerrancy," either to uphold the dogmas of previous popes or to pacify an evangelical constituency that might reduce financial support should the term be discarded. As one of the latter group told me, his institution does not really accept inerrancy, but they keep using the term because otherwise supporters would think they were becoming liberal(!).

But despite this haze in the current theological atmosphere, certain criteria serve as genuine indications of where people stand. (1) Those who resist inerrancy tend to express themselves on the mode of inspiration rather than on its extent. They may protest, for example, that the Bible *is* God's word as well as man's, or that its teachings are ultimately authoritative. But so long as these declaimers refuse to indicate which portions constitute "teaching" their protests decide little or nothing. (2) The parties of resistance may tacitly restrict Biblical truth to theological matters. Such delimitation is not infrequently camouflaged, as for example in last June's statement of the Wenham Conference on Inspiration, which affirmed: "The Scriptures are completely truthful and are authoritative as the only infallible rule of faith and practice." Splendid as this affirmation appears at first glance, could it be that the omission of a comma after "completely truthful"—so that this assertion likewise was limited by "as the only infallible rule of faith and practice"—provided the necessary restriction for those present at the conference who limit Biblical truthfulness to matters of faith and practice? (3) The resistance likes to remain noncommittal at points where disagreements with other sources are likely to appear. To suggest, for example, that the Bible will not duplicate what can be discovered by scientific research becomes but a backhanded way of setting aside its authority at such points.

The persistent question in all such declension, moreover, concerns the total authority of the Bible. This is not a semantic debate over how one defines "inerrant." Several times during the past year I have received critical inquiries as to what the Society means by saying, "The Bible is...inerrant," in its doctrinal affirmation. The not-so-veiled suggestion of the inquirers was that if the ETS would only adopt a more latitudinarian interpretation of inerrancy it could retrieve some of its errant colleagues. But this would only gloss over the real issue. Kenneth Kantzer's simple explanation at last year's meeting that an inerrant document "never wanders into false teaching" is quite clear. Could it be that those who oppose the use of the word "inerrancy" in stating their position on the authority and trustworthiness of the Bible are so keenly aware of its meaning that they purposely avoid it? Redefiners of inerrancy seem to contend for some form of partial inerrancy (*sic*), as opposed to the ETS affirmation that the Biblical autographs are never errant but that they are authoritative at every point. It boils down to this: that there are some who will no longer believe what they admit that the Bible believes but subscribe rather to *apeitheō*, "not persuaded."

## II. THE REASON FOR DISBELIEF

When those who resist Biblical inerrancy are asked for reasons why, forthrightness seems to come at even more of a premium. But answers are ascertainable. Originally, a rejection of Scripture was concomitant to an antisupernaturalistic opposition against Christianity. Of the disbelieving Pharisees Christ thus asked, "If ye believe not his [Moses'] writings, how shall ye believe my words?" (John 5:47). And to "the father of Old Testament criticism," Johann Gottfried Eichhorn (*Einleitung*, 1780-83), any miracle, including Christ's resurrection, had become absurd. But such is no longer necessarily the case. In the current English-speaking world at least, the personal piety of Samuel R. Driver (*Introduction*, 1891) pioneered a widespread adoption of negative criticism by men who were otherwise sincerely Christian. Scripture itself, moreover, distinguishes between church membership—"If thou shalt confess with thy mouth Jesus as Lord, and shalt believe in thy heart that God raised him from the dead, thou shalt be saved" (Rom 10:9)—and church leadership—"For the bishop must...hold to the faithful word which is according to the teaching, that he may be able to exhort in the sound doctrine" (Titus 1:9). There may therefore exist opponents of Biblical inerrancy whom we could never recognize as legitmate Church leaders—for example, by inviting them to share in our class platforms or pulpits—but who could still be brothers, even if inconsistent ones, in Christ.

Yet all resistance to Scripture, whether antisupernaturalistic or not, possesses the common denominator of a subjective authority: an assumption on the part of the critic of his own right to judge, as opposed to the NT concept of "bringing every thought into captivity to the obedience of Christ" (2 Cor 10:5) Irrespective of Christ's actual views on Scripture (see below), current Western thought remains irreconcilably antagonistic to the very idea of "captivity." As observed by H. H. Rowley, Britain's most outstanding present-day OT scholar:

> There were conservative writers who stood outside the general body of critical scholars and who rejected most of their conclusions, but they did not seriously affect the position. While many of them had considerable learning, they made little secret of the fact that they were employing their learning to defend positions which were dogmatically reached. Their work had little influence, therefore, amongst scientific scholars who were concerned only with the evidence, and the conclusions to which it might naturally lead.[1]

"After all," modern man inquires, "does not criticism go awry if subordinated to a presupposition? Do we not live by the scientific method of natural, uninhibited induction and free evaluation? Let the Bible speak for itself: Open-minded investigation will surely come out vindicating the truth."

In practice, however, an appeal to the scientific analogy seems unjustifiable, for Biblical revelation simply is not amenable to "natural" evaluation. It cannot be placed in a test tube for repeatable experimentation, like the data found in the natural sciences. It can only be appreciated through the testimony of competent witnesses, like the data found in the other historical disciplines. And God himself, through Christ (John 1:18), thus becomes the only authority who can really tell us about his own writing. Supernaturalism therefore replies to modern man: "A truly open-minded scientist must be willing to operate within those methods that are congruous to the object of his criticism, or his conclusions will inevitably go awry." This principle was what made James Orr's inductive attempt to construct a doctrine of inspiration upon the basis of his own evalutaion of the observable phenomena of Scripture, with all its various difficulties, basically illegitimate, and it is what made B. B. Warfield's approach of deductively deriving Biblical inerrancy from the revealed teaching of Christ and his apostles sound. Evangelicals, in other words, do not insist upon Warfield as though this latter scholar were immune to criticism, as those who resist inerrancy sometimes insinuate, but simply as one whose methodology is consistent with the object of his investigation. Neither do evangelicals wish to minimize the God-given significance of human intelligence or to inhibit those areas of thought that are pertinent to man's Spirit-directed exercise of his own rational responsibility: first, in examining the historical (resurrection) data that lead him to an acceptance of Jesus Christ (1 Cor 15:1-11); then, in seeking an exact understanding of what his Lord taught, specifically concerning Scripture (Luke 24:45); and lastly, in interpreting with diligence the truths therein contained (2 Tim 2:15). But evangelicals do deny the right of a man to contradict whatever it is that God may have said that he has said. If I were to do this I would effectively establish some other criterion over God himself, which amounts to nothing more nor less than idolatry. I would then also have to go on to accept the consequences of my rational subjectivism—namely, that doctrines such as the survival of my soul after death, or the atonement of my guilt through vicarious sacrifice, or the proofs for the very existence of my God, are apparently not supported by open-minded judgment in the light of natural evidence.

Yet have not our own Christian colleges, upon occasion, been guilty of conveying to some of their sharpest and most promising students the fallacy that a liberal arts education connotes an all-inclusive liberation, with a corresponding responsibility on the part of the individual to reserve to himself the final verdict on any given issue and to insist on his right to say, with *Porgy and Bess*, "It ain't necessarily so"? Within this past year there have arisen cases in one of our evangelical denominations in which, when its assembly resolved to include in its statement of faith an affirmation of Biblical inerrancy, some of its leading scholars and pastors indignantly withdrew from fellowship. Such infatuation with academic freedom produces the situation described in Acts 19:9, "Some were hardened and disobedient (*epeithoun*)" (ASV). Now it is true both that in theory the classical meaning of *apeitheō* is "to disobey" and that in practice a man's skepticism in respect to Scripture leads almost inevitably to overt acts of disobedience. But Arndt and Gingrich have searched more deeply and conclude:

> Since, in the view of the early Christians, the supreme disobedience was a refusal to believe their gospel, *apeitheō* may be restricted in some passages to the meaning *disbelieve, be an unbeliever*. This sense...seems most probable in John 3:36; Acts 14:2; 19:9; Romans 15:31, and only slightly less probable in Romans 2:8.[2]

The heart of the problem is thus an internal one, the primeval sin of pride, the prejudice of rebellious and fallen man, who refuses to go against his own "better judgment" and to take orders but who insists rather on his right to say, "*Apeithō*, I am not persuaded, I disbelieve" (cf. Acts 19:9 KJV, RSV).

A paradoxical feature in all this is that we who are committed to Biblical inerrancy may have contributed, albeit unwittingly, to the current resistance against the Bible's authority. Certain overly zealous Sunday-school materials have invoked a number of subjectively rationalistic bases for belief in Scripture, such as vindications from archaeology or fulfilled prophecies. And, as a result, when our better students uncover similar evidences with the opposite implications they are rendered an easy prey to rationalistic disbelief. Some of our finest Biblical introductions, moreover, contain statements like the following:

> If it [the Bible] presents such data as to compel an acknowledgment that it can only be of divine origin—and it does present such data in abundance—then the only reasonable course is to take seriously its own assertions of infallibility....Human reason is competent to pass upon these evidences ...in order to determine whether the texts themselves square with the claims of divine origin.[3]

The difficulty, however, is that most of today's outstanding Biblical scholars, those who are in the best position (humanly speaking) to know, fail to discover "such data in abundance." On the contrary they tend toward conclusions like the following:

In the field of the physical sciences we find at once that many mistaken and outmoded conceptions appear in the Bible....Much ink has been wasted also, and is still wasted, in the effort to prove the detailed historical accuracy of the biblical narratives. Archaeological research has not, as is often boldly asserted, resolved the difficulties or confirmed the narratives step by step. Actually they abound in errors, including many contradictory statements....Even in matters of religious concern the Bible is by no means of uniform value throughout.[4]

Moreover, even though most investigations do end up vindicating the Bible as far as inerrancy is concerned, one seeming discrepancy outweighs the significance of ninety-nine confirmations.

Others of our introductions have been more guarded about basing belief in Scripture upon inductive evaluations, cautioning, for example, that "unless we first think rightly about God we shall be in basic error about everything else" (cf. 1 Cor 2:14 or 2 Cor 4:3 on the blindness of the unregenerate mind). Yet this same source goes on to declare:

The Bible itself evidences its divinity so clearly that he is without excuse who disbelieves....Its "incomparable excellencies" are without parallel in any other writing and show most convincingly that the Bible is in a unique sense the Word of God.[5]

But had it not been for NT evidence on the canon, could even regenerate Christians have perceived that a given verse in Proverbs or Jeremiah was inspired while similar material from Ecclesiasticus or the Epistle of Jeremy was not? On the other hand, what of Scripture's unexplained difficulties? Are we going too far to say that, on the basis of the evidences presently available, Joshua's asserted capture of Ai or Matthew's apparent attribution (27:9) of verses from Zechariah 11 to Jeremiah favor Biblical errancy rather than inerrancy? Candor compels our admission of other cases too for which our harmonistic explanations are either weak or nonexistent. If therefore we once fall into the snare of subjectivism, whether liberal or evangelical, we also may conclude by saying, "*Apeithō*, I have had it."

## III. THE APPLICATION OF CHRISTIAN AUTHORITY

Turning then to God's own objective testimony in respect to Scripture, what if anything do we find? For we must recognize at the outset that we do not have to find anything. The syllogism, "God is perfect, and since the Bible stems from God, then the Bible must be perfect," contains a fallacy, as becomes apparent when we substitute the idea of Church for

Bible. God lay under no antecedent obligation to ordain inspiration along with his decree for revelation. Even as the Church continues to serve as a medium for men's redemption despite its obvious imperfections, so too a Bible of purely human origin could conceivably have proven adequate for human deliverance. Peter, John and Paul, for example, might have simply recorded their convictions about God's revealed plan of salvation in Christ, just as modern preachers do, without claiming inspiration (though actually they did: 1 Cor 2:13; 14:37; 2 Cor 13:3). Herein, moreover, lies the answer to one of liberalism's more persuasive arguments— namely, that since we today do not need an inerrant KJV, and since the early Church did not need an inerrant LXX (Rom 15:4), therefore the Biblical autographs need not have been inerrant either. For evangelicalism refuses to base its commitment to Biblical autographic inerrancy upon "needs," whether of God or man, except for that general need of maintaining the truthfulness of Jesus Christ. It is from this latter necessity that Christian authority comes historically into the picture. That is, until a man places his trust in Christ there appears to be no impelling reason why he should believe in the Bible or even in religious supernaturalism for that matter. But once a man does commit himself to the apostolically recorded person of Jesus, declared to be the Son of God with messianic power by his resurrection from the dead (Rom 1:4), then his supreme privilege as well as his obligation devolves into letting that mind be in him that was also in Christ Jesus (Phil 2:5; cf. Col 2:6; 1 John 2:6), and this includes Christ's mind toward Scripture. Specifically, how Christ's authority is to be applied may then be developed through the following two inquiries.

1. *Did Christ question the Bible?* Affirmative answers at this point seem more common than ever before. It is understandable, moreover, that professed Christians who have felt compelled on rationally subjective grounds to surrender their belief in Biblical inerrancy should seek support for their skepticism from some analogy discoverable with Jesus, since nobody really enjoys an inconsistent allegiance. Most modern writers seem content to dismiss inerrancy with generalizations about its being a "sub-Christian" doctrine.[6] Representative of a more straightforward analysis, however, is the Dutch neo-orthodox Biblical theologian T. C. Vriezen.[7] While granting that "the Scriptures of the Old Testament were for Him as well as for His disciples the Word of God," he adduces three areas in which Jesus "rises above the Holy Scriptures."

> Christ used the traditional text freely, and in doing so He showed Himself superior to all bondage to the letter: [yet the only evidence that Vriezen alleged is that] in Luke iv. 18ff., Isaiah lxi. 2 is quoted without the words "the day of vengeance of our God."

The example is irrelevant. It is one of those not uncommon instances of successive prophecies in one context: The year of Yahweh's favor, 61:2a, received fulfillment during our Lord's first advent (cf. v 1), but Christ apparently avoided reference to the day of vengeance described in v 2b, which was not to achieve fulfillment until his second coming. Real textual freedom, moreover, such as the NT use of the LXX no more necessarily subverts inerrancy than does a modern believer's missionary employment of accepted vernacular versions. In John 10:34-35, however, Jesus seemingly went out of his way to associate genuine inerrancy not even with copied mss of the original Hebrew but rather with the autographs themselves: "He [Yahweh] called them gods [judges (?) contemporary with the psalm writer Asaph] unto whom the word of God came [at that time, *egeneto*, aorist]... and the scripture cannot be broken." For similar associations of God's inspired words with their inscripturation in the original mss cf. Acts 1:16; 2 Pet 1:21.[8]

Vriezen next says of Jesus:

> Because of His spiritual understanding of the law, He again and again contradicts the Judaic theology of His days derived from it ("them of old time," Matthew v; Mark vii), and even repeatedly contradicts certain words of the law (Matthew v. 38ff.; xix. 1ff.).

The question, however, revolves in each case about what Christ was really contradicting. In Matthew 19 his opposition was to Pharisaic moral travesty in authorizing a man "to put away his wife for every cause" (v 2). For while he did go on to contrast Deuteronomic divorce for an '*erwat dābār*, "something indecent" (KB 735a), with Genesis' Edenic situation, he himself came out in favor of the Law because he too limited any absolute prohibition of divorce through his insertion of the words "except for fornication" (v 9; cf. 5:32). Likewise in the sermon on the mount Christ's opposition was directed against Pharisaism. While this sect, moreover, claimed its derivation from the Law, Vriezen's assumption that the words given "to them of old time," which Christ contradicted, must mean the original words of the Law appears gratuitous. In the preceding context our Lord specifically affirmed the inviolability of the Law (5:17) while singling out for criticism only the latter portions of such syndromes as "Love thy neighbor, *and hate thine enemy*" (v 44); and these latter words, far from being drawn from the Law, reflected rather those post-Biblical traditions that have been found among the self-righteous Qumran sectaries (1QS i 1-10). In the other alleged passages our Lord's opposition, for example, was directed against Pharisaic casuistry in the use of oaths (5:33-37; cf. 23:16-22)—he himself would accept an oath on proper occasion (Matt 26:63; cf. Heb 6:16-17)—and against their personally vindictive application of the *lex talionis* (Matt 5:38-42).

This ties in closely with Vriezen's concluding allegation: "The negative datum that nowhere in the New Testament is mention made of Jesus offering sacrifices may be considered important." Or should it be? For a law to lack particular applicability need not entail its derogation. Vriezen seems, moreover, to have answered his own argument when he states: "In imitation of Christ St. Paul recognized that there were certain commandments of God that were significant only in a certain age and a certain situation."

Ultimately, Vriezen is forthright enough to admit that neither liberals nor conservatives agree with his hypothesis of a Bible-questioning Christ, for he concedes, "This view of Jesus' critical attitude toward the law is contested from both the right and left." Apparently only the neo-orthodox, those with strongly vested loyalties toward both Christ and the critics, seem to have persuaded themselves of its validity, and even Vriezen cautions that he must not be understood "to mean that Jesus was 'critical of the Bible' in our sense of the word," or, as far as the present writer has been able to ascertain, in any other negative sense of the word either.

2. *Positively, then, did Jesus affirm the Bible as inerrantly authoritative?* Evangelicals seem at times to have failed to examine with sufficient rigor the exact Biblical affirmations of our Lord, or to consider with sufficient attention the neo-orthodox claim that the Bible does not teach its own inerrancy. Basically such examination demands an attempt to distinguish, and then to interrelate, two differing types of relevant evidence.

(1) Christ's general statements. While it seems clear that the prophets and apostles held to an authority of Scripture that was plenary in extent and hence inerrant—cf. 2 Sam 23:2; Jer 25:13; or Acts 24:14, "believing all things... which are written in the prophets"; or 2 Tim 3:16, "Every Scripture is *theopneustos*, God-breathed"—it remains possible for our Lord's own categorical statements to be so interpreted as to prove deficient, in themselves, of affirming infallibility for the whole Bible. Though they unmistakably teach its broad doctrinal authority, neo-orthodox writers have been able to produce explanations that keep them from finally establishing its inerrancy. The five following classic proof texts may serve as examples. In Matt 5:18 (cf. Luke 16:16-17) the words, "One jot or one tittle shall in no wise pass away from the law, till all things be accomplished," might be restricted to our Lord's inculcating of total obedience to the Law; cf. the next verse. In Luke 18:31 his affirmation that "all the things that are written through the prophets shall be accomplished unto the Son of man" may well be accepted at face value, without thereby promoting the prophets into anything more than uninspired reporters of valid revelations. The text of Luke 24:25 says, "O fool-

ish men and slow of heart to believe in all that the prophets have spoken"; but the ASV margin reads "...*after* all that the prophets have spoken." In Luke 24:44 could Christ perhaps insist that "all things must be fulfilled which are written in the law of Moses, and the prophets, and the psalms, concerning me," without necessarily including all things concerning other subjects? Finally John 10:35, "And the Scripture cannot be broken," might possibly be understood as an *ad hominem* argument: "If he called them gods...and if Scripture cannot be broken (as you believe, whether it actually be true or not), then..." The force of the above quotations, in other words, regarding inerrancy remains capable of evasion.

(2) Christ's specific statements. It is when our Lord discloses his mind over particular OT incidents and utterances that a recognition of his positive belief in the Bible becomes inescapable. At the outset, however, let it again be cautioned that not all of his citations carry equal weight. Christ's references, for example, to Elijah and Elisha (Luke 4:24-27), even when one allows for his confirmation of such factual details as the three years and six months of famine, can yet be treated as mere literary allusions to well-known OT stories, which he need not have considered as more than fictional, though possessed of inherent theological authority. Likewise his identifications of "the book of Moses" (Mark 12:26; Luke 16:29, 31; 24:44) might indicate nothing beyond an awareness of Moses as their central character, much like Samuel in the books of Samuel, without committing our Lord to fixed views on their Mosaic composition.

Yet on the other hand Jesus specifically compared down-to-earth marriage problems of his own and of Moses' days with what was to him the apparently equally real situation of Adam and Eve "from the beginning" (Matt 19:8; Mark 10:6); he associated Abel with the undeniably historical Zechariah (Luke 11:47-51); he described in detail the catastrophic days of Noah and Lot as transpiring "after the same manner" as the day in which the Son of man would be revealed (Luke 17:26-30); he lumped Sodom and Gomorrah together with certain first-century Galilean towns, as subject to equally literal judgments (Matt 10:15); and he connected the experiences of the Queen of Sheba, Jonah and the Ninevites with real events in the lives of himself and his contemporaries (Matt 12:39-41). He equated the narrative description of Gen 2:24 with the very spoken word of God the Creator (Matt 19:5). He said that God had uttered the words of Exod 3:6 to the man Moses (Mark 12:26) and that Moses "gave" Israel the law of Leviticus 12 (John 7:22), "commanded" the law of Leviticus 14 (Matt 8:4), "wrote" of the Messiah (John 5:46), and indeed "gave you the law" (John 7:19). He affirmed that an actual prophet named Daniel had predicted "the abomination of desolation" for a period still future to A.D. 30 (Matt 25:15) and that David, "in the Holy Spirit," composed the words of Ps 110:1 (Mark 12:36; Matt 22:43-45). Even if one allows for the sake of argument that the apostolic writers may not have reproduced Christ's exact phraseology, the impressions that he left about his views on the origin of the OT are still so unmistakable that George Adam Smith felt constrained to confess:

> If the use of his [Isaiah's] name [in the NT quotations]...were as involved in the arguments...as is the case with David's name in the quotation made by our Lord from Psalm cx, then those who deny the unity of the Book of Isaiah would be face to face with a very serious problem indeed.[9]

But this is just the point. Suppose a man were to go no farther than to acknowledge: "I will, as a Christian, accept Biblical authority in respect to those specific matters, and to those alone, which are affirmed by Jesus Christ." He would still find the mind of his Lord so hopelessly opposed to the consensus of modern "scientific" (subjective) criticism that his rationalistic autonomy would suffer automatic forfeit as a principle for Biblical research. He might then just as well accept the verdict of the apostles, whom Christ *did* authorize as his representatives (John 14:26; 16:13), on the unified authenticity of Isaiah as well (12:38-41). Furthermore, in the light of Christ's known attitude toward Adam and Abel, it appears rather pointless to question his belief over the literal truth of Elijah and Elisha and of all the other OT matters to which he refers.

(3) Interrelationships. In view of Christ's specific statements, his general affirmations (1, above), previously identified as in themselves inconclusive, now assume a more comprehensive significance. John 10:35, for example, no longer remains restricted at its *ad hominem* interpretation, for the unbreakableness of Scripture has been found to correspond to Christ's own beliefs. This Bible reference is therefore depicted on the seal of the Evangelical Theological Society, supported by the cross of Christ breaking in two the sword of criticism. Bernard's liberal International Critical Commentary on John states further that belief in

> the verbal inspiration of the sacred books...emerges distinctively in the Fourth Gospel, the evangelist ascribing this conviction to Jesus Himself. We may recall here some Synoptic passages which show that the belief that "the Scripture cannot be broken" was shared by Matthew, Mark, and Luke and that all three speak of it as having the authority of their Master (1. clii).

Older critics such as William Sanday thus conceded:

> When deductions have been made...there still remains evidence enough that our Lord while on earth did use the common language of His contemporaries in regard to the Old Testament.[10]

And modern liberals, such as F. C. Grant, freely admit that in the NT "it is everywhere taken for granted that Scripture is trustworthy, infallible, and inerrant."[11]

Two concluding questions remain then to be asked. The first directly parallels that which Pilate addressed to the Jewish leaders of his day: "What then shall I do unto Jesus who is called Christ?" (Matt 27:22). Are we going to recognize his authority, or are we going to take exception to it and deny his reliability by some theory of kenosis? Sigmund Mowinckel, a leading advocate of modern Scandinavian Biblical criticism, seems more squarely than most to have faced up to the implications of his views when he concludes:

> Jesus as a man was one of us except that he had no sin (Heb. 4:15)....He also shared our imperfect insight into all matters pertaining to the world of sense....He knew neither more nor less than most people of his class in Galilee or Jerusalem concerning history...geography, or the history of biblical literature.[12]

But can one then really maintain the belief in our Lord's sinlessness? This unreliability cannot be restricted to theoretical matters of incarnate omniscience, which few would wish to assert (cf. Mark 13:32), but it involves Christ's basic truthfulness in consciously committing himself to affirmations about Scriptures that he was under no antecedent obligation even to mention (cf. John 3:34).

In John 15 Jesus himself divided up his contemporaries between bond-slaves and friends, distinguishing the latter on the basis of their participation in his own convictions: "For all things that I have heard from my Father I have made known unto you" (John 15:15). What then is to be said of the man who is *apeitheō*, unpersuaded, about what Christ has made known? Is the man who rejects Biblical inerrancy simply an inconsistent Christian, perhaps through lack of understanding relative to the mind of Christ? Or having confessed Christ as his Savior is he failing to integrate his scholarship with the teachings of Christ in a logical manner (cf. Col 2:6)? God alone must judge. In either event, as J. I. Packer has so rightly observed, "any view that subjects the written word of God to the opinions and pronouncements of men involves unbelief and disloyalty toward Christ."[13] It is like Ephraim's worship on the high places after Jehu's removal of Pheonician Baalism: An overt invocation of the name of Yahweh, while persisting in a life opposed to his revealed authority, can result only, as previously suggested, in idolatry. Scripture moreover leaves us all with the wonderful and yet terrible pronouncement: "He that believeth, *ho pisteuon*, in the Son hath eternal life; but he who will not believe, *ho pisteuon*, the Son shall not see life, but the wrath of God abideth on him" (John 3:36).

But there is a second concluding question, which asks, "What are the implications for those who *are* willing to follow Jesus in his allegiance to Scripture?" Returning to John 15, one finds in v 15 Christ's words: "Greater love hath no man than this, that a man lay down his life for his friends." Christ's love for us was demonstrated on Calvary, but if we have become "friends" of his, then we too should demonstrate our love as we commit our lives to identification with both him and his commitments. For example, this last summer the Committee of Fifteen (formerly N.A.E.-Christian Reformed) on Bible Translation adopted a resolution to require affirmations on Biblical inerrancy from all who are to be associated with this major project. Their move took real courage in the face of current resistance to Scriptural authority. Sacrifice, moreover, is entailed, for in v 19 our Lord goes on to explain, "Because ye are not of the world, but I chose you out of the world, therefore the world hateth you." This Committee, as a result of its stand, suffered attack and withdrawal of support. Indeed, we should all take to heart Paul's admonition, "Strive together with me in your prayers to God for me, that I may be delivered from *tōn apeithountōn*" (Rom 15:30-31), those who will not be persuaded. Yet in v 27 Christ finished this discourse by observing: "And ye also bear witness, because ye have been with me from the beginning." We are persistently to proclaim submission to Christ, even as our Lord "in the spirit...went and preached unto them... that aforetime were *apeithēsasin*, unpersuaded, when the longsuffering of God waited in the days of Noah" (1 Pet 3:20). Should words themselves fail, we are to bear witness by lives of Christian love, so "that if any *apeithousin*, refuse to be persuaded, by the word, they may without the word be gained by the behavior of" (3:1) those who have experienced the power of lives yielded to Christ and to his Bible, the inerrant Scriptures.

---

[1]H. H. Rowley, *The Old Testament and Modern Study* (London: Oxford, 1961) xv.

[2]Arndt and Gingrich, *A Greek-English Lexicon of the New Testament and Other Early Christian Literature* (Chicago: University Press, 1959) 82.

[3]G. L. Archer, Jr., *A Survey of Old Testament Introduction* (Chicago: Moody, 1964).

[4]M. Burrows, *An Outline of Biblical Theology* (Philadelphia: Westminster, 1946) 44-45, 47.

[5]E. J. Young, *An Introduction to the Old Testament* (rev. ed.; Grand Rapids: Eerdmans, 1960) 7, 28-29.

[6]H. R. Mackintosh; cf. A.J. Ungersma, *Handbook for Christian Believers* (Indianapolis: Bobbs-Merrill, 1953) 80-81.

[7]T. C. Vriezen, *An Outline of Old Testament Theology* (Newton: Charles T. Branford, 1960) 2-5.

[8]Cf. J. B. Payne, "The Plank Bridge: Inerrancy and the Biblical Autographs," *United Evangelical Action* 24/15 (December 1965) 16-18.

[9]G. A. Smith, *The Book of Isaiah* (The Expositor's Bible; New York: Hodder and Stoughton, n.d.), 2. 6.

[10]W. Sanday, *Inspiration* (London: Longmans, Green, 1893) 393.

[11]F. C. Grant, *Introduction to New Testament Thought* (Nashville: Abingdon-Cokesbury, 1950) 75; cf. J. Knox, *Jesus Lord and Christ* (New York: Harper, 1958).

[12]S. Mowinckel, *The Old Testament as Word of God* (New York: Abingdon, 1959) 74.

[13]J. I. Packer, *"Fundamentalism" and the Word of God* (London: Inter-Varsity, 1958) 21.

# Ordinary Language Analysis And Theological Method

## ARTHUR F. HOLMES

The philosophical *bête noir* of the 1930s and 1940s is dead. Such at least is the case with that classical form of logical positivism that reduced all cognition to science and forced all science into a descriptivist and operational mold. Its principal tool, the verifiability theory of meaning, has been weakened beyond effectiveness; metaphysics, once eliminated from meaningful discourse, has been reintroduced into respectable philosophic society in a chastened but profitable form; and as a result theology has been given another chance to show what it is really talking about. From today's perspective we might even regard logical positivism as an unpleasant but instructive interlude in the history of traditional philosophic inquiry. It was unpleasant because of its radical reductionism, but it was instructive because of the attention it forced to questions of philosophic methodology and because of the repudiation it has won of eighteenth and nineteenth-century rationalisms.[1]

If theology is to take advantage of this new chance to explain itself, it must learn from the positivist interlude to avoid pouring theology into either a rationalistic or a scientistic mold. For—let us face it—theology has at times mistreated Biblical religion, whether by tying its meaning and truth to scientific-type verification or by uncritically adopting the rationalism of Thomas Aquinas or Thomas Reid or John Locke or even Hegel. Theology is undoubtedly a "rational inquiry" into redemptive history and revealed truth, but the thing we must watch is our definition of "rational" and the consequent method of "inquiry."

In British philosophy the *bête noir* has been succeeded by what is usually called "ordinary language analysis," a movement that had its roots in the Cambridge philosophers G. E. Moore, John Wisdom, and the later work of Ludwig Wittgenstein and that was further developed by such Oxford philosophers as Gilbert Ryle, J. L. Austin, P. F. Strawson, etc.[2]

Rather than imposing uniform standards of meaning and truth on all supposedly cognitive discourse, these analysts prefer to describe how language is actually used. They recognize a large variety of what Wittgenstein called "language games," in which the same players (words) may operate according to very different rules. Not all words name empirical objects, and not all language is descriptive. Rather than either formalizing arguments into deductive systems or insisting on empirical verification, the analyst engages in "logical mapwork," an attempt to map out the peculiar logic (or logos-structure, intelligible order) of moral language, or the language of freedom and responsibility, or the language of sense perception, or religious language. Each must be examined on its own terms; each has its own "informal logic." The task of philosophy is not to prescribe what is or is not logically legitimate, not to reduce one kind of language or logic to another. This sort of thing only creates needless puzzles and confusion. The task is not to revise but to describe the ways in which language works, and so to make explicit and clear the accumulated insight stored in linguistic use. While such mapwork begins at the local level and often appears trivial or fragmented, larger relational questions arise (what Wittgenstein calls "family resemblances" between language games), and these in turn lead to an analysis of the language, say, of behavioristic determinism in relation to that of individual freedom and responsibility, or of science in relation to religion. This illuminates traditional philosophic questions. It leads to more complete and integrated "logical maps" that tie things together by using philosophic categories, or models and constructs, or "integrator words" like "God." Systematic metaphysics is thus reborn.[3]

The "informalizing" of logic and methodology has reopened questions the positivists discarded as meaningless about the logic of religion and theology. Some analysts still ask what kind of experience religious discourse is about and what kinds of experience consequently bear on its verification or falsification. The various answers proposed reflect corresponding views of the nature of religious knowledge and experience, so that Schleiermacher reappears and Ritschl and Joseph Butler and Thomas Aquinas and Rudolph Otto and Karl Barth and Paul Tillich—in new forms and combinations.[4] Some of the better attempts to handle religious language preserve both its historical references and its cognitive content and its personal or existential character. Generally speaking, however, in less than orthodox hands the stress is on religious experience rather than historical revelatory situations and on existential rather than interpretive or metaphysical functions of language. This is, however, a matter of emphasis rather than exclusion and is more due to the absence of evangelicals from this phase of philosophical theology than to anything intrinsic to the analytic method.

In what follows let me make it clear that my concern is not with exegetical method, nor primarily with apologetics, but with systematic theology. It is sometimes customary to regard induction and deduction as the only two methods available for either concept-formation or system-building. If we take the analysts seriously, this is not necessarily so. Theology, like other "language games," must be handled on its own terms, not with the logics of other disciplines. Deduction is the logic of mathematics, native to that area, but it is of limited usefulness elsewhere. It is a logic of universals, of class concepts and universally distributed middle terms, and as such it cannot take every logical step we might need. It cannot draw inferences from logically particular statements nor derive concepts from unique events, nor can its logical necessities be applied to contingent truths. It may sometimes be useful, even necessary, but it is not sufficient.

If deduction were the logic of theology, (1) we would have to formalize in deductive fashion every movement of theological thought, (2) we would have to ignore the historical narrative except for illustrative purposes and work only with logically universal propositions, (3) we would have to reduce all Biblical analogy and metaphor and symbol and poetry and connotation to logically univocal as well as universal form, (4) we would have to regard all events in redemptive history and the consequent application of grace as logically necessary rather than contingent on the will of God. This I cannot do. (1) Deduction is, I want to point out later, not descriptive of all theological concept-formation and system-building. (2) Biblical history is important in theological concept-formation. It has its own revelational value, be it declarative, paradigmatic, symbolic or whatever. (3) Biblical language is too rich. Its literary diversity is more than an historic accident or a decorative device. It is a vehicle for imaginative thought and creative expression about things difficult to grasp. Analogy, metaphor, symbol, poetry—these and other forms cannot be translated without risking cognitive loss into univocal and pseudo-scientific form. Each must be examined on its own terms. (4) I do not subscribe to the view that God's sovereign acts in creation or history or grace occur out of logical necessity. I am not prepared to grant the rationalistic conception of God. For these reasons, then, deduction appears less than sufficient as the logic of theology.

It may be objected that theology nonetheless systematizes deductively, drawing logical implications from Biblical propositions and developing them into a formal system. I am not sure this is the whole story, that all doctrines are deduced and then interrelated in this specific way. Systematics begins with exegesis. The question is: How does systematization proceed from an exegetical beginning? What gives deductive order any edge on other kinds of systems? How, for instance, does the incarnation of God in Christ give the unity it does to systematic theology? Is it that everything else in theology is deduced from statements about the incarnation, or is it that everything else serves to extend and detail the meaning of this central event so that it becomes the recurring theme of a theological symphony? The doctrines of God, of creation, of revelation, of man, of redemption, of the Church, of history—all these areas of thought develop and detail, in their own Biblical and conceptual materials and to their own advantage, the fuller meaning of the central theme that God is in Christ.

In these terms, the analyst will have serious doubts about conforming the logic of theology entirely to deduction. Induction, moreover, is the logic of early empirical science (not of modern science, it should be noted). In what sense could theology be inductive? Is it (1) Aristotelian induction? For Aristotle, induction was the intuitive abstraction of universal principles from familiar classified data, and as such it presupposes the Aristotelian view of man and nature: potential and active intellect, hylomorphism, etc. To use Aristotelian induction intact would tie theology to Aristotle, and this I am not prepared to do. Is theological induction, then, (2) the very different method of Francis Bacon? You recall that he discarded the Greek view of man as contemplative intellect, seeking instead to know the laws of nature for pragmatic reasons, manipulating the variables to ensure that causes are correctly assigned to effects. This kind of induction—as also Mill's logic—is concerned with the experimental identification of causes, and this is obviously not what theology is doing. Induction of this sort is not the logic of theology. What then is induction in theology? I suggest that it is (3) a loose approximation to Aristotle's quest for generalized concepts based on an inspection of empirical data, in this case the Biblical data. But here two problems arise. (a) Is a complete induction ever possible? This was Hume's problem in another context, but it is equally applicable to any theologian present who is less than omniscient about Scripture and its historical context and languages, applicable also at any stage when the Church only knows in part or sees through a glass darkly. And if complete induction is impossible our theological concepts lack logical finality. (b) Is inductive generalization actually the way we construct our theological concepts? Is theological method just a repetitious collection and collation of proof texts that unambiguously dictate both their individual and their collective meaning? Or does it involve more than this, more complex procedures, postulates regarding language and logic, regarding the literature we call Scripture and so regarding life? Theology seems to me to involve hermeneutical assumptions and pre-understandings, the selection of materials, the choice of some preferred materials in interpreting others, the adoption of guiding hypotheses, the use of models, the gradual hesitating construction of conceptual maps.

This is neither deduction or induction. The logic of theological language is different from that of mathematics or early modern science. We are helped somewhat by the realization that modern science is not really inductive either, nor is it some easy combination of induction and deduction. Recent philosophy of science is increasingly explicit that concept-formation means adducing models and developing constructs, and some analysts have accordingly compared the logic of models and constructs in science and theology,[5] for these are different "language games."

For the sake of alliteration, let us call this third kind of logic "adduction." The questions for theological method become: (1) How are models adduced and conceptual or logical maps constructed? (2) How is their truth-value ascertained? To the first question, the evangelical replies that they are adduced from Scripture. But this is deceptively simple. Scripture uses a multiplicity of models in different contexts: For instance, God is Father and King and Fortress and Lover and Creator and Judge and Covenant-maker, all wrapped into one. He redeems from bondage, reconciles the alienated, forgives the offender, covers sin, regenerates the dead-in-sin—all of this wrapped in one. These are models. Theology analyzes their meaning without falsely literalizing them. Some creative and constructive mapwork is needed, to explore family resemblances between Father-language and Lover-language and King-language, and between bondage-language and alienation-language and dead-in-sin-language. The result is a doctrine of God, and a doctrine of sin and redemption. Then larger family resemblances are explored, perhaps using the covenant model as the integrating device, and the relation between God and sin and redemption appears. The statements of Scripture are frequently in model-contexts. The theologizing of the apostle Paul often uses models. The task of the theologian is not to dispense with them, not to reduce them to univocal or "literal" language, but to explore and develop them. It is very obscure what "literal" means in theology, if it is meant to exclude models and metaphors and symbols, those pregnant cognitive devices that make a literature intellectually alive, able to generate insight and understanding, able to reveal truth. The medievals were not altogether wrong when they developed a logic of analogy.

If theology is mapwork that explores the logical layout of the models adduced from Scripture, care should be taken to explore them in the total context of Scripture, its didactic as well as its historical and other materials. Particular caution is needed if the theologian uses non-Biblical models, whether those of Greek thought like "ens realissimum" or "Prime Mover" or "hypostasis," or those of Heideggerian ontology like "Ground of Being." These are rightly criticized if they force us to play a Greek or Heideggerian language game rather than that of Christian theology, that is to say—in more traditional terms—if they limit our conceptualization to the god of the philosophers rather than extending it to the God of Abraham and Isaac, the Father of our Lord Jesus Christ. The poverty of natural theology is as real today as in the past.

This logic of "adduction," models and constructive mapwork seems, then, to fit the needs of evangelical theology. It also accounts for theological diversity. If theology is neither rigorously deductive nor the result of a complete and pure induction but is sometimes conducted by less formal and conclusive means, then its systematic structure and to a certain extent its concept-formation will vary with the selection and creative interrelation of models. After all, Protestant theology is an open-ended and somewhat pluralistic venture. We do not usually claim to have one final theology to end all other and all future theologies. This, however, introduces our second question about adduction: the ascertaining of truth.

If the method were purely inductive, then some sort of Biblical correspondence or direct empirical verification would be sufficient. But not so if induction is not the only method, if there is not always a 1:1 correlation between theological construct and the heterogeneous Biblical models and statements it is intended to embrace. If the method were purely deductive, then some sort of formal self-consistency of the system would be the criterion—granted of course the truth of the Biblical premises—and we could establish one system to the exclusion of all others. But if deduction is not a sufficient logic for theology, then formal consistency is not an adequate criterion. This need not surprise us. In the history of philosophy a truth criterion has always been a function of a larger methodology for knowing. In recent philosophy it is recognized that different truth criteria may be appropriate to different kinds of knowing, to different language games. It has even been suggested that truth judgments may sometimes be "performative" rather than indicative. "It is true that..." may add no more to a proposition than a "Hear ye!" or an exclamation mark. In other words, the old schema on the problem of truth (correspondence, coherence, etc.) is breaking down with the breakdown of reductionist epistemologies.[6]

What sort of truth criteria, then, are appropriate in theological discourse? In evaluating conceptual schemes, interpretations, constructs and models, analytic philosophers tend to retain both an empirical and a rational criterion—though not the traditional ones. If a construct attempts to interpret a range of data, it must possess "empirical adequacy." That is, it must embrace the entire scope of relevant data, not ignoring some, not distorting others, but doing justice to all relevant factual considerations. If a model is intended to make certain facts more intelligible, then it should fit those facts properly. It must "fit" closely enough to avoid being the sort of generality that fits any conceivable facts at all. In these terms, Tillich's conception of God as Ground of Being, whether or not "adequate" to cover the relevant Biblical data, is so imprecise, it "fits" so loosely, that it could as well interpret naturalistic humanism as Biblical theism. This I suspect, is the way some post-Tillichians have taken the notion.

But empirical adequacy and fit are not the only criteria. If a model or construct is an attempt to unify what is given, and if larger logical maps attempt to interrelate and unify the whole, then we need some sort of coherence criterion, some index to logical unity and order. In fact, a theological construct may be adduced in a particular form precisely for this reason: It is the preferred way to round out a coherent conceptual scheme.

I suspect, by way of example, that such is the case with the conception of Biblical inerrancy. I am not convinced that, in its usual extension to all historical details, scientific allusions and literary references inerrancy is either explicitly taught in Scripture or is *deduced* therefrom without a fallacy of equivocation. Nor do I see it as the result of *inductive* study of the phenomena—the induction is too incomplete. In other words, I think both sides in the evangelical intramural debate on the subject are methodologically mistaken. Rather, I see inerrancy as a second-order theological construct that is *adduced* for systematic reasons. The first-order scriptural doctrine of revelation includes the affirmation that the Biblical literature was given by divine inspiration and constitutes our only final and sufficient rule of faith and practice. But inerrancy as we usually construct the concept is something further, something that I do not find logically entailed in the statement "Scripture speaks the truth," at least not in a form sufficiently precise to "fit" all the facts. Rather, inerrancy is adduced because of the high level of expectation (kind of truth demand) created by the Biblical doctrine, and the attractiveness of rounding out the doctrine with this further extrapolation. It is constructed and qualified so as to "fit" the actual phenomena and to "cohere" within the overall doctrine of Scripture. If the construct is modeled on twentieth-century standards of scientific accuracy or precision in documentation, it just does not "fit." I suspect therefore that some people's objection to "inerrancy" may be an objection to a term that evokes a malfitting model, rather than to the conceptual construct careful theologians try to delineate by a thousand qualifications. In that case the intramural debate is methodological and semantical rather than about substantive issues. Careful analysis might go a long way towards clearing it up.

There is, however, another ingredient in our theological truth-judgments that is more convictional and personal than it is systematic or empirical. Post-positivist analysis faces this squarely and explores the logic of conviction and personal involvement.[7] This means probing the relation of personal conviction to concept-formation, to system-building and to truth-judgments, and takes into account the I-Thou dimension of revelation, the witness of the Spirit, and kindred elements. But it is less a question for theological method than for apologetics and the philosophy of religion. It belongs to another occasion.

[1]On logical positivism and its demise see J. O. Urmson, *Philosophical Analysis* (Clarendon, 1956); G. J. Warnock, *English Philosophy Since 1900* (Oxford University, 1958); A. J. Ayer, ed., *Logical Positivism* (Free Press, 1959), and *The Revolution in Philosophy* (Macmillan, 1956); A. Plantinga, "Analytic Philosophy and Christianity," *Christianity Today* 8 (1963) 78.

[2]See for instance L. Wittgenstein, *Philosophical Investigations* (Macmillan, 1964), and *The Blue and Brown Books* (Harper, 1958); G. Ryle, *Dilemmas* (Cambridge University, 1954); J. L. Austin, *How To Do Things With Words* (Oxford University, 1962), and *Philosophical Papers* (Clarendon, 1961); V. C. Chappell, ed., *Ordinary Language* (Prentice-Hall, 1964).

[3]D. F. Pears, ed., *The Nature of Metaphysics* (Macmillan, 1957); I. Ramsey, ed., *Prospect for Metaphysics* (Allen and Unwin, 1961); E. Hall, *Philosophical Systems* (University of Chicago, 1960); F. Dilley, *Metaphysics and Religious Language* (Columbia University, 1964); P. F. Strawson, *Individuals* (Doubleday, 1963); F. Zabeeh, "Oxford and Metaphysics: A New Page in Contemporary Philosophy," *International Philosophical Quarterly* 3 (1963) 307.

[4]For instance A. Flew and A. MacIntyre, eds., *New Essays in Philosophical Theology* (SCM, 1955); B. Mitchell, ed., *Faith and Logic* (Allen and Unwin, 1957); I. Ramsey, *Religious Language* (SCM, 1957); F. Ferré, *Language, Logic and God* (Harper, 1961); W. Hordern, *Speaking of God* (Macmillan, 1964).

[5]M. Hesse, *Models and Analogies in Science* (University of Notre Dame, 1961); S. Toulmin, *Foresight and Understanding* (Hutchinson University Library, 1961); N. Hanson, *Patterns of Discovery* (Cambridge University, 1958); I. Ramsey, *Models and Mystery* (Oxford University, 1964), and *Religion and Science* (SPCK, 1964); F. Ferré, "Mapping the Logic of Models in Science and Theology," *The Christian Scholar* 46 (1963) 9, and "The Cognitive Possibilities of Theistic Language," in *Basic Modern Philosophy of Religion* (Scribners, 1967).

[6]See E. Hall, *Philosophical*, chaps. 5-6; G. Pitcher, ed., *Truth* (Prentice-Hall, 1964); F. Ferré and K. Bendall, *Exploring the Logic of Faith* (Association, 1962).

[7]See for instance D. D. Evans, *The Logic of Self-Involvement* (Ryerson, 1964); A. F. Holmes, "Philosophy and Religious Belief," *Pacific Philosophy Forum* 5 (May 1967) 4.3.

# THEOLOGICAL METHOD AND INERRANCY: A REPLY TO ARTHUR F. HOLMES

## NORMAN L. GEISLER

### I. THE POSITION OF HOLMES

In an address to the national meeting of the Evangelical Theological Society held in Toronto, Canada, 1967, Arthur Holmes of Wheaton College suggested that the doctrine of Biblical inerrancy is neither *deduced* from the doctrine of inspiration, nor is it the result of an *inductive* study of the phenomena. Rather, it is a second-order theological principle *adduced* to round out the first-order Biblical doctrine of inspiration. In his own words:

> I am not convinced that, in its usual extension to all historical details, scientific allusions and literary references inerrancy is either explicitly taught in Scripture or is *deduced* therefrom without a fallacy of equivocation. Nor do I see it as the result of *inductive* study of the phenomena—the induction is too incomplete....Rather, I see inerrancy as a second-order theological construct that is *adduced* for systematic reasons....But inerrancy as we usually construct the concept is something further [than inspiration], something that I do not find logically entailed in the statement "Scripture speaks the truth," at least not in a form sufficiently precise to "fit" all the facts. Rather, inerrancy is adduced because of the high level of expectation...created by the Biblical doctrine, and the attractiveness of rounding out the doctrine with this further extrapolation.

Holmes rejects the deductive method of system building in theology for four reasons:

> If deduction were the logic of theology, (1) we would have to formalize in deductive fashion every movement of theological thought, (2) we would have to ignore the historical narrative except for illustrative purposes and work only with logically universal propositions, (3) we would have to reduce all

Biblical analogy and metaphor and symbol and poetry and connotation to logically univocal as well as universal form, (4) we would have to regard all events in redemptive history and the consequent application of grace as logically necessary rather than contingent on the will of God. This I cannot do.

Likewise, Holmes denies the validity of the inductive method, both of the Aristotelian and of the Baconian forms. The former he considers insufficient because it involves "the intuitive abstraction of universal principles from familiar classified data, and as such it presupposes the Aristotelian view of man and nature.... To use Aristotelian induction intact would tie theology to Aristotle, and this," writes Holmes, "I am not prepared to do."

Further, Francis Bacon's method of "experimental identification of causes... is obviously not what theology is doing." According to Holmes, the usual theological method is "a loose approximation to Aristotle's quest for generalized concepts based on an inspection of empirical [Biblical] data." This procedure, however, he rejects because (1) a complete induction is impossible and hence our theological concepts would lack finality, and (2) theological method is more than a collection and collation of proof texts that unambiguously dictate their own meaning. "Theology seems to me," he says, "to involve hermeneutical assumptions and pre-understandings, the selection of materials, the choice of some preferred materials in interpreting others, the adoption of guiding hypotheses, the use of models, the gradual hesitating construction of conceptual maps."

As Holmes admits: "This is neither deduction nor induction. The logic of theological language is different from that of mathematics or early modern science." It is in fact consciously borrowed from contemporary science which "is not really inductive either, nor is it some easy combination of induction and deduction." Rather, it is a "language game" that adduces models and constructs that aid in system building. "I suspect," says Holmes, "that such is the case with the conception of Biblical inerrancy."

## II. A Critique of Holmes' Position

The main lines of our evaluation of "adduction" as the theological method of establishing inerrancy will include (1) an examination of the grounds upon which induction and deduction are rejected, (2) an appraisal of the method of "adduction" itself, and (3) a suggested alternative method.

To begin with, we must express a preliminary dissatisfaction with what is at least a very unfortunate description of the "adductive" method. For to define the doctrine of Biblical inerrancy, which rests at the very foundation of a consistent evangelical theology, as an "extrapolation," "a model," "a word game," or a "second-order theological construct," which is neither formally taught in Scripture nor logically entailed in the doctrine of inspiration is somewhat less than satisfactory. Whether or not this description is merely unfortunate or is really inadequate remains to be discussed. Prima facie it should do more than raise an evangelical eyebrow.

Now for an examination of the grounds upon which Holmes rejects the inductive and deductive methods. The form of the inductive method normally employed in systematic theology is dismissed on the grounds that a perfect induction is not possible and a limited induction is insufficient.[1] But this is scarcely an adequate reason for refusing it, for on that same basis one could deny the validity of many first-order Biblical doctrines. In fact granting—as any reasonable evangelical position must—that the Biblical revelation is self-consistent, it would follow that a perfect induction is not necessary to establish a Biblical doctrine. Definite doctrines can be established on the basis of a sound exegesis of several definite passages of Scripture. The virgin birth, for example, is founded on an incontrovertible interpretation of two clear passages of Scripture (Matt 1:18-19; Luke 1:26). The deity of Christ can be established on a handful of passages (John 1:1; 8:58; 10:30; Heb 1:8; etc.), even though there are many more passages to support it (cf. Mark 2:7; John 5:22-23; Rev 1:8; Col 1:16).[2] Of course the broader the induction, the more perfect is our understanding of a given doctrine. But this is not to say that a doctrine cannot be firmly based on a limited induction.

Prescinding for the moment from the question as to whether or not the Bible formally teaches its own inerrancy, we may safely conclude that if it did, the fact that there were only a few clear passages on the subject or that one had not examined all the phenomena of Scripture (although this is possible to do) would not be justifiable grounds for rejecting the doctrine. Once the doctrine is clearly established, the internal consistency of divine truth guarantees in advance that no correct interpretation of any other passage of Scripture will contradict it.

The second objection Holmes offers against induction is that it involves "hermeneutical assumption," "postulates" and "guiding hypotheses," which have a preferred position in the interpretation of other data—and none of these are inductively derived. Rather, they are "adduced" to round out the theological system. That is, since no Biblical texts unambiguously dictate their own meaning, it is necessary to adduce some models or patterns to map out the overall meaning.

Now granting that Holmes does not wish to deny the perspecuity of Scripture nor replace the Roman Catholic teaching magisterium with a kind of Protestant preferred-model system of interpretation, then it is difficult to see the validity of this objection to induction. Certainly Holmes does not wish to suggest that there is no factual or textual basis that demands that the data be interpreted in a given way. And whereas the data of Scripture do not always unambiguously dictate their own specific meaning, nevertheless they do usually set well-defined limits within which definite teachings can be clearly enunciated. Furthermore, we must understand that Holmes does not wish to suggest that the choice of models and conceptual maps is to be based purely on what he calls "personal involvement," or "conviction," for this would be to launch a rudderless ship of hermeneutics on the uncharted sea of subjectivity.

But, on the contrary, if there is some common basis for meaning and interpretation that arises out of the data of Scripture itself; if the Bible delineates some of its own paradigm principles or master models; if it in general maps out its own course of meaning, then the reasons offered for rejecting the inductive method are less than convincing. In fact, it is difficult to see how one could even know how to recognize and arrange the differing metaphors and models of Scripture unless he possessed a kind of supra-model of common meaning that transcends them. That is, unless the Scriptures themselves provide a definite basis for determining their own meaning, then there is no objective way of deciding which are the master models to be used in preference to others. In everyday language, the Bible "speaks for itself." And when it comes to preferential models, the answer is equally perspicacious: In the Bible the main things are the plain things, and the plain things are the main things. Fortunately, the Bible is not addressed to philosophers but to the common man!

As for Holmes' objections to a strictly deductive method, one may readily agree with them if deduction is limited to a logically rigid disregard for fact, particularly if the premises from which the deductions are made are themselves not sufficiently founded in fact. For certainly the claims of Scripture must be understood in the light of the character or phenomena of Scripture itself. Obviously what the Bible says about itself must be understood in the light of what the Bible shows itself to be.[3]

However, it is difficult to see what objections an evangelical could raise against deducing the doctrine of the trinity from the two firmly grounded scriptural truths that God is one (Deut 6:4; Mark 12:29) and yet that there are three distinct centers of consciousness that are called God (Matt 3:16-17; Acts 5:3, 5; John 14:26; etc.). Of course a careful scrutiny of all of Scripture will cast more light on this doctrine, which nevertheless can be deduced from two truths that themselves may be founded on only a limited induction.

Now to speak more precisely about the nature of the logical method that is involved in establishing the doctrine of inerrancy. Granting, as we shall, that the Scriptures do not clearly and formally teach their own inerrancy, we need not conclude that inerrancy is not logically entailed in the doctrine of inspiration, which *is* formally taught in Scripture. For if (as inspiration guarantees) whatever the Bibles teaches is true, and if the Bible does teach historical and factual matters, then it logically follows that whatever the Bible teaches about historical and factual matters is true. And that is what is meant by inerrancy—namely, that the Bible is without error in whatever it teaches.

As to the first of these premises, no evangelical need be in doubt. For Jesus said, "Thy word is true" (John 17:17). The Scriptures clearly claim to be the Word of God (cf. 2 Tim 3:16; 2 Pet 1:20-21), and "it is impossible that God should prove false" (Heb 6:18). Whatever else the doctrine of inspiration may imply, it certainly means that whatever the Bible teaches is true.

Concerning the second premise—that the Bible sometimes teaches or at least directly and logically implies historical and factual material—this is beyond reasonable doubt. For example, it was Jesus of *Nazareth* who was born in the city of *Bethlehem* under *Herod* the king and in the days of *Caesar Augustus* (cf. Matthew 2; Luke 2). The claim of these Scriptures is that these are specific historical places and persons. Any view that attempts to completely separate matters of "life and godliness" (2 Pet 1:3) or deed and doctrine (2 Tim 3:17) from matters of fact and history overlooks two basic facts. First, many times it is impossible to deny the historical truth of a passage without simultaneously destroying its spiritual truth. For example, what can the virgin birth mean if Mary had committed adultery? If it is not a biological fact, then it is a theological fiction too. What could the crucifixion mean if there were no nails and a wooden cross? It is senseless to speak of a resurrection unless Joseph's tomb was permanently vacated by Jesus of Nazareth (cf. 1 Cor 15:17). It must be clear to any unprejudiced observer that many of the truths of Scripture directly imply some physical, observable and verifiable facts about our time-space universe. Second, since not all Biblical teachings directly involve truths of an historical or factual nature, one's confidence in the doctrines that cannot be historically or factually verified is necessarily related to those that can be. To borrow the words from Jesus: "If I have told you earthly things and you do not believe, how can you believe if I tell you heavenly things?" (John 3:12). Plainly put, if we do not believe Jesus when he said, "Jonah was three days and three nights in the belly of the whale" (Matt 12:40), then how can we believe him when he said, "Before Abraham was, I am" (John 5:58), or "I am the way, and the truth, and the life; no one comes to the Father but by me" (John 14:6)? In other words, not only are some historical and spiritual truths inseparably connected, but, in the cases where they are not, they are logically (and/or psychologically) connected by the proposition: If the historical and factual truths of the Bible cannot be trusted as inerrant, then neither can the truths that are not directly connected to historical or factual matters. It would be specious to argue that the Scriptures are inerrant on truths that cannot be verified if they are errant on matters that can be tested. If the Scriptures are not inerrant when they teach matters of fact and history, which can be objectively tested, then how can one believe in the inerrancy of Scripture in matters of faith and theology?

In brief, there are two reasons for contending that the truth of the Bible extends beyond purely moral and spiritual matters: (1) Exegetically, some Biblical doctrines are inseparably connected to fact and history; and (2) logically, it is less than convincing to argue that the Bible should be trusted in the case of affirmations that are objectively unverifiable if it can be proven to be errant on statements that can be verified in this fashion.

The conclusion follows naturally. Inerrancy *is* logically entailed with inspiration. For inspiration (or, more properly, divine authority) guarantees that the Bible is true in whatever it teaches, and the teaching of the Bible sometimes clearly entails factual and historical material. Hence there appears to be no reason to weaken the methodological basis of the doctrine of inerrancy by resorting to any kind of "adduction" or extrapolation. Inerrancy can be derived from inspiration by a clear process of deduction.

Of course, to say that the Scriptures are inerrant in whatever they teach is not to imply that everything *contained* in the Bible is being *taught* by the Bible. The Scriptures sometimes illustrate the truth being taught by something that in itself is not necessarily correct. For example, Jesus once illustrated the persistence of prayer by a story in which God was represented by an unjust judge (Luke 18). But the point of the parable is not the justice of God but importunity in prayer, and it is only the point being taught that is inerrant. Also, merely because something is quoted in the Bible does not make it true, for Satan (Gen 3:4) and others (cf. John 8:48) are quoted as having said things that are clearly untrue.

The task of the interpreter is to determine whether the passage is approving or merely reporting what is said. What it is approving it is teaching, and that is without error. Admittedly it is not always easy to discover where to draw the line between what the Bible is reporting without approving, as anyone knows who has attempted to apply this principle to the discourses of Job's friends or to the apparent skepticism of the man "under the sun" in Ecclesiastes. However, in these cases the problem is an exegetical one and not a theological one. The theological principle is clear: Whatever the Bible is teaching is true and without error. It must be left to exegesis to determine precisely what the passage is teaching. In other words, there is no question that the passage is true. The question is: What is the truth of the passage?

Finally, it appears to me that it is both unnecessary and undesirable to relegate the doctrine of inerrancy to a "second-order theological construct," which is extrapolated in order to round out our theological system. It is unnecessary because inerrancy is logically implied in inspiration, as has been argued above. It is undesirable because this is a capitulation to contemporary methodology, which unduly weakens the basis of this crucial doctrine. For there can be no real certainty of a conclusion or principle that is arrived at by means of an extrapolation or "adduction." It seems to me that inerrancy is a first-order theological truth not unlike the doctrine of Christ's sinlessness. That Christ was without sin is based on (1) an inductive examination of several Biblical texts (cf. 2 Cor 5:21; Heb 4:15; 1 Pet 1:19; 2:22), (2) from which it can be deduced that this truth will not be contradicted by anything taught in the rest of Scripture, (3) and yet which truth must be understood in the light of how Christ actually behaved. For example, whatever understanding one may have of what is meant by the fact that Christ "knew no sin" (2 Cor 5:21), it must be inclusive of a person who could get angry, call down the judgment of God on religious hypocrisy, curse a fig tree, and even drown a herd of swine—for all of these Christ did, and yet he did them "apart from sinning" (Heb 4:15). Likewise even though it is known in advance (on the basis of some clear texts) that whatever the Bible teaches is true and therefore without error, nevertheless precisely what is meant by this inerrancy must be inclusive of the phenomena of Scripture itself. So in the cases of both Christ and the Bible the antecedent claim to be "without sin/error" must be understood in the light of the consequent character or performance of each.

Now let us briefly summarize the issue before us. Traditionally, there have been two suggested bases for inerrancy: (1) It is a doctrine clearly and formally taught in Scripture; (2) although inerrancy is not clearly and formally taught in Scripture, nevertheless it is logically implied in the doctrine of inspiration (or authority), which is clearly and formally taught in Scripture. In contrast to these two bases for the doctrine of inerrancy Holmes would offer a third alternative—namely, that inerrancy is neither founded on a purely inductive examination of the Bible nor is it a deductive conclusion from another truth found in the Scriptures but, rather, it is the result of an "adduction" or extrapolation from the text.

At this point it is perhaps not inappropriate to mention that while Holmes warned theologians against the danger of borrowing their method from other sciences, nevertheless he has admittedly borrowed his "adductive" method from the contemporary philosophy of science. However, the important question is not where one obtains his method but whether or not the method is appropriate and sufficient for his discipline. And as to this point, the method of deducing the doctrine of inerrancy from the divine authority of Scripture seems to be quite appropriate, and it is certainly more sufficient. For if the Bible is the Word of God written, then of course it is not in error in anything that it teaches. Nor is it necessary, as Holmes suggests, to modify this conclusion by "a thousand qualifications." In fact, there is only one inherent qualification to the doctrine of inerrancy—namely, the Scriptures are without error only in what they *teach* or in what is clearly implied therein, as opposed to what they may contain, allude to, or use to illustrate what they teach. It is true that there will no doubt be a further amplification and clarification of the precise meaning of inerrancy by the study of the phenomena of Scripture. However, when what the Bible says about itself is understood in the full light of what the Bible shows itself to be, there will be no contradiction but rather a further clarification of what is really meant by "speaking the truth without error." And if there is an apparent conflict between the claim of inerrancy and the facts of Scripture, then we must reexamine the meaning of both, always remembering that "it is impossible that God should prove false" (Heb 6:18).

[1]Actually a perfect induction is not intrinsically impossible with regard to a finite set of data, such as there is in the Bible.

[2]All Scripture quotations are taken from the RSV unless otherwise noted.

[3]For a more complete discussion of this point see N. L. Geisler and W. Nix, *A General Introduction to the Bible* (Moody, 1968), chap. 4.

# REPLY TO NORMAN L. GEISLER

## ARTHUR F. HOLMES

My paper on "Ordinary Language Analysis and Theological Method" was not about the doctrine of Scripture but part of a symposium on theological method. Had it been about Scripture I would have given the subject more than one paragraph! But it was about methodology: I suggested that the logic of models and constructs is neither strictly inductive nor strictly deductive and that induction and deduction are not the only logics available to theologians. How we formulate our theological concepts is a complex question: We do not derive all of them by direct exegesis. I used the concept of inerrancy (*not* inspiration *nor* revelation *nor* authority) as an example. I could as well have used the Chalcedonian formula or the congregational concept of Church government, both of which I accept but neither of which in its technical detail is, I think, derived either by inductive generalization or by strict deduction from Biblical statements alone. In the Chalcedonian formula the language of Greek metaphysics provides a model, but the resultant formula is still "true to" Scripture. In the congregational concept of the Church, I suspect seventeenth-century political concepts suggested how the Church might be regarded. The problem in each case is to distinguish the resultant construct from what Scripture plainly teaches. The construct is a second-order doctrine; what Scripture itself says is first-order. The same distinction must be made with regards to inerrancy, for we affirm an inerrant Scripture, not an inerrant logic nor an inerrant theological method nor inerrant theological constructs.

It seems to me that Geisler's response fails to understand this use of "first-order" and "second-order" doctrines, and to imply that all Christian theology is of the first order. In popular doctrinal teaching it may seem this way but not, I submit, in historical theology and the technicalities of systematics. He also overlooks two other crucial points in my paper:

1. I affirm that it is the doctrine of inerrancy *as technically formulated and qualified by careful theologians* that is not the result simply of pure induction or strict deduction. Geisler comes to this point only in his concluding paragraph and does not consider the possibility that extra-Biblical concepts of truth and error and accuracy have been adduced by theologians. A recent writer in this *Bulletin* claims, for instance, that the correspondence theory of truth is essential for evangelicals. Maybe or maybe not; but correspondence is an extra-Biblical philosophical theory, whatever its merits, rather than an exegetically derived doctrine. The truthfulness or inerrancy of Scripture defined on the correspondence model, or a scientific model, or a rationalistic model, is the sort of thing I have in mind. It is no use affirming truthfulness after all without a theory of truth. We have to use models of some sort.

2. I affirm that theological concepts that use models, concepts like inerrancy or the Chalcedonian formula *are* testable. Geisler implies I have no *objective truth criteria*, but in my paper I explicit discuss empirical adequacy and rational coherence as tests for our constructs. When I prefer a doctrinal formulation for systematic reasons, I do so because it coheres rationally in the whole body of theological understanding and because it adequately covers the Biblical data. My proposal, then, does not leave evangelicals up in the air. It serves rather to remind us that as Protestants we must reject an inerrant theology. We may be confident of what we believe, and with good and sufficient reasons, but we cannot claim inerrancy for ourselves, not even an inerrant theology of inerrancy. *Scriptura sola* is our rule.

# Baptists And Biblical Authority

## CLARK H. PINNOCK

The nature of Biblical inspiration and the extent of its authority has been the center of a vigorous controversy amongst Baptists, as it has been in every major Christian body, for over a hundred years. Let me start off on an autobiographical note. I myself was brought up in a Baptist congregation in Toronto, Canada, which was under the influence of the progressive theological views that had swept through scholarly Baptist circles in North America in the first decades of the twentieth century and were being disseminated at that time from the Canadian Baptist Seminary at McMaster University. I do not owe my conversion in 1949, humanly speaking, to that congregation or its ministers, but rather to a teacher in our Sunday school who, though deeply troubled by the lack of sound Biblical preaching in the pulpit, continued to teach the Word of God to his intermediate class of boys, aged twelve to fourteen. From the very beginning of my consciously Christian life, given this church situation, I was aware of the need to be alert to defections from the true faith and to maintain a theologically sound testimony. I can well recall a lectureship on Biblical subjects sponsored in one of the Toronto Baptist churches by the McMaster faculty in which higher-critical theories regarding the Pentateuch, the book of Daniel and the Psalms were put forth to a congregation of laymen. I can remember feeling then at the age of fifteen, as I still do today, how destructive to our confidence in the reliability of the Bible some of these views were, and how, upon seeking out reaction from other laymen present, I found that they either shared my concern and horror or else regarded the whole matter as the province of Biblical scholars whom they trusted meant no harm. (Trust is ordinarily a high Christian virtue, but on some occasions it can be quite dangerous. Alas, even Bible professors do not always deserve to be trusted, myself included, but must earn that right by being themselves faithful to Holy Scripture and thus worthy of trust.) It was a source of puzzlement to me to see how the Baptist faith, which I had been told rested squarely and solely upon the unique and final authority of the Bible, would be able to survive the new view of that Book that was being presented. Even today I do not believe that the educated Baptists who espouse the doctrine of a fallible Bible have yet been able to allay the fears of the people in the churches completely as to what the new theology means and where it leads. I do not believe that they can.

In the first section of my paper I wish to define the Scripture principle to which all Christian people, including Baptists, have traditionally adhered, and which has always seemed indispensable to a sound and coherent theology. Following that, I will describe the crisis of the Scripture principle since the rise of negative Biblical criticism and its effect on Baptist theology. Finally, I will call upon Baptists to maintain the Scripture principle in our day without equivocation, for the good of our own movement and for the sake of Christ and the gospel.

## I. The Scripture Principle

To confess the supreme authority of Holy Writ is to take a fundamentally Christian stand. Although it is a tenet of Baptist theology, it is likewise a historic Christian conviction that stands over and above merely sectarian interests. H. E. W. Turner has written: "No system of thought can be considered Christian which does not take the Biblical Revelation as its ultimate authority."[1] Christianity is after all a revealed religion and as such has been given to us by God's grace. Its truth was not discovered by human genius but delivered to us by God through the instrumentality of his apostles and prophets and deposited in the Scriptures. As Paul explained to young Timothy, the truth of the gospel, the "pattern of sound words," has been entrusted to us by the Spirit and must be guarded (2 Tim 1:13-14). Great care is to be exercised to ensure that the message is faithfully handed down by a succession of reliable teachers (2:2). He asks Timothy to continue stedfastly in his own apostolic teachings and to abide by the doctrine of the sacred and inspired writings of the OT (3:14-17). It is important that he preach the Word faithfully and not allow himself to turn away from listening to the truth (4:2, 4). (It has always amazed me when scholars have argued that 2 Timothy is primary evidence for nascent Catholicism in the NT. Surely a better case could be made for it as the earliest conservative evangelical tract!) In contending for the authority of the Bible we are simply asking that the truth that God gave in the history of salvation and definitively in Jesus Christ be granted undisputed priority and unlimited authority over us.

148

Ths historic Baptist doctrine of Biblical authority is one with the historic view of the Church. It is a simple historical fact that all the great doctors of theology as well as the mass of Christian faithful have maintained the highest possible regard for the written Word of God. Only for a hundred years or so has there been any significant dissent in this matter. As E. A. Litton put it: "If there ever was a general consent of the Church Catholic on any question, it exists on this. East and West, from the earliest to the latest times, concurred in assigning to Scripture a pre-eminence which consisted in its being—as no other collection of writings is—the Word of God."[2] We cannot but wonder whether the reasons that led theologians like Augustine, Luther, Calvin and Wesley to hold to the complete trustworthiness of Scripture might not be superior to the reasons that lead men today to reject it.

In order to refresh our memories as to how solid the historic doctrine of Scripture was, let us hear some eminent testimonies. In a letter to Jerome, Augustine wrote, "I confess to your charity that I have learned to defer this respect and honour to those Scriptural books only which are now called canonical, that I believe most firmly that no one of those authors has erred in any respect in writing."[3] In a sermon on John 3:16 Luther said:

> If a different way to heaven existed, no doubt God would have recorded it, but there is no other way. Therefore, let us cling to these words, firmly place and rest our hearts upon them, close our eyes and say: Although I had the merit of all the saints, the holiness and purity of all virgins, and the piety of St. Peter himself, I would still consider my attainment nothing. Rather I must have a different foundation to build on, namely, these words: God has given His Son so that whosoever believes in Him whom the Father's love has sent shall be saved. And you must confidently insist that you will be preserved; and you must boldly take your stand on His words, which no devil, hell or death can suppress.... Therefore no matter what happens, you should say: There is God's Word. This is my rock and anchor. On it I rely, and it remains. Where it remains, I, too, remain; where it goes, I, too, go. The Word must stand, for God cannot lie; and heaven and earth must go to ruins before the most insignificant letter or tittle of His Word remains unfulfilled.[4]

The *Institutes* of Calvin is likewise studded in the early chapters with references to Scripture as the true doctrine of God, from the mouth of God, given through the inspiration of the Spirit. And in his comment on 2 Tim 3:16 he utters these remarkable words:

> Whoever then wishes to profit in the Scriptures, let him first of all lay down as a settled point this—that the law and the prophecies are not teaching delivered by the will of men, but dictated by the Holy Ghost....Moses

and the prophets did not utter at random what we have from their hand, but since they spoke by divine impulse, they confidently and fearlessly testified, as actually was the case, that it was the mouth of the Lord that spoke.... We owe to the Scripture the same reverence which we owe to God, because it has proceeded from Him alone, and has nothing of man mixed with it.

Because they held this view of Scripture as the written Word of God, the leaders of the Reformation insisted that Scripture must rule the church and nothing must stand over it. *Sola scriptura* is the Protestant principle, Tillich notwithstanding. Scripture must constitute, determine and rule the entire theological endeavor. What it does not determine is no part of Christian truth.

This historic high view of Holy Writ is also the traditional Baptist view of it. Although the Baptist movement has not drawn up authoritative confessions of faith and used them as the basis of fellowship, still there are Baptist statements of faith that give us quite a clear impression of where Baptists have stood on this issue. Granted, some of the early brief statements lack altogether a paragraph on Biblical authority, as is also the case in the great ecumenical creeds of Christendom. But the reason for this is a simple one. The inspiration and supreme authority of Scripture was not being challenged then as it is today. Those who drew up the earliest statements had matters more pressing on their minds. Nevertheless, in the Second London Confession of 1677 and 1688, one of the most important of all Baptist statements, we read eloquent and extended testimony on Scripture modeled closely on the Westminster Confession of Faith:

The Holy Scripture is the only sufficient certain and infallible rule of all saving knowledge, faith, and obedience.... The supreme judge by which all controversies of religion are to be determined, and all decrees of councils, opinions of ancient writers, doctrines of men, and private spirits, are to be examined, and in whose sentence we are to rest, can be no other but the Holy Scripture delivered by the Spirit, into which Scripture so delivered, our faith is finally resolved (chap. 1).

More familiar to American Baptists is the masterful utterance of the New Hampshire Confession of 1833, taken over and repeated in the "Baptist Faith and Message" of the Southern Baptist Convention, which reads:

We believe that the Holy Bible was written by men divinely inspired and is a perfect treasure of heavenly instruction; that it has God for its author, salvation for its end, and truth, without any mixture of error, for its matter; that it reveals the principles by which God will judge us; and therefore is, and will remain to the end of the world, the true center of Christian union, and the supreme standard by which all human conduct, creeds, and religious opinions should be tried.

And, finally, from the continent we hear the confession of faith from the evangelical association of French-speaking Baptist churches, 1879:

> We believe that the canonical writings of the Old and the New Testaments are the Word of God and constitute the only and infallible rule of faith and Christian life and the only touchstone by which every doctrine, every tradition and every religious and ecclesiastical system as well as every method of Christian action are to be tested. We believe that the Holy Scripture is a providential document and that the Holy Spirit presided in sovereign manner at its origin and at the formation of the biblical story. We believe that He has Himself assured therein the perfect teaching and the entire historic truth, despite the imperfection of the human instruments who, by His divine inspiration and under His control, have contributed toward communicating to us the divine oracles.[5]

Early in this century the great Baptist theologian E. Y. Mullins set down his reflections on our subject of Baptists and the Bible. He wrote: "For Baptists there is one authoritative source of religious truth and knowledge. To that source they look in all matters relating to doctrine, polity, the ordinances, worship, and Christian living. That source is the Bible."[6] He went on in his article to discuss the sufficiency, certainty, dependability and divine authority of the Bible. Other important Baptist thinkers of the past, like John Smyth, John Gill and Andrew Fuller, all agree that the Bible is God's written Word and the supreme authority in life and thought.[7] Of course, being Baptists, they were individualists and did not agree on all that was involved in the outworking and development of that doctrine. Nevertheless they did agree on the divine origin and authorship of Scripture.

There is an historic view of the Bible, and Baptists have held to it. The conservative doctrine of inspiration has history on its side. It is a mistake often made by progressive theologians to suppose that belief in Biblical infallibility is a recent aberration of fundamentalist thought. As a matter of fact it is not. It has been the position of all the Christian churches for eighteen hundred years. And there is no mystery why it is so. It is the doctrine that Jesus taught his Church. The progressives in theology make much of Jesus and his authority over us. Yet it is more than strange how they seem to ignore the plain fact that Jesus himself trusted the Scriptures completely and without reservation. His own precept and practice is the firm foundation of the Scripture principle, and it is entirely natural that his disciples follow his example.[8]

## II. The Crisis of the Scripture Principle

Having reviewed, if only superficially, the encouraging story of Christian obedience in the matter of the Scripture principle, the mood changes as we attempt to characterize the sad and melancholy history of a great defection. For there has been, as everyone well knows, a noticeable modification of views regarding the Bible on the part of large segments of Christian thought today, a change that has brought with it a theological crisis of great scope.[9] Although Pannenberg is himself part of the problem, he is surely correct when he writes: "The dissolution of the traditional doctrine of Scripture constitutes a crisis at the very foundation of modern Protestant theology."[10] The saying is true! A very large number of Biblical scholars, preachers, and to a lesser extent Christian people have lost their confidence in the complete trustworthiness of Scripture. If it were a hesitating and reluctant change of mind we might be able to feel better about it. But what we face instead is a strident, self-confident and unabashed rejection of the view of the Bible that the Christian Church has always cherished. In the face of it our hearts are moved by both sadness and indignation. As the psalmist says, "My eyes shed streams of tears, because men do not keep thy law" (119:136). Our hearts should be saddened when people reject God's Word. But in the midst of sadness we cannot but be appalled by the ingratitude of the human heart. For after God had given us his Word to guide our minds and illumine our hearts, to teach us heavenly truths and lead us out of the darkness of our own fantasies, we find a company of so-called Christian leaders joining the chorus of unbelief in casting doubt upon the integrity and reliability of that priceless gift of the divine grace. The great defection from a high view of Holy Writ seems to us to be as perverse and ungrateful as it is disastrous.

Rather than describe the dreary story ourselves, let us listen to the words of Father Burtchaell who, although rejecting Biblical infallibility himself, understands precisely what has happened.

Christians early inherited from the Jews the belief that the biblical writers were somehow possessed by God, who was thus to be reckoned the Bible's proper author. Since God could not conceivably be the agent of falsehood, the Bible must be guaranteed free from any error. For centuries this doctrine lay dormant, as doctrines will; accepted by all, pondered by few. Not until the 16th century did inspiration and its corollary, inerrancy, come up for sustained review. The Reformers and Counter-Reformers were disputing whether all revealed truth was in Scripture alone, and whether it could dependably be interpreted by private or official scrutiny. Despite a radical disagreement on these issues both groups persevered in receiving the Bible as a compendium of inerrant oracles dictated by the Spirit. Only in the 19th century did a succession of empirical disciplines newly come of age begin to put a succession of inconvenient queries to exegetes. First, geology and paleontology discredited the view of the cosmos and the cosmogony of Genesis. Next, archeology suggested that there were serious historical discrepancies in the sacred narrative. Later, as parallel oriental literatures began to be recovered, much of Scripture lay under accusation of plagiarism from pagan

152

sources. Literary criticism of the text itself disclosed that the writers had freely tampered with their materials, and often escalated myth and legend into historical event. After all this, considerable dexterity was required of any theologian who was willing to take account of the accumulation of challenging evidence, yet continued to defend the Bible as the classic and inerrant Word of God.[11]

Putting aside for a moment the fact that Burtchaell has grossly exaggerated the actual results of legitimate criticism, he has certainly not exaggerated the magnitude of the shift in modern theology away from the historic doctrine of Scripture. Whereas orthodox theologians have always insisted that we regard Scripture as God-speaking and God-teaching, modern negative critics consistently refuse to identify God's Word with the written text of the Bible. In his essay "The Crisis of the Scripture Principle," Pannenberg expresses his skepticism about the history recorded in the gospels and his pessimism regarding the possibility of applying the Biblical text to present contexts. He speaks of "tendencies" in various Biblical writers and doubts the unity of the Bible. In his work on the Apostles' Creed he repudiates the miraculous conception of Jesus altogether, and in his book on Christology he refers to legendary elements in the resurrection narratives and elsewhere. I mention Pannenberg because he is not radically unorthodox, holding even it seems to the bodily resurrection of Jesus. Yet even in his work we are confronted with deep skepticism about the Bible. On the Catholic side we could mention Hans Küng, who has brought joy and encouragement to many in the last decade for his expression of evangelical truth from within the Roman Church. And yet he too has made it perfectly clear that he does not believe in any infallible authority, whether pope or Bible. The Bible contains, according to his judgment, numerous errors of every kind and cannot be trusted without reservation.

But the question that concerns us most in this paper is not the defection of Christians at large from the high view of Biblical inspiration, sad though that is, but rather the extent to which Baptists have shared in this shift of conviction. Though we do not have an historical study on this subject comparable to Lefferts A. Loetscher's *The Broadening Church*, which traces the shift in the northern Presbyterian denomination from 1869, we are priveleged to have a two-part article by Norman H. Maring entitled "Baptists and Changing Views of the Bible, 1865-1918" contained in the first volume of the periodical *Foundations* (1958). Although the article covers the very crucial years when liberalism entered into Baptist life and thought, we still need a further essay in which the research would be carried up to the present. Because the subject remains a hot and emotional one, perhaps it is not surprising why the work has not yet been done. Or it may be that contemporary Baptist theologians consider the matter settled and not in need of further controversy, which such research would inevitably stir up. In any case it is a project for someone to attempt.[12]

To what extent did Baptists share in the great defection from belief in the infallibile Scriptures? The answer has to be, at least in reference to the writing theologians of stature, to a large extent. This can be seen negatively from the almost complete silence of recent Baptist theologians to come out in defense of Biblical infallibility in the face of the blistering attack on it (two important exceptions being C. F. H. Henry and Bernard Ramm). And it can be seen positively in the historical documentation that Maring supplies. In the 1860s almost all Baptists, leaders and laymen, shared the historic Christian confidence in the inerrancy of the Bible. But after that time the influence of negative Biblical criticism from the continent began to eat away and erode that conviction, and scholars began to voice their disbelief in it. In the 1860s, for example, Thomas F. Curtiss, who had taught theology at a Baptist College in Lewisburg, Pennsylvania, and served for a brief time with the Southern Baptist Board of Domestic Missions, felt compelled to jettison belief in the infallibility of the Bible and publish that fact. Accepting documentary theories about the Pentateuch and other historical books, Curtiss found it necessary to revise his conception of inspiration. He began to emphasize instead the subjective experience of salvation and some of the ideas in the Bible he found to be experientially true even though communicated in fallible human terms. This stress upon personal experience as a substitute for objective infallibility was characteristic of liberal theology and would crop up again and again in later Baptist theologians like Ezekiel G. Robinson, president of the Rochester Seminary in the 1870s, and the justly famous William Newton Clarke (1841-1912), whose exegesis led him to conclude that his earlier confidence in the inerrancy of Scripture was untenable. He came to feel instead that the great ethical principles of the Bible, together with the person of Jesus, were enough to believe in. In his *Outline of Christian Theology* (1894) he wrote: "The Bible itself releases from all obligation to maintain its complete inerrancy, in the sense of freedom from all inaccuracy and incorrectness of statement, and shows us a higher quality, in which is manifest a higher purpose than that of inerrancy" (p. 35).[13] Further south there was the case of Crawford H. Toy, professor of OT at Southern Seminary in Louisville, who was one of the first Baptist professors forced to resign for his unorthodox views on the Bible. Though in the beginning of his teaching career he had held to strict Biblical inerrancy, later on he felt the pressure of Biblical problems and the necessity of broadening his views. Being a very honest man, Toy felt he could not suppress his views in the classroom as requested and was compelled to resign in 1879. Although the departure was a sad one, Toy subsequently became much more radical in his theology, no doubt justifying the wisdom of that decision. Obviously our account would be much extended if we were to include mention of the famous Baptists associated with the University of Chicago whose liberal views of inspiration and other Christian truths were far more radical than those I have mentioned. I refer to Shailler Matthews, E. de Wit Burton and Shirley Jackson Case. On the British side of the Atlantic one would have to mention H. Wheeler Robinson, who openly rejected Biblical infallibility. But the point is made and is a matter of public record. A considerable number of important Baptist leaders and thinkers publicly and unequivocally rejected and sometimes denounced belief in the complete trustworthiness of the Bible. And this continues to be true today.

Before leaving the subject of Baptists and the crisis of the Scripture principle, we should express some sympathy with the reasons that led men to this conclusion. For we would be sadly deluded if we concluded that the factors causing these Baptists to change their doctrine of inspiration were insubstantial and of their own making. Conservative Christians have a definitive tendency to minimize the force of Biblical difficulties, just as liberal Christians tend to exaggerate them. Often the orthodox stalwarts simply do not seriously confront well-formulated critical issues. This cannot be excused. These difficulties cannot be swept aside in a flood of rhetoric. It should give conservatives pause to remember that one no less than A. H. Strong felt the force of modern criticism so keenly that he too felt compelled to modify his earliest definition of inspiration and to speak of imperfections in the text. In the later editions of his *Systematic Theology* the whole idea of inerrancy and infallibility drops out of his discussion. He begins to write more of the religious efficacy of the Bible and of the accuracy of things essential to its "main purpose."

Nevertheless, however sympathetic we wish to be in the agonies of soul that accompanied this shift of viewpoint, we would be foolhardy indeed not to recognize the extreme dangers implicit in the new understanding of the Bible, which is a bog with no firm ground in it. And we must say that this shift of opinion has caused an ongoing and serious split between a large majority of Baptist people who hold the traditional Baptist and Christian view of the Bible and the majority of seminary and college professors who frankly do not.

## III. Maintaining the Scripture Principle

What exactly is at stake in this discussion on the nature of the Bible? There are some who believe very little is lost when trust in Scripture is given up. I believe that this hopeful and optimistic opinion is badly mistaken. On the contrary, I believe that *everything* is at stake. As Luther put it picturesquely, when men do not respect Scripture as God's Word "everyone makes a hole in it wherever it pleases him, and follows his own opinions, interpreting and twisting Scripture any way he pleases." Even William Newton Clarke sensed the danger when he wrote:

> I tell no secret—though perhaps many a man has wished he could keep it a secret—when I say that to the average minister today the Bible that lies on his pulpit is more or less an unsolved problem. He is loyal to it, and not for his right hand would he degrade it or do it wrong. He longs to speak with authority on the basis of its teaching, and feels that he ought to be able to do so. He knows that the people need its message in full power and clearness, and cannot bear to think that it is losing influence with them. Yet he is not entirely free to use it. Criticism has altered the book for his use, but just how far he does not know.[14]

On a much darker note still, A. H. Strong warned Baptists in 1918 of the severe potential and actual dangers in radical Biblical criticism. He wrote:

> What is the effect of this method upon our theological seminaries? It is to deprive the gospel message of all definiteness, and to make professors and students disseminators of doubts.... The result of such teaching in our seminaries is that the student, unless he has had a Pauline experience before he came, has all his early conceptions of Scripture and Christian doctrine weakened, has no longer any positive message to deliver, loses the ardor of his love for Christ; and at his graduation leaves the seminary, not to become preacher or pastor as he had once hoped, but to sow his doubts broadcast, as a teacher in some college, as editor of some religious journal, as secretary of some Young Men's Christian Association, or as agent of some mutual life insurance company. This method of interpretation switches off upon some sidetrack of social service many a young man who otherwise would be a heroic preacher of the everlasting gospel. The theological seminaries of almost all our demoninations are becoming so infected with this grievous error, that they are not so much organs of Christ as they are organs of Antichrist. This accounts for the rise, all over the land, of Bible schools, to take the place of seminaries.... We are losing our faith in the Bible, and our determination to stand for its teachings. We are introducing into our ministry men who have lost their faith in him and their love for him. The unbelief in our seminary teaching is like a blinding mist slowly settling down upon our churches, and is gradually abolishing, not only all definite views of Christian doctrine, but also all conviction of duty to "contend earnestly for the faith" of our fathers.... We are ceasing to be evangelistic as well as evangelical, and if this downward progress continues, we shall in due time cease to exist. This is the fate of Unitarianism today. We Baptists must reform or die.[15]

These are powerful sentiments and not, I think, exaggerated. What is at stake, quite frankly, is the possibility of normative theology, and with it the possibility of clear, bold preaching. If all that we have for revelational data is a Book tainted with errors, the extent of which no one can say, then we do not know what God has said and cannot pretend that we do. The alternative to a reliable Bible is human subjectivity, however we may define it. We are therefore faced with a choice between two versions of Christianity: one that depends on what God has spoken, and one that rests on human judgments. The crisis of the Scripture principle for theology is simply the fact that, if the new view of the Bible is correct, we do not know what constitutes revelational data and, not knowing that, cannot speak confidently about the truth of God.

Let me ask, "What doctrine is there that will survive this crisis?" None are safe from criticism. Each and every one is up for grabs today. Pannenberg, who accepts the bodily resurrection of Jesus, rejects his miraculous conception and is silent on the meaning of his death. There was a concerted effort only last year in Bangkok to define salvation in un-Biblical terms, formally and materially. Eschatology is being reduced to naturalistic dimensions and pressed into the service of Marxist guerrilla movements. Hardly a single prominent Catholic or Protestant theologian today accepts the historical fall of Adam into sin, though Scripture plainly teaches it. We are regularly subjected to Christologies that show the "human face of God" but do no justice to his eternal deity. The theory of universal salvation continues to undercut the necessity of world missions. The finality of Christ continues to be sacrificed in the name of a theology of world religions and a new syncretism. In order to gain an appreciation of the demonic, one had better turn to a Hollywood film like "The Exorcist" than to consult a modern theologian. Despite the fact that Biblical religion is supernaturalistic in its essence, Bultmann's barefaced and anachronistic naturalism continues to provide the starting point for scores of contemporary theologians. There is no point in going on with this dreary list of modern heresies, except to conclude that *none* of these aberrations, some of them every bit as serious as anything faced by the early fathers, would have been possible if Christians had held faithfully to the truth of the written Word of God. Of course it is true that a person holding to a low view of the Bible could—and many do—subscribe to any or all of the vital Biblical teachings. However, it would be *in spite of* his docrine of Scripture and not *because of it* that he did so. This fatal dualism between a reliable and sure gospel or theology and an unreliable and unsure Bible is intolerable, un-Biblical and unworkable. The Bible is a holistic book. Its "real" message is not floating like soap on murky waters of human fallibility. It is not possible to distinguish the religious truth of the Bible from the errant human dross that allegedly surrounds it. Many have tried it. None have succeeded. None ever will, because it cannot be done. The Bible is a seamless garment that deserves our total trust. Let us not deprive the world of the gospel it so desperately needs by our theological foolishness.

It might seem surprising that Baptists, for whom the Bible alone and not some creed is final authority, would succumb to a low view of the Bible. Though from one point of view their noncreedalism might seem to allow this defection, yet that very same fact that Baptists hold to Scripture alone ought to wed them indissolubly to a high view of it, having no other recourse. But it is less surprising when we consider the strong tendency of Baptists to locate truth in the saving encounter with Christ rather than in the objective truth outside themselves. (Cf. Strong's reference to a "Pauline experience" above!) The effects of revivalism upon them prepared the way, oddly enough, for them to be ravaged by liberal and later by neo-orthodox theology—and for this simple reason: Liberalism and neo-orthodoxy also emphasize that the doctrines of Christianity are grounded in personal religious experience and not upon external authorities. Therefore when untrained Baptists are confronted with subtle forms of liberal theology, classical or existential, they are not able to resist it intellectually even though their instinctive reaction is hesitant. In the extent to which Baptists make their subjective experience of salvation, rather than the objective Word of God, the main weapon in their defense of the truth, in the same measure they are vulnerable to theological compromise. Needless to say, this is even more true of the worldwide pentecostal movement, whose emphasis on religious subjectivity is even more complete. It is this very same factor that explains how at the present time evangelicals in various traditions are finding it possible to define revelation in terms of "encounter" rather than objective inerrancy. History is repeating itself. It is terribly important to remember that the truth of our salvation lies outside the soul in the objective act and word of the gospel. If we do not remember it, we may very well lose our convictions about Scripture and, worse still, our assurance of salvation itself. Luther's attitude seems much safer, at least to this Baptist, when he says:

> Unless I am convinced by the testimonies of the Holy Scriptures or evident reason (for I believe in neither the Pope nor councils alone, since it has been established that they have often erred and contradicted themselves), I am bound by the Scriptures that I have adduced, and my conscience has been taken captive by the Word of God; and I am neither able nor willing to recant, since it is neither safe nor right to act against conscience. God help me. Amen.

As we have already mentioned, we are not oblivious to the fact that there is work to be done if we are to maintain the Scripture principle intelligibly in our day of radical criticism. There are many tasks to which we must dedicate ourselves. Obviously there is critical work to be done. It is not enough to suspect naturalistic biases at the root of various critical objections to Scripture. It is necessary to show specifically what they are and where they are. Like Augustine, Luther and Calvin before us, we must work hard and long on the difficulties in the Biblical text and seek to find intellectually satisfying solutions to them. As proof that this can be done, and done with magnificent finesse, we need only mention the *Introduction to the Old Testament* written by R. K. Harrison, a book as thorough and scholarly as any liberal introduction today, yet one that vindicates the integrity of the Word of God at point after point, a book that shows how vulnerable are those very critical theories that caused so many Baptist leaders to defect from a high view of Scripture a century ago.

Beyond that, we have to be working at a unitive theology of the testaments. The opinion is widely held that the various writers of Scripture are moved by tendencies that are not mutually compatible and do not speak with a clear and united voice. Barr speaks of a multiplicity of theologies in the Bible, and he is not alone. The result of this would be to render impossible the use of the Bible as proof for anything, as criterion of anything. We must learn to replicate the method if not the theology of Calvin, in whose commentaries, which are still valuable today, he repeatedly showed the unity, consistency and coherence of the message of the Bible, whose ultimate author was God himself.

And in a more practical vein we must begin to hear profounder preaching, preaching like Ezra's, which gives the sense clearly and sends the people away rejoicing because they have understood the Word. So much conservative preaching is a travesty of the doctrine of Scripture. While holding out for our belief in the complete reliability of the Bible, preachers continue to wrench texts, to use and abuse them for whatever purpose thay happen to have in their minds, and to fail to enlighten the people as to what God has to say to them. Similarly, although the Bible we love is militant against injustice, violence and oppression, somehow we never get around to announcing to the congregation what this means for those who live in a society where all these things are practiced. It is not enough to maintain an orthodox view of the Bible unless at the same time we hear and obey God's Word.

When King Josiah discovered the Word of the Lord in the temple there came to pass a reformation of true religion in the land. The Church today needs the renewing impact of the Word of God. The Spirit wants to confront the Church afresh today with God's truth and lead her on to reformation and revival. God wants his people to believe and trust in him and all his promises. He has given us his written Word so that we might know his truth and walk in his light. Therefore let us delight in the Word of God. Let us sustain a doctrine of it that will make it possible for us to say with the psalmist:

> Oh, how love I thy law! It is my meditation all
> the day.
> Thou through thy commandments has made me wiser
> than mine enemies: for they are ever with me.
> I have more understanding than all my teachers:
> for thy testimonies are my meditation.
> I understand more than the ancients,
> because I keep thy precepts.
> I have refrained my feet from every evil way,
> that I might keep thy word.
> I have not departed from thy judgments:
> for thou hast taught me.
> How sweet are thy words unto my taste!
> Yea, sweeter than honey to my mouth!
> Through thy precepts I get understanding:
> therefore I hate every false way.
> (Ps 119:97-104)

[1]H. E. W. Turner, *The Pattern of Christian Truth* (London: Mowbray, 1954) 167.

[2]E. A. Litton, *Introduction to Dogmatic Theology* (London: Clarke, 1960) 19.

[3]Augustine, *Epistolae*, 82.1.3.

[4]Luther, *Weimarer Ausgabe*, 10.3.162.

[5]These materials are recorded in W. L. Lumpkin, *Baptist Confessions of Faith* (Philadelphia: Judson, 1959).

[6]E. Y. Mullins, "Baptists and the Bible," *Encyclopedia of Southern Baptists*, 1. 141-143.

[7]J. H. Watson, "Baptists and the Bible as Seen in Three Eminent Baptists," *Foundations* 16 (1973) 239-254; see also J. L. Garrett, Jr., "Representative Modern Baptist Understandings of Biblical Inspiration," *RevExp* 71 (1974) 179-195.

[8]See J. W. Wenham, *Christ and the Bible* (Downers Grove: Inter-Varsity, 1972). Our Lord's doctrine of Scripture gives us the norm for judging the so-called "phenomena" of the Bible. I do not agree with those evangelicals who reverse this order of things. Cf. B. Ramm, "Scripture as a Theological Concept," *RevExp* 71 (1974) 149-150.

[9]See W. B. Glover, *Evangelical Nonconformity and Higher Criticism in the 19th Century* (London: Independent Press, 1954).

[10]W. Pannenberg, *Basic Questions in Theology* (Philadelphia: Fortress, 1970), 1. 4.

[11]J. T. Burtchaell, *Catholic Theories of Biblical Inspiration Since 1810: A Review and Critique* (Cambridge: University Press, 1969) 1-2.

[12]Garrett, "Representative," does at least discuss H. Wheeler Robinson.

[13]See also W. N. Clarke, *The Use of the Scriptures in Theology* (New York: Scribner's, 1906); *Sixty Years With the Bible: A Record of Experience* (New York: Scribner's, 1912).

[14]Cited by H. E. Fosdick, *The Modern Use of the Bible* (New York: Macmillan, 1924) 2.

[15]A. H. Strong, *A Tour of the Missions: Observations and Conclusions* (Philadelphia: Griffith and Rowland, 1918) 170-174.

# Reconsidering "Limited Inerrancy"

## RICHARD J. COLEMAN

### I.

Surprisingly enough, the discussion of Biblical inerrancy swirls around us with almost the same ferocity as in the 1880s and the 1930s. The stance was taken then, namely by B. B. Warfield and J. Gresham Machen, that the traditional view of Biblical inerrancy should not be compromised by the promulgation of a limited view of inspiration. Well-fought issues do not die easily, and such is the case with the interrelationship between Scriptural inerrancy and its inspiration. The difficulties faced by Warfield and Machen in defending a strict view of inerrancy are still with us, if not more intensely, and thus the proponents of some kind of limited inspiration are still with us. The debate, however, has often been clouded by imprecisions and generalities. Thus my purpose is to unpack some of the commonly-used terms in this controversy, leading to a more careful definition of the alternatives.

When heresy charges were brought against Charles A. Briggs concerning, among other matters, his view of limited inerrancy, Henry P. Smith came to his defense.[1] As an OT scholar who accepted some of the results of the historical-critical method, Smith defined the issue thus: "Whether the Biblical writers were also divinely guided to remove from previous existing literary material every error of fact, *no matter how indifferent in its bearing on faith and morals*, and whether in giving their own observation and experience they were so far lifted above universal liability to error that they never *made a mistake*, even in the sphere of secular science or history." In this manner Smith carried the question of inspiration one step beyond that of the immediate recordings of the Biblical writers. In some matters—namely, those concerned with faith and morals—the authors gave evidence of being directly inspired, but on other matters the written text gave evidence of being dependent upon secondary sources, oral traditions, redactions and scribal errors. In other words, inspiration was limited to the unmediated parts of Scripture, and for that reason the Bible could be declared to be "the only infallible rule of *faith and practice*."[2]

Henry Smith was bound to lock horns with Benjamin Warfield. The latter took Smith to task on several fronts.[3] If we were willing to agree with Smith, Warfield argued, then we would find ourselves in the dangerous position of an un-Biblical separation between spiritual and secular matters. The consequences would be unfortunate for three reasons: (1) The objective basis of salvation history would be undermined, (2) we would lose confidence concerning the weightier matters if the veracity of the Biblical writer was doubted concerning the smaller details, and (3) Scripture gives no evidence that its inspiration is limited in any way.

As we look at this lively debate from hindsight, we notice that Smith weakened his position seriously by adopting the limiting formula that Scripture is infallible only in matters of faith and practice. It would have been far better if Smith had spoken of a "limited inerrancy" rather than a "limited inspiration"[4] and in speaking of limited inerrancy to have avoided any terminology that suggested a separation between faith and history. In 1884 John H. Newman had already charted a sounder course. Insisting upon the full inspiration of Scripture, yet finding unacceptable the doctrine of full Biblical inerrancy, Newman concluded that inerrancy was in effect extending to what was or was not material to God's purpose.[5] Rather than reducing Scripture to a single uniform level, Newman, as so many before him, sought a solution that would sustain the Bible's authority while accounting for the wide variety of linguistic and literary forms.

So long as divine inspiration is limited to matters of faith and morals and nothing besides, the criticisms raised by Warfield will have validity and force. But when the question is shifted from isolating spiritual and ethical matters to determining what the Biblical authors *intended* to teach as necessary for salvation, then a different set of arguments comes into play. Salvation is not robbed of its objective base because history and gospel are not artificially separated.[6] We can agree with Geisler that "many times it is impossible to deny the historical truth of a passage without simultaneously destroying its spiritual truth."[7] But at the same time we are free from reducing everything to a single level of infallibility. Since we are not judging inerrancy according to subject matter but according to *purpose*, we are permitted to weigh the importance of the historicity of Adam and Eve as opposed to the geographical location of the Garden of Eden.

The perennial difficulty with limited inerrancy is that it requires a hermeneutical principle to distinguish between what is necessary for salvation and what is incidental. Notwithstanding the tangled history of Church division over just this question, we must trust that we *are* able to make precisely this distinction. For if we cannot determine which doctrines and affirmations are necessary for salvation, then we are left sadly bewildered about what we should teach our children and what we say to the dying person, what we preach to our congregations and how to charge our missionaries.

We have reason to believe that the council fathers of Vatican II, acutely aware of the question of inerrancy,[8] framed its final draft in terms of a limited form of inerrancy without adopting a position of limited inspiration.

> Therefore, since everything asserted by the inspired authors or sacred writers must be held to be asserted by the Holy Spirit, it follows that the books of Scripture must be acknowledged as teaching firmly, faithfully, and without error *that truth* which God wanted put into the sacred writings *for the sake of our salvation*. Therefore "all Scripture is inspired by God and useful for teaching" (*Dei Verbum*, art. 11; emphasis added).

Choosing to avoid altogether such negative terms as "immune from all error," "inerrancy," or "an infallible Bible," the council spoke positively and specifically to that truth God wished to put there for our salvation. Inerrancy is no longer seen as an automatic effect resulting solely from the fact that the Church decided to canonize certain books. Not denying nor necessarily affirming that other kinds of truth are found in Scripture, whether historical or scientific, inerrancy is claimed only as it is the vehicle of a particular purpose. It should also be noted that Daniel Fuller in his defense of a limited form of inerrancy steered clear of the more traditional Westminster formula and chose to make his stand on "those statements that are able to make men wise unto salvation."[9]

## II.

It has been the standard assumption that any restriction of inerrancy logically entails a corresponding limitation of Biblical inspiration—namely, that some parts of Scripture are inspired while others are not, or that some are more inspired than others. Norman Geisler, following the usual evangelical position, asserts that "if the Bible does teach historical and factual matters, then it logically follows that whatever the Bible teaches about historical and factual matters is true."[10] Yet Geisler, being aware that, while everything contained in Scripture is inspired, not everything is necessarily what God teaches,"[11] qualifies his previous statement by adding that the interpreter is obligated to determine whether a passage is approving or merely reporting what is said. In other words, exegesis has a legitimate role when it distinguishes between what Scripture *intends* to teach as revelation and what it merely reports or transmits. Thus to the usual statement, "Whatever the Bible teaches is true and without error," I would only wish to add that the Scriptures are true and without error in what they *intend* to teach.[12] Is there a Biblical student among us who would deny that sound exegesis requires us to interpret each passage in light of its intended purpose?

In theory Geisler acknowledges this qualification of inerrancy when he begins by referring to cases where "historical and spiritual truths" are not inseparable. But he then rules it out when he continues: "They are logically (and/or psychologically) connected by the proposition: If the historical and factual truths of the Bible cannot be trusted as inerrant, then neither can the truths that are not directly connected to historical or factual matters."[13] But if logic and psychological feelings are all that support total inerrancy, then what about the honest Christian who reasons and feels just the opposite? Should he—following Geisler's assumptions—conclude that, since he cannot find Scripture entirely accurate concerning incidental factual matters, he should find untrustworthy what Scripture teaches concerning essential matters? It is unfortunately true that the conservative position would like to constrain all Christians into this "either-or" box. One of the tragedies of Christianity is that both liberals and evangelicals have tended to exclude persons who hold different opinions about inerrancy but affirm the inspiration and final authority of Scripture.

Undoubtedly the main reason why most evangelicals hesitate to limit inerrancy in principle is the nagging fear that the whole doctrine of inspiration will collapse.[14] If, as the consensus seems to be, the Scriptures do not explicitly or formally teach their own inerrancy, and inerrancy is only "logically entailed" in the doctrinal verses, then the sole question left is whether this is the only logical deduction.[15] The other equally logical and viable conclusion is that Scripture is inspired throughout but that inerrancy is limited to those matters necessary for our salvation. The scope of Biblical inspiration is much broader and varied than the scope of Biblical inerrancy. The latter is bounded as a result of the author's specific purpose in writing what he did. There were obviously times when one purpose took precedence over another, and in some instances a scientific historical description had to take second place to a literary existential description in order to teach a truth about God.[16] In other words inerrancy is a particular case of inspiration, but inerrancy is neither the end nor the sole consequence of inspiration. Plenary inspiration and limited inerrancy, when seen in this manner, are not logically inconsistent, as many would assert. In holding this position we are able to proclaim just as strongly as the most vehement conservative that inspiration guarantees that the Bible is true in whatever it intends to teach.

I have tenaciously avoided the term "limited inspiration" for the same reason I would avoid the problematic assertion that there are degrees of inspiration. The Spirit of God engulfed the totality of Scripture in such a way that discussion of degrees or levels of inspiration is downright misleading. Yet it is legitimate to say with the Reformers that while Scripture is equally inspired it is not equally profitable. Everything in Scripture was necessary for God's plan of salvation, but as that plan progressed and reached its culmination in Christ, some subjects, historical events, descriptions became less essential. The Holiness Code is no less inspired than the gospel of John, but if we had to choose between them we would have no difficulty deciding which is more important. The traditional monolithic conception of inspiration, almost invariably identified with plenary inspiration, simply cannot do justice to the Biblical phenomena. The rich variety of style, language, grammar, literary forms, author's intention, method of construction, leaves little doubt that all were inspired, but inspired differently. From the initial beginnings of oral traditions to the final compositions, God's Holy Spirit worked in an almost unthinkable diversity of ways. We can be thankful for this because mankind would be much the poorer if God spoke to us in a monolithic manner.

# III.

My third point of clarification, which is the most complex, concerns the imprecise way we use the word "inerrancy." When we speak of Scripture as being the inerrant word of God, several distinct levels of meaning might be implied.

1. *In its strictest and most rigid sense, inerrancy becomes identified and circumscribed by such qualifiers as immutable, absolute, and infallible.* The Biblical writers not only sufficiently stated what God intended but stated so perfectly what he willed that no further development is possible. The words of the authors are none other than the words of God. Thus no other words, regardless of time, can better express God's revelation of himself. Even if verbal dictation carries with it negative connotations, it is consistent with this understanding of inerrancy.

2. *The meaning to which most evangelicals subscribe is a middle position based upon a view of verbal inspiration.* Being inspired and superintended by the Holy Spirit, the authors of Scripture were so guided as to write those words necessary to sufficiently (but not necessarily defini-

tively) express the truth God willed. As I understand this interpretation of inerrancy and verbal inspiration, it does not decidedly rule out the possibility of further clarification by the Christian community.[17]

3. *Proponents of the third understanding of inerrancy would probably prefer a different word like "indefectibility."*[18] Inspiration and inerrancy do not turn on the individual words of Scripture but on the total reliability of the unified truth presented by the Bible. The absoluteness of Christian belief is not dependent upon unalterable concepts and immutable propositions but upon a continuity of development that guards against the dissolution of Christian commitment. Inspiration is not limited to the past but plays an essential role in the ongoing process of guaranteeing the essential integrity of Christianity.[19]

It is important to notice that all three definitions affirm the divine origin of the Bible, the truthfulness and trustworthiness of Scripture, the revelation of God in concepts and principles, and the intrinsic relationship between words and ideas. The latter is the most crucial and divisive. The debate is no longer whether the experience of faith can be separated from its verbal formulation but the consequence of the fact of their inseparability. The defenders of the first definition of inerrancy are in the difficult position of demonstrating how the Biblical writers, who were limited by the development of language and human conceptualization at their particular time, could so perfectly express God's truths that no later development or refinement is possible. To argue that the gift of inspiration permitted the writers to transcend their own cultural milieu in thought *and* expression must be supported by evidence that their vocabulary, grammar, literary forms, and conceptualization betray an advance era.

Since the second definition of inerrancy insists upon the immutability of only "primary words" and "basic concepts,"[20] the burden of evidence is not nearly as heavy. A degree of development is tolerated if not expected, both within the Biblical witness and after its finalization as the canon. What must be tested, therefore, is the complete adequacy of the basic truths and their verbal formulation.[21] Certainly a position of Biblical sufficiency and Biblical trustworthiness is much more defensible than total Biblical immutability.

The third definition of inerrancy carries with it another set of difficulties. Suffice it to say that since inspiration is understood as a continuing process, whether within the universal Church or the individual interpreter, the problem is not how to account for development but how to maintain scriptural authority within that development. For those of us who have felt that the admission of any form of development would destroy the objective basis for judging heresy, we have much to learn from

Roman Catholic scholars who are struggling with this question from another angle. I mention just two recent publications: Bruce Vawter, *Biblical Resources* (Westminster, 1972), and Jan Hendrik Walgrave, *Unfolding Revelation: The Nature of Doctrinal Development* (Westminster, 1972).

## Conclusion

By way of summary, three distinct arguments have been made. Past attempts to define the scope of inerrancy have unnecessarily circumscribed the question. Biblical inerrancy is not a quality unique to certain kinds of subject matter, such as faith and morals. Scripture is inerrant in whatever it intends to teach as essential for our salvation, whether it includes historical, scientific, biographical or theological materials. Undoubtedly not everything in Scripture is necessary for our salvation, and those that are cannot be determined by assumption or a priori but by their *context* and by the author's *principal* purpose.

Second, we argued that plenary inspiration and inerrancy are not synonymous or inseparable. Unequivocally the doctrinal verses teach the inspiration of Scripture as a whole. But to impose upon all Christians the deduction that plenary inspiration automatically guarantees total inerrancy is unwarranted. The gift of inspiration was granted not to insure the infallibility of every word and thought, though it did accomplish this in particular instances, but to secure a written Word that would forever be the singular instrument by which man learns and is confronted by God's will.

Third, we attempted to point out that inerrancy means different things to different people, the consequence being that each writer must take more care to define the meaning he has in mind. Even more importantly he must state clearly where he stands on the question of development. Roman Catholics are recognizing the necessity to reconcile the doctrine of infallibility with the actuality of human development. Evangelicals have the choice either to continue to react defensively or to advance positively a modified yet firm concept of inerrancy.

[1] The best discussion of the entire controversy is found in L. A. Loetscher, *The Broadening Church* (Philadelphia: University of Pennsylvania, 1957). H. P. Smith's full defense of the charges of heresy brought against him are recorded in *Inspiration and Inerrancy* (1893).

[2] The primary source of the limiting phrase, "the only infallible rule of faith and practice," is the Westminster Confession of Faith, chap. 1, art. 2; Larger Catechism, Q. 3. But probably even more important in its passage into the American tradition is its precise wording in the ordination questions of the Presbyterian Church in the U.S.A. (Form of Government, 19.4).

[3] B. B. Warfield, *Limited Inspiration* (Biblical and Theological Studies; Grand Rapids: Baker, 1961 [1894]).

[4] Smith, *Inspiration*, committed the common fallacy of assuming that a narrowing of Bib-

lical inerrancy means a parallel narrowing of Biblical inspiration (see below). Thus we have an explanation why Smith came up with clever interpretations of how the Biblical writers were inspired while Scripture as a whole was not.

[5]See his short treatise entitled "On the Inspiration of Scripture," which appeared as a pamphlet, then as an article in *The Nineteenth Century* (February 1884).

[6]C. E. Braaten, *History and Hermeneutics* (New Directions in Theology Today, Vol. 2; Philadelphia: Westminster, 1966) 26 ff., 37 ff. Here he reviews the objections to accepting a divorce between history and kerygma, *Historie and Geschichte*, etc.

[7]N. L. Geisler, "Theological Method and Inerrancy: A Reply to Arthur F. Holmes," *BETS* 11 (1968) 143.

[8]A discussion of the debate of the final wording of *Dei Verbum* is found in B. Vawter, *Biblical Inspiration* (Theological Resources; Philadelphia: Westminster, 1972) 143-148.

[9]D. P. Fuller, "Warfield's View of Faith and History," *BETS* 11 (1968) 75-83. Fuller, however, then proceeds to weaken his position when he says the doctrinal verses refer only to revealed knowledge (pp. 80-81). The term "revealed knowledge" is unfortunate because it again tends to unnecessarily restrict the scope of inerrancy. Fuller's distinction implies that Scripture contains both revelatory and nonrevelatory material; the latter, we are to assume, is not inspired? Finally, I find very weak his exegetical explanation that the author of the doctrinal verses had in mind such an artificial separation.

[10]Geisler, "Theologically" 142-143.

[11]For example, what Satan said to Jesus in the wilderness temptation or what Job's friends said to him in rebuttal.

[12]I certainly do not wish to imply that the change is a minor one. The interpreter is thereby obligated to go beyond the immediate literal meaning. He must begin to ask questions about the original meaning. The task is by no means simple, as J. G. Williams points out in "Exegesis-Eisegesis: Is There a Difference?", *Theology Today* 30 (October 1973) 218-227. It is interesting to note that in J. I. Packer's classic, *"Fundamentalism" and the Word of God* (Grand Rapids: Eerdmans, 1970), he argues for precisely this kind of limited inerrancy (see pp. 96-98).

[13]Geisler, "Theologically" 143.

[14]A close reading of the defense of inerrancy reveals that the doctrine is maintained "in principle" while in actuality it has been compromised by making a variety of restricted concessions. One can note, for example, the number of qualifying exceptions to a strict doctrine of inerrancy made by Clark Pinnock in *Biblical Revelation* (Chicago: Moody, 1971).

[15]I am only following Geisler's train of thought here because the acceptance of full Biblical inerrancy is not dependent solely upon how we interpret the doctrinal verses but upon an equal emphasis upon the historical-factual evidence Scripture presents. In the debate between Fuller and Pinnock, *JETS* 16 (Spring 1973) 67-69, I tend to side with Fuller, because Pinnock leaves the impression, just as Warfield did, of being indecisive about giving equal weight to the inductive method as it is employed by the historical-critical method.

[16]Whether it be Matthew's composition of the sermon on the mount, or the story of the tower of Babel, or the treatment of Jesus' feeding the multitude in John 6, we find other motives than pure historical ones at work. Redaction history has gone a long way in demonstrating that harmonization, even where it is possible, is not always the answer because it submerges the different literary means and ends of the individual writers. The very use of symbolic and mythological language means historical concerns were bracketed in order to teach a different kind of divine truth.

[17]Evangelicals have not clearly committed themselves on this important question. Are they willing to adopt the conservative Roman Catholic position, which states that revealed truths can change accidentally (in precision of expression) while remaining substantially unchanged? Thus development from the implicit to the explicit is allowed.

[18]Although this position has long been held by liberal Protestants, it is fast becoming identified with a number of prominent Roman Catholic scholars, such as Hans Küng, Edward Schillebeeckx, Karl Rahner, Leslie Dewart, Gregory Baum, John McKenzie and Avery Dulles (differences obviously exist between them).

[19]The idea of inerrancy as a process of continuity is well described by Paul de Voognt's statement: "Infallibility does not consist in a power to express irreformable formulas, but in

a power to reformulate throughout the centuries a number (a very limited number at that) of essential Christian truths." See *The Infallibility Debate* (ed. J. J. Kirvan; New York: Paulist, 1971) 33 n. 20.

[20]W. Künneth, *The Theology of the Resurrection* (St. Louis: Concordia, 1965) 56 (cf. pp. 67-68).

[21]The testing must take place in a twofold sense: (1) tested against internal criticism— namely, the development of God's revelation within Scripture must in no way contradict what has gone before it but adds to and supplements it; (2) tested against the development of language so it can be said that human history has added nothing that contradicts or substantially improves upon the original Biblical formulations, as for example the concept and wording of incarnation or resurrection.

# PARTIAL OMNISCIENCE: OBSERVATIONS ON LIMITED INERRANCY

## J. BARTON PAYNE

"Mr. Jones, who teaches at my school, is omniscient," says Johnny. "What, you mean he knows everything?" "Well, not exactly everything; but he does have an absolutely perfect knowledge of everything he's intended to teach—that is, third-grade multiplication tables."

Did somebody fudge in this dialogue? Theoretically, Johnny may be entitled to redefine the adjective "omniscient" so that it connotes a merely partial omniscience. But since in practice the word normally signifies an incommunicable divine attribute of knowledge—of knowledge without deficiency of any sort—we suspect that Johnny's assertion is a bit misleading. Similarly if inerrancy, as applied to the Bible, has normally been understood to signify its "*never* wandering into false teaching"[1] anywhere at all, did then Richard J. Coleman's article in *JETS* 17 (1974) 207-214 perhaps fudge in its advocacy of a "limited inerrancy"? Interaction with its proposals can lead to the following observations.

(1) We should all appreciate Coleman's antipathy toward H. P. Smith's view of "limited inspiration" and the writer's plea for the fully-inspired Scriptures—provided, of course, that one's definition of inspiration includes its divinely guaranteed truthfulness.[2] We can all appreciate his criticism of Daniel P. Fuller's attempt to limited inerrancy within Scripture to "revealed matters" and what Coleman sees as an artificial separation by Fuller of these passages from the supposedly nonrevelatory materials of Holy Writ. His disapproval of former Presbyterian U.S.A. attempts to limit Biblical authority to certain kinds of subject matter—that is, to faith and morals, separated from history—is similarly refreshing. Finally, his clarification of the various ways in which inerrancy is currently being defined, or redefined, is helpful,[3] together with the bibliographical detail with which his notes abound.

(2) Yet at certain points, particularly in its criticisms of Norman L.

Geisler,[4] one observes that this article in favor of "Reconsidering 'Limited Inerrancy' " seems to becloud issues rather than clarify them. It uses Geisler's acknowledgment, that the Bible does not teach everything it transmits, as a springboard for positing only a partial inerrancy. But Geisler's acknowledgment concerns speeches that the Biblical writers themselves abhor, such as words of Satan tempting Jesus (Matt 4:9) or of Sapphira lying to Peter (Acts 5:8), while the article's conclusion, drawn from it, concerns so-called "incidental factual matters," but ones that the Biblical writers positively assert, such as the two animals being present at the triumphal entry (Matt 21:2-7) or the mustard plant's having the smallest seeds that were sown in the soil of Palestine (Mark 4:31). Sound exegesis of the former passages hardly justifies a questioning of the latter. The article under discussion also misuses Geisler's acknowledgment that "historical and spiritual truths are not inseparable"—that is, that there might not have to be an historically accurate Bible, or even an inspired Bible of any kind, for Jesus to save men[5]—and his recognition that inerrancy is "logically entailed" in Biblical revelation. Both of these it uses as a basis for postulating a Biblical authority that is "limited to those matters necessary for our salvation." But when Coleman's article claims that inerrancy is "only" logically or psychologically entailed it fails to deal with what Geisler means by logic—namely, the force of the evidence that Jesus and the apostles did in fact teach the Bible's total historical reliability,[6] whether in the abstract they *had* to teach this or not.

(3) One's primary observation, however, concerns a gap in the article's own logic. For it shifts almost unconsciously from the basic evangelical position of accepting "what Scripture *intends* to teach"[7] to the more limited position of accepting only "what the Biblical authors *intended* to teach as necessary for salvation." And it never really defends this shift. It does argue that it is possible to distinguish "which doctrines and affirmations are necessary for salvation." True enough—but does an ability to make such a distinction justify one's disregard of those other doctrines that are not thus necessary?[8] It argues that the primary goal of Scripture is to make us wise unto salvation. True enough (John 20:31; 2 Tim 3:15)—but does this then deny the reality of other goals that are found in Scripture, such as making us wise about apocalyptic future history (Rev 1:1)? Or about that which is now past history (Dan 2:28)? Or about any history, together with what we can learn from its factuality (Gen 8:21; 39:9)? Or about things in general, "to make you know the certainty of the words of truth" (Prov 22:21)? It may be well and good to deny inerrancy in respect to "what was not material to God's purpose," but then what is one's basis for determining God's purpose or for deciding what constitutes his words? Is it human judgment about the trustworthiness of the phenomena of Scripture as sifted by the historico-critical method, or is it

Christ's judgment, as portrayed on the ETS seal, that "the Scripture cannot be broken" (John 10:35)? All its initial protestation to the contrary notwithstanding, the article seems to have ended up with a renewed separation between faith and history (at least, certain parts of the Bible's history) and a renewed enthronement of reason over faith (at least, over the NT's doctrine of the truthfulness of the OT). So would it not have been more straightforward for Coleman simply to have affirmed the errancy of Scripture, rather than to "reconsider limited inerrancy," thereby having to redefine the term inerrancy into the exact opposite of its normal meaning?

"But whatever ought to have been done," some will say, "what are we going to do now? Like it or not, men who doubt that the Bible 'never wanders into false teaching' are today affirming Biblical inerrancy [perhaps because of some vested interest in the term, such as the Roman Catholics, who have been committed to it by the dogmas of past popes]. What are the alternatives?" Three possibilities appear. (1) Everybody could give up inerrancy in fact. Then no one would have to keep using this (confessedly embarrassing) term in theory, and it could be relegated to the history books, like *massēbâ* or *taurobolium*. The catch to this approach is that as long as people keep believing that Jesus lives, his words about the unbreakable Scripture keep living too. (2) Those who are committed to inerrancy could so refine and amplify the term that it would continue to identify only those who believe all that the Bible has to say. For example, a doctrinal basis that has been advanced for the proposed North American Presbyterian and Reformed Council reads like this:

> [That the member churches] be committed to the total inerrancy of the autographs of Scripture, both in their central teaching on the saving revelation of God in Jesus Christ, and in all their other affirmations, whether on history, on cosmology, or on their own literary origins.[9]

Perhaps the ETS should tighten up its present, simple, doctrinal affirmation? It now reads: "The Bible alone, and the Bible in its entirety, is the Word of God written and therefore inerrant in the autographs." It might add: "—that is, it contains no falsehood, except in the case of quoted assertions that are opposed by the immediate context, such as the words of Sapphira in Acts 5:8." Or it might read something like the Council statement quoted above, so as to insure that the membership remain true to the entirety of the Bible. But is this necessary and/or desirable? (3) We can carry on as we do now, but making increasingly clear by unremitting research, interaction and publication what true ("unlimited") inerrancy is and must be. Biblical Christianity has always suffered from parasitic movements that would usurp its terminology and enter into its heritage, and today's believers can never finally avoid this, however much they may refine or sharpen their doctrinal bases. Furthermore, the implications of inerrancy are so clear that most negatively-minded critics react to it with undisguised hostility[10] (witness the deletion of inerrancy from the recently revised doctrinal statement of Fuller Theological Seminary).[11] Johnny may talk for a while about his partially omniscient Mr. Jones, but he will not fool many and will soon probably give up the term himself as an impossible fudging—just like limited inerrancy.

[1]K. S. Kantzer's definition; cf. *BETS* 10 (1967) 4.

[2]J. B. Payne, *Theology of the Older Testament* (Grand Rapids: Zondervan, 1962) 512. But this is precisely the provision that, as Coleman points out, modern Roman Catholicism (and he himself) refuses to accept, when it combines a belief in total inspiration with an assured truthfulness that extends only to what "God wanted put into the sacred writings for the sake of our salvation" (Vatican II, *Dei Verbum*, art. 2).

[3]Though his description of the strict view of inerrancy lapses into caricature when he refuses to recognize the distinction between limited and yet absolute truth and complete— i.e, undevelopable—truth. The fact that "the words of the [Biblical] authors are none other than the words of God," and as truthful as if God himself spoke them, need by no means imply that no other words could ever express God's revelation better or more fully (p. 212).

[4]In *BETS* 11 (1968) 139-146.

[5]J. B. Payne, "*Apeitheō*: Current Resistance to Biblical Inerrancy," *BETS* 10 (1967) 8.

[6]Geisler, *BETS* 11, p. 143; cf. F. C. Grant's widely quoted conclusion that in the NT "it is everywhere taken for granted that Scripture is trustworthy, infallible, and inerrant," *Introduction to New Testament Thought* (Nashville: Abingdon-Cokesbury, 1950) 75.

[7]Cf. Coleman again: "Inspiration guarantees that the Bible is true in whatever it intends to teach."

[8]Similarly, that we are able to decide which things in Scripture are "more important" provides no brief for dismissing the less important, or of castigating the retention of them in our belief as entailing a monolithic concept of truth. Instead, it should be clear that the theory that the Bible consists partly of truth to be believed and partly of error to be disbelieved is not NT teaching. It has been imposed on Scripture from without.

[9]Such wording reflects the troubles that have arisen in recent years within the Reformed Ecumenical Synod, with the proven insufficiency of its more general assertion of Biblical authority.

[10]Payne, "*Apeitheō*" 4.

[11]See *Christianity Today*, May 7, 1971.

# Problems For Limited Inerrancy[1]

## VERN S. POYTHRESS

Richard Coleman's recent article, "Reconsidering 'Limited Inerrancy,' "[2] presents for our consideration some new positions on the inerrancy of Scripture. I should like to respond with some observations in defense of a more traditional view. My observations are of two kinds. First, almost all if not all the proffered formulations of "limitations" on inerrancy contain some disturbing vagueness. Second, limited inerrancy has some problems to face of which its defenders as yet show little awareness.

## I. Vaguenesses About the "Limitations"

Coleman's article is vague about just how far the limitations extend. Most of the time he can be interpreted either as defending a traditional view or as making enormous concessions. Let us see how this works.

1. The first position that Coleman presents in an approving light is something like the following: The Bible is inerrant in those things that the Biblical authors intend to teach as necessary for salvation.[3]

A major difficulty here is with the phrase "necessary for salvation." This could mean a number of things. (a) A Biblical teaching is necessary for salvation if no fallen human being can be saved without believing this teaching. (b) A Biblical teaching is necessary for salvation if God saw fit to record the teaching for the sake of salvation. (c) A Biblical teaching is necessary for salvation if, in some circumstances, not believing it puts one's salvation in question. Still other interpretations are possible.

Under condition (a), none of the NT is necessary for salvation, since people were saved before it was written. Some of the NT *teaching* may be necessary, insofar as it simply repeats teaching in the OT. Moreover, since some people have been saved by reading the gospel of Mark alone or the gospel of John alone, only what is common to both is necessary. Thus interpretation (a) makes enormous concessions. Under condition (c), everything the Bible teaches is necessary for salvation, since a person who believed that the Bible was unconditionally God's Word and knew that it taught $x$, yet out of sheer stubbornness refused to acknowledge $x$, would thereby raise questions about whether his relation to God was a saving one.

What Coleman later says is more consistent with interpretation (b). But this would normally be put, "For the sake of our salvation."[4] Let us formulate it thus:

2. The Bible is inerrant in what the Biblical authors intended to teach for the sake of our salvation.

"For the sake of our salvation" is still unclear. "Salvation" could have in view either (a) those things centrally related to establishing and maintaining our relation to Christ, or (b) everything that obviously and decidedly helps us in our life, both in relation to God and neighbor, or (c) everything that can morally affect any attitudes, dispositions or actions. Sometimes Coleman apparently has (a) in mind (for example, where he asks what we say to the dying person). In that case the scope may be quite narrow. Generally we do not talk to the dying about Adam and Eve, Josiah's reign, the virgin birth, or Paul's instructions concerning elders. Under (c) the whole Bible is included since, of anything that the Bible says, we may decide to believe or disbelieve it. And our belief has a moral component to it. Moreover, incidentals in the Bible are instructive because they show us that, for the sake of our salvation, God speaks about all kinds of things, even incidentals.

3. Let us therefore try a third variation: The Bible is inerrant in what the Biblical authors intended to teach.[5]

Our first reaction to this may be favorable. "Ah," we say, "surely now this is saying what advocates of inerrancy have always said." Indeed, as redoubtable a defender of inerrancy as Clark Pinnock can explain his view in similar terms. Pinnock talks about inerrancy of "the intended teaching of each passage of Scripture."[6] Does Coleman agree with Pinnock? Perhaps. But having had a taste of the dangers of vagueness, we take a second look.

There is vagueness in "intend." (a) There is evidence that the Biblical authors did not always fully grasp what they said (1 Pet 1:10-11). How can we tell in such cases what was their "intention"? (b) Bultmann could claim that, centrally, the NT writers intended to teach the possibility of authentic existence through the kērygma. But the bodily resurrection in

1 Corinthians 15 is not *per se* included in the "intention." (c) Intention could be interpreted broadly to include what the Biblical authors do in fact succeed in teaching. (This is what Pinnock means, as he makes clear in a footnote.)

4. Consider also another formulation: The Bible is inerrant in what it intends to teach.

This has the same difficulty as position 3, compounded by the fact that, since the Bible is not a person, saying that "the Bible intends" is slightly metaphorical.

5. To avoid the problem of "intention," we can try the following formulation: The Bible is inerrant in what the human authors teach.

Here there is still a problem with "teach." "Teach" is normally used of a somewhat formal, structured situation where the teacher is pretty self-conscious about what he asserts. But it can be used more loosely, as when we say that Paul teaches that Demas has deserted him (2 Tim 4:10). Thus as extremes we could have: (a) The Bible is inerrant in what the human authors most formally and explicitly set themselves to teach (Gal 1:11; Prov 1:8 ff.; 1 Cor 15:33 ff.; and a few other passages[7]); (b) the Bible is inerrant in what it says.

6. A safer formulation, therefore, is the following: The Bible is inerrant in what it says is the case.

This position is an alternative that Coleman does not mention. But I think that it comes closest to what advocates of inerrancy have in mind. There is still a certain vagueness in the expressions "inerrant" and "is the case." But a sympathetic reading of position 6 leads to reasonable treatment of the problems. It means the "There is no God" is false and that "The fool says in his heart, 'There is no God' " is true. It also allows Biblical writers to paraphrase, summarize, translate, use their own favorite words, and use metaphor, hyperbole and the like. It allows for historical telescoping (Matt 9:18; cf. Luke 8:41, 49) and for omission of pedantic qualifications (Mark 1:5). It allows, in other words, that Biblical writers use ordinary language rather than hyper-precise language. It does *not* allow us to say that Demas in fact had good reasons for leaving Paul (2 Tim 4:10), or that Zimri did *not* reign in Tirzah (1 Kgs 16:15), or that Noah sent out birds only twice, not four times (Gen 8:7-12).

Part of the attractiveness of positions 1-5, I submit, is that they can be construed in a way virtually identical to position 6, *or* in a way that allows enormous concessions to the Bible's trustworthiness. Thus they can give us a comfortable illusion. On the one hand, we appear to maintain what the pre-modern Church and indeed the Bible itself has always maintained about its trustworthiness (the tight interpretation of 1-5); on the other hand, we are able to make peace with the literature of modern critical scholarship (the loose interpretation of 1-5).

This form of argument I call "argument by slipperiness." It is remarkable that such slipperiness should occur in an article that concludes by expressly saying that "each writer must take more care to define the meaning [of inerrancy] that he has in mind. Even more importantly he must state clearly where he stands on the question of development." But it is less remarkable when one realizes that argument by slipperiness seems to be standard procedure among evangelicals who advocate "limitations" on Biblical authority. The word "infallibility" was greased up and made to slide around some time ago. "Error" is greased up by those who move from the "errors" of approximate figures, paraphrases, quotations of falsehoods, and departures from modern literary and historiographical conventions to the "errors" of historical, geographical and scientific mistakes and (sometimes) moral blemishes. "Revelation" can slide from matters included under the classic idea of inspiration to matters relating to illumination, and from there even to matters involving learning anything that one did not know before. Or "revelation" may be confined to only those things that we could not come to know by ordinary means.[8]

After so much encounter with slipperiness, the unconvinced reader begins to wonder. Is slipperiness the sophisticated way of bridging a chasm that straightforward people know cannot be bridged? In other words, can one have his cake and eat it too?

## II. Problems for Limited Inerrancy

The first problem for limited inerrancy, then, is to define itself, to demonstrate that the chasm between ordinary inerrancy and ordinary fallibility can be bridged.

But to say where the chasm is takes some doing. So let us begin with some easy observations. Generally speaking, when God speaks to someone or something he speaks in a context formed by other things that he says and does as well as by the person or thing to which he speaks. His words have, as it were, a contextual coloring. Hence, in the case of men a thorough understanding of what he says in a Biblical passage demands attention to the historical and linguistic context of the passage. One asks, "What language is it in? To whom did God speak? Who is the human author? What situation were the addressees in?" And so forth. The sophisticated interpreter therefore approaches the text with a linguistic-historical framework, to endeavor to bridge the cultural and temporal gap between himself and the original words. Textual criticism as well as many other techniques are included. The framework may of course have to be modified on the basis of what the passage is found to say. Everyone grants that from time to time there are difficulties with this approach, and disagreements may arise. But in more respects the difficulties are not qualitatively different from the difficulties involved in understanding a contemporary document coming from another cultural setting. Here, then, we have a procedure of grammatical-historical exegesis such as the ordinary view of inerrancy allows. Let us call this procedure "using a framework."

But those who speak of "limitations" on inerrancy appear to want something more. They are saying that, at certain points, the human reader must be prepared to encounter "mistakes" or "errors" or "peccadilloes" in certain nonessential matters that the Bible says are the case. Various attempts have been made to circumscribe what is nonessential—none very successful. Let us call these nonessential matters where the Bible makes errors or at least does not say things in quite the right way "muck." I know that "muck" is an emotionally laden term. I doubt whether it is more emotionally laden than "error." At any rate, it will perhaps help to convey to the limited inerrantist how things really look to the opposing party.

According to this view, then, the Bible contains muck, but it is a *very* small amount in proportion to the clear and pure teaching. To avoid swallowing the muck the reader must use a sieve, which filters out only those Biblical statements that lead to intolerable historical, scientific or (perhaps) moral difficulties. Drawing the line as to just what is "intolerable" is hard, but let us assume that it can be done. Even if a position of limited inerrancy is dressed up in fancy language, I think that it boils down in practice to some such sieve procedure.

I will admit that the boundary between using a framework and using a sieve is not always clear. There may be some points on which people will disagree about which is being done. For example, take the quotation in Heb 2:7 from Ps 8:5. Did the original of Ps 8:5 read "little less than God" as in the MT or "little less than the angels" as in the LXX and Heb 2:7? Suppose A argues that the MT is original. B claims that this is using a sieve to exclude the implication of Heb 2:7. A replies that, within the framework of ordinary-language quotation (as opposed to technical and pedantic quotation), Heb 2:7 can quote from the LXX without necessarily claiming that the LXX goes back to the original more faithfully than the MT. I side with party A in this case. But I am not greatly disturbed by B, provided he understands that A is at least trying not to use a sieve.

As a second example, take the mention of Jannes and Jambres in 2 Tim 3:8. A argues that within the framework of ordinary communication Paul simply makes use of traditional names for convenience, without a claim for their phonetic authenticity. B claims that A is using a sieve. Again I side with A.

A third example will show how the idea of a framework can be abused. A argues that Matthew and Luke do not claim that the virgin birth really happened as described. They use the stories only to illustrate the greatness of Jesus. Within the framework of first-century culture, this was acceptable. B replies that Biblical writers can distinguish fact from fiction as easily as we can (Luke 1:1-4; John 21:23; Gal 1:20; 2 Pet 1:16). When a fictional narrative parable is presented, the context tells us *that* it is fictional. In this case, B is the one who has really understood what "using a framework" means.

The important question is this: Have advocates of "limitation" thought that they could move easily from the use of a framework to the use of a sieve? Have they been deceived by a fuzzy boundary into believing that there is no boundary? Has argument by slipperiness been exploited to make this transition? The temptation is great because the whole liberal scholarly world slides easily from framework to sieve with no detectable jar. Both are called "grammatical-historical exegesis" and "critical method."

Of course, advocates of "limitation" may claim that they have never intended to do anything more than use a framework. In charity, I will grant that this may be true in some cases. Some "limiters" may be simply confused or vague. But we must ask the question: Is the claim to use a framework another case of slipperiness, where now the idea of "framework" has itself been made slippery? Many people cannot but feel that there is some slipperiness here. Why are "limiters" so addicted to using language ambiguous or vague enough to allow for a sieve, when all they really want is a framework? Why do they even bring up the issue at all, since representative evangelicals have always seen the need for a framework?

Now let us assume (for the sake of argument) that there is muck in the Bible and see some of the difficulties this causes. In the first place, it comes into immediate conflict with the teaching of Scripture: "The words of the Lord are pure words: as purified in a furnace of earth, purified seven times" (Ps 12:6). "I have seen an end of all perfection: but thy commandment is exceedingly broad" (Ps 119:96). "Every word of God is pure" (Prov 30:5). More passages could be cited, but the arguments of this kind are already well known. One possible reply is that these passages are themselves contaminated with muck. This objection represents a serious alternative that might actually be taken by many liberals. But it is not my purpose to deal with it. As far as I know, advocates of limited inerrancy do not want to escape in this way.

But direct conflict with Scripture is not the only difficulty that limited inerrancy faces. It faces other difficulties due to the overarching role of God's words. One significant point made in the Bible is that other things *besides* the Bible are God's words. God's word includes (a) words of Jesus not recorded in the Bible (John 21:24-25), (b) the direct speech of God to

*179*

Abraham, Moses and others when he appeared to them ("personal address"),[9] (c) God's word of power by which he rules the universe (Heb 1:3; cf. Ps 33:6), and (d) the Son, the second Person of the trinity (John 1:1; Rev 19:13). If the Bible, the Word of God, contains muck, perhaps some of these other words contain muck too. How can we be sure that they do not? Several positions are possible: (1) Muck (or the possibility of muck) is in fact introduced only when there is a human intermediary such as Moses or Paul. God's words of personal address and God's ruling word of power are always and infallibly free of muck. (2) Muck may occur even in God's words of personal address to Abraham, Moses, etc. (3) Muck may occur even in God's words in the intratrinitarian communication and in God the Son.[10]

All these positions have difficulties of a severe kind. The most serious is position 3. To be sure, we must remember that the muck consists only in complete nonessentials, in details of the minutest kind. But, nevertheless, the conclusion is inescapable: God himself is mucked up. The Persons of the trinity do not communicate exhaustively. Consequently a separation is introduced in the trinity, and one obtains incipient tritheism. If the Son alone has muck, one descends to a form of Arianism.

Let us see where position 2 leads. Can muck occur also in God's words to other creatures besides men? Only men are fallen, it is true, but creation is under a curse. And one must remember the possibility that muck is introduced by man's ignorance as well as by his sin. Other creatures are still more ignorant than man, so may we suppose that there is more muck? Perhaps, then, there is muck scattered through the word of power by which God upholds the universe. If the clear passages speaking of the purity of the Bible do not exclude muck, much less can we exclude muck from these other words, which are much less essential to salvation.

But see how disastrous this is. Nothing at all happens apart from God's will (Eph 1:11), or apart from God's command (Lam 3:37-38; cf. Ps 147:15; Heb 1:3). Hence *everything* gets contaminated with muck.

Now suppose that L (a limited inerrantist) claims that Luke has introduced muck in Acts 5:37 by confusing the order in which Gamaliel placed Theudas and Judas the Galilean. L bases himself on Josephus. Josephus may have erred in the ordinary way, as humans do. But he may also have erred in an extraordinary way—namely, the word of God ordering the universe may have introduced muck into Josephus' researches. In fact, muck in *this* word of God is far more likely than muck in the more "essential" word of God in Acts 7. Similarly, Gamaliel may have been mucked up.

But there are worse possibilities as well. Muck may have been introduced into L's perception of the page of Acts that he is reading. Muck may have been introduced into his memory of Josephus. Muck may have been introduced so that he does not know what a contradiction is. Muck may have been introduced so that a demon has deluded him at this one point. Surely these are matters of nonessential character. Surely here, if anywhere, God could be expected not to be so careful about whether every last jot and tittle of his word that orders the universe is correct. The name of this view is skepticism.

Let us, then, consider position 1. Most of the problems here are well known. (a) Position 1 seems to do injustice to Exod 20:18-20 and Deut 5:22-33. These passages explain the transition from God's word of personal address at Mount Sinai (reported in Exod 20:1-17) to God's word through Moses, both oral and written. On the surface of things they imply that God's words did not lose any purity, veracity, power, authority or inerrancy by being mediated through Moses rather than being "direct." But position 1 would have us believe otherwise. Position 1 would have us believe that the Israelites, in asking for Moses' mediation, made a choice that committed them to the introduction of muck. Many a servant of God would rather die than have this happen to God's word. Yet Israel is approved for her choice.

Let us pass on to some other difficulties. (b) Position 1 seems to involve a view of limited inspiration or, rather, noninspiration. It denies that the words of Moses to Israel are really, without qualification, the words of God. The "real" word of God is the word of personal address to Moses. But this contradicts the testimony of Scripture. (c) The exegetical arguments of Benjamin B. Warfield, Edward J. Young and others remain to be answered.[11] (d) It does not seem to do justice to Psalm 119. Can we ourselves conscientiously adopt the psalmist's attitude now that we know that there is muck and do not know just how far it extends?

But beyond this, there is an additional difficulty. It appears that sometimes angels may be employed in executing some words of God by which he rules the universe (Ps 103:20-21; cf. Dan 10:13; 11:1; 12:1). The introduction of finite, nonomniscient intermediaries raises questions. Does their execution of God's word introduce muck? If so, where? Is there muck in Josephus' researches? In my memory? And so on. If so, we are back in a position as bad as position 2.

There are also ethical difficulties. God's speech is in certain ways the standard to which human speech ought to conform. One can easily argue that if God's own speech makes a "mistake" about Theudas and Judas, then we are permitted to make the same "mistake" in our speech. Perhaps we even *ought* to make it. So let us go ahead and say that Judas followed Theudas. In fact, let us say so boldly and without fear. No one can blame us or reproach us for doing what *God* does.[12]

There are two lessons to be learned from this exercise. First, it is easy for the guns of criticism employed by limited inerrantists to be selectively aimed at the Bible, far more than at their modern environment, their own techniques, their own ethical standards, their own persons, or their own language. It is easy to imitate the bulk of critical scholarship that practices selective aim. But one wonders whether it is conducive to a healthy spiritual attitude.

Second, muck can be conclusively found in the Bible only by those who have some source that is in some respect more free of muck than the Bible itself. In other words, they must have a superior source of revelation. Of course it will be claimed that the source is superior only in certain specific, minute areas of historical or scientific detail. Now we agree that a person can know more about certain areas of history and science than what the Bible says. But can one be sure that it is muck-free? Sure enough to detect muck in the Bible? It appears, moreover, that a person must have purer ethics than the Bible in order to ethically justify speaking about the Bible's muck. The reader must judge whether this can succeed.

All this leads us to the topic of "development" in revelation and/or inspiration, discussed in Coleman's third section. As one might expect, Coleman's argument for "development" is another case of slipperiness. He offers us three positions (p. 212). The first position is that "no further development is possible [beyond Scripture]." This could mean: (a) From the time of the completion of the canon onward, God gives to men no new words, in addition to the Bible, which have the same inspired status, purity, authority, etc.; (b) from the time of the completion of the canon until the parousia or its immediate precursors, God gives to men no new words, in addition to the Bible, which have the same inspired status; (c) in the period mentioned in (b), no one comes to have an ethics higher than the ethics that the Bible holds forth; (d) in the period (b), no literary work is produced that says what God wanted to say in (for example) Esther better than Esther said it;[13] (e) in the period (b), no individual or church comes to understand what God says in the Bible better than the apostle Paul understood it; (f) in the period (b), no individual or church comes to understand what God says in the Bible, even at a single point, better than the apostle Paul; (g) in the period (b), no individual or church comes to understand what God says in the Bible better than his or their predecessors; (h) in the period (b), no translations appear communicating the Bible to a given cultural group in a fashion better than the original language alone would have; (i) in the period (b), no men learn things not recorded in the Bible. And so on and on.

Several types of distinctions need to be made. There is a distinction between development within the canon (God teaches new things when Paul writes Romans) and development outside the canon (supposed new teachings beyond the canon). There is a distinction between development in our subjective understanding of the text and development in the objective text. Between effectiveness for modern communications and effectiveness as a final standard. Between change in language and improvement in language. Between the amount of teaching that God might, in the abstract, have given us and what he in fact gives us.

Most if not all of these distinctions Coleman slides over. The reader who returns to his article will easily see that Coleman (rightly) dismisses in a few lines positions like (f), (g) and (h). But he imagines himself to have shown the difficulties of (b), (c) and (d).

Anyone who has abandoned (b) and (c) is in serious trouble. He has, I think, virtually denied the *sola scriptura* of the Reformation. I would like to believe that Coleman does not go this far. But he says:

> Since inspiration is understood as a continuing process, whether within the universal Church or the individual interpreter, the problem is not how to account for that development but how to maintain scriptural authority within that development.

What shall we say to this? I was surprised at first to see that Coleman introduced the idea of continuing inspiration. I supposed that it loaded the position of limited inerrancy with an unnecessary and odious burden. But now it seems to me that Coleman has real insight. In order to detect muck in the Bible one must be in a superior position of "development." Like the critic of Luke 6:40-42, one must be without muck in order to see the muck.

Here arises an even more serious problem: How can the Lordship of Christ still remain effective? With the abandonment of (c), the advancing moral consciousness of the Christian can, at crucial points, be opposed to what the Bible only "seems" to say (but not "teach"?). With the abandonment of (b), the advancing knowledge of our scholars or our "prophets" can, at crucial points, be opposed to what the Bible only "appears" to hold. If we have no words that are beyond challenge, there is no rule that we *must* obey, and the Lordship of Christ becomes a sounding gong and a clanging cymbal.[14] We still cite the Bible as the voice of the greatest religious and moral experts, but it is *we* who ultimately decide where and how they are experts. We will acknowledge that Christ is Lord, provided that this takes place in a way that does not cause too great embarrassment to the modern world and to our modern notions.

A final lesson, then, is this. Attempting to modify significantly the doctrine of inspiration is playing with fire. The clumsiness of those who have so far attempted it does not inspire confidence. Nor does their clumsiness tend to increase our confidence in the superior purity of their modern sources of revelation.

Some may wonder why I do not say more about all the particular cases of supposed muck in the Bible. I have nothing special to contribute. Most of the major problems have received possible explanations during the last one hundred years.

I will say this. I do not think that the problems will all go away or the chasm between fallibility and ordinary inerrancy be bridged. Does that mean that ordinary inerrancy is condemned to defensiveness and unsatisfying argument? No. It is helpful sometimes to remember that questions of inerrancy can be seen as a spiritual battle as well as a scholarly nicety. Those who hold for ordinary inerrancy do not have a more difficult trial than Abraham had when he was commanded to sacrifice Isaac. Abraham was faced with a seeming conflict in God's word. According to Heb 11:19, he arrived at a tentative explanation for it in God's power to raise the dead. One wonders what the limited inerrantist of Abraham's day would have said. Would he have been tempted to say that Abraham's resurrection explanation was incredibly improbable and farfetched and that in view of the possibility of muck Abraham had best call the whole project off? Perhaps, when we meet with difficulties in the Bible, we ought to rejoice that in some small way we can demonstrate that we are followers of Abraham rather than his detractors.

[1]In composing this article I have profited from suggestions and criticisms from Don A. Carson, Wayne A. Grudem, John J. Hughes, and other colleagues at Tyndale House, Cambridge, England.

[2]*JETS* 17 (1974) 207-214.

[3]The actual words of Coleman are as follows:

"But when the question is shifted from isolating spiritual and ethical matters to determining what the Biblical authors *intended* to teach as necessary for salvation, then a different set of arguments comes into play [and the limited inerrantists can make a better case]." Later he adds:

"The perennial difficulty with limited inerrancy is that it requires a hermeneutical principle to distinguish between what is necessary for salvation and what is incidental."

[4]The phrase "for the sake of our salvation" appears in an approving quotation from Vatican II.

[5]Coleman says, "Thus to the usual statement, 'Whatever the Bible teaches is true and without error,' I would only wish to add that the Scriptures are true and without error in what they *intend* to teach." This is more like position 4 than position 3.

[6]C. H. Pinnock, "Limited Inerrancy: A Critical Appraisal and Constructive Alternative," in *God's Inerrant Word: An International Symposium on the Trustworthiness of Scripture* (ed. J. W. Montgomery; Minneapolis: Bethany Fellowship, 1974) 148.

[7]This can easily lead to absurdities if it is pushed. Does John teach only John 20:31, using the rest "merely" as fallible supportive illustration? Does Luke in Luke 1:1-4 claim to teach all of Luke-Acts? Will we in that case prefer Luke to Matthew and Mark when we confront synoptic problems?

[8]I do not object to vagueness as such. Absolutely perfect precision is not only unnecessary but impossible. I object to the use of vagueness to slide over the crucial differences.

[9]I owe to John M. Frame an appreciation for the significance of personal address, as well as some of the other ideas in this article.

[10]Still other positions are possible. These three are chosen simply as illustrations of the problems.

[11]I am thinking especially of B. B. Warfield, *The Inspiration and Authority of the Bible* (ed. S. G. Craig; Philadelphia: Presbyterian and Reformed, 1948) and E. J. Young, *Thy*

*Word Is Truth* (Grand Rapids: Eerdmans, 1957). For a fuller bibliography of works in defense of inerrancy see J. W. Montgomery, ed., *God's Inerrant Word.*

[12]This argument must not be used unfairly. God, speaking through Paul, does not always quote the OT verbatim. But *we* are not free to paraphrase in a framework of literary convention that leads people to expect verbatim quotation. So too if God deliberately makes a mistake in one situation, it does not necessarily mean that *we* have the liberty to make a deliberate mistake in another situation where mistakes are not tolerated. It does not *necessarily* mean that, but still it *may* mean that. And it may mean that we should tell people to tolerate our deliberate errors. It may mean, in fact, a complete breakdown of communication. That is unsettling.

[13]There is a difficulty here with "better." Better in what sense? A translation might be better for the purpose of communicating to a group that did not know Hebrew. What we want is something like, "Better as a standard to which one may return as final court of appeal" (see the Westminster Confession of Faith 1.10).

[14]See the remarks on Lordship in J. Frame, "Scripture Speaks for Itself," in *God's Inerrant Word*, pp. 182-185.

# REDACTION CRITICISM AND THE GREAT COMMISSION: A CASE STUDY TOWARD A BIBLICAL UNDERSTANDING OF INERRANCY

## GRANT R. OSBORNE

A great deal of misunderstanding about redaction criticism exists among evangelicals. Too often we have accepted the negative criteria of the radical critics as the only mode within which redactional work may be done. But redaction criticism, properly used, is a positive tool for Biblical research, and evangelicals should be in the forefront of research into its constructive possibilities. The purpose of the present study is to apply redactional techniques to the great commission (Matt 28:16-20) in order to understand that pericope better. We shall then examine the implications for a Biblical understanding of inerrancy by stressing the attitude of the Biblical writers themselves to the question rather than the twentieth-century philosophical approach we employ all too often.

## I. A REDACTIONAL STUDY OF THE GREAT COMMISSION

Matthew 28:16-20 not only concludes the resurrection narrative and the book of Matthew as a whole but, many believe,[1] also summarizes the message of the first gospel itself. Otto Michel et al.[2] argue that the heading "great commission" is inappropriate, since the passage is mainly an epiphany or exaltation story directed to the new status of the Risen One. However, an exegesis of the passage bears out the traditional title. The early Church must have thought that the message of vv 18-20 centered on its universal mission, since the comments before and after v 19 center on that verse and provide the means (v 18) and the encouragement (v 20) for accomplishing the task.

The *Traditionsgeschichte* of the passage shows some evidence of a traditional origin, but also a great deal of Matthean themes and language throughout. In the introductory section there is some evidence of tradition in the phrase "to which Jesus had appointed them" (v 16), for *tassō* is not Matthean and the phrase is probably taken from tradition,[3] alluding to an event not recorded in the gospels. Also *hoi de edistasan* (v 17) favors a traditional source, because Matthew normally avoids critical comments regarding the disciples.

Although the message itself contains a large proportion of Matthean phrases, there are indications of tradition. Many of the terms, such as "give," "authority" and "heaven and earth," are just as frequent among the other evangelists and may not be Matthean. The command to "disciple" is expressed in Matthean style but may reflect tradition, since there are parallels in the other resurrection narratives (Luke 24:47; John 20:21). As Wenham notes,[4] the combination of mission and authority also occurs in Luke and John and is hardly a Matthean peculiarity. The command to baptize probably goes back to Jesus himself because no other explanation can suffice for the institution of the practice among early Christians.[5] "Teach" is more frequent in Mark and Luke, and "keep" is more common to John and Acts. While many scholars believe that v 20b is a Matthean composition,[6] the theology is echoed in many places, especially in John and Paul. In short, there is good evidence for asserting that this pericope has its foundation in tradition, though it is expressed predominantly in Matthean language.

Another difficulty is deciding whether the passage is a single whole delivered on one occasion or a combination of separate traditions. Many scholars assert that the latter is more probable due to the close connection with Matthew's themes.[7] This would also fit both the fact that the missionary command is found in different contexts in the other gospels and Matthew's common practice of combining speeches of the Lord given on separate occasions (for example, the sermon on the mount).

However, there are good grounds for considering it a single tradition that was redacted by Matthew. There is some basis for saying it may reflect the lost Markan ending,[8] and the three points of the message are paralleled in the other gospels and may not be truly Matthean. For instance, authority and mission are linked in Luke and John (cf. John 4), and the presence of the Lord is connected with mission in John 20:19 ff. Strecker argues that the three form a homogeneous whole and would hardly have circulated independent of context.[9] Furthermore, Matthew's practice of combining traditions does not normally extend to phrases. It would seem that the tradition came to Matthew, possibly via Mark, as a single whole but that he stated it in his own style and words.

The literary context of the message itself is also debated. The major hypotheses are as follows:

(1) Many believe that the background is found in OT prophecies (especially Daniel) that the Son of man would have power and dominion.[10]

The passage would then consummate the Matthean Son-of-man emphasis.

(2) Others argue that the Son of man is not indicated in v 18 since the eschatological Judge is not present.[11] The passage instead reflects Ps 2:8 and the royal-enthronement motif of Judaism. Jesus is the anointed King and appointed Messiah who here assumes his throne.

(3) Bornkamm denies the first two, arguing that neither lordship nor parousia are in mind.[12] He believes Matthew stresses the *mystērion* of the mission to the Gentiles.

(4) B. J. Malina sees a similarity to the decree of Cyrus, which concluded 2 Chronicles (36:23) and therefore the Hebrew Bible.[13] Matthew 28:18 would thus be an official decree of the King.

(5) Evans claims the passage does not fit any theory and was an original Christian composition intended to stress discipleship—that is, what it means to be a Christian in the present.[14]

The problem with the above theories is that they are set in opposition to one another. The Son-of-man background, as we shall see below, is definitely predominant in v 18. The enthronement pattern fits in with the possibility that Matthew sees a royal emphasis in the speech and uses it to conclude his previous stress on the "lowly King" motif.[15] Bornkamm's thesis fits the implicit universalism of the passage. Evans' "discipleship" theme is also prominent in v 19. Only Malina's hypothesis is speculative, since he stretches the similarities to 2 Chronicles. In short, the theories catch varying nuances of a kaleidoscopic theme, and the title "great commission" best expresses the central emphasis. As Jesus' followers studied the speech they must have noted its richness.

There are two major sections in the pericope: the setting (vv 16-17), and the message (vv 18-20). The latter may be subdivided into three parts: the statement of authority (v 18), the command to evangelize (vv 19-20a), and the promise of Jesus' presence (v 20b).

1. *The setting (vv 16-17).* There are several important points in this section. "Eleven" is found only here in the gospels apart from four times in Luke-Acts and may have come from tradition, although it might also have been used because it fits Matthew's stress on Judas in the passion narrative. An important concept is seen in *eis to oros*, for "mountain" has an important place in the first gospel (found sixteen times). It is connected with the temptation, sermon on the mount, and transfiguration, as well as with times of special communication between the Father and the Son. W. D. Davies and others state that Matthew has in mind here a "new-Sinai" motif, in which Jesus is viewed as a "new Moses" providing a "new Torah" for the "new Israel."[16] However, this thesis suffers when one notes first of all that there is little Moses typology in Matthew. It is better

to say with Bornkamm that Matthew viewed the mountain as the place of divine revelation.[17]

The worship theme in v 17 parallels v 9 and is part of the contrast between the hatred in vv 11-15 and the homage in vv 8-9 and 16-17. Matthew's resurrection discourse is shaped by a series of contrasts between the enmity of the officials and the triumph of Christ. In vv 16-20 that triumph is finalized. The phrase "but some doubted," however, seems at first glance to jar with the worship theme. While doubt is a central motif of the appearance narratives,[18] it is found only here in Matthew.

Various attempts have been made to explain its presence: that it is a scribal error,[19] that it refers to "other" disciples who were present,[20] that it means lack of recognition rather than true doubt.[21] The context, however, shows that the disciples were the doubters. As I. P. Ellis has noted,[22] the verb is found only in Matthew in the NT (14:31 and here) and refers not to unbelief but to hesitation or uncertainty. The disciples worship, but waver. There is twofold connection here: a contrast with the worship theme, which adds even greater stress to the victorious promise of v 18; and a transition to the reassurance of vv 18 ff.[23] This is Matthew's message to the believer: In the midst of uncertainty he may trust the authority of the Lord. In the other gospels doubt is assuaged by the physical presence of the Risen One.[24] Here it is dispelled by the authority of his word.

2. *The Message (vv 18-20).* (1) The statement of authority (v 18). This verse stems from Dan 7:14, as a comparison with the LXX shows. The Son-of-man motif receives special attention in Matthew. As Albright demonstrates,[25] Matthew consciously adds to Mark the concept of the glory of the Son that he receives from the Father (cf. 10:23; 12:32; 13:41; etc.). The title itself is probably omitted for two reasons: (1) It would be misunderstood and given a parousia interpretation; (2) he wished to teach that the parousia power and glory were his now and were offered to his followers during the interval between the two advents.[26]

There are several emphases. *Edothē*, which is also first in Dan 7:14 LXX, is used temporally for the resurrection event as the enthronement of the Messiah,[27] with the passive force presupposing an act of the Father (cf. the creedal passive in 1 Cor 15:3-4). The *exousia* is the authority originally given Christ by the Father "within the limits of His earthly calling and commission" (Matt 9:8; 11:27) but now his absolutely (*pas*).[28] The term is more comprehensive than "power" and refers to position as well as function. The kingdom of heaven (a favorite Matthean phrase) is already present in the form of the Risen One.[29]

A key word throughout the message is *pas*, found in all three parts. It binds the sections together, stressing the universal reign of Christ. In fact we may have here a type of rabbinic "pearl-stringing" midrash centering on the "all-ness" of Yahweh transferred to the risen Lord. It looks at Christ positionally (all authority), locally (all the earth), individually (every creature), and temporally (always). The concept includes the exaltation theology reflected in Eph 1:21, Phil 2:9 ff., and Col 1:15 ff. Absolutely "all" things are under his dominion. The first phrase of the four includes the other three and sums up the partial claims to authority made in the first gospel regarding his earthly sojourn.[30] This authority is "heavenly" as well as "earthly," a sweeping concept that implies divine status. When we add v 20, the divine status of Christ reveals its theological purpose here.[31] Jesus as the Risen One has the authority of Yahweh.

(2) The command to make disciples (vv 19-20a). This is paralleled in pseudo-Mark 16:15 but is a different tradition from those in Luke 24:47-48 and John 20:21. On the basis of his claim to authority (*oun*) Jesus now gives his command. The use of the participle before the verb is found often in the first gospel and is used for two aspects of the same act: "Go and make disciples."[32] *Mathēteuō* is found only in Matthew (13:52; 27:57 and here) and Acts (14:21). It is one of Matthew's major emphases and refers to discipleship, both on the part of the disciples and of those they evangelize. One notes a deeper meaning than the one normally given to evangelization, for there is implicit in the word "a call which leads to discipleship."[33] It is a central theme of Matthew's ecclesiology and, as Barth states,[34] denotes both imitation and obedience. The followers of Christ must act, suffer and walk as he did, trusting the authority of his Person.

*Panta ta ethnē* consummates the implicit universalism of the gospel. The entire thought refers to the interim period between the resurrection and the "consummation" (v 20; cf. Matt 24:14 ═ Mark 13:10) and implies that some time will pass before those closing events. This motif of universal mission is part of the exaltation theme. As Bornkamm says,[35] "all the nations" is part of the universal Lordship theme "elaborated in various ways" by the early Church (cf. Phil 2:9-10; Rom 14:9; Col 1:19-20; etc.). Here we see a striking contrast with the seeming emphasis of Matthew's previous mission sayings, which show that it was confined to Israel (10:5-6, 16; 15:24). Yet there are several hints of an implicit universalism (12:18 ff.; 13:38; 24:14; 26:13), and these set the stage for the command here. The full explication had to await Jesus' sacrificial death and authenticating resurrection.

Two modal participles, "baptizing" and "teaching," describe the process of making disciples. The baptismal motif seems strange here. Many scholars believe it resulted from later Church tradition read back into the resurrection events. But as we have already argued, it probably came from the original tradition as expressed here. Baptism is not stressed in the first gospel; Matthew only uses the verb seven times (versus twelve for

Mark and ten for Luke) and the noun twice (versus four each for the other synoptists). The major problem is that elsewhere the baptismal formula includes only one member ("in the name of Jesus") while the trinitarian formula is found here (nowhere else in the NT in a baptismal context; but see *Did.* 7:1).

Most scholars today believe it is a Matthean addition, perhaps due to his own *Sitz im Leben* but probably taken from a late tradition and inserted here (cf. 1 Cor 12:4-6; 2 Cor 13:14; Gal 4:6; Eph 5:5-6; 1 Pet 1:2). The concept is prepared for in Matthew's gospel, as in Jesus' baptism (3:11, 16-17), the Father/Son relationship (11:27//Mark 13:32; 24:36), and the Son-of-man/Spirit connection (12:32). E. F. Harrison argues that Acts simply reports the baptism and never seeks to reproduce the creedal formula, as seen in the variation between the titles "Jesus Christ" (2:38; 10:48) and "Lord Jesus" (8:16; 19:5).[36] However, recent studies in NT creedal formulae make this argument difficult to uphold. For one thing, the very presence of "in the name of" indicates that Luke was repeating a creedal statement; and for another, the titles of Jesus were somewhat interchangeable within the creeds, depending on the theological emphasis.[37] It seems most likely that at some point the tradition or Matthew expanded an original monadic formula. The implications of this will be explored in the second major section. Here we will simply point out two things: (1) Matthew was not freely composing but sought to interpret the true meaning of Jesus' message for his own day; (2) both *ipsissima verba* and *ipsissima vox* are inspired words of God. Harrison himself agrees "that the words in Matthew need not be identical with the actual words of Jesus...for where we have parallel accounts in the synoptic Gospels the language frequently differs."[38]

The purpose of the triadic formula here is connected with the exalted *pas*-imagery. In order to show that the baptized disciples would enjoy full participation in the fulness of the divine activity, Matthew stressed each member of the Godhead (as implied in the original *eis to onoma*). While recognizing the growing similarity between *eis* and *en* in NT times, we must agree with Allen and Albright that *eis* is used deliberately here.[39] They say that "in the name" generally refers to the ceremonial rite invoking the name of Jesus, while "into the name" speaks of the results of the act—namely, incorporation "into" the fellowship of the Godhead. Therefore the phrase is more than a liturgical formula; it is an experiential reality. Baptism is not only an act of obedience but is also an entrance into fellowship. As part of the discipling activity, it has certain rights and obligations associated with discipleship.

The second aspect, teaching, comes after baptism and may well reflect the practice of post-baptismal instruction.[40] It is based, however, on the tradition of Jesus' own teaching ministry, a central emphasis of Matthew's gospel. Where Mark stresses action, Matthew emphasizes teaching, constructing his gospel around five major teaching sections (chaps. 5-7, 10, 13, 18, 24-25) that center on the believer's life and his relation to the world. Again, although Davies and others (see n. 16) believe Matthew has a "new-Torah" theology, we do not believe this fits Matthew's view of the Law. R. A. Guelich has shown that Jesus is seen as the fulfilment of the Law; it still has validity but is "at the same time transcended and set aside by Jesus' own demand for conduct representative of the present age of salvation."[41] There was no programmatic "new Law" to supersede the old but rather a radical demand for a changed life. *Panta* would therefore refer to the totality of Jesus' teaching,[42] especially as presented in the first gospel, centering on the coming kingdom of heaven and man's relation to it as well as on the Person of Jesus.

(3) The promise of his presence (v 20b). This is a proper conclusion to the speech and to the gospel as a whole. It is paralleled in 1:23, where we read that "his name shall be called Emmanuel (which means, God with us)," and in 18:20: "Where two or three are gathered in my name, there am I in the midst of them."[43] These verses are part of the evangelist's emphasis on the deity of Christ. Michel finds parallel statements in Exod 3:12 and Josh 1:5, 9.[44] The theme of these passages—God's presence among men—is consciously applied to the Risen One as omnipresent among us.[45] The divine comfort (Michel calls it "divine succor"), given by God to his people throughout the periods of the OT and intertestamental literature, is offered to the Church. The Risen One here supplies the means of performing the obedience required in v 20a. As Bornkamm puts it, "The gospel ends with the 'Immanuel' with which it began (1:23)."[46]

"Until the consummation of the ages" is also in keeping with the theology of the first gospel. *Synteleia* is found five times in Matthew (13:39-40, 49; 24:3 and here) and only in Heb 9:26 elsewhere in the NT. It is an apocalyptic concept, and the risen Christ is saying that the authority of the kingdom age is present with his disciples at every moment and that its extent is limitless,[47] ceasing only when the kingdom appears and the presence becomes a physical as well as spiritual reality. Therefore the mission itself is an integral part of the parousia expectation and becomes, as already stated, a "proleptic parousia."[48]

Verse 20b is meant to fill the gap between the ages. In Matthean theology, Jesus' radical demand is to become the life-style for the Church as the people of God during the interval between the ages. This statement, then, provides comfort for his people via the promise of his continued presence during that time. With this in mind Matthew concludes his study with a summary of his ecclesiology: The "church" is God's chosen messenger during the interim before the "consummation" and as such is promised the presence of the authoritative One in executing that task.[49]

This final pericope in the gospel has a twofold relation: to the resurrection narrative, and to the gospel as a whole. To the former it climaxes and focuses the entire section. Matthew builds contrast upon contrast to emphasize the glory and authority of the Risen One who is at work in this aeon. To the gospel itself it sums up much of Matthew's most important teaching, including his messianic Lordship Christology, his discipleship ecclesiology, and his inaugurated eschatology.

A great deal more could be done with this pericope if space permitted, especially in the area of *Traditionsgeschichte*. A preliminary conclusion, however, would indicate that Matthew has redacted an actual tradition (perhaps taken from Mark) of a threefold statement of the Risen One on a mountain in Galilee. The statement itself contained a claim of authority, a command to evangelize, and a promise of help.

## II. A Biblical Understanding of Inerrancy

In the twentieth century the Church is experiencing in bibliology the same growth pangs it encountered in Christology in the third and fourth centuries. Radical criticism takes an Arian approach by divorcing the human words of the Bible from the Word of God, which it defines as existential encounter. Fundamentalism, on the other hand, takes a docetic approach by effectively removing the human element from the Biblical text. Evangelicalism is trying to discover an Athanasian middle ground, combining the human and divine elements in a God-ordained tension that recognizes the interplay between both aspects behind the origin of the sacred text.

The current debate in evangelicalism centers on the question of limited versus full inerrancy. Daniel Fuller argues that inerrancy should be limited to those areas necessary to salvation,[50] while Robert Coleman believes that it should be limited to what Scripture "intends" to teach—that is, didactic purpose rather than incidental details.[51] Both separate inspiration from inerrancy and argue that the latter is not a necessary part of the former. Several others, notably Geisler, Pinnock, Payne and Poythress,[52] have written that inerrancy is unlimited and must be an integral part of any concept of plenary inspiration. Not only the primary purpose but also the secondary details are trustworthy. To deny the latter is the first step to a denial of the former.

The key to a proper concept is the meaning of the word "error." It is here that we must be careful to note the Biblical understanding rather than the twentieth-century definition. In fact, a logical mapwork of the term must carefully note the "language games" that are played with "inerrancy" in our time. Both liberals and evangelicals are guilty of a too-easy acceptance of certain facts as error. For instance, many assume that because the gospels are not biographies in the modern sense of the term, they contain error. Others assume that because Matthew quotes Christ in a different way than Mark does, the *Logia Jesu* contains errors. In this way the gospels are the logical testing ground for the doctrine of inerrancy, for they claim to contain factual historical data and to portray accurately the life of Christ. Synoptic differences, then, are the necessary battleground for any discussion of this topic.

Is it true that the *Logia Jesu* must contain *ipsissima verba* in order to be inerrant? Or is *ipsissima vox* equally inspired? We must note first that the quotations are, at the very best, translations of the original Aramaic and therefore cannot be the *actual* words of Jesus. Moreover, synoptic differences at nearly every point show that the evangelists did not attempt to give us *ipsissima verba* but rather sought to interpret Jesus' words for their audiences.[53] In other words, they wished to make Jesus' teachings meaningful to their own *Sitz im Leben* rather than to present them unedited. Relevancy triumphed over verbal exactness.[54]

This does not mean that the evangelists had no concern for the teachings themselves and freely composed their own materials. It simply means that they selected and paraphrased Jesus' teachings so that the true meaning of them would be revealed to their readers. Matthew's trinitarian formula and theologically colored phrases are not error but are inspired interpretations of Jesus' actual message. How can we know that his is the correct interpretation rather than an erroneous compilation of inaccuracies? We know via our belief in inspiration, by our acceptance of the promise in John 14:26:[55] "The Holy Spirit...will bring to your remembrance all that I have said to you."[56]

This leads us into the whole question of history and theology in the Biblical texts. Radical scholars tend to say that there is an absolute dichotomy between history and theology. Because the gospels are theological, they cannot be historical. For the same reason many evangelicals have neglected the theological ramifications of the historical narratives in the Bible.[57] Both sides are wrong.[58] One cannot blindly assume that redaction always involves the creation of material rather than the rephrasing of an existing tradition. Nor can one presuppose that theology does not exist because one is writing history. History and its interpretation must always exist side by side. The critic should take cognizance of the possibility that a passage is traditional but has been reconstructed to provide a particular theological interpretation of the evangelist (while remaining true to the event itself).

What value, then, does redaction criticism have for the evangelical, and how should he approach it? When one removes the negative presuppositions of the radical critics, one has in redaction criticism a tremendous, positive tool for understanding the early Church and its theology. It is hoped that this study has shown the greater insight into the great commission that a redactional approach has provided. A better understanding of the evangelist's theology and a deeper insight into the meaning of the passage has resulted.

But what of the dangers? Is the domino theory correct, and will such research weaken the structure of Biblical authority until it falls? There is no reason why it should. In fact, it is hoped that this study will provide a further insight into the true relation between fact and interpretation in the Biblical text.[59] Both aspects are true, and both are inspired. In this case it is difficult, if not impossible, to trace the exact words that Jesus spoke on the mountain in Galilee. However, we can know that Matthew has faithfully reproduced the intent and meaning of what Jesus said. In fact, we can rejoice because Matthew has rephrased it in such a way that it illuminates his entire gospel and applies the meaning of Jesus' life and ministry to the present mission and responsibility of the Church. Matthew did not simply repeat that command. He lived it—and so must we. For Matthew, it summed up his entire theology. We must ask whether it summarizes ours.

[1]O. Michel, "Der Abschluss des Matthäusevangeliums," *EvT* 10 (1950-51) 16-21, esp. p. 21; G. Bornkamm, "The Risen Lord and the Earthly Jesus—Matthew 28, 16-20," in *The Future of Our Religious Past* (ed. J. M. Robinson; London, 1971). W. Trilling, *Das Wahre Israel* (München, 1964) 21-22, bases his entire study of Matthew's theology on the insight given in this pericope.

[2]Michel, "Abschluss" 22-23, calls it an "enthronement scene"; Bornkamm in *Future* (ed. Robinson) 212, a "hidden mystery scene"; R. Bultmann, *The History of the Synoptic Tradition* (Oxford, 1963) 286, a "cult legend."

[3]It occurs elsewhere in the gospels only in Matt 8:9 = Luke 7:8.

[4]D. Wenham, "The Resurrection Narratives in St. Matthew's Gospel," *TB* 24 (1973) 20-54, esp. pp. 40-41, 51-52. He notes that in Luke the mission is connected with the sovereign power of God and the authority of Scripture and that in John the disciples are sent out with authority. This is not a free composition but a Matthean version of the tradition.

[5]O. Cullmann, *Baptism in the New Testament* (London, 1950) 19-20, argues that Qumran, proselyte baptism, John the Baptist's practice, etc., are all insufficient reasons for the reappearance of baptism in the early Church.

[6]See Bornkamm in *Future* (ed. Robinson) 223-224; G. Barth in *Tradition and Interpretation in Matthew* (ed. G. Bornkamm, G. Barth and H. J. Held; London, 1963) 136-137. The best presentation of this position is found in J. D. Kingsbury, "The Composition and Christology of Matt. 28:16-20," *JBL* 93 (1974) 573-584. His extensive linguistic study certainly shows that Matthew redacted the message, but it falls short of proving Matthean composition for two reasons: (1) He draws too much from words that are found elsewhere in Matthew, and (2) he fails to consider words and phrases common to all the evangelists.

[7]See E. Lohmeyer, *Das Evangelium des Matthäus* (Göttingen, 1963) 423-424; Michel, "Abschluss" 17; Barth in *Tradition* (ed. Bornkamm) 131. Lohmeyer believes the traditions were combined in the pre-Matthean period, while the others believe Matthew did the combining himself.

[8]For the possibility of a lost ending see C. F. D. Moule, "St. Mark XVI 8 Once More," *NTS* 2 (1955-56) 58-59; G. W. Trompf, "The First Resurrection Appearance and the Ending of Mark's Gospel," *NTS* 18 (1972) 308-330, esp. pp. 316-319. There are similarities with

Mark in both the theme and structure of Matt 28:16-20. The Galilean setting and commission would fit the promise of Mark 16:7. Furthermore, the themes of the message also fit Markan motifs.

[9]G. Strecker, *Der Weg der Gerechtigkeit* (Göttingen, 1962) 210-211; see also E. F. F. Bishop, "The Risen Christ and the 500 Brethren (I Cor. 15, 6)," *CBQ* 18 (1956) 341-344.

[10]See Barth in *Tradition* (ed. Bornkamm) 133; Lohmeyer, *Evangelium* 413, 416-417; Michel, "Abschluss" 22; R. H. Fuller, *The Formation of The Resurrection Narratives* (London, 1972) 83.

[11]See K. H. Rengstorf, "A Formula of the Judean Royal Ritual," *NovT* 5 (1961) 229-244. J. Jeremias, *Jesus' Promise to the Nations* (London, 1959) 38-39, sees an echo of the enthronement pattern here: authority, proclamation, acclamation.

[12]Bornkamm in *Future* (ed. Robinson) 207-208, *contra* R. H. Lightfoot, *Locality and Doctrine in the Gospels* (London, 1938) 72, who argues that it does look to consummation in the parousia.

[13]B. J. Malina, "The Literary Structure and Form of Matthew XXVIII 16-20," *NTS* 17 (1970-71) 87-103. He also sees overtones of OT proof passages used to authenticate the message.

[14]C. F. Evans, *Resurrection and the New Testament* (London, 1970) 89-91.

[15]Matthew has a definite stress on Jesus' kingship but includes it during his earthly ministry. In his triumphal entry account (21:1-11) he uses OT messianic testimonia from Isa 62:11; Zech 9:9 but excludes the important phrase "righteous and triumphant is he" from the latter. In so doing Matthew makes Jesus the "lowly King," pointing the way to the death of the Messiah. Only afterward can Jesus become "triumphant King."

[16]W. D. Davies, *The Setting of the Sermon on the Mount* (Cambridge, 1964) 85, 99; see also Fuller, *Formation* 81; Lohmeyer, *Evangelium* 75-76.

[17]Bornkamm in *Future* (ed. Robinson) 204. Many scholars would say this is a Matthean addition to the pericope. However, the connection with the following phrase, which is distinctly non-Matthean (see above), may well indicate that it is taken from tradition. There is no reference to such a command in Matthew, and it is doubtful that he would have included it if it were not in his source.

[18]C. H. Dodd, "The Appearances of the Risen Christ: An Essay in Form Criticism," in *More New Testament Studies* (London, 1968) 12, says that "the appearance of the Lord does not bring full or immediate conviction to the beholders who require some form of assurance: the sight of His wounds, contact with His body, or His word of authority."

[19]See W. D. Morris, "Matt. xxviii 17," *ExpTim* 47 (1953-367) 142, who conjectures that *edistasan* was originally *diestēsan*, meaning "they stood apart" in reverential awe. However there is no manuscript evidence for this.

[20]See A. N. McNeile, *The Gospel According to Matthew* (London, 1961) 434. He argues that Matthew always tones down Mark's derogatory comments regarding the disciples. But this is not always true, and Matthew here has a special reason for the doubt motif.

[21]See F. V. Filson, *A Commentary on the Gospel According to St. Matthew* (New York, 1960) 305. However, lack of recognition would more likely precede than follow worship.

[22]I. P. Ellis, "But Some Doubted," *NTS* 14 (1968) 574-580. Michel, "Abschluss" 16-17, and Barth in *Tradition* (ed. Bornkamm) 132, note this same theological emphasis.

[23]C. H. Giblin, "A Note on Doubt and Reassurance in Matt. 28:16-20," *CBQ* 37 (1975) 68-75, argues against the contrast and for the reassurance theme here. But there is no reason why both cannot be correct, for the contrast strengthens the reassurance (especially in light of Matthew's outline in chap. 28, as already noted).

[24]See E. M. Howe, " '...But Some Doubted' (Matt. 28:17). A Re-Appraisal of Factors Influencing the Easter Faith of the Early Christian Community," *JETS* 18/3 (1975) 173-180, for the setting of this in the larger context of the doubt motif in the early Church as a whole. What she neglects is the *Sitz im Leben* of the motif in the post-Easter community. Its prominence is probably due to the fact of doubt in the risen Lord on the part of many later disciples. The evangelists wished to identify themselves with it and show solutions. John is especially strong here.

[25]W. F. Albright and C. S. Mann, *Matthew* (New York, 1971) lxxxviii. D. Senior, "The Passion Narrative of St. Matthew," in *L'Evangile selon Matthieu* (ed. M. Didier; Gembloux,

1972) 343-357, esp. pp. 354-356, says Matthew deliberately underscores Mark's Christological elements in his passion narrative, especially in the Son-of-man theme, "as a preparation for and a preinterpretation of the passion as a revelation of the Messiah."

[26]As Bornkamm in *Future* (ed. Robinson) 207 says, the title does not belong in this context since the speech stresses Jesus' universal Lordship rather than the consummation of the ages, *contra* Barth in *Tradition* (ed. Bornkamm) 142, who states that the eschatological judge is implied here. Kingsbury, "Composition" 580-584, argues that Son of God, not Son of man, is the predominant Christology of the pericope. In this light Matthew stresses the unique personhood and authority of the risen Son. This is an excellent qualification of the above, but in light of the exaltation motif predominant here it seems that Matthew uses this pericope to culminate and fuse the two titles. Son of man is given divine status, Son of God eschatological overtones.

[27]Lohmeyer, *Evangelium* 416-417; Michel, "Abschluss" 22; and Barth in *Tradition* (ed. Bornkamm) 133 interpret this more in the sense of eschatological ruler and judge; they see exaltation, rather than resurrection, as the central thrust. However, they read too much from Son-of-man eschatology into the context.

[28]W. Foerster, "*Exousia*," *TDNT*, 2. 568-569.

[29]Barth's reformulation of Lightfoot's parousia thesis, in *Tradition* (ed. Bornkamm) 134 n., that "the Christophany in 28.16 f." is "a kind of proleptic parousia," is certainly preferable, for the kingdom has now been made available to believers in the interim age.

[30]Cf. 4:23-24; 7:29; 8:32; 9:6, 35; 10:1; 12:22; 17:18.

[31]Albright, *Matthew* clviii, shows that the combination of "Son" and "Lord" in Matthew points to a person who surpasses a messianic role.

[32]Barth in *Tradition* (ed. Bornkamm) 131 n. follows Schlatter in saying that "when two actions are linked in an event Matthew uses for the preparatory action the aorist participle before the aorist of the main verb."

[33]K. H. Rengstorf, "*Matheteuō*," *TDNT*, 4. 461. Bornkamm in *Future* (ed. Robinson) 218-219 notes that "disciple" is a major ecclesiological term in Matthew and defines his attitude to the Church as following Jesus in "obedience, humility, and readiness to suffer."

[34]Barth in *Tradition* (ed. Bornkamm) 105-106, 119-120.

[35]Bornkamm in *Future* (ed. Robinson) 210-212. See also Davies, *Setting* 327-328. Bornkamm declares that the addition here is mythical and not historical. This, however, is hardly necessary, especially in view of the strong flavor of universalism throughout the gospels.

[36]E. F. Harrison, "Did Christ Command World Evangelism?", *Christianity Today* 18 (November 23, 1973) 6-10, esp. p. 9.

[37]For a more detailed study of the creeds see A. M. Hunter, *Paul and His Predecessors* (London, 1940); O. Cullmann, *The Earliest Christian Confessions* (London, 1949); W. Kramer, *Christ, Lord, Son of God* (London, 1966).

[38]Harrison, "Christ" 9. He uses differences between Mark 14:24 and Matt 26:28 as an example.

[39]W. C. Allen, *A Critical and Exegetical Commentary on the Gospel According to Matthew* (ICC; Edinburgh, 1922) 306-307; Albright, *Matthew* 362-363, *contra* J. A. Robinson, "In the Name," *JTS* 7 (1905-06) 186-202.

[40]See Fuller, *Formation* 88-89. This does not mean, however, that it was read into the tradition from later Church practice. It more likely was the other way around—i.e., later Church practice stemmed from it.

[41]R. A. Guelich, *Not to Annul the Law; Rather, to Fulfill the Law and the Prophets* (Hamburg, 1967) 246 (cf. pp. 216-266).

[42]Note the use of *entellō* with *panta*; the verb stresses the authority of Jesus' teaching. It occurs in 4:6; 15:4; 17:9 and here (versus three total in Mark and Luke) and refers twice to the Father's commands and twice to Jesus' commands.

[43]Fuller, *Formation* 89-90, states that 18:20 and 28:20 are separate developments of a single logion. This is improbable, however, since only *eimi* is common between them and since they occur in different settings (the binding of sins and the missionary charge).

[44]Michel, "Abschluss" 18-19. Fuller, *Formation* 89, adds *Pap. Oxy.* 10.1, *Gos. Thom.* 77, and *'Abot* 3.2 (which describes the shekinah glory of Yahweh).

[45]Many, such as Barth in *Tradition* (ed. Bornkamm) 136-137 and Bornkamm in *Future* (ed. Robinson) 223-224, say this is a Matthean composition, due to the omnipresence doctrine, which they believe is late in the Christological development of the early Church. However, this is paralleled in several of the early creeds (Col 1:15 ff.; Rom 6:2-3; Heb 7:25) and was more likely in early tradition.

[46]Bornkamm in *Future* (ed. Robinson) 228.

[47]McNeile, *Gospel* 437, asserts that *pasas tas hēmeras* occurs only here in the NT but is common in the LXX. The detailed time-note here stresses the extent of the presence—i.e., "all the days" of the interim period.

[48]Barth in *Tradition* (ed. Bornkamm) 136-137 says that Matthew makes the presence contiguous with the proclamation of Jesus' teaching. This expands the motif in 'Abot 3:2-3, which says that the shekinah glory is present only through the proclamation of the Torah.

[49]Matthew's is the only gospel to employ the term "church" (16:18; 18:17), and he programmatically stresses her origins and heritage. He emphasizes the choice and purpose of the twelve (10:2 ff.; 13:11-12; 16:12 ff.; 18:18 ff.; 19:28) and looks at the Church as the inheritor of Israel's mantle. His stress on Israel's rejection underscores the Church as God's chosen people. However, as D. Hill, *The Gospel of Matthew* (London, 1972) 72, argues, "all nations" in 28:19 includes Israel (cf. Acts 1:8).

[50]D. Fuller, "Warfield's view of Faith and History," *BETS* 11 (1968) 75-83. See also his "The Nature of Biblical Inerrancy," *Journal of the American Scientific Affiliation* 24 (1972) 47-50.

[51]R. J. Coleman, "Reconsidering Limited Inerrancy," *JETS* 17 (1974) 207-214; reprinted in this volume.

[52]N. L. Geisler, "Theological Method and Inerrancy: A Reply to Professor Holmes," *BETS* 11 (1968) 139-146 (reprinted in this volume); C. Pinnock, "Limited Inerrancy: A Critical Appraisal and Constructive Alternative," in *God's Inerrant Word* (ed. J. W. Montgomery; Minneapolis, 1974) 143-158; J. B. Payne, "Partial Omniscience: Observations on Limited Inerrancy," *JETS* 18 (1975) 37-40 (reprinted in this volume); V. S. Poythress, "Problems for Limited Inerrancy," *JETS* 18 (1975) 93-104 (reprinted in this volume).

[53]Many evangelicals cloud this fact with an overzealous use of "harmonizing." While this interpretive key answers many difficulties, it can by no means remove every problem.

[54]For an excellent discussion of this see R. T. France, "Inerrancy and New Testament Exegesis," *Themelios* 1/1 (Autumn 1975) 12-18.

[55]The question regarding whether or not this was the actual teaching of Jesus does not concern us here (although we believe it was). At the very least, it proves a sense of inspiration on the part of the early Church regarding the gospels.

[56]This does not mean that we take a Barthian "leap of faith." There is good evidence that the evangelists themselves believed they were inspired and that this involved accurate historical portrayal (Luke 1:1-4; John 19:35; 21:24).

[57]This is readily seen in the paucity of references to evangelical works in this study. There are very few who have delved into the theological ramifications of the data.

[58]See the excellent critique of both sides in relation to the gospels in G. C. Berkouwer, *Studies in Dogmatics: Holy Scripture* (Grand Rapids, 1975) 9-24, 250-253, 265-266. On pp. 181-187 he argues against a mechanical view of inerrancy that removes itself from an honest consideration of scriptural development and differences.

[59]See also Berkouwer's closing chapter, "Faith and Criticism," in *Studies* 346-366.

# INDUCTIVISM, INERRANCY, AND PRESUPPOSITIONALISM

## GREG L. BAHNSEN

At the heart of contemporary evangelical bibliology and apologetics is the question of scriptural inerrancy—in particular, the most appropriate and effective method of its exposition and defense. The three elements mentioned in the title of this paper have been derived from a short but potentially significant interchange between Daniel Fuller and Clark Pinnock in the *Christian Scholar's Review*.[1] Their brief discussion of Biblical authority is a noteworthy skirmish, one that puts a particular epistemological and apologetical outlook to a critical test. An analysis of the Fuller-Pinnock encounter may very well offer evangelicals unexpected but sound guidance through the thicket of present-day theological and apologetical questions impinging on inerrancy. To begin this recommended analysis we can rehearse how Fuller and Pinnock relate the three topics of inductivism, inerrancy and presuppositionalism to each other. Three major theses emerge from a reading of the two published letters exchanged between these two writers and each can be substantiated by quotation from the relevant literature. Thesis I may be stated as follows: *Presuppositionalism is opposed to empirical procedures and inductive investigation.*

Fuller says to Pinnock: "If faith really has to *begin* the approach to Scripture, then I don't think you can talk very meaningfully about induction. I would argue that really, after all, you are on Van Til's side, not on Warfield's" (p. 331). "I am trying to do as Warfield and let induction control from beginning to end. You say on page 185 [of Pinnock's *Biblical Revelation*] that following Christ's view of Scripture 'will always prove safe'.... This is the language of an unassailable starting point—the language of deductive thinking—of Van Til" (p. 332).

Pinnock replies to Fuller: "It is more common to be criticized by our fideistic evangelical colleagues for being *too* concerned about questions of factual verification. Dr. Fuller recognizes that I wish to follow the epistemology of the Princeton apologetic as it was developed by B. B. Warfield, but he believes that I am inconsistent in this and tend to lapse into presuppositional modes of expression, if not thought. He would even place me on Van Til's side, *Mirabile dictu*" (p. 333). Pinnock wants us to understand that "Dr. Fuller and I share a view of the constructive relation between faith and history" (p. 333).

Thus it is that both Pinnock and Fuller set an inductive, empirical approach (like that of Warfield and the Princeton school) over against the approach of presuppositionalism (as found in an apologist like Van Til). On the one side you have a constructive relation between history and faith where induction controls from beginning to end the questions of factual verification, whereas on the other side you have mere deductivism and fideism. Presuppositionalism and inductivism are accordingly portrayed as polar opposites, as conflicting epistemologies. To this antagonism Fuller and Pinnock both give assent.

Here now is Thesis II: *Inductivism and empirical apologetics are independent of presuppositional commitments, letting neutral reason and critical thinking control the knowing process from beginning to end.* On this point Fuller and Pinnock are again agreed. In their discussion with each other, both men make much of the alleged "inductive" nature of their epistemologies and their approach to Biblical authority (and hence apologetics). It is indispensable at this point to rehearse what they mean by their commitment to "inductive" procedures. Let us once more have them speak for themselves to this question.

"Induction, as I understand it, means letting criticism control all aspects of the knowing process from beginning to end" (Fuller, p. 330). "All knowing, including the knowledge which faith claims to have, comes by but one way" (Fuller, p. 332). This one way is the empirical approach, which is committed to factual verification (Pinnock, p. 333). With inductivism faith does not begin the approach to Scripture, nor does it start the knowing process at all (Fuller, pp. 331-332). On the other hand, true empiricism does not let negative criticism and naturalistic presuppositions control thought (Pinnock, p. 333). Therefore Fuller and Pinnock are saying that one begins with neither a commitment to Scripture nor a commitment against Scripture. Apparently, then, one is to be completely "open-minded" or neutral from the outset. Indeed, this is precisely what they both claim. For inductivism maintains that no mere claim to authority is self-establishing (Fuller, p. 330), and it refuses to claim "an unassailable starting point" (Fuller, p. 332). Moreover, it will not permit circular reasoning and argumentation (Fuller, p. 330). Hence inductivism on this account does not resort to self-attesting starting points, nor does its chain of explanations and evidences ever bend around and ultimately hook into itself, forming a wide argumentative circle. Clearly, then, this outlook holds to "the right of reason and criticism to be sovereign" (Fuller, p. 330). It will "let critical thinking prevail" (Fuller, p. 332)—"to go all the way" (p. 333), because "you can't just have it 'in part' " (Fuller, p. 332). According to Fuller and Pinnock, if one is "consistently inductive" (p. 332) his every commitment will be based totally on empirical evidences and critical thinking. In particular, belief in inspiration and the security of Biblical authority will rest, we are told, totally on inductive evidence (Fuller, p. 332) and well-authenticated credentials (Pinnock, p. 333). This, then, is the nonpresuppositional inductive (or empirical) approach that Fuller and Pinnock claim to be utilizing. It makes a radical, all-encompassing demand on us epistemologically—"you either have it or you don't" (Fuller, p. 332).

We would formulate Thesis III as follows: *The question of Biblical inerrancy can be settled only inductively.* It should be rather obvious that this thesis is demanded by the previous two. Presuppositionalism has been shunned, and the radical demand to let inductive empiricism answer every question in the knowing process has been affirmed. Thus the question of the Bible's errant or inerrant nature must be answered, if at all, in an inductive manner. Fuller and Pinnock would both say as much.

However, these two committed empiricists and anti-presuppositionalists do not come to the same conclusion about the inerrant nature of Scripture—that is, in the application of their common inductive approach they have reached contrary positions. Fuller maintains the full inerrancy of "any Scriptural statement or necessary implication therefrom which involves what makes a man wise to salvation" (p. 331); "if it errs where historical control is possible in matters germane to 'the whole counsel of God' which 'makes men wise unto salvation,' then all the Bible becomes questionable" (p. 332). Pinnock calls this unacceptable: "Though convenient for sidestepping certain biblical difficulties, this dichotomy is unworkable and unscriptural" (p. 334). We must, instead, take the view of the Biblical authors: "The attitude of Jesus and the Apostles toward Scripture was one of *total* trust.... What Scripture said, with *a priori* qualification, God said, was their view. The whole *graphē* is God-breathed and fully trustworthy" (p. 334). Consequently "the theological truth is discredited to the extent that the factual material is erroneous" (p. 335). So we observe that Fuller and Pinnock have agreed on all three of the aforementioned theses, but they have not ended up in the same place. These two empirical apologists do not see eye to eye with respect to scriptural inerrancy and authority.

What makes this divergence of conclusion so interesting to us today is the additional fact that, in their differing conclusions about scriptural inerrancy, Fuller and Pinnock make decided counter-accusations that the other writer is really less than true to the radical demand of inductivism.

Each man considers himself to be the genuine champion of inductive empiricism in the attempt to relate faith to history. Says Fuller, "I would argue that really, after all, you are on Van Til's side, not on Warfield's" (p. 331); "there is a part of you that wants to be inductive, to let critical thinking prevail. But you can't go all the way" (p. 332). Fuller challenges Pinnock with these words: "Are you willing to be as consistently inductive as he [Warfield] was?" (p. 332), and after mentioning resistance to the thunderous veto against induction in Pinnock's book on *Biblical Revelation* Fuller asks, "Are you willing to go all the way in resisting this veto?" (p. 333). Thus Fuller thinks that Pinnock has arrived at his viewpoint on scriptural inerrancy by a manner inconsistent with inductivism.

Nevertheless, and on the other hand, Pinnock feels that it is, rather, Fuller who has not been faithful to the inductive epistemology we have just outlined. He declares: "Fuller is less empirical at this point than Warfield and I, because if he were more careful in his induction, he would see at once that the dichotomy he has proposed [between revelational and nonrevelational statements in Scripture] is untenable in the light of what he calls 'the doctrinal verses' " (p. 334). Indeed, Pinnock says that Fuller's view of inerrancy would "make it relative to some dubious *a priori* standard, inaccurately derived from the doctrinal verses" (p. 334). Pinnock concludes that Fuller "is less than fully consistent in the way he relates faith and history.... Most of the material which in his view would belong to the 'revelational' category lies outside the reach of science and history, safe from their critical control" (p. 334)—even though in reality the theological and factual materials "are so inextricably united in the text" (p. 335). And so there we have the counter-allegations. Pinnock feels that Fuller is not consistently inductive; Fuller says the converse is true.

Let us now explore and respond to the three Fuller-Pinnock theses seriatim, aiming to draw out of this telling interchange principles and insights that can give us basic guidance in such theological and apologetical issues as center on the inerrancy of Scripture.

As to Thesis I, we must rather flatfootedly challenge its accuracy. Both Fuller and Pinnock have counterfeited the presuppositional outlook by aligning it with fideistic deductivism over against empirical and inductive methods. A perusal of Van Til's many publications is sufficient to falsify this preconceived misrepresentation. For instance:

> The greater the amount of detailed study and the more carefully such study is undertaken, the more truly Christian will the method be. It is important to bring out this point in order to help remove the common misunderstanding that Christianity is opposed to *factual investigation*.[2]

> What shall be the attitude of the orthodox believer with respect to this? Shall he be an *obscurantist* and hold to the doctrine of authority of the Scrip-

ture though he knows it can empirically be shown to be contrary to the facts of Scripture themselves? It goes without saying that such should not be his attitude.[3]

The Christian position is certainly not opposed to *experimentation and observation*....It is quite commonly held that we cannot accept anything that is not the result of a sound scientific methodology. With this we can as Christians heartily agree.[4]

Surely the Christian, who believes in the doctrine of creation, cannot share the Greek depreciation of the things of the *sense world*. Depreciation of that sense world inevitably leads to a depreciation of many of the important facts of historic Christianity which took place in the sense world. The Bible does not rule out every form of empiricism any more than it rules out every form of *a priori* reasoning.[5]

Now this approach from the bottom to the top, from the particular to the general, is the *inductive aspect* of the method of implication....All agree that the immediate starting point must be that of our everyday *experience* and the "*facts*" that are most close at hand....But the favorite charge against us is that we are...employing the deductive method. Our opponents are thoughtlessly identifying our method with the Greek method of deduction....We need only to observe that *a priori* reasoning, and *a posteriori* reasoning, are equally anti-Christian, if these terms are understood in their historical sense....On the other hand, if God is recognized as the only and the final explanation of any and every fact, neither the inductive nor the deductive method can any longer be used to the exclusion of the other.[6]

Every bit of historical investigation, whether it be in the directly biblical field, archaeology, or in general history is bound to confirm the truth of the claims of the Christian position....A really fruitful historical apologetic argues that every fact *is* and *must be* such as proves the truth of the Christian theistic position.[7]

Far from being indifferent or antagonistic to inductive and empirical science, Van Til has devoted much of his scholarly labors to the constructive analysis of the philosophy of science. He has always insisted that Christians relate their faith positively to science and history, finding unequivocal evidence—indeed, a definite demand—for distinctively Christian conclusions in all inductive study of the facts themselves.[8] On the other hand he has persistently and apologetically attacked unbelieving philosophies on the telling ground that they render inductive science impossible.[9]

Consequently it is not at all surprising that Van Til has been unfailing in his opposition to fideism, apologetic mysticism, and the notion that belief cannot argue with unbelief. He is highly critical of those who saw no way of harmonizing the facts of the Christian religion with the "constitution and course of nature." They gave up the idea of a philosophical apologetics entirely. This *fideistic* attitude comes to expression frequently in the statement of the experiential proof of the truth of Christianity. People will say that they know that they are saved and that Christianity is true no matter what the philosophical or scientific evidence for or against it may be. ...But in thus seeking to withdraw from all intellectual argument, such fideists have virtually admitted the validity of the argument against Christianity. They will have to believe in their hearts what they have virtually allowed to be intellectually indefensible.[10]

It might seem that there can be no *argument* between them. It might seem that the orthodox view of authority is to be spread only by testimony and by prayer, not by argument. But this would militate directly against the very foundation of all Christian revelation, namely, to the effect that all things in the universe are nothing if not revelational of God. Christianity must claim that it alone is rational....An evangelical, that is a virtually Arminian theology, makes concessions to the principle that controls a "theology of *experience*"...and to the precise extent that evangelicalism makes these concessions in its theology, does it weaken its own defense of the infallible Bible.[11]

These pro-inductive or pro-empirical attitudes of Van Til are conspicuous: To miss them one would need to approach his writings, if at all, with far-reaching and vision-distorting preconceived notions. We cannot but conclude that the Fuller-Pinnock Thesis I is simply mistaken. Presuppositionalism is not opposed to empirical procedures or inductive investigation, nor does it discourage them.

What Van Til and the presuppositionalists *do* say—and this point will be crucial to understanding subsequent parts of this paper—is that not only must one utilize inductive empiricism but he must press beyond this and examine the foundations of science and inductive method. That is, we must not stop short in our philosophical analysis but rather inquire into the presuppositions necessary for an intelligent and justified use of empiricism. As Van Til puts it: "I would not talk endlessly about facts and more facts without challenging the non-believer's *philosophy* of *fact*."[12] Van Til makes it clear that presuppositionalism does not "disparage the usefulness of arguments for the corroboration of the Scripture that came from archaeology. It is only to say that such corroboration is not of independent power."[13] The apologist "must challenge the legitimacy of the scientific method as based upon an assumed metaphysic of chance."[14]

So hopeless and senseless a picture must be drawn of the natural man's methodology, based as it is upon the assumption that time or chance is ultimate. On his assumption his own rationality is a product of chance.... Our argument as over against this would be that the existence of the God of Christian theism and the conception of his counsel as controlling all things in the universe is the only presupposition which can account for the uniformity of nature which the scientist needs.[15]

Christianity does not thus need to take shelter under the roof of "known facts." It rather offers itself as a roof to facts if they would be known. Christianity does not need to take shelter under the roof of a scientific method independent of itself. It rather offers itself as a roof to methods that would be scientific.[16]

The point is that the "facts of experience" must actually be interpreted in terms of Scripture if they are to be intelligible at all.[17]

With this background we can better understand the general thrust of presuppositional method in apologetics:

To argue by presupposition is to indicate what are the epistemological and metaphysical principles that underlie and control one's method.[18]

The Reformed method of argument is first constructive. It presents the biblical view positively by showing that all factual and logical discussions by men take place by virtue of the world's being what God in Christ says it is. It then proceeds negatively to show that unless all facts and all logical relations be seen in the light of the Christian framework, all human interpretation fails instantly.... What we shall have to do then is to try to reduce our opponent's position to an absurdity. Nothing less will do.... We must point out to them that univocal reasoning itself leads to self-contradiction, not only from a theistic point of view, but from a non-theistic point of view as well. It is this that we ought to mean when we say that we must meet our enemy on their own ground. It is this that we ought to mean when we say that we reason from the *impossibility of the contrary*.[19]

Having challenged Thesis I and having briefly explained the nature of presuppositional reasoning with respect to inductivism, we can now proceed to correct the dubious allegation of Thesis II that inductive empiricism is independent of presuppositions, allowing neutral and critical thinking (which assents to nothing except upon evidential strength) to control the knowing process completely from beginning to end. We already have had occasion above to note that inductive empiricism is intelligible and justified within the context of certain metaphysical and epistemological precommitments or basic assumptions. Thus we have already challenged the alleged neutrality of the inductivist. As hard as Fuller and Pinnock may try to hide it from themselves, the stubborn fact remains that, for them both, critical and neutral reasoning does not prevail and reign supreme throughout their knowing processes. They have their covert presuppositions. I would like to illustrate this observation by means of a series of considerations that can be conveniently summarized under three headings.

## I. Unargued Philosophical Baggage

In discussing issues under this rubric, my aim is to point out that inductive empiricism is not a philosophically neutral or unproblematic tool by which evangelical apologetics may proceed.

(1) Inductivists are not as thoroughly inductive as they think, for the reflexive theoretical statements of the inductivists about their procedure and practice, its merits and criteria are not inductive or empirical in nature. Hence extra-inductive commitments are immediately discernible.

(2) Should the Christian inductivist assume universal uniformity or regularity in nature and history so as to provide the metaphysical precondition of his inductivism—but thereby exclude miracles? Or should he begin by allowing miracles (which, by the way, is a supra-empirical commitment to the range of the possible)—but thereby dismiss the reliability and uniformity needed for inductive knowledge?

(3) What sort of rational basis or evidence does the inductivist have for his implied belief in natural uniformity (for example, against Hume's skeptical attack on induction)? Such issues as the nature of induction, its preconditions, and the basis for a commitment to the uniformity of nature are rarely discussed by evangelicals. But this is at the heart of inductive epistemology, and it is still central in philosophical disputes today.

(4) Of course the nature of evidence that should be given for the theory of induction will be determined by the nature of that theory's objects and methods. So we can ask, "What kind of entity is spoken of in the inductivist's self-referential theoretical statements?" Once this is answered, if ever, we must go on and ask, "What is a proposition, an idea, a belief, a standard of evidence, a directive, a rule, etc.?" For instance, are they properties, relations, substances, individuals, dispositions, functions, modes of cognition, or what? These are all categorically different things in metaphysics, and therefore without dealing with the demands of such questions an incomplete, inadequate, inconsistent and self-delusory apologetic may inevitably be the outcome.

(5) The foregoing questions, along with the upcoming one, all indicate that one's metaphysic must be formulated correctly at the outset if epistemological headaches are to be avoided later. For instance, cognizance is a familiar kind of fact to epistemologists (for example, "I see $x$," "I know $p$," being conscious of, believing, remembering, etc.), and cognizance is just as much a reality as what scientists study directly. Thus we ask how cog-

nizance is to be categorized, so as to avoid category mistakes about it. The common tendency is to hold that cognizance is a relation between a subject and an object. But this leads to the obvious epistemological problem of seeking an object of cognition. As a relation, cognizance would require something that cognizance is about, for relations require the existence of their terms. But, then, to what is a belief related in cases of past belief? What is its object? More generally, what is the nature of the objects of cognition, especially in cases of error and illusion?

(6) So to be intelligible and reasonable an inductive epistemology cannot be understood, accepted, and followed without an ontology. With reference to empiricism and metaphysics, it should be noted that no valid argument has ever been given for the statement, "Only perceivable individuals exist." And indeed such a proposition is highly suspect in light of the importance of abstract entities. Without abstract entities (a) there would be no sense in talking about validity and invalidity in argument; (b) there could be no induction, for nothing would be repeatable (that is, the future would have to be different from the past); and (c) there would be no objective knowledge, since we could not transcend the individuality of experience and gain a community of knowledge (that is, we could not experience the same thing). So, then, abstract entities seem necessary for inductive epistemology, but of course abstract entities are precisely the kind of things we cannot and do not experience empirically and inductively.

(7) Given Fuller's and Pinnock's notion of inductive empiricism where neutral, critical thinking controls the knowing process from beginning to end, their alleged epistemology commits them to the view that all synthetic and meaningful ideas derive from experience, that all nondemonstrative (inductive) reasoning is empirical generalization from observations, and that empirical knowledge is founded upon a set of independently intelligible and separately credited observation claims. The credibility of this outlook is subject to serious challenge: (a) If held consistently from beginning to end, it would preclude the use of certain ideas necessary to inductive science (for example, normal observer, location, etc.) that cannot be empirically specified in the above way; and (b) it would involve saying that what one directly experiences are his own sensations and thoughts, and, therefore, since words derive their meaning from observation and stipulation, some theory of private language must be affirmed. Against this, however, such a theory is not intelligible; language calls for a consistent application of words, but to speak of a privately consistent application is meaningless since there is no possible way to tell independently (that is, objectively or publicly) that a word is in fact being used consistently (that is, given the same private sense now that it was given in the past). Fuller and Pinnock must *either* show that they

are not committed to the views that lead to the above two problems and yet are consistently following inductive empiricism from beginning to end, *or* they must present refutations to these problems in a way that consistently follows inductive empiricism from beginning to end. Whatever response they choose, it will soon be clear that their inductive method is committed to a great deal of philosophical fare that was not "critically" or "neutrally" established. Moreover, the view that there are independently intelligible and separately credited observation claims should also be cross-examined and rejected in light of the following considerations: (c) Observation claims derive their credibility from background assumptions (for example, what counts as a "fact," and how facts are discerned, is determined within a broader theoretical framework; every observational claim takes one beyond his present direct experience—for instance, assuming normalcy of perception in the particular instance, uniformity of category scheme, constancy of observational subject, commonality of language, etc.); (d) observation claims indeed derive their meaning within the network of background assumptions (for example, there are no purely ostensive words since an observational term—"red"—will not retain a constant meaning through a change of theory—for example, from Aristotelian to quantum physics); and (e) observations themselves are theory-infected—that is, are interpretations of stimuli in light of assumptions, beliefs, categories and anticipations (for example, the work of *Gestalt* psychology, indicating the ambiguity of objects of perception, etc.). Again we have compelling reason to doubt that inductive empiricists actually do or can let critical and neutral thinking control the knowing process from beginning to end; the very appeal to observation is governed by presuppositions that transcend the particular observation itself. To acquiesce to these considerations, Fuller and Pinnock would have to retract or radically qualify their thorough inductivism. But on the other hand if they wished to dispute these considerations, could they do so on purely empirical and inductive grounds without engaging in philosophical assumptions and reasoning?

(8) Given the inductivist's commitment to empirical procedures, we can press even harder philosophically and ask whether sense perception is reliable, in light of (a) the problem of illusion (since the nonveridical nature of an illusion is not recognized while the illusion is experienced, how can veridical perception ever be distinguished reliably from illusions?), and (b) the problem of perspectival variation (since various visual images I receive from different perspectives on an object cannot reasonably be atributed to the changing qualities of that object itself, perception seems not to be telling me the truth about those objects).

(9) Space will not permit us to speak further about such problems as (a) the traditional way of distinguishing inductive and deductive arguments

and how it undermines the use of probability, (b) how to rate probability and explicate its nature in inductive study (especially in cases of the testimony of historical writers), or (c) how to explain the analytic/synthetic distinction that inductivism assumes, and especially how to explain the distinction in a way that does not commit us to such awkward and extra-empirical metaphysical furniture as necessity or essences. Suffice it to say that each of these issues presents a solid challenge to the credibility of Fuller's and Pinnock's espousal of exhaustive inductivism. How are they to delineate and delimit sharply their "inductive" method or the "synthetic" area to which it is applied with the calculus of "probability"?

(10) In the very nature of their historical discipline, Fuller and Pinnock are *not* the presuppositionless inductivists that they make themselves out to be. The historian studies not the direct phenomena but the sources that report the past. The historian must interpret his sources, attempting to reconstruct the past. He does not simply accept the facts as a passive observer. He is faced with the chore of cross-examining his sources (which cannot but be silent in response), knowing what questions are appropriately addressed to the various types of sources, knowing when he is pushing the sources too far for desired information, etc. Moreover, the historian's inquiry must be directed toward a specific goal from its inception; he does not simply string together anything and everything he learns about a certain period or event, but rather is seeking particular kinds of answers to particular questions, certain lines of evidence for various sorts of hypotheses, different conceptions of relevance, etc. History as a science is also inherently value-impregnated. The ordinary language that historians use is quite a bit more than merely descriptive. And this is only to be expected, since they cannot properly reduce human history to the history of natural objects. To do so would be to screen out that which is peculiar to humans: intentions, desires, motives, morals, etc. In approaching the evidence the historian is also forced to use a criterion of selectivity, and this itself involves personal value judgments. Such selectivity enters right into the historian's attempt to find solutions, and not simply into his choice of problems to study. In this selectivity the historian either utilizes a notion of historical causation or a standard of historical importance. In the former case his causal explanations are not value-neutral, for he has to judge that certain conditions were relevant as causes and some were not. Furthermore, a causal analysis of human action and social history is itself a matter of assigning responsibility (thus involving moral judgment). If the historian follows out the idea of historical causation in his selectivity, then he is faced with the selection between competing models of "explanation" (that is, shall he seek to render covering laws as suggested by Hempel, nondeducible generalizations [Gardner], joint-sufficiency conditions [Goudge], or necessary conditions [Dray; Danto]?). On

the other hand, if the historian's selectivity is guided by a standard of historical importance (for example, what is memorable, intrinsically valuable, etc.), then he is *ipso facto* doing more than simple description of the past. Thus in all these ways we see how strong the case is against the common conception of objective, neutral historiography.

After a sober consideration of the ten issues we have briefly surveyed it ought to be quite clear that neutral and presuppositionless reasoning does not and cannot have full control in Fuller's or Pinnock's inductivism. The very use of that epistemology commits one to a great deal of unargued philosophical baggage. By its use one wittingly or unwittingly endorses certain crucial assumptions. And in connection with a commitment to inductivism, one inescapably must face difficult philosphical questions pertaining to epistemology and ontology, questions that can be left unanswered only at the price of theoretical arbitrariness and disrespect for the very justifying considerations that inductivism demands for our every commitment—from beginning to end.

## II. Evident Precommitments

When we read the letters Fuller and Pinnock have exchanged, we see quite obviously that each man is committed in advance to so conducting his empirical studies that the teachings of Scripture will be vindicated. Says Fuller, "I sincerely hope that as I continue my historical-grammatical exegesis of Scripture, I shall find no error in its teaching" (p. 332), for "if there is one error anywhere in what Scripture intends to teach, then everything it intends to say is suspect and we have not even one sure word from God" (p. 331). Likewise Pinnock declares that he will not permit naturalistic presuppositions to control his thought, lest he no longer speak as a Biblical supernaturalist (p. 333). Even apart from having verified every particular statement of the Scriptures, Pinnock generally indicates in advance that "the whole *graphē* is God-breathed and fully trustworthy" (p. 334). Indeed he does not want to dichotomize the Bible into factual and revelational truths, lest the revelational material shrink "before the advance of the latest critical charge" (p. 335).

Therefore it is manifest on the very surface of their letters that Fuller and Pinnock are *not* after all neutral and without their scholarly precommitments. The kind of thing we have just witnessed them saying would, in a hostile atmosphere, be sufficient to indict and convict them for failing to be impartial and requisitely objective (or "open-minded") in their approach to the Bible's veracity. These two writers simply need to be honest with themselves and recognize that, because they are saved by God's redeeming grace and have submitted in faith and love to Jesus Christ, they are dedicated in advance to protecting their Savior's word from discredit. That, however, is *not* presuppositionless, neutral inductivism.

## III. SCRIPTURAL DECLARATIONS

Finally, we know that presuppositionless impartiality and neutral reasoning are impossible and undesirable because God's Word teaches that (1) all men know God, even if suppressing the truth (Romans 1); (2) there are two basic philosophic and presuppositional outlooks—one after worldly tradition, the other after Christ (Colossians 2); (3) thus there is a knowledge falsely so-called that errs according to the faith (1 Timothy 6) and genuine knowledge based on repentant faith (2 Timothy 2); consequently, (4) some men (unbelievers) are "enemies in their minds" (Romans 8) while others (believers) are "renewed in knowledge" (Colossians 3), and characteristic of these two mindsets is the fact that the former cannot be subject to God's Word (Romans 8) but sees it as utter foolishness (1 Corinthians 1), while the latter seeks to bring every thought captive to the obedience of Christ (2 Corinthians 10) in whom is found all the treasures of wisdom and knowledge (Colossians 2) because the fear of the Lord is the beginning of knowledge (Proverbs 1). This mindset submits to Christ's word, just as the wise man builds his house upon a rock (Matthew 7); and it views the alleged foolishness of preaching as indeed the wisdom and power of God (1 Corinthians 1). Presuppositionless neutrality is both impossible (epistemologically) and disobedient (morally): Christ says that a man is either *with* him or *against* him (Matt 12:30), for "no man can serve two masters" (6:24). Our *every* thought (even apologetical reasoning about inerrancy) must be made captive to Christ's all-encompassing Lordship (2 Cor 10:5; 1 Pet 3:15; Matt 22:37).

Therefore in response to the Fuller-Pinnock Thesis II we must say: As a matter of fact, no man is without presuppositional commitments. As a matter of philosophical necessity, no man can be without presuppositional commitments. And as a matter of scriptural teaching, no man ought to be without presuppositional commitments.

We come, then, finally to Thesis III—namely, that the question of Biblical inerrancy must be settled inductively, not presuppositionally.

Is this doctrine *about* Scripture to be formulated on the basis of what Scripture says about itself (and thus presuppositionally), or rather do we take the phenomenological approach of handling the various Biblical phenomena and claims (among which are the problem passages) inductively with a view to settling the question of Scripture's inerrancy only in light of the discovered facts of empirical and historical study?

Another way of laying out the different approaches here is to point out that the Bible makes a large set of indicative claims (for example, that David was once king of Israel, that Jesus was born at Bethlehem, that Jesus was divine, that salvation is only through his shed blood, etc.). Needless to say, this set is very large indeed. Now among this set of scriptural assertions are to be found certain self-referential statements about the set as a whole (for example, "Thy word is truth," "The Scripture cannot be broken," "All Scripture is inspired by God," etc.). The question then arises: Does one decide the question of scriptural inerrancy by an inductive examination of the discursive and individual assertions of Scripture one by one, or by settling on the truth of these special self-referential assertions and then letting them control our approach to all the rest?

It is clear to anyone who will reflect seriously on this question that the statements of Scripture *about* Scripture are primary and must determine our attitude toward all the rest. Why is this so? (1) An exhaustive inductive examination cannot be carried out in practice. The doctrinal profession of the Bible's absolute truthfulness such that alleged errors or discrepancies are only apparent could take inductive scholarship as its sole or central foundation only if each and every assertion had been examined and publicly vindicated (the requirements of which stagger the imagination), but even then all the external inductive evidence cannot be presumed to be in (future discoveries and refinements of evidence might pervasively change the complexion of the pool of relevant data)—in which case the theologian could legitimately (that is, by cautious, circumspect, presuppositionless, inductive warrant) profess only a provisional and qualified inerrancy, even if he had successfully completed the enormous task of inductively confirming all of the Bible's numerous assertions. (2) By their very character, many scriptural assertions cannot be tested inductively but must be accepted, if at all, on Scripture's own attestation (for example, Christ's interpretation of his person and work as being divine and redemptive).[20] We must not forget that the necessity of special revelation does not arise as a shortcut for the intellectually ungifted who do not pursue their inductive homework thoroughly and accurately, but rather stems from the fact that there are divine truths that all men, especially as fallen, could never discover on their own but that must be unveiled by God to them (cf. Matt 16:17). Such revealed truths (for example, that the ascended Christ now makes continual intercession for us to the Father) are not subject to our inductive examination and confirmation; they are accepted on the authority of God speaking in Scripture itself. And yet they are just as much members of the set of scriptural assertions (and as such included in the range of the set-reference statements) as are the apparently more mundane historical assertions (for example, that Judas of Galilee rose up after Theudas). (3) As we have seen already, inductive study itself has crucial presuppositions that cannot be accounted for except on a Biblical basis, and therefore in a profound sense an inductive study is already committed to the content of these self-referential statements of Scripture.

We see, then, that the self-referential statements are and must be primary in our approach to the nature of Scripture and the question of its authority. The question of Biblical inerrancy must be resolved presuppositionally. Central to evangelical bibliology and apologetics is the issue of inerrancy and inductivism, and yet we must see that the latter is in no position to serve as the foundation for the former. If intelligibility in our doctrinal affirmation of inerrancy depends on the intelligibility of the presuppositionally pure inductive theory of apologetics, then the doctrine has been scuttled for sure.

And so we can agree with Pinnock against Fuller. One cannot but let the Bible speak for itself about its own nature and attributes, and consequently one cannot choose to submit to scriptural truths at some points (for example, Christ's deity and redeeming work are beyond the adjudication of empirical criticism) and reserve self-sufficient critical authority elsewhere (for example, historical data are accepted or rejected on the strength of empirical examination). Fuller's inductive approach is epistemologically and theologically impossible. It is double-minded.

On the other hand, we can agree with Fuller against Pinnock when he says Pinnock has not really been thoroughly inductive, for Pinnock allows certain scriptural statements a privileged and controlling position—one that is not subject to the radical demand to let critical thinking prevail.

Before we are tempted to reply to this charge that nonetheless Pinnock does take an inductive and evidential apologetical approach to these self-referential statements of Scripture, let us hesitate and observe that such a reply is hardly tenable. (1) If Pinnock really took a thoroughly inductive approach to such statements, that could only mean that he verified the set-reference statement itself by inductively confirming every particular assertion covered by it—that is, every claim that is within its range. This then would collapse into the phenomenological approach we have just rejected. It would be subject to its crucial defects, and Pinnock would be prey to Fuller's taunt that a part of him wants to be inductive but that he cannot go all the way. (2) Moreover, it must be observed that the very empirical apologetic pursued by Pinnock in defense of the Bible's divine credentials is of necessity grounded in metaphysical and epistemological presuppositions for which only the Bible can account. That is, he is intellectually dependent on the Bible's veracity even while examining the Bible's claims. (3) Nor should it be thought that Pinnock can credibly work toward an empirical confirmation of *some* of Scripture's historical details and then inductively infer that the *other* statements of Scripture can also be accepted, for (a) the argument would be thoroughly fallacious (just as if someone argued that because *some* [even many] statements in the Koran, or in Churchill's *Gathering Storm*, etc., are empirically confirmed, we can infer that *all* of the statements in these writings must be accepted as without error); (b) the historical details may very well be veracious without the theological interpretation of them being inductively substantiated (for example, that Paul was correct in historically asserting that Christ was "born of a woman" is hardly warrant for saying that Paul was also correct in soteriologically asserting that Christ "condemned sin in the flesh"); and (c) this approach would be subject to the same criticism as we have made of Fuller (albeit in a slightly different way)—that is, the inductive approach to inerrancy by an empirical apologist like Pinnock submits to Scripture's self-testimony at some places (for example, the interpretation of Christ's person and work is absolutely inerrant) but relies on self-sufficient critical reasoning elsewhere (for example, the historical data are provisionally inerrant to the extent of empirical confirmation or infirmity). Pinnock operates inconsistently on two different and incompatible epistemologies: On the one hand the Bible's assertions are endorsed as true, although admitted as possibly untrue, only on the basis of a neutral and critical evaluation of external evidence and independent reasoning (strictly gauged to inductive and empirical credentials), but on the other hand the Bible's assertions are accepted as true without qualification on its own sufficient authority (and in spite of apparent empirical difficulties). He double-mindedly defends a conception of Biblical authority in a way that compromises that very authority by its methodological assumptions. The question is this: What exercises control over our speculation, evaluation, and conclusions—God's revealed word in Scripture, or some authority external to God's revelation? Do empirical difficulties render the Bible's inerrancy only apparent, or does the Bible's inerrancy render empirical difficulties only apparent? Does critical thinking reign supreme only over *part* of the Bible? The errors of Fuller and Pinnock are epistemological and theological twins.

## SIGNIFICANCE AND CONCLUSION

The reason it is important for us to consider and analyze this important exchange on inerrancy between Pinnock and Fuller is simply that it brings to the surface certain latent issues and inconsistencies in the popular evangelical witness today. There is a basic intramural dispute that must be resolved in our approach to inerrancy, and this resolution is a necessary first step toward our apologetic reply to those who are antagonistic to an evangelical understanding of Scripture and its authority. Fuller correctly observes, "But we evangelicals have a basic question we must settle before we can talk very coherently with those farther afield" (p. 330).

That basic question is epistemological in nature—namely, whether we should take an inductive or presuppositional approach to the nature and authority of the Bible. We must conclude from our previous discussion that Christ's Lordship—even in the area of thought—cannot be treated like a light switch, to be turned on and off at our own pleasure and discretion. Christ makes a radical demand on our thinking that we submit to his Word as self-attesting. To do otherwise leads away from a recognition of his divine person and saving work, for it leads away from an affirmation of Scripture's inerrancy. Moreover, it simultaneously leads away from the intelligibility of all experience and every epistemic method. One must begin with the testimony of Scripture to itself rather than with the allegedly neutral methods of inductivism. And this means acknowledging the veracity of Scripture even when empirical evidence might appear to contradict it (following in the steps of the father of the faithful, Abraham: Rom 4:16-21; Heb 11:17-19). The classic interschool encounter between Pinnock and Fuller points beyond itself to the basic and inescapable need for a presuppositional apologetic rather than the allegedly pure inductivism espoused by Pinnock and Fuller. Speaking of such a presuppositional approach to the issue of inerrancy, J. I. Packer said:

> It is only unmanageable for apologetics if one's apologetic method is rationalistic in type, requiring one to have all the answers to the problems in a particular area before one dare make positive assertions in that area, even when those positive assertions would simply be echoing God's own, set forth in Scripture. But it might be worth asking whether it is not perhaps a blessing to be warned off apologetics of that kind.[21]

---

[1]"Daniel Fuller and Clark Pinnock: On Revelation and Biblical Authority," *Christian Scholar's Review* 2 (1973) 330-335; reprinted in *JETS* 16 (1973) 67-72.

[2]C. Van Til, *A Survey of Christian Epistemology*, Vol. 2 of the series "In Defense of Biblical Christianity" (den Dulk Christian Foundation, 1932; reprinted 1969) 7.

[3]C. Van Til, *A Christian Theory of Knowledge* (New Jersey: Presbyterian and Reformed, 1969) 35.

[4]C. Van Til, *Christian-Theistic Evidences* (mimeographed syllabus, Westminster Theological Seminary, 1961) 62, ii.

[5]C. Van Til, *An Introduction to Systematic Theology* (mimeographed syllabus, Westminster Theological Seminary, reprinted 1966) 45.

[6]*Survey* 7, 120, 9, 10.

[7]*Theory* 293.

[8]For example, Van Til has consistently criticized allegedly "Christian" approaches to science that maintain either that the circle of naturalistic interpretation vaguely points beyond itself to certain religious truths (that is, projection into theology) or that the autonomous scientific interpretation of the facts can also be supplemented with a religious perspective (i.e., imposition of a theological dimension). E.g., see Van Til's articles "Bridgewater Treatises" and "Butler, Joseph," *The Encyclopedia of Christianity* (ed. G. G. Cohen: Marshallton,

Delaware: National Foundation for Christian Education, 1968), 2. 178-179, 238-239, and Van Til's reviews of *The Scientific Enterprise and Christian Faith* by M. A. Jeeves, *WTJ* 32 (May 1970) 236-240; *The Philosophy of Physical Science* by A. Eddington, *WTJ* 3 (November 1940) 62; and *The Logic of Belief* by D. E. Trueblood, *WTJ* 5 (November 1942) 88-94.

[9]E.g., see Van Til's analysis of Dewey in his review of *The Philosophy of John Dewey* (ed. P. A. Schilpp), *WTJ* 3 (November 1940): "We would humbly but firmly maintain that only Christianity makes sense and philosophy as well as other forms of human experience intelligible" (p. 72). The same theme can be traced throughout Van Til's many writings; for instance, "I think that science is absolutely impossible on the non-Christian principle" (*The Defense of the Faith* [Philadelphia: Presbyterian and Reformed, 1955] 285) since it undermines the inductive procedure (pp. 283-284). Speaking of the non-Christian's method Van Til says: "Its most consistent application not merely leads away from Christian theism but in leading away from Christian theism leads to the destruction of reason and science as well" (p. 119).

[10]*Evidences* 37. Van Til's clear opposition to fideism is not sufficiently countenanced and credited by some fellow apologists (e.g., N. Geisler, *Christian Apologetics* [Grand Rapids: Baker, 1976] 56 ff. In fact Van Til has made a very similar, but much earlier, critique of fideism than Geisler!).

[11]C. Van Til, "Introduction," in B. B. Warfield, *The Inspiration and Authority of the Bible* (Philadelphia: Presbyterian and Reformed, 1948) 38, 67.

[12]*The Defense of the Faith* (1955) 258; also, in *Theory* 293.

[13]"Introduction" 37.

[14]*Evidences* 63.

[15]*Defense* 119-120.

[16]*Evidences* 56.

[17]*Theory* 26.

[18]*Defense* 116-117.

[19]*Survey* 225, 204-205.

[20]Lest it be thought that Christ's interpretation, rather than being self-attestingly established, is tested and vindicated by some informal logic such as "If Jesus rose from the dead, then he is God and accordingly speaks the truth at every point," it should be commented that this very logic is far from reflecting the unbiased, accepted and uniform conclusion or thinking of the world of advanced scholarship! That is, the logic of such an argument is itself derived from and warranted by the Scriptures (if they are in fact properly interpreted as teaching this line of reasoning), which means that Christ's interpretation is after all still based on Christ's own word. That this reasoning is subject to dispute is perhaps illustrated by considering just three aspects of it: (1) The inference "if resurrected, then divine" is hardly acceptable if applied in a discriminating and special pleading fashion so as to avoid concluding that Lazarus was also God; (2) the committed secularist would almost certainly look upon such an inference pattern as a manifestation of primitive, mythic, God-of-the-gaps thinking and present an alternative inference pattern congenial to naturalism (e.g., "If Jesus rose from the dead, then very complex and sophisticated biological principles and factors surpassing those presently recognized and utilized by scientists remain to be discovered and rendered in natural formulas"); and (3) one clearly begs many important questions, the unbelieving philosopher will note, if he simply reasons that "if Jesus was God, he always spoke the truth," for this naively utilizes only one of many competing conceptions of deity—e.g., the Greek gods were not unfailing truth-tellers! The evangelical apologist must finally realize that what should count as an acceptable test for recognizing and acknowledging something as a divine revelation can only be set forth and warranted by God himself—which could only be done by revelation. That is, the criteria for identifying revelation would themselves have to be revealed if they were to be objectively trustworthy and properly accepted over against the competing and mistaken options of man's imagination. Divine revelation *must* be self-attesting, for God alone is adequate to witness to himself; cf. J. Murray, "The Attestation of Scripture," in *The Infallible Word* (3d rev. ed.; ed. P. Woolley: Philadelphia: Presbyterian and Reformed, 1967 [1946]) 6, 10, 46-47.

[21]J. I. Packer, "Hermeneutics and Biblical Authority," *Themelios* 1/1, p.12.

# STEPHEN'S SPEECH: A CASE STUDY IN RHETORIC AND BIBLICAL INERRANCY

## REX A. KOIVISTO

The speech delivered by Stephen before the Jerusalem Sanhedrin bristles with perplexing problems for any who would approach it exegetically. Some have concluded that its lengthy character forms a foreign intrusion into the well-balanced progression of Acts.[1] Others, more favorable to the present speech text, have puzzled over the apparent divergency between the text and the judicial allegations it was supposed to have addressed.[2] Although these problems prove quite real, the speech of Stephen empties even a larger basket of difficulties on the heads of those who posit a factually inerrant text of Scripture, for this speech alone contains approximately fifteen apparent historical inaccuracies and other blunders.[3]

These problems in the speech have coaxed many conservatives into redefining the relationship of inerrancy to the speech as a unit, even though a number of those same scholars have carefully displayed solutions for the other apparent inaccuracies in Scripture. Their approach, followed by an expanding number of expositors and apologists, is to relegate the content of the speech to the realm of "allowable errancy," while preserving actual inerrancy only for Luke's accuracy in recording the speech.[4]

This approach, posit many of its adherents, preserves the doctrine of factual inerrancy by limiting the inerrancy claim only to Luke's scrupulously accurate record of what Stephen had said before the Sanhedrin. The speech may thus be admitted as having as many errors as Stephen was inclined to commit, for inerrancy extended not to *Stephen* but only to *Luke* as an author of Scripture.

The implications for this kind of approach to the difficulty are large, for by placing Stephen's speech on the shelf of secondary authority these scholars have removed that speech from the pool of revelational data suitable for constructing Biblical history and systematic theology. The data gleaned by theologians from the speech as revelational support for specific doctrines, such as the Mosaic authorship of the Pentateuch (drawn from 7:22),[5] the aseity of God (7:25),[6] the "church" of Israel (7:38),[7] the sin-restraining work of God (7:51)[8] and the truth that the striving of the Holy Spirit does not lead to repentance at times (7:51)[9] would have to be gained from other Biblical texts. The historical statements frequently taken from the speech as further revelation or clarification of OT accounts (such as the call of Abraham while in Ur as against an initial call in Haran, Acts 7:2; cf. Gen 12:1) would need to be posited merely as erroneous ideas that were held by Hellenistic Jewish Christians—or, more precisely, by Stephen—and not as being true per se as a part of direct, inerrant divine revelation.

This problem of Stephen's speech uncovers a greatly neglected area in the study of Biblical inerrancy. Little has been done to construct a working formula for determining how to approach rhetorical content in Scripture theologically.[10] Should all Biblical speeches be taken as some would take Stephen's, or should all be deemed inerrant in what they teach? Or, better yet, is there some criterion that if consistently applied would help us know which rhetoric in Scripture is or is not to be considered divinely authoritative? It is the purpose of this paper to seek answers to these crucial questions regarding the application of inerrancy by looking closely at its application to Stephen's speech as a working model.

## I. SECONDARY INERRANCY AND STEPHEN'S SPEECH

Several lines of support have been mustered to release Stephen's speech from a claim to its own inerrancy. The first factor lies in the necessity of this kind of approach in other portions of Scripture. Clark Pinnock refers to the recorded speeches of liars in the book of Job as a parallel issue.[11] The content of those speeches cannot be claimed as inerrant, but the historical actuality of the recording must be; hence a distinction of approach *must* be employed. A more obvious example may be observed in the blatant lies spoken by the serpent in the garden (Gen 3:1-3).[12] His words contradict God and are manifestly intended to deceive. Inerrancy, if applied to *all* of Scripture,[13] must here be further refined in view of context and author use. A distinction is therefore legitimately suggested between primary inerrancy of speech *content* and secondary inerrancy of speech *occurrence*.

The statement of the Amalekite before David affords a further example. Clearly, the unity of the books of Samuel and the immediate contexts denote that the Amalekite invented his tale of slaying Saul with the intention of gaining David's favor (2 Samuel 1), yet this lie is also recorded as God-breathed Scripture. A distinction between inerrancy of content and occurrence again solves the dilemma. The conclusion must be that the phenomenon of rhetoric as a form in Scripture allows for the possibility of viewing all rhetorical statements as mere inerrant records rather than as inerrant, divinely approved revelation.

In addition to the necessity of taking this kind of approach on occasion, the value of acknowledging the difficulties of Stephen's speech as obvious errors is alleged by Stokes as a solid confirmation of the truth of Biblical inerrancy. Stokes' reasoning follows these lines:

> Surely any man composing a speech to put into the mouth of one of his favorite heroes and champions would not have represented him as making such grave errors when addressing the Jewish senate.... We conclude, then, that the inaccuracies reported as made by St. Stephen are evidences of the genuine character of the oration attributed to him.[14]

The difficulties of Acts 7 are not deftly pushed away as phenomenological disclaimers for inerrancy but rather are carefully roped and dragged into the corral as support for the doctrine as a whole.[15]

The implications of this transfer of Stephen's message into the realm of secondary inerrancy are manifold. One of the implications ties in with the motive and methodology of any who would seek reconciliation, who are held to employ "strange and forced expedients of an exegetical and critical nature."[16] Stokes curtly sparks his attitude on the matter: "I would not waste the time endeavoring (if I was able) to reconcile such a variance."[17] Those who look upon themselves as valiant apologetes of Scripture suddenly emerge as those who pervert the intent of Scripture, a common allegation against those who try to reconcile difficult phenomena with the doctrine of Biblical inerrancy.[18]

In addition to this accusation of artificiality that hovers over the necks of those who would attempt a reconciliation, a more serious implication arises. As noted previously, a deletion of inerrancy claims from Stephen's speech ejects that portion of Scripture from the source-pool of revelation utilized by Biblical theologians. While this endangers no cardinal point of doctrine per se,[19] it should demand a much closer analysis of the bases for such a rejection in view of the implications carried for other doctrinal sources in Scripture.

In view of these implications, and the clear reality that some rhetorical statements of Scripture are explicable only as secondarily inerrant, a close analysis of this viewpoint is necessary.

## II. ANALYSIS OF A SECONDARY INERRANCY

To begin with, it must be admitted that some rhetorical statements in Scripture must be deferred into secondary inerrancy. This does not mean, however, that *all* rhetorical statements must be. The issues to be dealt with, then, are (1) the bases for determining which speeches must be so relegated, and (2) those criteria as applied specifically to Stephen's speech.

Two difficulties lie in the path of those claiming the ejection approach: first, a tendency not to distinguish between intentions of the Biblical writers in quoting their sources; and second, a failure to apply this in Luke's case in order to discern accurately his intention in using Stephen and his defense.

1. *Failure in source-quote distinctions.* There must be some way to distinguish the inerrancy claim of a given rhetorical statement in Scripture. Although some statements are clearly untrue (as shown earlier), it may be demonstrated that some speakers and writers used as a source are clearly understood to be true and correct in their teaching by the Biblical authors. A few of the more obvious examples of the nonrhetorical type are the quotations from the books of Jashar (Josh 10:12-13) and of the Wars of Yahweh (Num 21:14). These statements, since given author sanction in the specific texts quoted,[20] must be viewed as having divine sanction as well and hence as partaking of the quality of inerrancy, irrespective of any phenomenological difficulties contained in the quotation.[21] To relegate all quoted material with inexplicable phenomena to the labyrinths of secondary inerrancy may fail to exert adequately the critical criterion of discernment.

2. *Failure in determining clear criteria.* If it is admitted that a distinction must be enforced among the extra-scriptural quoted material, the immediate problem becomes that of determining the criteria for accepting or rejecting a given quotation as valid, inerrant revelational data. If the only criterion is the presence of some sort of difficulty within the quote, then the same arguments may be applied that are set forth against those who insist that difficulties demand an alteration of the entire doctrine of inerrancy. E. J. Young has stated the weakness of this kind of reasoning:

> The fundamental assumption, often uncritically adopted, is that the mind of man, without the assistance of divine revelation, can make pronouncements as to whether certain parts of the Bible are from God or not.[22]

There are enough *unquoted* phenomena of the Scriptures that are beyond the scope of natural man to accept; so how can one judge whether a quoted portion is revelational simply by the presence of phenomenological problems?

One way around these difficulties has been proposed by Leonard Myers in his study of the problem. Realizing the importance of some sort of distinguishing standard in handling the different speeches in Scripture, Myers concludes with the following reasoning:

The question we must now ask is how far down the line we must go before we cut off those whose pronouncement is not to be regarded as infallible truth? Between Jesus and John, or John and Stephen, or Timothy and the Samaritan woman, or who? This is the crux of the problem. The answer is that only what God Himself says is to be regarded infallible. The only exception to this is that which God Himself sanctions as coming from Him. The lies of Satan do not lie in any of these categories, so they are to be regarded as not infallible. The same goes for the book of Ecclesiastes. However, there is much which can fall in the category of infallibility: the "thus saith the Lord's" of the Old Testament, the record of biblical history, church epistles, etc. Even the apostles in their public teaching were regarded as infallible, as shown by the upper room discourse. But this infallibility does not extend beyond the apostolic circle. Therefore, Peter's sermon in Acts 2 is to be regarded as infallible, inerrant, but not Stephen's in Acts 7. Luke was granted inerrancy in recording the events in the book of Acts (inerrancy of speaking and recording are two different things). Thus Luke inerrantly records what Peter had inerrantly spoken on the day of Pentecost and inerrantly records what Stephen had errantly spoken in Acts 7.[23]

The essence of Myers' approach is that only God's direct statement in Scripture and the direct statements of those whom he specifically sanctions as authoritative spokesmen (that is, prophets, apostles, etc.) may be viewed as infallible and inerrant. Myers, however, fails to realize that inerrancy essentially applies to the inspired text of Scripture as the concurrent result of God's superintending breath and the literary work of men. In speaking of delegated men, he has been forced to distinguish between "inerrancy of speaking and recording" and has lost sight of the fact that inspiration does not simply cover recorded history but also instruction in the truth of that history. This instruction comes from the inspired writers themselves, many of whom "externally" would not have had God's sanction since they were not apostles or prophets.[24]

In a recent dissertation on Stephen's speech, Arthur B. Walton has confronted this difficulty of quotation-distinction as it relates to the phenomena in the speech. He begins by noticing the two poles that are clearly distinguishable: the lies of Satan in Genesis 3 (inerrantly recorded), and the words of Jesus (inerrantly recorded and inherently inerrant). Between these two, he notes, are the words of mortal men. He suggests that they may be distinguished by the following criteria:

(1) If the character of the speaker is inherently evil, his words may well be false, as in the words of Satan; (2) if the character of the speaker is shown by the Scripture to be deficient in spiritual perception, the statements may well be false, as in Psalm 53:1, "the fool hath said..."; (3) the context of a passage may reveal that the contents are erroneous, as in the case of Job's friends and

in the case of the natural reasoning recorded in Ecclesiastes; (4) a rebuke may reveal the fallacy of a statement by one who elsewhere makes divinely directed inerrant statements, illustrated by the rebuke of Peter by Christ (Matt. 16:23).[25]

Walton's analysis shows keener insight than Myers' into the issues involved, but it still leaves the door open somewhat for subjective decisions. The first criterion, for example, bases choice on character. This criterion could, if not carefully applied, delete the magnificent speech of Nebuchadnezzar from authoritativeness (hence inerrancy) as to its contents:

> I blessed the Most High
>     and praised and honored Him who lives forever;
> For His dominion is an everlasting dominion,
>     and His kingdom endures from generation to generation.
> And all the inhabitants of the earth are accounted
>     as nothing,
> But He does according to His will
>     in the host of heaven and among the inhabitants
>     of the earth;
> And no one can ward off His hand
>     or say to Him, "What hast Thou done?"[26]

Although it may be argued that this statement came after a regeneration experience, that is hardly demonstrable since that point is absent from the text.[27] The only conclusion to be drawn, then, is that the speech is given by one who is "inherently evil." If the text of the speech teaches correct, inspired truths about God, then that factor cannot be gained by the character of the speaker itself.[28]

Walton hit upon what appears to be the answer but did not capitalize on it: The only way hermeneutically to determine what God intends to communicate in a particular passage (and thus what substance is to partake of the quality of inerrancy) is objectively to determine what the Biblical author intends to communicate.[29] If this principle is true, then Walton's third criterion is the primary and only valid principle for analyzing cited material. When fully employed this principle thus supplies the contextual basis for discovering the data needed to determine whether the speaker is "deficient in spiritual perception," or his character is "inherently evil," or he is "rebuked" for a statement.

The central principle, then, for determining how to understand a quotation used by a Biblical writer (whether in brief or extended rhetorical statement) is this: If the author gives tacit approval to a quoted text in his manner of citation, then God gives it tacit approval; hence it must partake of the characteristic of inerrancy. Pinnock came to the same basic conclusion regarding a criterion for differentiation:

> This rule would seem to be a safe one: Where the sacred writer records data in such a way that it is apparent he regards it to be true and expects us to take it as such, we must assume that it is. Inspiration is posited in reference to writing. For that reason, whatsoever it asserts as true and free from error is to be received as such.[30]

This principle preserves quotations of unknown, pagan or evil men and allows them to be viewed as inerrant statements of divine truth. Paul thus uses the pagan writer Epimenides with patent approval of his words (Acts 17:28;[31] Titus 1:12), Jude incorporates material from the apocryphal book of Enoch with matter-of-fact certainty as to the truth of those statements (Jude 14), and the author of Daniel employs a beautiful quotation of the pagan Nebuchadnezzar in Dan 4:34-35.[32] Each of these quotations, then, should be deemed inerrant based on the principle of author sanction.

The validity of this sole principle as a dividing line between that which is primarily inerrant and that which is secondarily inerrant among Biblical quotations may be observed in its application to several questionable texts. In Gen 3:1, for example, the author notes that the "person" about to speak to Eve was "more subtle than any other wild creature that the LORD God had made" (RSV). From this introductory note it is evident that the author does not expect the reader to express much confidence in the character of the serpent; hence the serpent's statements are not to be looked on as reliable in the absolute sense. They must be relegated to the sphere of secondary inerrancy.

Another example may be evinced from the statement of the Amalekite in 2 Sam. 1:10. Here the Amakekite is recorded as saying that he killed Saul, although the preceding narrative in 1 Samuel 31 depicts Saul's self-invoked death by his armor-bearer on Gilboa. The unity of the books of Samuel may be called on as a clear factor in determining whether the Amalekite's claim before David is to be regarded as true by the reader. The author's gruesomely detailed narrative of Saul's death reveals that he was obviously not ignorant of the facts, yet the narrator gives no hint that the report of that death had been relayed to David.

In order to depict the conveyance of the information to David in the next chapter (2 Samuel 1), the author shows David returning from his skirmish against the Amalekites. The victory over the Amalekites at this time is described by the author as a vengeful slaughter due to David's painful loss to them at Ziklag (1 Sam 30:1-6). The tenor is clearly anti-Amalekite at this point, yet the one who shuttles the report of Saul's death to David is himself an Amalekite. The overt inference is that the Amalekite, gazing into David's fuming eyes, had ulterior motives of putting himself in David's favor; thus he boasts that he killed David's nemesis.

In view, then, of the author's selection of words and distinct emphases, it becomes apparent that he did not intend the Amalekite's story to be taken as an actual account of Saul's death. The context demands that we understand the Amalekite as an enemy of David and a deliberate liar.[33] Here too, then, the author did not intend the statement to be regarded as true, so secondary inerrancy may be fairly posited.

In like manner the speeches of Job's comforters must be viewed. The claims they set forth regarding the character of Job and God in their verbal tête-à-tête runs *against* the direct statements of the author in his narrative of the first two chapters. In addition, the falseness of their words may be seen in the conclusive verdict delivered by God himself: "My wrath is kindled against you [Eliphaz] and your two friends; for you have not spoken of me what is right, as my servant Job has" (Job 42:7, RSV). By virtue of the author's intention in the context of his book it is clear that the speeches in the narrative given by the "comforters" are not to be viewed as infallible; thus secondary inerrancy finds its home here as well.

3. *Conclusion.* The observation has been made that the crux of the matter in determining the inerrancy of a given rhetorical quotation in Scripture is not the difficulty of any phenonema that may appear in that quotation, nor is it the character of the speaker, nor is it the speaker's implicit rank or delegated divine authority attributed to him as an individual. The only valid, testable and objective criterion for ascertaining the inerrancy of quoted material (extra-Biblical or not) is this: "Does the writer condone or approve the substance of the statement quoted?" It now remains to apply this criterion to the presentation of Stephen's speech by Luke.

## III. Stephen's and Luke's Inerrancy

There is sufficient evidence to demonstrate that Stephen received a strong backing of approval by Luke and hence to posit that we must take Stephen's speech in an inerrant sense. Five factors tilt the scales in this direction: (1) Luke's portrait of Stephen's character; (2) Luke's editorial comments on Stephen; (3) Luke's judicial foil; (4) Luke's nontendency toward error; and (5) Luke's speech usage in Acts.

1. *Stephen's character.* Stephen's entrance into the forefront of Luke's narrative is relatively rapid. His first appearance in Acts 6:5 is melted into the list of seven particularly noteworthy men who were put forth by the multitude of believers for the distributionary task. This clearly denotes that he was acknowledged by the group and ratified by the apostles (6:6) as having attained the threefold character requirements previously set forth. Stephen, as one of the seven, was recognized by the Christian community as possessing "good repute" and as being "full of the Holy Spirit

and wisdom" (6:3). Although this in itself is not an independent criterion for determining the inerrancy of Stephen's speech, it does show that Luke as an author paints a positive portrait of Stephen.

2. *Luke's comment.* Although this portrait in itself initiates a positive tenor to Stephen's character, a further factor arises in Luke's treatment of Stephen in his catalog of the seven. Not only does Luke begin the list with Stephen, but Stephen also is one of two in that list with Lukan comments attached to his name. The other one, Nicolas, receives the added note concerning his distinct station as a proselyte to Judaism. Stephen, however, receives an expansion on the integrity of his character. Luke does not merely list him as "Stephen," but "Stephen, a man full of faith and of the Holy Spirit" (6:5). The very fact that he would reiterate these issues almost to the point of redundancy shows that Luke himself holds Stephen in a unique place among the seven noteworthy men.

3. *Luke's judicial foil.* A third factor in the narrative demonstrates that Luke intends to put his stamp of approval on Stephen. Luke devotes a full paragraph to the activities that sparked his arrest and gives no hint that the arrest was legally justifiable. On the contrary, he goes to notable lengths to bring to the reader's attention the fact that the arrest was totally unjust. In 6:8 Luke describes Stephen's activities as motivated by the fact that he was "full of grace and power," while in v 10 he notes that the verbal attack on Stephen was curtailed because the opposition "could not withstand the wisdom and Spirit with which he spoke." The negative tenor in this introductory section does not apply to Stephen but is instead slapped upon those who are in opposition to Stephen. Luke records that this sinister group "secretely instigated men" (v 11), "stirred up the people and the elders and the scribes" (v 12), and "set up false witnesses" against Stephen (v 13).

From the foregoing, it is clear that Luke intended to show that Stephen's was a mock trial on "trumped-up" charges.[34] There is no hint that Luke intended to display Stephen in a bad light at his trial. The *contrary* is true, however, for after painting his portrait of the opposition with such dark colors Luke focuses his narrative on Stephen and records that even the opposition noticed that "his face was like the face of an angel" (v 15).[35] This strong contrast within the trial backdrop itself gives fair indication that Luke was siding himself personally with Stephen and his cause. It seems highly improbable that Luke would do this sort of thing and yet place the central contribution of Stephen—his speech—into the narrative, knowing that his hero was teaching erroneous Biblical history. Luke must have accepted what Stephen taught as true. Walton observes the logical outgrowth of this data:

Yet, neither his character, nor the context of the speech, nor Luke's treatment of the speech, suggest that his words were to be questioned. Indeed, it seems clear that Luke included the speech of Stephen in detail and at length, without criticism, but with obvious approval, because he considered the teachings of Stephen to be his own. This is one of the strongest arguments for inerrancy in the content of the speech.[36]

4. *Luke and possible error.* In view of Luke's presentation of positive character in the person of Stephen, it has been concluded that Luke approved of Stephen. Earlier it was argued by Stokes as a chief proponent of the secondary inerrancy school that the multiplicity of error within the speech commends the doctrine of Biblical inerrancy by showing Luke's scrupulous objectivity. However, with Luke's clear approval of Stephen's character as a deliberate backdrop to the speech, this conclusion proves untenable. Alexander has written a more probable conclusion to the phenomena of multiple difficulties at this point in the speech:

> This last hypothesis, that Stephen erred, even if admissable in the case of exegetical necessity, is far less natural than either of the others. With respect to the concurrence or accumulation of supposed inaccuracies in this one verse (as to Jacob's burial, that of the patriarchs and Abraham's purchase), so far from proving one another, they only aggravate the improbability of real errors having been committed in such quick succession, and then gratuitously left on record, when they might have been so easily corrected or expunged.[37]

In view, then, of Luke's presentation of Stephen's character and innocence, the probability of known factual error in the speech is low.

5. *Luke and the speeches.* Luke's general handling of the speeches in Acts in correlation to the gospel words of our Lord forms the final argument against assuming that Luke acknowledged and integrated factual error into the speech. Bruce notes the necessity that "the speeches in *Ac.* must not be considered in isolation from those in *Lk.*, where we have the other Synoptists for comparison."[38] At this point the attitude of Luke toward recording the words of our Lord may serve as a viable pattern for determining his attitude toward the words of the apostolic band in Acts. Concerning Luke's treatment of the Lord's discourses, Bruce notes that "it is agreed by Synoptic students that Luke reports with great faithfulness the sayings and speeches which he found in his Gospel sources."[39] Longenecker has made this same observation:

> Comparing the third Gospel with the first, it can be demonstrated that Luke did not invent sayings for Jesus. On the contrary, he seems to have been more literally exact in the transmission of the words of Jesus than in the recording of the events of His life.[40]

The relationship of Luke's scrupulousness in his gospel to his record in Acts implies that extreme care would be afforded the recording of a proclamation in Acts by virtue of parallel intent and continuity of message. Longenecker concludes the relationship in this way:

> There is, therefore, it must still be insisted, a presumption in favor of a similarity of treatment in Luke's recording of the words of Jesus and his recording of the addresses of Peter, Stephen, Philip, James and Paul. And though it is certainly true that his respect for the latter never rivaled his veneration for the former, it is difficult to believe that such a difference would have appreciably affected his desire for accuracy of content, if not also of word, which he evidences in his Gospel.[41]

Given the reality of similarity of treatment between the two works, and given the high priority Luke gives to the place of Christian proclamation in his book of apostolic history, it becomes extremely unlikely that Luke would insert a speech that is a defense of the universal scope of that faith knowing that it contained clear and observable historical errors.

## Conclusion

In view of the foregoing data, it seems quite clear that Stephen's speech fits the essential criterion of author sanction, which demands that we take the speech as primarily inerrant and not simply secondarily inerrant.

We have used Stephen's speech as a pivotal test case to hammer out a suitable method for approaching rhetorical content in Scripture theologically. The only scientific approach is an objective criterion that is detachable and applicable to all the speech-segments in Holy Writ. It has been concluded that the simplest and safest criterion is author sanction. Stephen's speech receives author sanction. Therefore we must use the content of his speech as another source-pool of divinely revealed truth.

---

[1]F. J. Foakes Jackson, "Stephen's Speech in Acts," *JBL* 49 (1930) 283-286; B. W. Bacon, "Stephen's Speech: Its Argument and Doctrinal Relationship," in *Biblical and Semitic Studies* (New York: Yale, 1901) 213-229.

[2]For a brief survey of these difficulties see L. W. Barnard, "St. Stephen and Alexandrian Christianity," *NTS* 7 (1960) 31-32.

[3]R. B. Rackam cites fifteen difficulties in his *Acts of the Apostles* (14th ed.; Grand Rapids: Baker, 1964) 99-102, while H. J. Cadbury is content to leave them at ten in *The Book of Acts in History* (New York: Harper, 1955) 102-103.

[4]C. H. Pinnock, *Biblical Revelation* (Chicago: Moody, 1971) 78-79.

[5]A. H. Strong, *Systematic Theology* (Valley Forge: Judson, 1907) 169.

[6]L. Berkhof, *Systematic Theology* (4th ed.; Grand Rapids: Eerdmans, 1939) 58.

[7]Ibid., pp. 409, 572.

[8]Ibid., p. 442.

[9]Ibid. Thiessen argues along a similar line from this last Stephenic statement; *Lectures in Systematic Theology* (Grand Rapids: Eerdmans, 1949) 144.

[10]I know of only two unpublished sources that deal seriously with the question: L. Myers, "Acts 7:15-16" (M. Div. thesis; Grace Theological Seminary, 1969), and A. B. Walton, "Stephen's Speech" (ThD. dissertation; Grace Theological Seminary, 1972). C. Pinnock touched on the issue in *Biblical Revelation* 78-79, but did not explore to the fullest the difficulties involved.

[11]Pinnock, *Revelation* 78. Cf. C. W. Carter and R. Earle, *The Acts of the Apostles* (Grand Rapids: Zondervan, 1959) 96.

[12]W. R. Cook, *Systematic Theology in Outline Form* (Portland: Western Conservative Baptist Seminary, 1970), 1. 44.

[13]This follows as a logical outgrowth of the plenary doctrine of 2 Tim 3:16.

[14]G. T. Stokes, *The Acts of the Apostles* (New York: Armstrong, 1837) 311-312.

[15]This is particularly supportive in view of the apparent Thucydidean historical procedure of "supplying" speeches for his characters (*History*, 1.22): "My habit has been to make the speakers say what was in my opinion demanded of them by the various occasions, of course adhering as closely as possible to the general sense of what was said." Thucydides, *The History of the Peloponnesian War* (trans. Richard Crawley; New York: Dutton, 1950).

[16]H. A. W. Meyer, *Critical and Exegetical Handbood to the Acts of the Apostles* (New York: Funk and Wagnalls, 1883) 145.

[17]Stokes, *Acts* 317.

[18]Mounce refers to this approach to inerrancy as artificial. R. A. Mounce, "Clues to Understanding Biblical Accuracy," *Eternity* 17/6 (June 1966) 16-18.

[19]I say this with caution, due to the use of Stephen's speech as a sole source of appeal by some theologians for particular doctrines.

[20]This of course does not mean that all the books from which quotes are extracted receive sanction by the authors.

[21]Thus the "standing still" of the sun at Gibeon must be viewed as actual history because of the author's approval of that quote in spite of the scientific tremors it causes some.

[22]E. J. Young, "Scripture—God-breathed and Profitable," *Grace Journal* 7/3 (Fall 1966) 4.

[23]Myers, "Acts" 28-29.

[24]Luke himself serves as an example. Even though both Luke and Mark gain external authority due to their association with specific apostles, that association does not give them intrinsic apostolic authority. The same holds true for other canonical yet nonprophetic or nonapostolic books.

[25]Walton, "Speech" 202-203

[26]Dan 4:34b-35 (NASB).

[27]All that the text states is that his "reason" returned to him after he had been humbled by God, and he blessed God for it.

[28]An even clearer example is the beautiful inspired truths implanted in the Balaam oracles by God himself *against* the "inherently evil" prophet's will (Numbers 22-24).

[29]Unless of course the text itself states that the author did not understand what he was writing (e.g., some apocalyptic literature; cf. Rev 17:6-7).

[30]Pinnock, *Revelation* 78-79.

[31]A verse taken by many theologians as divine revelation on the immensity/omnipresence of God; see Strong, *Theology* 280; Berkhof, *Theology* 61.

[32]A verse taken by theologians to teach the *independentia* of God; see Berkhof, *Theology* 58.

[33]"His description of himself as an Amalekite, twice repeated, must have made his action seem all the more horrible in the eyes of David and his men, newly returned from the battle against Amalek. Amalekites remain Amalekites, even if they are sojourning in Israel; these born robbers do not even shrink from the Lord's anointed! Doubtless this is the only way the narrative was understood and judged....Moreover, the man betrays himself as an obvious liar, out for what he can get. True, it is not expressly said that David sees through him and therefore holds him responsible. But the narrator seems to think that his death is just punishment." H. W. Hertzberg, *I and II Samuel: A Commentary* (Philadelphia: Westminster, 1964) 237.

[34]This leads to the further possibility that Luke was intending to show a definite correla-

tion between the trial of our Lord and the trial of Stephen. This certainly appears to be a valid correlation in view of the singularly unique statements of both our Lord and Stephen as they are at the point of unjust execution. Luke records that Stephen stated, "Lord, do not place this sin against them," which is remarkably similar to our Lord's statement, recorded by Luke alone, "Father, forgive them, for they do not know what they are doing" (Luke 23:34). Although many (including B. M. Metzger, *A Textual Commentary on the Greek New Testament* [London: United Bible Societies, 1971] 180) question the Lukan origin of this reading, its genuineness as a logion of Christ is still acceptable.

[35]This same contrast between Stephen and his opponents is depicted at the conclusion of the speech, when the opposition "were enraged and ground their teeth at him," but he, "full of the Holy Spirit, gazed into heaven and saw the glory of God" (v 55).

[36]Walton, "Speech" 203.

[37]J. A. Alexander, *The Acts of the Apostles Explained* (3d ed.; New York: Scribners, 1864), 1. 268-269.

[38]F. F. Bruce, *The Acts of the Apostles: The Greek Text* (Chicago: InterVarsity, 1952) 18-19.

[39]Ibid.

[40]R. Longenecker, *Biblical Exegesis in the Apostolic Period* (Grand Rapids: Eerdmans, 1975) 82.

[41]Ibid., pp. 82-83.

# THE CHICAGO STATEMENT ON BIBLICAL INERRANCY

## Preface

The authority of Scripture is a key issue for the Christian Church in this and every age. Those who profess faith in Jesus Christ as Lord and Savior are called to show the reality of their discipleship by humbly and faithfully obeying God's written Word. To stray from Scripture in faith or conduct is disloyalty to our Master. Recognition of the total truth and trustworthiness of Holy Scripture is essential to a full grasp and adequate confession of its authority.

The following Statement affirms this inerrancy of Scripture afresh, making clear our understanding of it and warning against its denial. We are persuaded that to deny it is to set aside the witness of Jesus Christ and of the Holy Spirit and to refuse that submission to the claims of God's own Word that marks true Christian faith. We see it as our timely duty to make this affirmation in the face of current lapses from the truth of inerrancy among our fellow Christians and misunderstanding of this doctrine in the world at large.

This Statement consists of three parts: a Summary Statement, Articles of Affirmation and Denial, and an accompanying Exposition. It has been prepared in the course of a three-day consultation in Chicago. Those who have signed the Summary Statement and the Articles wish to affirm their own conviction as to the inerrancy of Scripture and to encourage and challenge one another and all Christians to growing appreciation and understanding of this doctrine. We acknowledge the limitations of a document prepared in a brief, intensive conference and do not propose that this Statement be given creedal weight. Yet we rejoice in the deepening of our own convictions through our discussions together, and we pray that the Statement we have signed may be used to the glory of our God toward a new reformation of the Church in its faith, life and mission.

We offer this Statement in a spirit, not of contention, but of humility and love, which we purpose by God's grace to maintain in any future dialogue arising out of what we have said. We gladly acknowledge that many who deny the inerrancy of Scripture do not display the consequences of this denial in the rest of their belief and behavior, and we are conscious that we who confess this doctrine often deny it in life by failing to bring our thoughts and deeds, our traditions and habits, into true subjection to the divine Word.

We invite response to this Statement from any who see reason to amend its affirmations about Scripture by the light of Scripture itself, under whose infallible authority we stand as we speak. We claim no personal infallibility for the witness we bear, and for any help that enables us to strengthen this testimony to God's Word we shall be grateful.

# I. Summary Statement

1. God, who is Himself Truth and speaks truth only, has inspired Holy Scripture in order thereby to reveal Himself to lost mankind through Jesus Christ as Creator and Lord, Redeemer and Judge. Holy Scripture is God's witness to Himself.

2. Holy Scripture, being God's own Word, written by men prepared and superintended by His Spirit, is of infallible divine authority in all matters upon which it touches: It is to be believed, as God's instruction, in all that it affirms; obeyed, as God's command, in all that it requires; embraced, as God's pledge, in all that it promises.

3. The Holy Spirit, Scripture's divine Author, both authenticates it to us by His inward witness and opens our minds to understand its meaning.

4. Being wholly and verbally God-given, Scripture is without error or fault in all its teaching, no less in what it states about God's acts in creation, about the events of world history, and about its own literary origins under God, than in its witness to God's saving grace in individual lives.

5. The authority of Scripture is inescapably impaired if this total divine inerrancy is in any way limited or disregarded, or made relative to a view of truth contrary to the Bible's own; and such lapses bring serious loss to both the individual and the Church.

# II. Articles of Affirmation and Denial

Article I.    We affirm that the Holy Scriptures are to be received as the authoritative Word of God.

We deny that the Scriptures receive their authority from the Church, tradition, or any other human source.

Article II.      We affirm that the Scriptures are the supreme written norm by which God binds the conscience, and that the authority of the Church is subordinate to that of Scripture.

We deny that church creeds, councils, or declarations have authority greater than or equal to the authority of the Bible.

Article III.      We affirm that the written Word in its entirety is revelation given by God.

We deny that the Bible is merely a witness to revelation, or only becomes revelation in encounter, or depends on the responses of men for its validity.

Article IV.      We affirm that God who made mankind in His image has used language as a means of revelation.

We deny that human language is so limited by our creatureliness that it is rendered inadequate as a vehicle for divine revelation. We further deny that the corruption of human culture and language through sin has thwarted God's work of inspiration.

Article V.      We affirm that God's revelation in the Holy Scriptures was progressive.

We deny that later revelation, which may fulfill earlier revelation, ever corrects or contradicts it. We further deny that any normative revelation has been given since the completion of the New Testament writings.

Article VI.      We affirm that the whole of Scripture and all its parts, down to the very words of the original, were given by divine inspiration.

We deny that the inspiration of Scripture can rightly be affirmed of the whole without the parts, or of some parts but not the whole.

Article VII.      We affirm that inspiration was the work in which God by His Spirit, through human writers, gave us His Word. The origin of Scripture is divine. The mode of divine inspiration remains largely a mystery to us.

We deny that inspiration can be reduced to human insight, or to heightened states of consciousness of any kind.

Article VIII.     We affirm that God in His work of inspiration utilized the distinctive personalities and literary styles of the writers whom He had chosen and prepared.

We deny that God, in causing these writers to use the very words that He chose, overrode their personalities.

Article IX.     We affirm that inspiration, though not conferring omniscience, guaranteed true and trustworthy utterance on all matters of which the Biblical authors were moved to speak and write.

We deny that the finitude or fallenness of these writers, by necessity or otherwise, introduced distortion or falsehood into God's Word.

Article X.     We affirm that inspiration, strictly speaking, applies only to the autographic text of Scripture, which in the providence of God can be ascertained from available manuscripts with great accuracy. We further affirm that copies and translations of Scripture are the Word of God to the extent that they faithfully represent the original.

We deny that any essential element of the Christian faith is affected by the absence of the autographs. We further deny that this absence renders the assertion of Biblical inerrancy invalid or irrelevant.

Article XI.     We affirm that Scripture, having been given by divine inspiration, is infallible, so that, far from misleading us, it is true and reliable in all the matters it addresses.

We deny that it is possible for the Bible to be at the same time infallible and errant in its assertions. Infallibility and inerrancy may be distinguished but not separated.

Article XII.     We affirm that Scripture in its entirety is inerrant, being free from all falsehood, fraud, or deceit.

We deny that Biblical infallibility and inerrancy are limited to spiritual, religious, or redemptive themes, exclusive of assertions in the fields of history and science. We further deny that scientific hypotheses about earth history may properly be used to overturn the teaching of Scripture on creation and the flood.

Article XIII.     We affirm the propriety of using inerrancy as a theological term with reference to the complete truthfulness of Scripture.

We deny that it is proper to evaluate Scripture according

233

to standards of truth and error that are alien to its usage or purpose. We further deny that inerrancy is negated by Biblical phenomena such as a lack of modern technical precision, irregularities of grammar or spelling, observational descriptions of nature, the reporting of falsehoods, the use of hyperbole and round numbers, the topical arrangement of metrical, variant selections of material in parallel accounts, or the use of free citations.

Article XIV.    We affirm the unity and internal consistency of Scripture.

We deny that alleged errors and discrepancies that have not yet been resolved vitiate the truth claims of the Bible.

Article XV.    We affirm that the doctrine of inerrancy is grounded in the teaching of the Bible about inspiration.

We deny that Jesus' teaching about Scripture may be dismissed by appeals to accommodation or to any natural limitaton of His humanity.

Article XVI.    We affirm that the doctrine of inerrancy has been integral to the Church's faith throughout its history.

We deny that inerrancy is a doctrine invented by scholastic Protestantism, or is a reactionary position postulated in response to negative higher criticism.

Article XVII.    We affirm that the Holy Spirit bears witness to the Scriptures, assuring believers of the truthfulness of God's written Word.

We deny that this witness of the Holy Spirit operates in isolation from or against Scripture.

Article XVIII.    We affirm that the text of Scripture is to be interpreted by grammatico-historical exegesis, taking account of its literary forms and devices, and that Scripture is to interpret Scripture.

We deny the legitimacy of any treatment of the text or quest for sources lying behind it that leads to relativizing, dehistoricizing, or discounting its teaching, or rejecting its claims to authorship.

Article XIX.    We affirm that a confession of the full authority, infallibility and inerrancy of Scripture is vital to a sound understanding of the whole of the Christian faith. We

234

further affirm that such confession should lead to increasing conformity to the image of Christ.

We deny that such confession is necessary for salvation.
However, we further deny that inerrancy can be rejected without grave consequences, both to the individual and to the Church.

# III. Exposition

Our understanding of the doctrine of inerrancy must be set in the context
of the broader teachings of Scripture concerning itself. This exposition
gives an account of the outline of doctrine from which our Summary
Statement and Articles are drawn.

A. *Creation, Revelation and Inspiration*

The Triune God, who formed all things by His creative utterances and
governs all things by His Word of decree, made mankind in His own image for a life of communion with Himself, on the model of the eternal fellowship of loving communication within the Godhead. As God's
image-bearer, man was to hear God's Word addressed to him and to respond in the joy of adoring obedience. Over and above God's self-
disclosure in the created order and the sequence of events within it,
human beings from Adam on have received verbal messages from Him,
either directly, as stated in Scripture, or indirectly in the form of part or
all of Scripture itself.

When Adam fell, the Creator did not abandon mankind to final judgment but promised salvation and began to reveal Himself as Redeemer in
a sequence of historical events centering on Abraham's family and culminating in the life, death, resurrection, present heavenly ministry and
promised return of Jesus Christ. Within this frame God has from time to
time spoken specific words of judgment and mercy, promise and command, to sinful human beings, so drawing them into a covenant relation
of mutual commitment between Him and them in which He blesses them
with gifts of grace and they bless Him in responsive adoration. Moses,
whom God used as mediator to carry His words to His people at the time
of the exodus, stands at the head of a long line of prophets in whose
mouths and writings God put His words for delivery to Israel. God's purpose in this succession of messages was to maintain His covenant by causing His people to know His name—that is, His nature—and His will both
of precept and purpose in the present and for the future. This line of prophetic spokesmen from God came to completion in Jesus Christ, God's incarnate Word, who was Himself a prophet—more than a prophet, but
not less—and in the apostles and prophets of the first Christian genera-

tion. When God's final and climactic message, His word to the world concerning Jesus Christ, had been spoken and elucidated by those in the apostolic circle, the sequence of revealed messages ceased. Henceforth the Church was to live and know God by what He had already said, and said for all time.

At Sinai God wrote the terms of His covenant on tablets of stone as His enduring witness and for lasting accessibility, and throughout the period of prophetic and apostolic revelation He prompted men to write the messages given to and through them, along with celebratory records of His dealings with His people, plus moral reflections on covenant life and forms of praise and prayer for covenant mercy. The theological reality of inspiration in the producing of Biblical documents corresponds to that of spoken prophecies: Although the human writers' personalities were expressed in what they wrote, the words were divinely constituted. Thus what Scripture says, God says; its authority is His authority, for He is its ultimate Author, having given it through the minds and words of chosen and prepared men who in freedom and faithfulness "spoke from God as they were carried along by the Holy Spirit" (1 Pet 1:21). Holy Scripture must be acknowledged as the Word of God by virtue of its divine origin.

B. *Authority: Christ and the Bible*

Jesus Christ, the Son of God who is the Word made flesh, our Prophet, Priest and King, is the ultimate Mediator of God's communication to man, as He is of all God's gifts of grace. The revelation He gave was more than verbal; He revealed the Father by His presence and His deeds as well. Yet His words were crucially important; for He was God, He spoke from the Father, and His words will judge all men at the last day.

As the prophesied Messiah, Jesus Christ is the central theme of Scripture. The Old Testament looked ahead to Him; the New Testament looks back to His first coming and on to His Second. Canonical Scripture is the divinely inspired and therefore normative witness to Christ. No hermeneutic, therefore, of which the historical Christ is not the focal point is acceptable. Holy Scripture must be treated as what it essentially is—the witness of the Father to the incarnate Son.

It appears that the Old Testament canon had been fixed by the time of Jesus. The New Testament canon is likewise now closed, inasmuch as no new apostolic witness to the historical Christ can now be borne. No new revelation (as distinct from Spirit-given understanding of existing revelation) will be given until Christ comes again. The canon was created in principle by divine inspiration. The Church's part was to discern the canon that God had created, not to devise one of its own.

The word *canon*, signifying a rule or standard, is a pointer to authority, which means the right to rule and control. Authority in Christianity belongs to God in His revelation, which means, on the one hand, Jesus

Christ, the living Word, and, on the other hand, Holy Scripture, the written Word. But the authority of Christ and that of Scripture are one. As our Prophet, Christ testified that Scripture cannot be broken. As our Priest and King, He devoted His earthly life to fulfilling the law and the prophets, even dying in obedience to the words of messianic prophecy. Thus as He saw Scripture attesting Him and His authority, so by His own submission to Scripture He attested its authority. As He bowed to His Father's instruction given in His Bible (our Old Testament), so He requires His disciples to do—not, however, in isolation but in conjunction with the apostolic witness to Himself that He undertook to inspire by His gift of the Holy Spirit. So Christians show themselves faithful servants of their Lord by bowing to the divine instruction given in the prophetic and apostolic writings that together make up our Bible.

By authenticating each other's authority, Christ and Scripture coalesce into a single fount of authority. The Biblically-interpreted Christ and the Christ-centered, Christ-proclaiming Bible are from this standpoint one. As from the fact of inspiration we infer that what Scripture says, God says, so from the revealed relation between Jesus Christ and Scripture we may equally declare that what Scripture says, Christ says.

C. *Infallibility, Inerrancy, Interpretation*

Holy Scripture, as the inspired Word of God witnessing authoritatively to Jesus Christ, may properly be called *infallible* and *inerrant*. These negative terms have a special value, for they explicitly safeguard crucial positive truths.

*Infallible* signifies the quality of neither misleading nor being misled and so safeguards in categorical terms the truth that Holy Scripture is a sure, safe and reliable rule and guide in all matters.

Similarly, *inerrant* signifies the quality of being free from all falsehood or mistake and so safeguards the truth that Holy Scripture is entirely true and trustworthy in all its assertions.

We affirm that canonical Scripture should always be interpreted on the basis that it is infallible and inerrant. However, in determining what the God-taught writer is asserting in each passage, we must pay the most careful attention to its claims and character as a human production. In inspiration, God utilized the culture and conventions of his penman's milieu, a milieu that God controls in His sovereign providence; it is misinterpretation to imagine otherwise.

So history must be treated as history, poetry as poetry, hyperbole and metaphor as hyperbole and metaphor, generalization and approximation as what they are, and so forth. Differences between literary conventions in Bible times and in ours must also be observed: Since, for instance, non-chronological narration and imprecise citation were conventional and acceptable and violated no expectations in those days, we must not regard these things as faults when we find them in Bible writers. When total precision of a particular kind was not expected nor aimed at, it is no error not to have achieved it. Scripture is inerrant, not in the sense of being absolutely precise by modern standards, not in the sense of being absolutely precise by modern standards, but in the sense of making good its claims and achieving that measure of focused truth at which its authors aimed.

The truthfulness of Scripture is not negated by the appearance in it of irregularities of grammar or spelling, phenomenal descriptions of nature, reports of false statements (for example, the lies of Satan), or seeming discrepancies between one passage and another. It is not right to set the so-called "phenomena" of Scripture against the teaching of Scripture about itself. Apparent inconsistencies should not be ignored. Solution of them, where this can be convincingly achieved, will encourage our faith, and where for the present no convincing solution is at hand we shall significantly honor God by trusting His assurance that His Word is true, despite these appearances, and by maintaining our confidence that one day they will be seen to have been illusions.

Inasmuch as all Scripture is the product of a single divine mind, interpretation must stay within the bounds of the analogy of Scripture and eschew hypotheses that would correct one Biblical passage by another, whether in the name of progressive relation or of the imperfect enlightenment of the inspired writer's mind.

Although Holy Scripture is nowhere culture-bound in the sense that its teaching lacks universal validity, it is sometimes culturally conditioned by the customs and conventional views of a particular period, so that the application of its principles today calls for a different sort of action.

D. *Skepticism and Criticism*

Since the Renaissance, and more particularly since the Enlightenment, world views have been developed that involve skepticism about basic Christian tenets. Such are the agnosticism that denies that God is knowable, the rationalism that denies that He is incomprehensible, the idealism that denies that He is transcendent, and the existentialism that denies rationality in His relationships with us. When these un- and anti-Biblical principles seep into men's theologies at presuppositional level, as today they frequently do, faithful interpretation of Holy Scripture becomes impossible.

E. *Transmission and Translation*

Since God has nowhere promised an inerrant transmission of Scripture, it is necessary to affirm that only the autographic text of the original documents was inspired and to maintain the need of textual criticism as a means of detecting any slips that may have crept into the text in the course of its transmission. The verdict of this science, however, is that the Hebrew and Greek text appears to be amazingly well preserved, so that we are amply justified in affirming, with the Westminster Confession, a singular providence of God in this matter and in declaring that the authority of Scripture is in no way jeopardized by the fact that the copies we possess are not entirely error-free.

Similarly, no translation is or can be perfect, and all translations are an additional step away from the *autographa*. Yet the verdict of linguistic science is that English-speaking Christians, at least, are exceedingly well served in these days with a host of excellent translations and have no cause for hesitating to conclude that the true Word of God is within their reach. Indeed, in view of the frequent repetition in Scripture of the main matters with which it deals and also of the Holy Spirit's constant witness to and through the Word, no serious translation of Holy Scripture will so destroy its meaning as to render it unable to make its reader "wise for salvation through faith in Christ Jesus" (2 Tim 3:15).

## F. *Inerrancy and Authority*

In our affirmation of the authority of Scripture as involving its total truth, we are consciously standing with Christ and His apostles, indeed with the whole Bible and with the main stream of Church history from the first days until very recently. We are concerned at the casual, inadvertent and seemingly thoughtless way in which a belief of such far-reaching importance has been given up by so many in our day.

We are conscious too that great and grave confusion results from ceasing to maintain the total truth of the Bible whose authority one professes to acknowledge. The result of taking this step is that the Bible that God gave loses its authority, and what has authority instead is a Bible reduced in content according to the demands of one's critical reasonings and in principle reducible still further once one has started. This means that at bottom independent reason now has authority, as opposed to Scriptural teaching. If this is not seen and if for the time being basic evangelical doctrines are still held, persons denying the full truth of Scripture may claim an evangelical identity while methodologically they have moved away from the evangelical principle of knowledge to an unstable subjectivism, and will find it hard not to move further.

We affirm that what Scripture says, God says. May He be glorified. Amen and Amen.

# EVANGELICAL THEOLOGY: WHERE SHOULD WE BE GOING?

## STANLEY N. GUNDRY

What is appropriate for a presidential address? Those who have been in this position will recognize how unique the demands of this assignment are. The difficulties are obvious. We sit here with full stomachs after a long and full day of travel and meetings. One more session is still on the agenda. And it is only realistic for me to recognize that our interests are varied. Consequently, I suspect that there are only two fond hopes for this address that you all hold in common: (1) that I will not put you to sleep with a subject of no personal interest to you, and (2) that I will keep the length of my remarks within appropriate limits. This certainly presents me with a challenge, but not with a subject.

When I considered the theme of this thirtieth annual meeting, "Evangelical Theology: Where Are We and Where Are We Going?" I discovered that no one had been assigned to give an overview of where evangelical theology *should* be going. I did not choose my subject; my subject chose me. Presumptuous though it may be of me to address this topic, I come to it with the conviction that we each are prone to be isolated within the specialties of our own discipline, with a consequent loss of direction, perhaps within that discipline itself, and even more likely a loss of direction with reference to matters outside that discipline. We need a sense of direction across the countryside while wending our way through the cities, villages and hamlets. I will give my perception of where evangelical theologians should be going in the years ahead. I will not be so presumptuous, however, as to suggest conclusions that should be reached; we must do our homework first. But I will point to the possibilities and problems that, in my judgment, we either cannot or dare not ignore.

One direction we will find ourselves going, whether we want to or not. You all know what I am referring to: the inerrancy question. Neither side in this discussion can be expected to let the subject go away. One pole will be sharpening and defending the concept but may be in danger of so narrowing inerrancy that it will depart from the Biblical basis and the historical understanding of the concept. The other pole in the discussion can be expected to continue to repudiate the concept altogether or to continue to use the term "inerrancy" but to so qualify it as to evacuate the concept of any significant meaning.

Few if any evangelicals look with relish upon the possible polarizations and divisions that may develop within their ranks if trends known to exist back in the 1950s and 1960s, but only recently publicly identified,[1] continue. But I submit to you that no matter where you stand on this issue there could hardly be one more crucial for the future health and vigor of evangelical theology. Perhaps Lindsell's historical and theological argument can be faulted in certain minor details. But the "slippery-slide" theory (or maybe you prefer to call it the "banana-peel" or "domino" theory) is pretty hard to refute in either its historical or theological version. In saying that, I am not arguing that inerrancy is the *essence* of what it means to be evangelical or Christian (as Bernard Ramm accuses some of saying[2]). But I am saying that historical precedents and epistemological considerations seem to indicate that one's position on inerrancy is a kind of watershed indicating the logical, and perhaps eventual, direction of one's theology. As Kenneth Kantzer has put it, the doctrine of inerrancy is "essential for *consistent* evangelicalism and for a full Protestant orthodoxy."[3]

Just because the developing discussion of inerrancy is so critical, I appeal for an attitude of candor and openness bathed in familial Christian love. We should not forget that even James Orr, who did not subscribe to inerrancy, was a contributor to *The Fundamentals* and a valiant defender of orthodoxy.[4] J. Gresham Machen is not remembered as one who evaded critical theological issues. Yet even Machen admitted, "There are many who believe that the Bible is right at the central point, and yet believe that it contains many errors. Such men are not really liberals, but Christians." Machen could say this while also emphatically saying that "the mediating view of the Bible" was not "logically tenable."[5] We who subscribe to inerrancy should continue to value the contribution to the cause of Christ made by those who have modified their position on inerrancy even while we express concern over those very modifications and departures.

Furthermore, just because we do believe the noninerrantist position of our brethren to be historically, Biblically and logically indefensible, there must continue to be forums where the two sides can continue to discuss the issues. Specifically, inerrantists need to press the issues of logical consistency and epistemology, Scripture's view of itself, Christ's view of and use of Scripture, and the historic view of the Church. In my judgment, noninerrantists have either been in actual error on these matters or else have evaded the key issues.[6] Is it too much to hope that open confrontation of issues, not people, would elicit serious rethinking among some errantists? Perhaps it would prove to be wishful thinking, but is there not much more to be gained by assuming the integrity and intellectual honesty of those with whom we disagree? It is to be hoped that the International Council on Biblical Inerrancy can successfully follow through on its announced intention of engaging the opposing view in open discussion.

If truly open discussions take place, however, inerrantists should not be so foolish as to assume that they will not be confronted with some rather difficult questions themselves. We may have individually resolved these matters to our own satisfaction, but on them there is no consensus among inerrantists. It is far from evident that there is even a common, univocal meaning ascribed to the word "inerrancy." Among those whose inerrancy credentials are considered to be impeccable, there are differing explanations of the implications of the concept.

Unresolved differences of hermeneutical approach becloud the unity of our subscription to inerrancy. Let me illustrate. Is there any responsible inerrantist who would not say that it is the intended meaning of the author's words that is without error? Lindsell, for instance, admits to such in his discussions of the missing thousand and the mustard seed.[7] But once that legitimate and necessary principle is admitted, we might as well candidly acknowledge the presence of a whole host of other problems. Is there a single concurrent divine-human authorial intention in Scripture, or the possibility of double authorial intention—one human (and possibly errant) and the other divine (and hence inerrant)? If recognition of authorial intention is necessary to the proper perception of inerrancy, how round can a round number be and still be inerrant? If approximations are admissible, how approximate can an approximation be and still be inerrant? If phenomenological language or the language of appearances is admissible, what is the dividing line between errancy and inerrancy? If apparent errors in recorded speeches in Scripture can be dismissed as inerrant records of errant speeches, how may the reader know which speeches, or parts of speeches, come to him with absolute binding authority? If it is admitted that the Bible is a piece of literature containing a variety of figurative language (at least simile, metaphor and hyperbole) and literary genre (at least poetry, discourse, historical narrative, parable, epistle and apocalyptic), then on the basis of authorial intention can an inerrantist admit the possibility of pseudonymous literature in Scripture? If not, why not? Or can a NT scholar who subscribes to inerrancy legitimately argue that the evangelists created a distinctively Christian type of literary genre called "gospel," somewhat akin to Jewish midrash, in which historical accuracy, in the author's intention, took second place to the author's exposition of the Christian message, with the result that there are *actual* discrepancies and contradictions among the gospels in reportorial details? Can it be argued, then, that fictional elements, mixed with historical facts, are consistent with the inerrancy of the author's intention because the fictional elements serve the author's theological purpose? Using the assumptions and methodology of redaction criticism, evangelical NT scholars are raising these questions. The broader community of evangelical scholarship would do well to address these very questions posthaste.

There is another interesting twist to inerrancy and authorial intention. Inerrantists have legitimate interest in harmonization and elimination of apparent discrepancies in Scripture. On the really tough problems we usually resort to one of two approaches. We can propose a solution that theoretically or technically is possible, but that is something less than a natural or obvious meaning we would assign the passage were it not for the existence of an apparently discrepant parallel. The other approach is to suspend judgment and speak of it as an apparent discrepancy incapable of natural resolution at this time. I prefer the latter approach. However, proponents of both alternatives have to be ready to defend themselves against the charge that neither takes the words of Scripture as seriously as the word "inerrancy" suggests. Why? Because, it is charged, neither will accept the obvious conclusion based on the most natural meaning of the passages: An actual discrepancy exists. It can be argued that both contorted harmonization and suspension of judgment deny the clarity of Scripture, which is to deny the view of inspiration they are intended to uphold. In fact, with such reasoning errancy is being defended in the name of inerrancy and verbal inspiration!

Just what does inerrancy of the author's intended meaning allow for? We are driven from inerrancy into hermeneutics. But hermeneutics can also become a guise to evacuate the inerrancy concept of any real meaning. The pages of our Society's *Journal* testify to the fact that we inerrantists still have homework to do.[8]

William Wells concludes his review of James Barr's recent book, *Fundamentalism*, with this challenge:

> If inerrancy is worth defending, then it is worth articulating more carefully. Barr's questions and barbs make it apparent that we do not yet have a satisfactory formulation of the doctrine. Second, the evangelical community has in fact been accommodating itself to critical scholarship. The question is: How far should that process go? Until now, conservative theologians and Bible scholars have worked on this problem, but they have rarely worked together closely. It is time they did.[9]

I happen to believe inerrancy is worth defending, and hence worth articulating more carefully. It is also worth working toward a consensus on the hard problems.

I read with skepticism James Boice's statement in a letter to invited participants to the summit meeting of the ICBI. He wrote that after the summit "the church and the world will know exactly what we mean by the term 'Biblical Inerrancy,' and that we are in agreement concerning its definition."[10] Although Boice expressed a legitimate goal, his predicted fulfillment seems premature. The "Chicago Statement on Biblical Inerrancy" resulting from that meeting is a remarkably balanced and comprehensive document, especially considering the theological diversity of the participants and the time limitations within which they operated. Even so, the papers and discussions leading up to the document clearly showed that inerrantists themselves disagree on the definition and implications of inerrancy, the apologetics of inerrancy, the determination of authorial intention, the question of single or dual intention, the use of the historical-critical method, the uses of literary genre, and the cultural conditioning of Scripture. A comprehensive consensus has not yet emerged. As a body, evangelical theologians, apologists and Bible scholars committed to inerrancy need to squarely face these questions.

The Evangelical Theological Society has this statement as its doctrinal basis: "The Bible alone, and Bible in its entirety, is the Word of God written and is therefore inerrant in the autographs." Allegations have occasionally appeared to the effect that some in our membership continue to sign this statement with mental reservations.[11] That such is the case is not all that evident to me. But it may be true that the alleged mental reservations are in fact differing understandings of what "inerrancy" means or perhaps even uncertainty with respect to its precise meaning.

The Evangelical Theological Society should be a forum where those with a commitment to inerrancy can come to grips with the problems of definition and hermeneutics. We (and our critics) should remember that our statement was never intended as a creed adequately summarizing what it means to be Christian or evangelical. The statement on Scripture is exactly what our constitution says it is. It is the doctrinal basis on which we have agreed to do our scholarly work, theological and Biblical. Part of that work in the days immediately ahead should be to challenge and confront the errantist position. But in all candor we should admit that another part of our work is to clarify and sharpen our own position, attempting to come to a common understanding of what inerrancy means and how it functions within the hermeneutical problems surrounding our use and appropriation of Scripture for our day in history.

Important as it is, though, the discussion of inerrancy should not be allowed to become the preoccupation of evangelical theology.[12] Theology is more than prolegomena. Our theological task is to move beyond and build on that theological foundation. If we do not do this, in a few years we will discover that our work has only been an eddy in the ongoing stream of theological discussion in our time. We may have won a battle (over inerrancy) but have lost the war (the construction of a Biblically-based evangelical theology addressing the issues of our time). I make a special point of this, because in the past we have been prone to this kind of narrow focus. It is important that a building have a foundation; but of what value is a foundation with no adequate structure atop it?

Just what are these areas of theology that we need to address constructively in the immediate future? Without suggesting that there are no other candidates, I submit to you that the area most in need of serious theological discussion in the near future will be ecclesiology. This in turn can be divided into two large subject areas: the nature of the Church (what we might call ecclesiology proper) and the mission of the Church (an aspect of missiology). The theologian and Biblical scholar who does not tune his/her ear to the discussion of these related issues simply will not be where the action is; and, worse yet, the Church of Jesus Christ worldwide will be the poorer for that failure.

Keep in mind, please, that this is an essay proposing an agenda for evangelical theology, identifying the crucial questions with which evangelical theologians should be wrestling. As with inerrancy, I will not attempt to resolve the issues. It is sufficient for my purposes to identify them and indicate how they impinge on the theological task. First, we turn to ecclesiology proper.

One of the most interesting concerns surfacing among some evangelicals is the search for Church continuity and connection with tradition. Even from the earliest years of the Reformation, the Reformers asked these same kinds of questions. Consider for instance Luther's lengthy discussions of the marks of the true Church and its continuity as the Church of Christ through history.[13] Protestants indeed do need to ask such questions.

But recent years have seen a renewed interest in the question in American evangelical circles. It has been marked by the turn of some well-known evangelical personalities to the Episcopal Church and the issuance of the Chicago Call.[14] What seems to have influenced some in this direction are the emphases on continuity and tradition, liturgy and worship, and the sacraments and the historic creeds of early Christendom. That such an interest should emerge in American evangelicalism at this time is not surprising. Except for those denominations with a particular national origin, North American evangelicals have characteristically had little sense of history or of their connection with the Christian past. Independence has been so idealized as to make it appear that a church can exist without a context in or connection with the Christian past. Faith and worship have been so highly individualized in the North American evangelical experience that the corporate aspects of these seem all but lost in many instances. It is no wonder, then, that some evangelicals are searching for roots, even if it means grafting themselves into the episcopal trunk.[15] They apparently feel that there they find a continuity of faith, practice, worship, community and ecclesiastical authority.

This mood can hardly be ignored. For one thing it is a response to a very real deficiency in North American evangelical Christianity. It will not be enough to ignore or criticize the crypto-episcopalism of the Chicago Call and some of its signers, though there will undoubtedly be some of us who will want to do that. We must address those felt needs to which the Chicago Call and the turn to episcopalism are a response.

Another of the critical ecclesiological issues of our day is Church unity. It confronts Christians worldwide. It concerns inclusivists and exclusivists, ecumenists and separatists. Each position from its own perspective wrestles with the problems. Is the oneness for which Jesus prayed and about which Paul wrote exclusively spiritual, or is it to also have structural and visible manifestations? And if there are to be the latter, what should be the shape of that structure? How inclusive should the theological basis be? Would subscription to the Apostles' Creed be sufficient? Or should it be a distinctly Protestant evangelical unity? If so, how is "evangelical" to be defined? Or should the basis of unity be experiential (such as a born-again or a charismatic experience) rather than creedal-theological? And once these issues are resolved, how is such unity to be effected within the diversity reflected within Christendom-Protestantism-evangelicalism?

Or perhaps the preoccupation with problems of structural unity is misplaced. Is the Biblical model of the Church organic rather than institutional? If Howard Snyder is right, the current preoccupation with super-churches, with super-pastors, with super-plants, with super-bus fleets is misplaced.[16] But if he is right, it seems to me that denominational and transdenominational structures of all types must also be radically revalued.

As long as we are discussing the problems of Church structure, the whole problem of parachurch organizations needs to be theologically addressed. Are they in fact arms of the church, or have some of them in effect become "church" for their staffs and constituency? To whom are they accountable theologically, financially, and in terms of methodology, priorities and goals? The contemporary proliferation of organizations with multimillion-dollar budgets and staffs numbering in the hundreds or thousands, accountable to no one but an ill-defined constituency, is certainly as much a theological question as it is a practical question.

Intertwined with several of these issues is the nature of the Christian ministry. Is it to be authoritarian or serving? Singular or plural? Ordained or lay? Male alone or male and female? Indeed, what roles of leadership and service may women scripturally assume in the cause of Christ? Has the traditional subjection of women to male leadership preserved the divine order for home, Church, and society, or has it in fact perpetuated sinful male dominance and deprived the Church of the feminine perspective and the full use of fifty per cent of its human resources? Is the traditional position a Biblical absolute or culturally conditioned? Are evangelical feminists self-assertive females with no regard for Biblical authority and order, or are they prophetic voices calling on the Church to incarnate the full implications of oneness and equality in Christ? Are they selfishly demanding a piece of the ecclesiastical pie or simply insisting that they be allowed to use fully the gifts sovereignly given them? Let us not be so naive as to think these questions will go away by ignoring them or by dismissing them with jokes. Furthermore, we must all face these questions aware of our own culturally conditioned rationalizations, submitting them to the full authority of what Scripture teaches as the ideal that transcends culture.

Most of the matters I have mentioned so far are most directly related to the daily life and function of the Church in the world. One remaining item is less so, but it is no less important for one's theological understanding of the Church and its place within redemptive history. What is the Church, and what is its relationship to OT Israel and its covenants? Many interrelated concepts are at issue in this discussion: Israel, Israel of God, spiritual Israel, seed of Abraham, OT Church, people of God, body of Christ, old covenant, new covenant, and kingdom. Nearly the whole of social eschatology is also bound up with this aspect of ecclesiology.

In the past our discussions have usually polarized around two standards: covenant theology and dispensationalism. I do not call for a renewal of the old polemics or for the ill feeling that all too frequently passed back and forth in that discussion. But I wonder if the time has not come for a reopening of the discussion that would go beyond that of our predecessors. I am no starry-eyed optimist who would ask that the opposing views put aside deeply-held convictions in the interests of finding the lowest common denominator. The great gulf between the two, however, may not be so great as it once was. I cannot speak for the covenant theologians, and I confess that I am not conversant with their recent literature on this subject. But what I have picked up in casual conversation with some of you suggests to me that many of you have made some significant modifications in your so-called covenant theology and that you may even be less doctrinaire than you once were. But equally significant is the fact that dispensational theology is not now what it once was or perceived to be. Even a comparison of the old *Scofield Reference Bible* with the *New Scofield Reference Bible* gives some evidence of shifting. Or one might compare older dispensationalism with Charles Ryrie's *Dispensationalism Today* or his recently published *Study Bible*. Other younger dispensational theologians have made even more significant changes in their views on the kingdom concept, the new covenant, the sermon on the mount, Matthew 13, the people of God, and so on. I wonder whether we are mutually aware of these shifts. May there now exist the possibility of a new level of discussion? Does a focus for renewed discussion exist in Walter Kaiser's proposal of a promise theology?[17] As Kaiser has so often insisted, one's hermeneutical theory and practice are hinge issues.[18] Maybe this is where a new level of ecclesiological-eschatological engagement should occur. I urge evangelical theologians to explore this route.

As we stand back and look at the panorama of Church-related issues that need to be seriously addressed by theologians, we are struck by their diversity and complexity. In the past most of them have been marked by deadlocks and in some cases ugly animosities. But these very issues continue to press in upon us, some with renewed urgency. We might prefer not to address them anew because of pessimism as to the outcome. Or could it be that even the suggestion of renewed discussion also suggests the possibility of flexibility and modification—something theologians are not noted for? But the facts are that a great deal of literature has recently appeared on some of these subjects. Unfortunately, much of it is historically and theologically uninformed, or at least ill-informed. The Church of Jesus Christ is in a critical period just in terms of its perception of itself. It needs the services of its theologians. Decisions and directions are influenced and/or made by popular authors, charismatic personalities, congregational votes, general assemblies, commissions, congresses, continuation committees, parachurch organizational hierarchies, and so on. Evangelical theologians need to get their ecclesiological act together and on the road. Only then can we expect to have a meaningful impact on the Church as Church at the end of the twentieth century.

The Church and its mission, or missiology, has emerged as an even more critical area of theological discussion in the last few years. Missiologists are addressing issues that many feel make the inerrancy question pale into relative insignificance by way of comparison. And yet with only a few notable individual exceptions North American evangelical theologians seem to be unaware of and unconcerned about the missiological discussion and literature. Few of us have become involved in the discussion in meaningful ways.

Shortly after I was elected president of ETS, I had a brief discussion with a highly placed individual in the World Evangelical Fellowship about the relationship of ETS to the WEF's Theological Commission (they list us as an association with whom fraternal contact has been established). I wanted to explore the possibility of more meaningful involvement of ETS members in the work of the Theological Commission. Frankly, I was given the cold shoulder. Why? I was told that North American evangelical theologians tend to exercise a theological imperialism over their peers around the world and that as a group we were largely unaware of the missiological issues. That indictment may not be fully justified, but there is enough truth to it that it should give us cause for concern. If we are to avoid a theological provincialism we must tune in to missiological literature and discussions. Frankly, many of us will need to assume the role of student before we can become full participants.[19]

Some of the missiological issues are better known to us than others. The theological issues arising from the church growth movement and principles are generally well known. Is the concept of socially homogeneous churches consistent with the nature of the Church as developed in Pauline literature? Are people movements, or the newer phrase "multi-individual conversions," consistent with the personal nature of repentance, faith and new birth? Is the concept of winnable peoples consistent with the universal character of the great commission? Do the quantitative means of measuring church growth tend to minimize discipleship and qualitative growth? Does the church growth movement have a well-defined theological basis, or is it fundamentally a success-oriented set of principles primarily indebted to the findings of the behavioral sciences? Church growth theoreticians have sharpened some of their terminology, modified some of their concepts, and corrected some mistaken outside perceptions of their principles as they have interacted with those not identified with the movement. But more of this sort of interaction is needed, and theologians need to be more active participants in the discussion.

The missiological issue that we most urgently need to come to grips with is contextualization. I wonder if we really recognize that all theology represents a contextualization, even our own theology? We will speak of Latin American liberation theology, black theology, or feminist theology; but without the slightest second thought we will assume that our own theology is simply theology, undoubtedly in its purest form. Do we recognize that the versions of evangelical theology held to by most people in this room are in fact North American, white, and male and that they reflect and/or address those values and concerns?

Contextualization is concerned with the communication of the substance of divine revelation into the forms and structures of the recipients' culture in such a way that the integrity of the gospel and Christianity are not compromised, but also in such a way that the gospel and the Christian way can be fully internalized by the person in that culture. Contextualization aims to address the person in his actual situation.

The gospel and Christianity are never known to exist outside of a cultural context, not even within Scripture itself. So we are first faced with the hermeneutical problem of discerning essential substance from nonessential form within Scripture itself. What is normative and what is merely descriptive within Scripture? Our present norms of Biblical hermeneutics do not adequately deal with this problem. Next, the one communicating to those of another culture must be sensitive to the fact that his own expression and practice of the faith is a contextualized one. And finally, that essential substance must be contextualized in the culture of the recipient.

Some elements of cultures, however, need to be judged by divine revelation. By what standard and methodology do we discern which aspects of a culture need to be adapted to and which to be judged? How can the gospel and theology be related to a culture without becoming relativized in the process? How do we avoid accommodation (in a bad sense) to a culture in the interests of communication to a culture? In short, how can contextualization avoid becoming syncretism? The one taking the gospel to another culture is not the only one who must be sensitive to the danger of accommodation and syncretism in the process of contextualization. We must examine our own contextualized theologies for evidence of accommodation and syncretism to and with prevailing non-Christian values and concepts.

We must also recognize that contextualization properly involves not only readily identifiable cultural forms and values but also the mentality, concepts and ways of thinking peculiar to a particular culture. Samuel Rowen has stated this point well by asking:

> If creeds and confessions are our contextualized expressions of the gospel, then what is their proper place in the continuing process of contextualization? In what ways do we legitimately build upon what the Spirit of God has done through the church in the past?[20]

Must an Asian Christian express his understanding of the incarnation in Chalcedonian form?

The more one becomes aware of the peculiar problems faced in contextualization the more one is impressed with the complex and critical nature of the issues. We must adequately prepare our students to participate in the process, and we ourselves must begin to participate in and contribute to that process in meaningful ways.

This then is where I believe evangelical theology should be going in the years ahead of us. But I have one final observation. I have argued that the challenge to evangelical theology is to make new advances in the definition and implications of inerrancy, the nature of the Church and its ministry, and missiological issues loaded with theological implications. You may have noticed that one theme is a common ingredient in all three: hermeneutics. Many, perhaps most, of the unresolved problems relating to the definition and implications of inerrancy can be boiled down to one word: hermeneutics. The same can be said of many of the issues I have identified in ecclesiology: It has long been recognized that hermeneutics is at the heart of the debate between covenant and dispensational ecclesiology and eschatology.[21] And what is contextualization except cross-cultural hermeneutics? Hermeneutics is the unfinished item on our agenda of theological prolegomena. It must be seriously and comprehensively addressed by all evangelical theologians and Biblical scholars in the immediate future. Without a hermeneutical consensus, any hope for a consensus in theology and ethics is mere wishful thinking. We evangelicals rightly make a great deal of the normative nature of the Biblical text. Our views must be judged in the light of Scripture. But our agreement on this point has real significance only to the extent that we "correctly handle the word of truth."

---

[1]H. Lindsell, *The Battle for the Bible* (Grand Rapids: Zondervan, 1976).

[2]B. Ramm, "Is 'Scripture Alone' the Essence of Christianity?", *Biblical Authority* (ed. J. Rogers; Waco: Word, 1977) 109-123.

[3]K. Kantzer, "Evangelicals and the Inerrancy Question," *Evangelical Roots* (ed. K. Kantzer; Nashville: Nelson, 1978) 91.

[4]Orr contributed to vols. 1, 4, 6, 9 of *The Fundamentals* (Chicago: Testimony Publishing, 1910-1913).

[5]J. G. Machen, *Christianity and Liberalism* (New York: Macmillan, 1923) 75.

[6]As examples I cite J. Rogers, ed., *Biblical Authority*, and the special 1976 issue of Fuller Theological Seminary's *Theology, News and Notes*: "The Authority of Scripture at Fuller."

[7]Lindsell, *Battle* 167-169.

[8]Consider these articles from the last ten years of *BETS* and *JETS*: D. P. Fuller, "Benjamin B. Warfield's View of Faith and History," 11 (1968) 75-83; A. F. Holmes, "Ordinary Language Analysis and Theological Method," 11 (1968) 131-138; N. L. Geisler, "Theological Method and Inerrancy: A Reply to Professor Holmes," 11 (1968) 139-146; A. F. Holmes, "A Reply to N. L. Geisler," 11 (1968) 194-195; G. H. Clark, "Guest Editorial," 12 (1969) 69-71; D. Fuller and C. Pinnock, "On Revelation and Biblical Authority," 16 (1973) 67-72; R. J. Coleman, "Reconsidering 'Limited Inerrancy,'" 17 (1974) 207-214; J. B. Payne, "Partial Omniscience: Observations on Limited Inerrancy," 18 (1975) 37-40; V. S. Poythress, "Problems for Limited Inerrancy," 18 (1975) 93-103; G. R. Osborne, "Redaction Criticism and the Great Commission: A Case Study Toward a Biblical Understanding of Inerrancy," 19 (1976) 75-85; P. B. Payne, "The Fallacy of Equating Meaning with the Human Author's Intention," 20 (1977) 243-252; G. H. Clark, "Beegle on the Bible: A Review Article," 20 (1977) 265-286.

[9]W. W. Wells, "Blasting Bible Believers," *Christianity Today* 22/17 (June 2, 1978) 34.

[10]Letter dated June 22, 1978.

[11]Such allegations often take the form of vague, oral rumor. A few are in print and more specific. Cf. Lindsell, *Battle* 128-131; R. Quebedeaux, *The Worldly Evangelicals* (New York: Harper, 1978) 18, 22-23, 163-164; J. Montgomery, "Whither Biblical Inerrancy?", *Christianity Today* 21/20 (July 29, 1977) 40; also "Relief from Payne," *Christianity Today* 22/8 (January 27, 1978) 39-40.

[12]Cf. Kantzer, "Evangelicals" 88-100.

[13]These may be found throughout vols. 39, 40, 41 of *Luther's Works* (American edition), but note especially 40. 7-44.

[14]M. A. Noll, "Evangelicals on the Canterbury Trail," *Eternity* (March 1978) 15-19, 40, 42.

[15]Cf. R. Webber, *Common Roots* (Grand Rapids: Zondervan, 1978).

[16]H. Snyder, *The Problem of Wineskins: Church Structure in a Technological Age* (Downers Grove: InterVarsity, 1975), and *The Community of the King* (Downers Grove: InterVarsity, 1977).

[17]W. C. Kaiser, "The Davidic Promise and the Inclusion of the Gentiles (Amos 9:9-15 and Acts 15:13-18): A Test Passage for Theological Systems," *JETS* 20 (1977) 97-111. This paper, read at the spring 1976 meeting of the mid-western section of ETS, was the focus of prepared responses by an amillennialist, a covenant premillennialist and a dispensationalist. The results of that discussion tend to support the point I am making here, but there must be a purposeful effort to continue such exploratory dialogue.

[18]W. C. Kaiser, "The Current Crisis in Exegesis and the Apostolic Use of Deuteronomy 25:4 in 1 Corinthians 9:8-10," *JETS* 21 (1978) 3-18.

[19]The literature is enormous, although largely ignored by evangelical Biblical scholars and theologians. One could begin with G. W. Peters, "Current Theological Issues in World Missions," *BSac* 135 (1978) 153-164, and *Theology and Mission* (ed. D.J. Hesselgrave; Grand Rapids: Baker, 1978). Journals such as *Missiology, International Review of Mission, Occasional Bulletin* and *Evangelical Missions Quarterly* quickly plunge one into the issues. Also see *The Willowbank Report—Gospel and Culture* (Wheaton: Lausanne Committee for World Evangelization, 1978).

[20]S. Rowen, "Response," in *Theology and Mission* (ed. Hesselgrave) 114.

[21]The literature is replete with examples of this recognition. I cite only one recent example: R. Clouse, ed., with contributions by G. Ladd, H. Hoyt, L. Boettner and A. Hoekema, *The Meaning of the Millennium* (Downers Grove: InterVarsity, 1977) 18-29, 41-44, 55, 65-69, 104-111, 134-138, 172-176.

# Select Bibliography On Inspiration And Inerrancy

(Inclusion in the following lists does not imply wholesale acceptance of methodology or contents.)

## I. Books

Achtemeier, Paul J. *The Inspiration of Scripture: Problems and Proposals* (Philadelphia: Westminster, 1980).

Aland, Kurt. *The Problem of the New Testament Canon* (London: A. R. Mowbray, 1962).

Anderson, Bernhard. *The Living Word of the Bible* (Philadelphia: Westminster, 1979).

*The Authority of Scripture at Fuller*: special issue of *Theology, News and Notes* (1976).

Barclay, William. *By What Authority?* (London: Darton, Longman and Todd, 1974).

Barr, James. *The Bible in the Modern World* (New York: Harper, 1960).
——.*Fundamentalism* (Philadelphia: Westminster, 1978).

Barth, Karl. *The Word of God and the Word of Man* (New York: Harper, 1957).

Bartlett, David L. *The Shape of Scriptural Authority* (Philadelphia: Fortress, 1983).

Beegle, Dewey. *The Inspiration of Scripture* (Philadelphia: Westminster, 1963).
——.*Scripture Tradition and Infallibility* (Grand Rapids: Eerdmans, 1973).

Berkouwer, G. C. *Holy Scripture* (Grand Rapids: Eerdmans, 1965).

Boer, Harry R. *Above the Battle? The Bible and Its Critics* (Grand Rapids: Eerdmans, 1977).

Brown, Raymond. *The Critical Meaning of the Bible: How a Modern Reading of the Bible Challenges Christians, the Church and the Churches* (New York: Paulist, 1981).

Bruce, F. F. *Tradition Old and New* (Grand Rapids: Zondervan, 1970).

Burtchaell, J. T. *Catholic Theories of Biblical Inspiration Since 1810* (Cambridge: University Press, 1969).

Carnell, E. J. *The Case for Orthodox Theology* (Phildaelphia: Westminster, 1959).

Carson, D. A. *Scripture and the Truth* (Grand Rapids: Zondervan, 1983).

Christensen, Michael J. *C. S. Lewis on Scripture: Thoughts on the Nature of Biblical Inspiration, the Role of Revelation, and the Question of Inerrancy* (Waco: Word, 1979).

Coats, George W. *Canon and Authority* (Philadelphia: Fortress, 1977).

Coleman, Richard. *Issues of Theological Warfare: Evangelicals and Liberals* (Grand Rapids: Eerdmans, 1972).

Criswell, W. A. *Why I Preach That the Bible Is Literally True* (Nashville: Broadman, 1969).

Davis, S. T. *The Debate About the Bible: Inerrancy Versus Infallibility* (Philadelphia: Westminster, 1977).

Forsyth, P. T. *The Gospel and Authority* (Minnepolis: Augsburg, 1972).

———. *The Principle of Authority* (London: Independent, 1952).

France, R.T. *Jesus and the Old Testament* (London: Tyndale, 1971).

Geisler, Norman L. *From God to Us* (Chicago: Moody, 1974).

———. *Inerrancy* (Grand Rapids: Zondervan, 1979).

Harris, R. Laird. *Inspiration and the Canonicity of the Bible* (Grand Rapids: Zondervan, 1969).

Henry, Carl F. H. *God, Revelation and Authority* (Waco: Word, 1979).

Johnson, S. Lewis. *The Old Testamtent in the New: An Argument for Biblical Inspiration* (Grand Rapids: Zondervan, 1980).

Kelsey, David H. *The Use of Scripture in Recent Theology* (Philadelphia: Fortress, 1975).

Kline, Meredith. *The Structure of Biblical Authority* (Grand Rapids: Eerdmans, 1972).

Klug, Eugene F. A. *From Luther to Chemnitz: On Scripture and the Word* (Grand Rapids: Eerdmans, 1971).

Kooiman, Willem Jan. *Luther and the Bible* (Philadelphia: Muhlenberg, 1967).

Lewis, Gordon R. *Testing Christianity's Truth Claims: Approaches to Christian Apologetics* (Chicago: Moody, 1976).

Lightner, Rob P. *The Saviour and the Scriptures* (Nutley: Presbyterian and Reformed, 1973).

Lindsell, Harold. *Battle for the Bible* (Grand Rapids: Zondervan, 1976).

———. *God's Incomparable Word* (Wheaton: Victor, 1977).

Longenecker, R. *Biblical Exegesis in the Apostolic Period* (Grand Rapids: Eerdmans, 1975).

Loretz, Oswald. *The Truth of the Bible* (New York: Herder and Herder, 1968).

MacArthur, John F. *Take God's Word For It* (Glendale: Regal, 1978).

———. *Why Believe the Bible?* (Glendale: Regal, 1978).

MacKenzie, John L. *Authority in the Church* (New York: Image, 1971).

Marquart, Kurt. *Anatomy of an Explosion: Theological Analysis of the Missouri Synod Controversy* (Grand Rapids: Baker, 1978).

Marshall, I. Howard. *Biblical Inspiration* (Grand Rapids: Eerdmans, 1982).

Martin, James. *The Reliability of the Gospels* (London: Hodder and Stoughton, 1959).

McDowell, Josh. *Evidence That Demands A Verdict* (Campus Crusade, 1972).

———. *More Evidence That Demands A Verdict* (Campus Crusade, 1975).

McKim, Donald. *The Authoritative Word: Essays on the Nature of Scripture* (Grand Rapids: Eerdmans, 1983).

Montgomery, John W. *God's Inerrant Word* (Minneapolis: Bethany Fellowship, 1974).

Morris, Henry M. *Many Infallible Proofs* (San Diego: Creation Life, 1974).

Newman, J. H. *On the Inspiration of Scripture* (Washington: Corpus, 1967).

Newman, John Cardinal. *Cardinal Newman's Doctrine of the Holy Scriptures* (Louvain: Oxford, 1953).

Nicole, Roger R. *Inerrancy and Common Sense* (Grand Rapids: Baker, 1980).

Nineham, Dennis. *The Use and Abuse of the Bible* (New York: Barnes and Noble, 1976).

Packer, J. I. *"Fundamentalism" and the Word of God* (Grand Rapids: Eerdmans, 1958).

———. *God Has Spoken: Revelation and the Bible* (London: Hodder and Stoughton, 1965).

Phillips, John Bertram. *Ring of Truth: A Translator's Testimony* (New York: Macmillan, 1967).

Pinnock, Clark H. *Biblical Revelation: The Foundation of Christian Theology* (Chicago: Moody, 1971).

———. *A Defense of Biblical Infallibility* (Philadelphia: Presbyterian and Reformed, 1967).

Polman, A. D. R. *The Word of God According to St. Augustine* (Grand Rapids: Eerdmans, 1961).

Rahner, K. *Inspiration in the Bible* (New York: Herder and Herder, 1961).

Ramm, Bernard L. *Protestant Christian Evidences* (Chicago: Moody, 1953).

——. *Special Revelation and the Word of God* (Grand Rapids: Eerdmans, 1961).

Reid, J. K. S. *The Authority of Scripture* (London: Methuen, 1957).

Reventlow, H. Graf. *The Authority of the Bible and the Rise of the Modern World* (Philadelphia: Fortress, 1984).

Rice, John R. *Our God-Breathed Book, the Bible* (Murfreesboro: Sword of the Lord, 1969).

Ridderbos, N. H. *Studies in Scripture and Its Authority* (Grand Rapids: Eerdmans, 1978).

——. *The Authority of the New Testament Scriptures* (Philadelphia: Presbyterian and Reformed, 1963).

Ridenour, Fritz. *Who Says?* (Glendale: Regal, 1967).

Rogers, Jack. *Biblical Authority* (Waco: Word, 1977).

——. *Scripture and the Westminster Confession* (Grand Rapids: Eerdmans, 1967).

Sanders, James. *Torah and Canon* (Philadelphia: Fortress, 1972).

Saucy, Robert L. *The Bible Breathed from God* (Wheaton: Victor, 1978).

Schaeffer, Francis. *No Final Conflict* (Downers Grove: InterVarsity, 1980).

Schoekel, L. A. *The Inspired Word* (New York: Herder and Herder, 1980).

Shelton, Raymond Larry. *Martin Luther's Concept of Biblical Interpretation in Historical Perspective* (doctoral dissertation, Fuller Theological Seminary, 1974).

Stott, John R. *The Lausanne Covenant: An Exposition and Commentary* (Minneapolis: Lausanne Committee for World Evangelization, 1975), esp. p. 10.

Tavard, George. *Holy Writ or Holy Church* (London: Burnes and Oates, 1959).

Tenney, Merrill C. *The Bible: The Living Word of Revelation* (Grand Rapids: Zondervan, 1968).

Van Kooten, Tenis. *The Bible: God's Word* (Grand Rapids: Baker, 1972).

Vawter, Bruce. *Biblical Inspiration* (Philadelphia: Westminster, 1972).

Vos, H. *Can I Trust the Bible?* (Chicago: Moody, 1963).

Wenham, John F. *Christ and the Bible* (Downers Grove: InterVarsity, 1973).

Wilson, Cliff A. *Rocks, Relics and Biblical Authority* (Grand Rapids: Zondervan, 1977).

Wood, A. Skevington. *Captive to the Word* (Grand Rapids: Eerdmans, 1969).

Young, Edward J. *Thy Word Is Truth: Some Thoughts on the Biblical Doctrine of Inspiration* (Grand Rapids: Eerdmans, 1957).

## II. Monograph Essays and Journal Articles

Ashcroft, Morris. "The Theology of Fundamentalism." *RevExp* 79 (Winter 1982) 31-44.

Austin, M. R. "How Biblical is 'The Inspiration of Scripture?' " *ExpTim* 93 (December 1981) 75-79.

Bahnsen, Gregory. "Autographs, Amanuenses and Restricted Inspiration." *EvQ* 45 (April 1973) 100-110.

Balmer, Randall H. "The Princetonians, Scripture and Recent Scholarship." *Journal of Presbyterian History* 60 (Fall 1982) 267-270.

Barnhouse, Donald Grey. "When God-Breathed." *Eternity* 12 (February 1961) 15 ff.

Barr, James. "The Interpretation of Scripture: Revelation Through History in the Old Testament and in Modern Theology." *Int* (April 1963) 201-202.

Baum, G. "The Bible as Norm." *The Ecumenist* 9/5 (1971) 71 ff.

Biddle, John. "John Locke's Essay on Infallibility: Introduction, Text and Translation." *Church and State* 19 (Spring 1977) 300-327.

Blaiklock, E. M. "More and More, Scriptures Live." *Christianity Today* 17 (September 28, 1973) 13-19.

Blocher, Henri. "The Biblical Concept of Truth." *Themelios* 6/1 (1969).

Bloesch, Donald. "The Sword of The Spirit: The Meaning of Inspiration." *RefR* 33 (Winter 1980) 65-72.

———. "Crisis In Biblical Authority." *TToday* 35 (January 1979) 455-462.

Branson, Mark. "A Break in the Battle." *TSF Bulletin* 5/1 (1981) 11-12.

Brown, Raymond E. " 'And the Lord Said': Biblical Reflections on Scripture as the Word of God." *TS* 42 (March 1981) 3-19.

Bube, Richard H. "A Perspective on Scriptural Inerrancy." *Journal of the American Scientific Affiliation* 15/3 (September 1963) 86-92.

Buursma, Bruce. "The Sound and Fury of Canon Fire (Congress on the Bible—March '81)." *Christian Century* 99 (April 14, 1982) 438-439.

Cahill, P. J. "Scripture, Tradition and Unity." *CBQ* 27 (October 1965) 315-335.

Carroll, Robert F. "Canonical Criticism: A Recent Trend in Biblical Studies." *ExpTim* 92 (December 1980) 73-78.

Chapman, Sidney. "Bahnsen on Inspiration." *EvQ* 47 (July-September 1975) 162-167.

Chirico, Peter. "Infallibility: Rapprochement between Küng and the Official Church." *TS* 42 (December 1981) 529-560.

Clark, Gordon H. "Beegle on the Bible: A Review Article." *JETS* 20 (September 1977) 265-286.

Coleman, Richard. "Biblical Inerrancy: Are We Going Anywhere?" *TToday* 31 (January 1975) 295-303.

Cook, W. R. "Biblical Inerrancy and Intellectual Honesty." *BSac* 125 (April-June 1968) 157-175.

Daane, James. "The Odds on Inerrancy." *Reformed Journal* 26/10 (1976).

Dayton, Donald W. "Battle for the Bible: Renewing the Inerrancy Debate." *Christian Century* 93 (November 10, 1976) 976-980.

———. "The Church in the World: The Battle for the Bible Rages On." *TToday* 37 (April 1980) 79-84.

———. "Wrong Front: A Review of the Battle and the Bible." *The Other Side* (May/June 1976) 36-37.

Douglas, J. D. "The Living Bible: For Children Only: Infallibility Attaches Only to Scripture, Not to the Words of Its Self-appointed Champions." *Christianity Today* 23 (October 5, 1979) 78 ff.

Edwards, O. C., Jr. "Historical-Critical Method's Failure of Nerve and a Prescription for a Tonic: A Review of Some Recent Literature." *ATR* 59 (1977) 115-134.

Ellis, E. E. "Authority of Scripture: Critical Judgments in Biblical Perspective." *EvQ* 39 (October-December 1967) 196-204.

Fouke, Dan. "B. B. Warfield vs C. A. Briggs: The 19th Century Debate Over Inerrancy." *Canadian Journal of Religious Studies* 10 (Fall 1982) 15-33.

France, R. T. "Inerrancy and New Testament Exegesis." *Themelios* 1/1 (Autumn 1975) 12-18.

Fuller, Daniel P. "The Nature of Biblical Inerrancy." *Journal of the American Scientific Affiliation* 24/2 (June 1972) 47-51.

———. "Benjamin B. Warfield's View of Faith and History." *BETS* 11 (1968) 75-83.

Garrett, J. L. "Representative Modern Baptist Understandings of Biblical Inspiration." *RevExp* 71 (Spring 1974) 79-95.

Geisler, Norman. "The Concept of Truth in the Inerrancy Debate." *BSac* 137 (October-December 1980) 327-339; reprinted with minor editorial changes in M. Inch and R. Youngblood, *The Living and Active Word of God* (Winona Lake: Eisenbrauns, 1983) 225-236.

Gerstner, John H. "Church Historian Warns: Presbyterians Are Demoting the Bible." *Christianity Today* 10 (December 3, 1965) 11-14.

Goldingay, John. "Inspiration, Infallibility and Criticism." *Churchman* 90 (January-March 1976) 6-23.

Graham, Billy. "The Authority of the Scriptures." *Decision* (June 1963) 1 ff.

Groff, W. F. "Is the Bible Something to Believe In." *Brethren Life* 18 (Summer 1973) 131-136.

Grounds, V. C. "Building on the Bible." *Christianity Today* 11 (November 25, 1966) 9-12.

Hagner, Donald A. "The Old Testament in the New Testament" in *Inter-*

*preting the Word of God* (ed. S. J. Schultz and M. A. Inch; Chicago: Moody, 1976) 78-104.

Harrison, Everett F. "Criteria of Biblical Inerrancy." *Christianity Today* 2/8 (January 20, 1958) 16-18.

Hefley, James. "Another Round on the Elusive Term 'Inerrancy': Theologians Debate The Bible on T.V." *Christianity Today* 26 (January 22, 1982) 36-37.

Heick, O. W. "Biblical Inerrancy and the Hebrew Mode of Speech." *LQ* 20 (Fall 1968) 7-19.

Henry, Carl F. H. "Review of Harold Lindsell, *The Battle for the Bible.*" *The New Review of Books and Religion* 1/1 (September 1976) 7.

Hill, Joseph A. "The Bible and Non-Inspired Sources." *BETS* 3 (1960) 78-81, 92.

Hill, R. "St. John Chrysostom's Teaching on Inspiration in Six Homilies on Isaiah." *VC* (April 22, 1968) 19-37.

Hindson, Edward. "The Inerrancy Debate and the Use of Scripture in Counseling." *Grace Theological Journal* 3/2 (1982) 207-219.

Hoffman, Thomas. "Inspiration, Normativeness, Canonicity and the Unique Sacred Character of the Bible." *CBQ* 44 (July 1982) 447-469.

Holmes, J. D. "Newman's Attitude Towards Historical Criticism and Biblical Inspiration." *LQ* 230 (May 1971) 118-137.

Holmes, Michael W. "Origen and the Inerrancy of Scripture." *JETS* 24 (Spring 1981) 221-231.

Horning, E. "Biblical Authority: God's Word for God's People." *Brethren Life* 18 (Summer 1973) 145-148.

House, H. Wayne. "Biblical Inspiration in II Timothy 3:16." *BSac* 137 (March 1980) 54-63.

Hughes, John J. "Review of W. W. Gasque and W. S. LaSor: *Scripture, Tradition and Interpretation.*" *WTJ* 42/2 (1980) 422 ff.

Hughes, P. E. "Reason, History and Biblical Authenticity." *Christianity Today* 13 (September 12, 1969) 3-7.

——. "What Is the Bible For?" *Christianity Today* 10 (November 19, 1965) 6-9.

Hultgren, Leland. "Interpreting Scripture in a Theological Context." *Dialogue* 21 (Spring 1969) 87-94.

Hyers, Con. "Biblical Literalism: Constricting the Cosmic Dance." *Christian Century* 99 (August 4, 1982) 823-827.

"Inerrancy: Clearing Away Confusion." *Christianity Today* 25 (March 1981) 12-13.

"Inerrantists on the March." *Christian Century* 95 (November 22, 1978) 1126.

Isaacson, Carl. "Facing Fundamentalism." *Christian Ministry* 11/3 (1980) 27-28.

Johnston, Robert K. "Facing the Scriptures Squarely." *Christianity Today* 24 (April 18, 1980) 24-27.

Jungkuntz, R. P. "Church in Tension: In Teaching the Truth." *CTM* 37 (December 1966) 693-702.

Kalin, E. "The Inspired Community: A Glance at Canon History." *CTM* 42/8 (1971) 541-542.

Kantzer, Kenneth. "The Authority of the Bible," in *The Word for This Century* (ed. Merrill C. Tenney; New York: Oxford, 1960) 21-51.

——. "Evangelicals and the Inerrancy Question: The Current Debate." *Christianity Today* 22 (April 21, 1978) 16-21.

Kaufmann, G. D. "What Shall We Do with the Bible?" *Int* 25 (January 1971) 95-112.

Keck, Leander. "The Presence of God Through Scripture." *Lexington Theological Quarterly* 10 (July 1975) 10-18.

Kelso, J. L. "Inspiration of Scripture." *Christianity Today* 14 (June 5, 1970) 6-9.

Knight, Douglas. "Revelation Through Tradition," in *Tradition and Theology in the Old Testament* (ed. D. Knight; Philadelphia: Fortress, 1977) 143-180.

Koivisto, Rex A. "Clark Pinnock and Inerrancy: A Change in Truth Theory." *JETS* 24 (June 1981) 139-151.

Kraus, C. N. "American Mennonites and the Bible (1750-1950)." *Mennonite Quarterly* 41 (October 1967) 309-329.

Kucharsky, David. "The Year of the Evangelical." *Christianity Today* 21 (October 22, 1976) 12 ff.

Lancashire, A. "Authority of Scripture." *CQ* 167 (October-November 1966) 425-431.

Lasor, W. S. "Life Under Tension—Fuller Theological Seminary and The Battle For the Bible." *Theology, News and Notes*: special issue (1976) 5-6.

Lindsell, Harold. "Biblical Infallibility from the Hermeneutical and Cultural Perspectives." *BSac* 133 (October-December 1976) 312-318.

——. "The Infallible Word." *Christianity Today* 16 (August-September 1972) 8-12.

——. "Biblical Infallibility: The Reformation and Beyond." *JETS* 19 (Winter 1976) 25-37.

——. "Whither Southern Baptists?" *Christianity Today* 14 (April 24, 1970) 3-5.

Lohfink, N. "The Inerrancy of Scripture" in *The Christian Meaning of the Old Testament* (Milwaukee: Bruce, 1968).

Lyles, Jean Caffey. "Losing Battles: Those Old Inerrancy Blues." *Christian Century* 99 (July 7, 1982) 751-753.

Maatman, Russell W. and Richard H. Bube. "Inerrancy, Revelation and

Evolution." *Journal of the American Scientific Affiliation* 24 (June 1972) 80-88.

Mattill, Andover. "Bible and the Battle of Faith." *Personal Religious Studies* 5 (September 1978) 54-58.

Mavrodes, G. I. "The Inspiration of the Autographs." *EvQ* 41/1 (January-March 1969) 19-29.

McCarthy, D. J. "Personality, Society and Inspiration." *TS* 24/4 (1968) 55-56.

McCartney, Daryl. "Early Wesleyan Views of Scripture." *WTJ* 16 (Fall 1981) 95-105.

McKenzie, J. L. "The Social Character of Inspiration." *CBQ* 24/2 (1962) 115-129.

McKim, Donald. "Archibald Alexander and the Doctrine of Scripture." *Journal of Presbyterian History* 54 (Fall 1976) 355-375.

———. "John Owen's Doctrine of Scripture in Historical Perspective." *EvQ* (October-December 1973) 195 ff.

Miller, E. L. "Plenary Inspiration and II Timothy 3:16." *LQ* 17 (Fall 1965) 56-62.

Minnery, Tom. "The Battle for the Battle, 1982: Scholars and Laymen Rally for Inerrancy in San Diego." *Christianity Today* 26 (April 9, 1982) 40-42.

Montgomery, John W. "Relevance of Scripture for Current Theology." *Christianity Today* 12 (November 10, 1967) 14-16.

———. "Whither Biblical Inerrancy." *Christianity Today* 21 (July 29, 1977) 40-42.

Morris, Leon. "The Authority of the Bible." in *I Believe in Revelation* (Grand Rapids: Eerdmans, 1976) 136-147.

———. "Biblical Authority and the Concept of Inerrancy." *Churchman* 31 (Spring 1967) 22-38.

Murphy, R. E. "Biblical Inspiration: Dead or Alive?" *JR* 51 (October 1971) 301-305.

Murray, R. "How Did the Church Determine the Canon of Scripture?" *HeyJ* 11 (1970) 115-126.

Nicole, R. "Dialogue on the Bible Continues." *Christianity Today* 11 (December 23, 1966) 16-17.

Noll, Mark. "Word of God and the Bible: A View from the Reformation." *Christian Scholars Review* 8/1 (1978) 25-31.

Noyce, Gay. "How Shall We Use the Bible Now?" *Christian Century* 96 (April 4, 1980) 370-373.

Ogden, Schubert M. "The Authority of Scripture for Theology." *Int* 30 (July 1976) 242-261.

———. "Sources of Religious Authority in Liberal Protestantism: For Van A. Harvey on His 50th Birthday." *JAAR* 44/3 (1976) 403-416.

Oliver, H. H. "The Impact of Nineteenth Century Philosophy on Biblical Authority." *Perspective: Religious Studies* 1 (Spring 1974) 29-42.

Olson, A. L. "Constitution on Divine Revelation." *Dialogue* 5 (September 1966) 182-187.

Osborne, G. "A Biblical Understanding of Inerrancy." *JETS* 19 (Spring 1976) 73-85.

Oswalt, John. "The Myth of the Dragon and Old Testament Faith." *EvQ* 49 (1977) 163-172.

Parsons, Mike. "Warfield and Scripture." *Churchman* 91 (July 1977) 198-220.

Payne, P. B. "Fallacy of Equating Meaning with the Human Author's Intention." *JETS* 20 (September 1977) 243-252.

Payne, J. Barton. "The Plank Bridge: Inerrancy and the Biblical Autographs." *United Evangelical Action* 24 (December 1965).

Phillips, Timothy R. "The Argument for Inerrancy: An Analysis." *Journal of the American Scientific Affiliation* 31/2 (June 1979) 80-88.

Piepkorn, A. C. "What Does Inerrancy Mean?" *CTM* 36 (September 1965) 577-593.

Pinnock, Clark. "Inspiration and Authority: A Truce Proposal." *The Other Side* (May-June 1976) 61-65.

———. "Our Source of Authority: The Bible." *BSac* 124 (April 1967) 150-156.

———. "Review of Harold Lindsell, *The Battle for the Bible*." *Eternity* (June 1976) 40-41.

———. "Southern Baptists and the Bible." *Christianity Today* 10 (May 27, 1966) 30-31.

———. "Three Views of the Bible in Contemporary Theology" in *Biblical Authority* (ed. J. Rogers; Waco: Word, 1977) 49-73.

———. "The Treasure of the Earthen Vessels: The Inspiration and Interpretation of the Bible." *Sojourners* 10 (October 1980) 16-19.

Piper, John. "Authority and the Meaning of the Christian Canon: A Response to Gerald Sheppard on Canon Criticism." *JETS* 19 (Spring 1976) 87-96.

Preus, R. D. "Notes on the Inerrancy of Scripture." *CTM* 38 (June 1967) 363-375.

Raitt, Thomas M. "Horizontal Revelation." *Religious Life* 47 (Winter 1978) 423-429.

Ramm, Bernard. "The Relationship of Science, Factual Statements and the Doctrine of Biblical Inerrancy." *Journal of the American Scientific Affiliation* (December 1969) 98-104.

——— "Scripture as a Theological Concept." *RevExp* 71 (Fall 1974) 149-161.

"Rhetoric About Inerrancy: The Truth of the Matter." *Christianity Today* 24 (September 4, 1981) 16-19.

Ricoeur, Paul. "Toward a Hermeneutic of the Idea of Revelation" in *Essays in Biblical Interpretation* (ed. L. Mudge; Philadelphia: Fortress, 1980).

Ridderbos, Hermann. "An Attempt at the Theological Definition of Inerrancy, Infallibility and Authority." *International Reformed Bulletin* 32-33 (1968) 27-41.

——. "Canon of the Old Testament" in *The New Bible Dictionary* (ed. J. D. Douglas; Grand Rapids: Eerdmans, 1962) 187-194.

Ritschl, D. "Plea for the Maxim: Scripture and Tradition." *Int* 25 (January 1971) 113-129.

Robinson, W. C. "Inspiration of Holy Scripture." *Christianity Today* 13/1 (October 11, 1968) 6-9.

Runia, K. "Modern Debate Around the Bible." *Christianity Today* 12 (August 16, 1968) 8-12.

——. "What Do Evangelicals Believe About the Bible?" *Christianity Today* 15 (December 18, 1970) 8-10.

Ryrie, C. "Some Important Aspects of Biblical Inerrancy." *BSac* 136 (January-March 1979) 16-24.

Sanders, J. A. "Re-opening Old Questions About Scripture." *Int* 28 (July 1974) 321-330.

Scaer, David C. "Apostolicity, Inspiration and Canonicity: Opinion of the Department of Systematic Theology." *CTM* 44 (January 1980) 46-49.

——. "Problems on Inerrancy and Historicity in Connection with Genesis 1-3." *CTM* 41 (January 1977) 21-25.

——. "Theological Observer: International Council on Biblical Inerrancy." *CTM* 43 (January 1979) 45-46.

Scharlemann, Martin. "Reu and the Doctrine of the Holy Scriptures." *Concordia Journal* 1 (January 1979) 12-20.

Rehwaldt, T. H. "Other Understanding of the Inspiration Texts." *CTM* 43 (June 1972) 355-357.

Schneider, Sandra. "The Literal Sense of Scripture." *TS* 39/4 (1978) 719-736.

Sheppard, Gerald. "Biblical Hermeneutics: The Academic Language of Evangelical Identity." *USQR* 32 (Winter 1977) 81-94.

——. "Canon Criticism: The Proposal of Brevard Childs and an Assessment for Evangelical Hermeneutics." *Studia Biblica et Theologica* 6 (1976) 3-17.

Shurden, W. B. "The Inerrancy Debate: A Comparitive Study of Southern Baptist Controversies." *Baptist History and Heritage* 16/2 (1981) 12-19.

Smith, T. C. "Canon and the Authority of the Bible." *Perspective: Religious Studies* 1 (Spring 1974) 43-51.

Stigers, Harold. "Preservation: The Corollary of Inspiration." *JETS* 22 (September 1979) 217-222.

Strieter, T. W. "Luther's View of Scripture." *CurTM* 1 (December 1974) 91-97.

Sundberg, Albert. "Bible Canon and the Christian Doctrine of Inspiration." *Int* 29 (October 1975) 352-379.

Soulen, Richard N. "Unity, Truth and the Validity of the Bible." *Int* 29 (October 1975) 391-405.

Tarr, Leslie. "Group Voices Alternative to Verbal Inspiration (Conference June 1981)." *Christianity Today* 25 (August 7, 1981) 34-35.

Taylor, G. Aiken. "Is God As Good As His Word?" *Christianity Today* 21 (February 4, 1977) 22-25.

Thomas, K. J. "The Old Testament Citations in Hebrews." *NTS* 11 (1964-65) 303-325.

Thomas, W. H. Griffith. "Inspiration." *BSac* 118 (1961) 41-45.

Thorson, Walter R. "The Concept of Truth in the Natural Sciences." *Themelios* 5/2 (1968) 27-38.

Tinder, Don. "Pro-Inerrancy Forces Draft Their Platform—October 26-28." *Christianity Today* 23 (November 17, 1978) 36-37.

Vasady, B. "Revelation, Scripture and Tradition." *Theology Life* 9 (Summer-Winter 1966) 106-117, 206-219, 318-334.

Warfield, B. B. "The Westminster Confession and the Original Autographs (DeKoster Editorials)." *The Banner* (August 19, 26; September 2, 1977).

Wenham, G. J. "Inspiration of Scripture—A Received Tradition?" *Churchman* 84 (Winter 1970) 286-288.

"What the Bible Means: Evangelical Scholars Come to Agreement on the Issue of Hermeneutics." *Christianity Today* 26 (December 17, 1982) 45-46.

Wiseman, D. J. "Archaeology and Scripture." *WTJ* 33 (May 1971) 133-152.

Woodbridge, John. "Biblical Authority: Toward an Evaluation of the Rogers and McKim Proposal." *Trinity Journal* 1 (Fall 1980) 165-236.

Wright, David. "Soundings in the Doctrine of Scripture in British Evangelicalism in the First Half of the Twentieth Century." *TB* 31 (1980) 87-106.

Wright, J. Stafford. "The Perspecuity of Scripture." *Theological Students' Letter* (Summer 1969).

Young, Davis. "Nineteenth-Century Christian Geologists and the Doctrine of Scripture." *Christian Scholar's Review* 11/3 (1982) 212-228.

Young, E. J. "The Verbal Plenary Inspiration of the Scriptures, IV: The Bible and History." *BSac* 122 (January-March 1965) 16-22.